American Contempt
for Liberty

American Contempt
for Liberty

Walter E. Williams

HOOVER INSTITUTION PRESS
STANFORD UNIVERSITY | STANFORD, CALIFORNIA

www.hoover.org

Hoover Institution Press Publication No. 661
Hoover Institution at Leland Stanford Junior University
Stanford, California, 94305–6010

First printing 2015
23 22 21 20 19 18 17 16 15   9 8 7 6 5 4 3 2 1
Manufactured in the United States of America

The paper used in this publication meets the minimum Requirements of the American National Standard for Information Sciences—Permanence of Paper for Printed Library Materials, ANSI/NISO Z39.48–1992. ∞

Cataloging-in-Publication Data is available from the Library of Congress.
ISBN 978–0–8179–1875–0 (pbk. : alk. paper)
ISBN 978–0–8179–1876–7 (e-pub)
ISBN 978–0–8179–1877–4 (mobi)
ISBN 978–0–8179–1878–1 (ePDF)

For my grandson Harrison Edward Mulhollen,
who is my ticket to the future.

Contents

PART II

Politics   43

PART III

Race   131

PART IV

Education   205

PART V

Environment and Health   269

PART VI

International 299

PART VII

Potpourri 341

Preface

Most of mankind's history has been one featured by arbitrary abuse and control by people who deem themselves as betters. Personal liberty, free markets, and peaceable, voluntary exchange have always been roundly denounced by tyrants and often greeted with suspicion by the general public. Once a conspicuous exception to this historical pattern, Americans have increasingly accepted the tyrannical ideas of reduced private property rights, reduced rights to profits, and have become enamored with restrictions on personal liberty and control by government.

People who seek to reduce our liberties see themselves as more intelligent and have superior wisdom to the masses. Plus, they believe that they have been ordained to forcibly impose that wisdom on the rest of us. Of course, they have what they consider good reasons but every tyrant has had what he saw as good reasons for restricting the freedom of others. Their plan requires the elimination, or at least attenuation, of the free market. Why? Tyrants do not trust that people acting voluntarily will do what the tyrant thinks they should do. Therefore, they want to replace the market with economic planning. Economic planning is not a very complex concept. It is nothing more than the forcible superseding of other people's plans by the powerful elite.

Here are a couple of examples, among thousands, of the elite vision. My daughter might plan to work at the ice cream parlor down the street for $4 an hour. She agrees with $4 an hour and so does the proprietor and so does her mother and father. The powerful elite will supersede that transaction because it is not being transacted at the wage they think—currently $7.25 an hour, the minimum wage. Or, a refrigerator manufacturer might plan to purchase sheet metal from a Japanese producer. The powerful elite, through tariffs and quotas, will supersede that transaction because they think it is better for him to make his purchases from an American producer.

Most supporters of restrictions on personal liberty claim that they are doing it in the name of good. In the case of minimum wages, it is to protect the worker. In the cases of import tariffs and quotas, it is to protect American jobs. Do-gooders fail to realize that most good is not done in the name of good but done in the name of self-interest. In other words, in the process of people trying to get more for themselves they promote what might be seen as the social good. This concept is not popularly held so let's look at a couple of examples to make the point.

During cold winter nighttime blizzards, one might find Texas cattlemen braving the weather to run down stray cows and care for them. They make this personal sacrifice to help ensure that New Yorkers have beef on their grocery shelves. During hot summers, one can see Idaho potato farmers getting up in the morning, doing back-breaking, dirty work—making this personal sacrifice to ensure that New Yorkers also have potatoes on their grocery shelves. It would be the height of naiveté to think that Texas cattle ranchers and Idaho potato farmers are making these personal sacrifices because they care about New Yorkers. In fact they might hate New Yorkers but they make sure that beef and potatoes get to New Yorkers every day of the week. Why? The no-brainer reason is that they do so because they want more for themselves. Most good things get done because of the pursuit of self-interest and private property rights.

This is precisely what Adam Smith was writing about in *An Inquiry into the Nature and Causes of the Wealth of Nations* when he wrote, "It is not from the benevolence of the butcher, the brewer, or the baker that we expect our dinner, but from their regard to their own interest." Smith's other insightful observation was, "I have never known much good done by those who affected to trade for the public good."

Pope Francis, in his 2013 apostolic exhortation, levied charges against free market capitalism, denying that "economic growth, encouraged by a free market, will inevitably succeed in bringing about greater justice and inclusiveness in the world," concluding that "this opinion . . . has never been confirmed by the facts." He went on to label unfettered capitalism as "a new tyranny." The Pope's stinging critique of capitalism is shared by many, but let's examine this tragic vision shared by many.

First, let's acknowledge that capitalism fails miserably when compared to heaven or a utopia. In fact, any earthly system is going to compare badly. The fact of business is that mankind must make choices among alternative economic systems that actually exist on Earth. For the common man, capitalism is superior to any system yet devised to deal with his everyday needs and desires.

Capitalism is relatively new in human history. Prior to capitalism, the way people amassed great wealth was by looting, plundering, and enslaving their fellow man. With the rise of capitalism, it became possible to amass great wealth by serving and pleasing one's fellow man. Capitalists seek to discover what people want and then produce and market it as efficiently as possible as a means to wealth. For example: J. D. Rockefeller, whose successful marketing drove kerosene prices down from 58 cents a gallon in 1865 to 7 cents in 1900. Henry Ford became rich by producing cars for the common man. Both Ford and Rockefeller became immensely wealthy, but the benefits they created for the common man by having cheaper kerosene and cheaper transportation far exceeded their personal gains. There are literally thousands of examples, such as wonder drugs, vacuum cleaners, and refrigerators, of how the common man's life has been made better by those in the pursuit of profits. Here's my question: Are these entrepreneurs who, by their actions, created unprecedented convenience, longer life expectancy, and a more pleasant life for the ordinary person—and became wealthy in the process—deserving of all the scorn and ridicule heaped upon them by intellectuals, politicians?

The pursuit of profits by pleasing one's fellow man in a cost-efficient manner is praiseworthy but it should not be confused with crony capitalism. Free market capitalism is unforgiving. In order to earn a profit and stay in business, producers must please customers and wisely use resources to do so. If they fail to do so, they face losses or bankruptcy.

It is this market discipline of profits and losses that many businessmen seek to avoid. That's why they descend upon Washington calling for government bailouts, subsidies, tariffs, licenses, and other special privileges. They do not want to be held strictly accountable to consumers and stockholders, who hold little tolerance or sympathy for economic blunders and will give them the ax on a moment's notice. However, with a campaign contribution here and a gift there, they can get Congress and the White House to legislate against the best interests of consumers and investors. What our nation needs is a separation of "business and state" as it has a separation of "church and state." That would mean crony capitalism and crony socialism could not survive.

Another emphasis of my columns is the massive and little appreciated decline in moral values. Evil acts are given an aura of moral legitimacy by noble-sounding socialistic expressions, such as spreading the wealth, income redistribution, caring for the less fortunate, and the will of the majority. At least two-thirds of all federal spending can be described as Congress taking the rightful property of one American and giving it to another to whom it does not belong. Examples of this process run the gamut from farm subsidies and business bailouts to food stamps and welfare.

The immorality of these acts becomes apparent when one recognizes that Congress has no resources of its very own. Moreover, there is no Santa Claus or Tooth Fairy who comes up with the resources. The recognition of the fact that Congress has no resources of its own forces us to acknowledge that the only way Congress can give one American one dollar is to first, through intimidation, threats, and coercion, confiscate that dollar from some other American. If a private citizen did the same thing that Congress does, we would call it an immoral act—namely theft. Acts such as theft that are immoral when done privately do not become moral when done collectively. The moral tragedy that has befallen Americans is our belief that it is okay for government to forcibly use one American to serve the purposes of another—that in my book is a working definition of slavery.

The columns contained in this selected collection represent my efforts to sell my fellow Americans on the moral superiority of personal liberty and its main ingredient—limited government.

Acknowledgments

One of the greatest things about our country is that just because you know where a person ended up in life you cannot be sure about where he started. Americans enjoy a level of economic mobility not seen at any time in human history or any other place in the world. I have had the opportunity to share in that mobility—starting out poor and ending up with more wealth than I could have dreamed as a youngster.

No one who starts out at the bottom, and winds up near the top, does so without a lot of luck, help, and goodwill from others along the way. The greatest luck that I enjoyed was to meet and marry Connie, my wife of nearly forty-eight years before she passed away in 2007. She shared my vision of hard work and sacrifice that enabled both of us to escape poverty. Long before I met Connie I benefited from a determined mother who would always tell my sister and me that we had a beer pocketbook but champagne tastes.

After a two-year stint in the U.S. Army, Connie and I moved to Los Angeles. I enrolled at California State College Los Angeles and earned a bachelor of arts degree in economics in 1965. A number of professors saw promise in me and went beyond the call of duty to assist and later encourage me to continue my education. I took that advice and enrolled in UCLA's master's, and later PhD, economics program. Through the assistance of many professors, and what I called trial by ordeal, I was awarded a doctorate degree in economics in 1972. One of the greatest gifts that all of my professors gave me was to treat me as an individual. They made no exceptions and gave me no slack because of the nation's history of discrimination. They treated me just as they treated other students. I often tell people that I am happy that I received virtually all of my education before it became fashionable for white people to like black people and before teachers cared about a student's self-esteem.

Writing syndicated columns is an education in and of itself. There is the task of being able to write on potentially complicated subjects while economizing on the number of words. There is the added task of being able to explain things in a fashion that is understandable to the ordinary person without economic training. Professor Armen Alchian, one of my most tenacious mentors at UCLA, told me that the true test of whether one knows his subject comes when he can explain it to someone who does not know a darn thing about it. That is a challenge that I welcome and enjoy.

Much of the education that I have received from writing a nationally syndicated weekly column for the best part of thirty-five years comes from reader responses. I have benefited from letters that ask whether I thought about this or that aspect of an issue. Or, they write, "Here is an example of what you are saying." Then there have been letters criticizing what I have written. Criticism is always beneficial in the sense that it gets one to abandon a weak position or do a better job of explaining it. Speaking of errors, I should acknowledge the due diligence of my editor Mr. David Yontz, who has spared me embarrassment on more than one occasion.

PART I

Constitution

My view of the US Constitution is that it represents the rules of the game—namely the relationship between the citizenry and our government. Most of what the framers of the Constitution saw as the legitimate role for the federal government is found in Article I, Section 8, of our Constitution. Briefly quoting sections thereof, it says that "The congress shall have the power to lay and collect taxes, Duties, Imposts and Excises to pay the Debts and provide for the common Defense and general Welfare of United States . . . to borrow money on the credit of the United States . . . to regulate commerce with foreign Nations, and among the several States, and with Indian tribes . . . to coin money . . . to establish Post Offices and post Roads . . . to raise and support Armies." The framers granted Congress taxing and spending powers for these and a few other activities.

Nowhere in the Constitution do we find authority for Congress to tax and spend for up to three-quarters of what Congress taxes and spends for today. In other words, there is no constitutional authority for farm subsidies, bank bailouts, food stamps, Social Security, Medicare, and thousands of other federal spending programs. I think we can safely say that we have made a significant departure from the constitutional principles of individual freedom and its main ingredient limited government that made us a rich nation in the first place. These principles of freedom were embodied in our nation through the combined institutions of private ownership of property and free enterprise.

Through numerous successful attacks, private property and free enterprise, which the framers envision, are mere skeletons of their past. Thomas Jefferson anticipated this when he said, "The natural progress of things is for government to gain ground and for liberty to yield." The best way to look at this process is to look at what has happened to government taxation and spending.

Taxes represent government claims on private property. As government taxes increase our claims to our personal property decrease. And taxes are going up. A much better measure of our loss of private property is to look at what has happened to spending. In 1902 expenditures at all levels of government totaled $1.7 billion whereas the average taxpayer paid only $60 a year in taxes. In fact, from 1787 to 1920, federal expenditures were only 3 percent of GNP, except during war times. Today federal expenditures alone are nearly $4 trillion, nearly 25 percent of the GDP. State and local governments spend close to $3.5 trillion. The average taxpayer pays more than $10,000 a year in federal, state, and local taxes.

The significance of all of this means that as time goes by we own less and less of our most valuable property—ourselves and the fruits of our labor. Another way to look at this is to recognize that the average taxpayer works from January 1st to the end of April to pay federal, state, and local taxes. That means that we work four months out of the year and we have no rights to determine how the fruits of our labor will be used. Someone else makes that decision. Keep in mind that a working definition of slavery is that you work all year and it is someone else who decides how the fruits of the slaves' labor are used. Most federal government spending can be characterized as taking what belongs to one American and giving it to another to whom it does not belong. That is no less than the forcible use of one person to serve the purposes of another—which is also a good working definition of slavery.

My columns in this section share the radical vision of the men who founded our nation and sought to make a significant break from the most dominant characteristic of mankind's history—the arbitrary abuse and control by others.

The Hell with Our Constitution

February 11, 2009

Dr. Robert Higgs, senior fellow at the Oakland-based Independent Institute, penned an article in *The Christian Science Monitor* (2/9/2009) that suggests the most intelligent recommendation that I've read to fix our current economic mess. The title of his article gives his recommendation away: "Instead of stimulus, do nothing—seriously."

Stimulus package debate is over how much money should be spent, whether some should be given to the National Endowment for the Arts, research sexually transmitted diseases, or bail out Amtrak, our failing railroad system. Dr. Higgs says, "Hardly anyone, however, is asking the most important question: Should the federal government be doing any of this?" He adds, "Until the 1930s, the Constitution served as a major constraint on federal economic interventionism. The government's powers were understood to be just as the framers intended: few and explicitly enumerated in our founding document and its amendments. Search the Constitution as long as you like, and you will find no specific authority conveyed for the government to spend money on global-warming research, urban mass transit, food stamps, unemployment insurance, Medicaid, or countless other items in the stimulus package and, even without it, in the regular federal budget."

By bringing up the idea of constitutional restraints on Washington, I'd say Dr. Higgs is whistling Dixie. Americans have long ago abandoned respect for the constitutional limitations placed on the federal government. Our elected representatives represent that disrespect. After all I'd ask Higgs: Isn't it unreasonable to expect a politician to do what he considers to be political suicide, namely conduct himself according to the letter and spirit of the Constitution?

While Americans, through ignorance or purpose, show contempt for our Constitution, I doubt whether they are indifferent between a growing or stagnating economy. Dr. Higgs tells us some of the economic history of the United States. In 1893, there was a depression; we got out of it without a stimulus package. There was a major recession of 1920–21; though sharp, it quickly reversed itself into what has been call the "Roaring Twenties." In 1929, there was an economic downturn, most notably featured by the stock market collapse, after which came massive government intervention—you might call it the nation's first stimulus package. President Hoover and Congress responded to what might have been a two- or three-year sharp downturn with many of the policies President Obama and Congress are urging today. They raised tariffs, propped up wage rates, bailed out farmers, banks, and other businesses, and financed state relief efforts. When Roosevelt came to office, he became even more interventionist than Hoover and presided over protracted depression where the economy didn't fully recover until 1946.

Roosevelt didn't have an easy time with his agenda; he had to first emasculate the US Supreme Court. Higgs points out that federal courts had respect for the Constitution as late as the 1930s. They issued some 1,600 injunctions to restrain officials from carrying out acts of Congress. The US Supreme Court overturned as unconstitutional the New Deal's centerpieces such as the National Industrial Recovery Act, the Agricultural Adjustment Act, and other parts of Roosevelt's "stimulus package." An outraged Roosevelt threatened to pack the Court, and the Court capitulated to where it is today giving Congress virtually unlimited powers to tax, spend, and regulate. My question to my fellow Americans is: Do we want a repeat of measures that failed dismally during the 1930s?

A more fundamental question is: Should Washington be guided by the Constitution? In explaining the Constitution, James Madison, the acknowledged father of the Constitution, wrote in Federalist Paper No. 45: "The powers delegated by the proposed Constitution to the federal government are few and defined. Those which are to remain in the State governments are numerous and indefinite. The former will be exercised principally on external objects, as war, peace, negotiation, and foreign commerce." Has the Constitution been amended to permit Congress to tax, spend, and regulate as it pleases or have Americans said, "To hell with the Constitution"?

Good Ideas

March 11, 2009

During winter months, I work out ten minutes on the treadmill and lift weights at seven stations four mornings a week. Over the years, during the spring through fall months, I racked up about two thousand miles on my road bike. This level of exercise helps account for why, at seventy-three years, I'm in such good health and physical fitness. So my question to you is whether you think regular exercise is a good idea. I think the answer is definitely yes, if nothing other than its beneficial effects on health care costs. Since exercise is a good idea, would you support a congressional mandate that all Americans engage in regular exercise?

Instead of simply saying, "Williams, you're a lunatic!" and rejecting such a congressional mandate out of hand, let's ask why it should be rejected. We should keep in mind that there's precedent for congressionally mandated measures to protect our health and safety. Seatbelt and helmet laws are examples. If you're in an accident and wind up a vegetable, you will be a burden on taxpayers; therefore, it's argued, Congress has a right to mandate seatbelt and helmet usage. Wouldn't the same reasoning apply to people who might burden our health care system because of obesity or sedentary lifestyles? If it is a good idea for Congress to force us to buckle up and wear a helmet on a motorcycle, isn't it also a good idea to force us to regularly exercise?

There is only one question to ask were there to be a debate whether Congress should mandate regular exercise. Whether regular exercise is a good idea or a bad idea is entirely irrelevant. The only relevant question is: Is it permissible under the Constitution? That means we must examine the Constitution to see whether it authorizes Congress to mandate exercise. From my reading, the Constitution grants no such authority.

You say, "Aha, Williams, you've blown it this time. What about Article I, Section 8, of the Constitution, which says Congress shall provide for the 'general welfare of the United States'? Surely, healthy Americans contribute to the nation's general welfare." That's precisely the response I'd expect from your average law professor, congressman, or derelict US Supreme Court justice. Let's look at what the men who wrote the Constitution had to say about its general welfare clause. In a letter to Edmund Pendleton, James Madison, the father of the Constitution, said, "If Congress can do whatever in their discretion can be done by money, and will promote the General Welfare, the Government is no longer a limited one, possessing enumerated powers, but an indefinite one. . . ." Madison also said, "With respect to the two words 'general welfare,' I have always regarded them as qualified by the detail of powers connected with them. To take them in a literal and unlimited sense would be a metamorphosis of the Constitution into a character which there is a host of proofs was not contemplated by its creators." Thomas Jefferson said, "Congress has not unlimited powers to provide for the general welfare, but only those specifically enumerated."

If you compare the vision of our nation's founders to the behavior of today's Congress, White House, and US Supreme Court, you would have to conclude that there is no longer rule of law where there is a set of general rules applicable to all persons. Today, we are commanded by legislative thugs who, with Supreme Court sanction, issue orders commanding particular people to do particular things. Most Americans neither understand nor appreciate the spirit and letter of the Constitution and accept Congress's arbitrary orders and privileges based upon status.

What to do? Thomas Jefferson advised, "Whensoever the General [federal] Government assumes undelegated powers, its acts are unauthoritative, void, and of no force." That bit of Jeffersonian advice is dangerous. While Congress does not have constitutional authority for most of what it does, it does have police and military power to inflict great pain and punishment for disobedience.

Why a Bill of Rights?

July 1, 2009

Why did the founders of our nation give us the Bill of Rights? The answer is easy. They knew Congress could not be trusted with our God-given rights. Think about it. Why in the world would they have written the First Amendment prohibiting Congress from enacting any law that abridges freedom of speech and the press? The answer is that in the absence of such a limitation Congress would abridge free speech and free press. That same distrust of Congress explains the other amendments found in our Bill of Rights protecting rights such as our rights to property, fair trial, and to bear arms. The Bill of Rights should serve as a constant reminder of the deep distrust that our founders had of government. They knew that some government was necessary but they rightfully saw government as the enemy of the people and they sought to limit government and provide us with protections.

After the 1787 Constitutional Convention, there were intense ratification debates about the proposed Constitution. Both James Madison and Alexander Hamilton expressed grave reservations about Thomas Jefferson's, George Mason's, and others' insistence that the Constitution be amended by the Bill of Rights. Those reservations weren't the result of a lack of concern for liberty. To the contrary, they were concerned about the loss of liberties.

Alexander Hamilton expressed his reservation in Federalist Paper No. 84, "[B]ills of rights . . . are not only unnecessary in the proposed Constitution, but would even be dangerous." Hamilton asks, "For why declare that things shall not be done [by Congress] which there is no power to do? Why, for instance, should it be said that the liberty of the press shall not be restrained, when no power is given [to Congress] by which restrictions may be imposed?" Hamilton's argument was that Congress can only do what the Constitution specifically gave it authority to do. Powers not granted belong to the people and the states.

Another way of examining Hamilton's concern: Why have an amendment prohibiting Congress from infringing on our right to picnic on our back porch when the Constitution gives Congress no authority to infringe upon that right in the first place?

Alexander Hamilton added that a Bill of Rights would "contain various exceptions to powers not granted; and, on this very account, would afford a colorable pretext to claim more [powers] than were granted. . . . [it] would furnish, to men disposed to usurp, a plausible pretense for claiming that power." Going back to our picnic example, those who would usurp our God-given liberties might enact a law banning our right to have a picnic. They'd justify their actions by claiming that nowhere in the Constitution is there a guaranteed right to have a picnic.

To mollify Alexander Hamilton's and James Madison's fears about how a Bill of Rights might be used as a pretext to infringe on human rights, the Ninth Amendment was added that reads: "The enumeration in the Constitution of certain rights shall not be construed to deny or disparage others retained by the people." In essence, the Ninth Amendment says it's impossible to list all of our God-given or natural rights. Just because a right is not listed doesn't mean it can be infringed upon or disparaged by the US Congress. The Tenth Amendment is a reinforcement of the Ninth saying, "The powers not delegated to the United States by the Constitution, nor prohibited by it to the states, are reserved to the states respectively, or to the people." That means if a power is not delegated to Congress, it belongs to the states or the people.

The Ninth and Tenth Amendments mean absolutely nothing today as Americans have developed a level of naive trust for Congress, the White House, and the US Supreme Court that would have astonished the founders, a trust that will lead to our undoing as a great nation.

Constitutional Contempt
November 11, 2009

At Speaker Nancy Pelosi's October 29 press conference, a CNS News reporter asked, "Madam Speaker, where specifically does the Constitution grant Congress the authority to enact an individual health insurance mandate?" Speaker Pelosi responded, "Are you serious? Are you serious?" The reporter said, "Yes, yes, I am." Not responding further, Pelosi shook her head and took a question from another reporter. Later on, Pelosi's press spokesman Nadeam Elshami told CNSNews.com about its question regarding constitutional authority mandating that individual Americans buy health insurance. "You can put this on the record. That is not a serious question. That is not a serious question."

Suppose Congress was debating a mandate outlawing tea-party-type protests and other large gatherings criticizing Congress. A news reporter asks Nancy Pelosi where specifically does the Constitution grant Congress the authority to outlaw peaceable assembly. How would you feel if she answered, "Are you serious? Are you serious?" and ignored the question. And what if, later on, someone from her office sent you a press release, as was sent to CNS News, saying that Congress has "broad power to regulate activities that have an effect on interstate commerce," pointing out that demonstrations cause traffic jams and therefore interfere with interstate commerce?

Speaker Pelosi's constitutional contempt, perhaps ignorance, is representative of the majority of members of both the House and the Senate. Their comfort in that ignorance and constitutional contempt, and how readily they articulate it, should be worrisome for every single American. It's not a matter of whether you are for or against Congress's health care proposals. It's not a matter of whether you're liberal or conservative, black or white, male or female, Democrat or Republican, or member of any other group. It's a matter of whether we are going to remain a relatively free people or permit the insidious encroachment on our liberties to continue.

Where in the US Constitution does it authorize Congress to force Americans to buy health insurance? If Congress gets away with forcing us to buy health insurance, down the line, what else will they force us to buy; or do you naively think they will stop with health insurance? We shouldn't think that the cure to Congress's unconstitutional heavy-handedness will end if we only elect Republicans. Republicans have demonstrated nearly as much constitutional contempt as have Democrats. The major difference is the significant escalation of that contempt under today's Democrat-controlled Congress and White House with the massive increase in spending, their proposed legislation, and the appointment of tyrannical czars to control our lives. It's a safe bet that if and when Republicans take over the Congress and White House, they will not give up the massive increase in control over our lives won by the Democrats.

In each new session of Congress since 1995, John Shadegg, R-Ariz., has introduced the Enumerated Powers Act, a measure "To require Congress to specify the source of authority under the United States Constitution for the enactment of laws, and for other purposes." The highest number of cosponsors it has ever had in the House of Representatives is fifty-four and it has never had cosponsors in the Senate until this year, when twenty-two senators signed up. The fact that less than 15 percent of the Congress supports such a measure demonstrates the kind of contempt our elected representatives have for the rules of the game—our Constitution.

If you asked the questions: Which way is our nation heading, tiny steps at a time? Are we headed toward more liberty, or are we headed toward greater government control over our lives? I think the answer is unambiguously the latter—more government control over our lives. Are there any signs on the horizon that the direction is going to change? If we don't see any, we should not be surprised. After all, mankind's standard fare throughout his history, and in most places today, is arbitrary control and abuse by government.

The Census and the Constitution

February 17, 2010

The Census Bureau estimates that the life-cycle cost of the 2010 Census will be from $13.7 billion to $14.5 billion, making it the costliest census in the nation's history. Suppose you suggest to a congressman that given our budget crisis, we could save some money by dispensing with the 2010 census. I guarantee you that he'll say something along the lines that the Constitution mandates a decennial counting of the American people and he would be absolutely right. Article I, Section 2, of our constitution reads: "The actual Enumeration shall be made within three Years after the first Meeting of the Congress of the United States, and within every subsequent Term of ten Years, in such Manner as they shall by Law direct."

What purpose did the Constitution's framers have in mind ordering an enumeration or count of the American people every ten years? The purpose of the headcount is to apportion the number of seats in the House of Representatives and derived from that, along with two senators from each state, the number of electors to the Electoral College.

The Census Bureau tells us that this year, it will use a shorter questionnaire, consisting of only ten questions. From what I see, only one of them serves the constitutional purpose of enumeration—namely, "How many people were living or staying at this house, apartment, or mobile home on April 1, 2010?" The Census Bureau's shorter questionnaire claim is deceptive at best.

The American Community Survey, long form, that used to be sent to one in six households during the decennial count, is now being sent to many people every year. Here's a brief sample of its questions, and I want someone to tell me which question serves the constitutional function of apportioning the number of seats in the US House of Representatives: Does this house, apartment, or mobile home have hot and cold running water, a flush toilet, a bathtub or shower, a sink with a faucet, a refrigerator, a stove? Last month, what was the cost of electricity for this house, apartment, or mobile home? How many times has this person been married?

After each question, the Bureau of the Census provides a statement of how the answer meets a federal need. I would prefer that they provide a statement of how answers to the questions meet the constitutional need as expressed in Article I, Section 2, of the US Constitution.

The Census Bureau also asks questions about race, and I want to know what does my race have to do with apportioning the US House of Representatives? If I'm asked about race, I might respond the way I did when filling out a military form upon landing in Inchon, Korea, in 1960; I checked off Caucasian. The warrant officer who was checking forms told me that I made a mistake and should have checked off "Negro." I told him that people have the right to self-identify themselves and I'm Caucasian. The warrant officer, trying to cajole me, asked why I would check off Caucasian instead of Negro. I told him that checking off Negro would mean getting the worse job over here. I'm sure the officer changed it after I left.

Americans need to stand up to Washington's intrusion into our private lives. What business of government is the number of times a citizen has been married or what he paid for electricity last month? For those who find such intrusion acceptable, I'd ask them whether they'd also find questions of their sex lives or their marriage fidelity equally acceptable.

What to do? Unless a census taker can show me a constitutional requirement, the only information I plan to give are the number and names of the people in my household. The census taker might say, "It's the law." Thomas Jefferson said, "Whensoever the General Government [Washington] assumes undelegated powers, its acts are unauthoritative, void, and of no force."

Constitutional Awakening

March 24, 2010

If there is anything good to say about Democrat control of the White House, Senate, and House of Representatives, it's that their extraordinarily brazen, heavy-handed acts have aroused a level of constitutional interest among the American people that has been dormant for far too long. Part of this heightened interest is seen in the strength of the tea party movement around the nation. Another is the angry reception that many congressmen received at their district town hall meetings. Yet another is seen by the exchanges on the nation's most popular radio talk shows such as Rush Limbaugh, Sean Hannity, Mark Levin, and others. Then there's the rising popularity of conservative/libertarian television shows such as Glenn Beck, John Stossel, and Fox News.

While the odds-on favorite is that the Republicans will do well in the fall elections, Americans who want constitutional government should not see Republican control as a solution to what our founders would have called "a long train of abuses and usurpations." Solutions to our nation's problems require correct diagnostics and answers to questions like: Why did 2008 presidential and congressional candidates spend over $5 billion campaigning for office? Why did special interests pay Washington lobbyists over $3 billion that same year? What are reasons why corporations, unions, and other interest groups fork over these billions of dollars to lobbyists and into the campaign coffers of politicians?

One might say that these groups are simply extraordinarily civic-minded Americans who have a deep and abiding interest in elected officials living up to their oath of office to uphold and defend the US Constitution. Another response is these politicians, and the people who spend billions of dollars on them, just love participating in the political process. If you believe either of these explanations, you're probably a candidate for some medicine, a straitjacket, and a padded cell.

A far better explanation for the billions going to the campaign coffers of Washington politicians and lobbyists lies in the awesome government power and control over business, property, employment, and other areas of our lives. Having such power, Washington politicians are in the position to grant favors and commit acts that if committed by a private person would land him in jail.

Here's one among thousands of examples: Incandescent light bulbs are far more convenient and less expensive than compact fluorescent bulbs (CFL) that General Electric now produces. So how can General Electric sell its costly CFLs? They know that Congress has the power to outlaw incandescent light bulbs. General Electric was the prominent lobbyist for outlawing incandescent light bulbs and in 2008 had a $20 million lobbying budget. Also, it should come as no surprise that General Electric is a contributor to global warmers who help convince Congress that incandescent bulbs were destroying the planet.

The greater Congress's ability to grant favors and take one American's earnings to give to another American, the greater the value of influencing congressional decision-making. There's no better influence than money. The generic favor sought is to get Congress, under one ruse or another, to grant a privilege or right to one group of Americans that will be denied another group of Americans.

House Speaker Nancy Pelosi covering up for a corrupt Ways and Means Committee chairman, Charles Rangel, said that while his behavior "was a violation of the rules of the House. It was not something that jeopardized our country in any way." Pelosi is right in minimizing Rangel's corruption. It pales in comparison, in terms of harm to our nation, to the legalized corruption that's a part of Washington's daily dealing.

Hopefully, our nation's constitutional reawaking will begin to deliver us from the precipice. There is no constitutional authority for two-thirds to three-quarters of what Congress does. Our Constitution's father, James Madison, explained, "The powers delegated by the proposed Constitution to the federal government, are few and defined ... [to be] exercised principally on external objects, as war, peace, negotiation, and foreign commerce."

The Founders' Vision versus Ours

July 7, 2010

The celebration of our founders' 1776 revolt against King George III and the English Parliament is over. Let's reflect how the founders might judge today's Americans and how today's Americans might judge them.

In 1794, when Congress appropriated $15,000 to assist some French refugees, James Madison, the acknowledged father of our Constitution, stood on the floor of the House to object, saying, "I cannot undertake to lay my finger on that article of the Constitution which granted a right to Congress of expending, on objects of benevolence, the money of their constituents." He later added, "[T]he government of the United States is a definite government, confined to specified objects. It is not like the state governments, whose powers are more general. Charity is no part of the legislative duty of the government." Two hundred years later, at least two-thirds of a multitrillion-dollar federal budget is spent on charity or "objects of benevolence."

What would the founders think about our respect for democracy and majority rule? Here's what Thomas Jefferson said: "The majority, oppressing an individual, is guilty of a crime, abuses its strength, and by acting on the law of the strongest breaks up the foundations of society." John Adams advised, "Remember democracy never lasts long. It soon wastes, exhausts, and murders itself. There never was a democracy yet that did not commit suicide." The founders envisioned a republican form of government, but as Benjamin Franklin warned, "When the people find they can vote themselves money, that will herald the end of the republic."

What would the founders think about the US Supreme Court's 2005 Kelo v. City of New London decision where the court sanctioned the taking of private property of one American to hand over to another American? John Adams explained: "The moment the idea is admitted into society that property is not as sacred as the laws of God, and that there is not a force of law and public justice to protect it, anarchy and tyranny commence. If 'Thou shalt not covet' and 'Thou shalt not steal' were not commandments of Heaven, they must be made inviolable precepts in every society before it can be civilized or made free."

Thomas Jefferson counseled us not to worship the US Supreme Court: "[T]he opinion which gives to the judges the right to decide what laws are constitutional and what not, not only for themselves in their own sphere of action but for the Legislature and Executive also in their spheres, would make the Judiciary a despotic branch."

How might our founders have commented about last week's US Supreme Court's decision upholding our rights to keep and bear arms? Justice Samuel Alito, in writing the majority opinion, said, "Individual self-defense is the central component of the Second Amendment." The founders would have responded "Balderdash!" Jefferson said, "What country can preserve its liberties if its rulers are not warned from time to time that their people preserve the spirit of resistance? Let them take arms."

George Mason explained, "[T]o disarm the people [is] the best and most effectual way to enslave them." Noah Webster elaborated: "Before a standing army can rule, the people must be disarmed.... The supreme power in America cannot enforce unjust laws by the sword; because the whole body of the people are armed, and constitute a force superior to any band of regular troops that can be, on any pretense, raised in the United States. A military force, at the command of Congress, can execute no laws, but such as the people perceive to be just and constitutional; for they will possess the power, and jealousy will instantly inspire the inclination, to resist the execution of a law which appears to them unjust and oppressive."

Contrary to Alito's assertion, the central component of the Second Amendment is to protect ourselves from US Congress, not street thugs.

Today's Americans have contempt for our founders' vision. I'm sure our founders would have contempt for ours.

What Our Constitution Permits

January 12, 2011

Here's the House of Representatives new rule: "A bill or joint resolution may not be introduced unless the sponsor has submitted for printing in the *Congressional Record* a statement citing as specifically as practicable the power or powers granted to Congress in the Constitution to enact the bill or joint resolution." Unless a congressional bill or resolution meets this requirement, it cannot be introduced.

If the House of Representatives had the courage to follow through on this rule, their ability to spend and confer legislative favors would be virtually eliminated. Also, if the rule were to be applied to existing law, they'd wind up repealing at least two-thirds to three-quarters of congressional spending.

You might think, for example, that there's constitutional authority for Congress to spend for highway construction and bridges. President James Madison on March 3, 1817, vetoed a public works bill saying: "Having considered the bill this day presented to me entitled 'An act to set apart and pledge certain funds for internal improvements,' and which sets apart and pledges funds 'for constructing roads and canals, and improving the navigation of water courses, in order to facilitate, promote, and give security to internal commerce among the several States, and to render more easy and less expensive the means and provisions for the common defense,' I am constrained by the insuperable difficulty I feel in reconciling the bill with the Constitution of the United States and to return it with that objection to the House of Representatives, in which it originated."

Madison, who is sometimes referred to as the father of our Constitution, added to his veto statement, "The legislative powers vested in Congress are specified and enumerated in the eighth section of the first article of the Constitution, and it does not appear that the power proposed to be exercised by the bill is among the enumerated powers."

Here's my question to any member of the House who might vote for funds for "constructing roads and canals, and improving the navigation of water courses": Was Madison just plain constitutionally ignorant or has the Constitution been amended to permit such spending?

What about handouts to poor people, businesses, senior citizens, and foreigners?

Madison said, "Charity is no part of the legislative duty of the government."

In 1854, President Franklin Pierce vetoed a bill to help the mentally ill, saying, "I cannot find any authority in the Constitution for public charity. [To approve the measure] would be contrary to the letter and spirit of the Constitution and subversive to the whole theory upon which the Union of these States is founded."

President Grover Cleveland vetoed a bill for charity relief, saying, "I can find no warrant for such an appropriation in the Constitution, and I do not believe that the power and duty of the General Government ought to be extended to the relief of individual suffering which is in no manner properly related to the public service or benefit."

Again, my question to House members who'd vote for handouts is: Were these leaders just plain constitutionally ignorant or mean-spirited, or has our Constitution been amended to authorize charity?

Suppose a congressman attempts to comply with the new rule by asserting that his measure is authorized by the Constitution's general welfare clause. Here's what Thomas Jefferson said: "Congress has not unlimited powers to provide for the general welfare, but only those specifically enumerated."

Madison added, "With respect to the two words 'general welfare,' I have always regarded them as qualified by the detail of powers connected with them. To take them in a literal and unlimited sense would be a metamorphosis of the Constitution into a character which there is a host of proofs was not contemplated by its creators."

John Adams warned, "A Constitution of Government once changed from Freedom, can never be restored. Liberty, once lost, is lost forever." I am all too afraid that's where our nation stands today and the blame lies with the American people.

Why We're a Divided Nation

January 19, 2011

Some Americans have strong, sometimes unyielding preferences for Mac computers, while most others have similarly strong preferences for PCs and wouldn't be caught dead using a Mac. Some Americans love classical music and hate rock and roll. Others have opposite preferences, loving rock and roll and consider classical music as hoity-toity junk. Then there are those among us who love football and Western movies, and find golf and cooking shows to be less than manly. Despite these, and many other strong preferences, there's little or no conflict. When's the last time you heard of rock and roll lovers in conflict with classical music lovers, or Mac lovers in conflict with PC lovers, or football lovers in conflict with golf lovers? It seldom if ever happens. When there's market allocation of resources and peaceable, voluntary exchange, people have their preferences satisfied and are able to live in peace with one another.

Think what might be the case if it were a political decision of whether there'd be football or golf watched on TV, whether we used Macs or PCs, and whether we listened to classical music or rock and roll. Everyone had to comply with the politically made decision or suffer the pain of fines or imprisonment. Football lovers would be lined up against golf lovers, Mac lovers against PC lovers, and rock and rollers against classical music lovers. People who previously lived in peace with one another would now be in conflict.

Why? If, for example, classical music lovers got what they wanted, rock and rollers wouldn't. Conflict would emerge solely because the decision was made in the political arena.

The lesson here is that the prime feature of political decision-making is that it's a zero-sum game. One person's gain is of necessity another person's loss. As such, political allocation of resources is conflict-enhancing, while market allocation is conflict-reducing. The greater the number of decisions made in the political arena, the greater the potential for conflict. It would not be unreasonable to predict that if Mac lovers won, and only Macs could be legally used, there would be considerable PC-lover hate toward Mac lovers.

Most of the issues that divide our nation, and give rise to conflict, are those best described as a zero-sum game where one person's or group's gain is of necessity another's loss. Examples are: racial preferences, school prayers, trade restrictions, welfare, Obamacare, and a host of other government policies that benefit one American at the expense of another American. That's why political action committees, private donors, and companies spend billions of dollars lobbying. Their goal is to get politicians and government officials to use the coercive power of their offices to take what belongs to one American and give it to another or create a favor or special privilege for one American that comes at the expense of some other American.

You might be tempted to think that the brutal domestic conflict seen in other countries can't happen here. That's nonsense. Americans are not super-humans; we possess the same frailties of other people. If there were a catastrophic economic calamity, I can imagine a political hustler exploiting those frailties, as have other tyrants, blaming it on the Jews, the blacks, the conservatives, the liberals, the Catholics, or free trade.

The best thing the president and Congress can do to reduce the potential for conflict and violence is reduce the impact of government on our lives. Doing so will not only produce a less-divided country and greater economic efficiency, but bear greater faith and allegiance to the vision of America held by our founders—a country of limited government. Our founders, in the words of Thomas Paine, recognized that, "Government, even in its best state, is but a necessary evil; in its worst state, an intolerable one."

Democracy versus Liberty

February 23, 2011

It is truly disgusting for me to hear politicians, national and international talking heads, and pseudo-academics praising the Middle East stirrings as democracy movements. We also hear democracy as the description of our own political system. Like the founders of our nation, I find democracy and majority rule a contemptible form of government.

You say, "Whoa, Williams, you really have to explain yourself this time!"

I'll begin by quoting our founders on democracy. James Madison, in Federalist Paper No. 10, said that in a pure democracy, "there is nothing to check the inducement to sacrifice the weaker party or the obnoxious individual." At the 1787 Constitutional Convention, Virginia Gov. Edmund Randolph said, "that in tracing these evils to their origin every man had found it in the turbulence and follies of democracy." John Adams said, "Remember, democracy never lasts long. It soon wastes, exhausts, and murders itself. There was never a democracy yet that did not commit suicide." Alexander Hamilton said, "We are now forming a Republican form of government. Real Liberty is not found in the extremes of democracy, but in moderate governments. If we incline too much to democracy, we shall soon shoot into a monarchy, or some other form of dictatorship."

The word "democracy" appears nowhere in the two most fundamental documents of our nation—the Declaration of Independence and the US Constitution. Our Constitution's Article IV, Section 4, guarantees "to every State in this Union a Republican Form of Government." If you don't want to bother reading our founding documents, just ask yourself: Does our pledge of allegiance to the flag say to "the democracy for which it stands," or to "the Republic for which it stands"? Or, did Julia Ward Howe make a mistake in titling her Civil War song "The Battle Hymn of the Republic"? Should she have titled it "The Battle Hymn of the Democracy"?

What's the difference between republican and democratic forms of government? John Adams captured the essence when he said, "You have rights antecedent to all earthly governments; rights that cannot be repealed or restrained by human laws; rights derived from the Great Legislator of the Universe." That means Congress does not grant us rights; their job is to protect our natural or God-given rights.

For example, the Constitution's First Amendment doesn't say Congress shall grant us freedom of speech, the press, and religion. It says, "Congress shall make no law respecting an establishment of religion, or prohibiting the free exercise thereof; or abridging the freedom of speech, or of the press. . . ."

Contrast the framers' vision of a republic with that of a democracy. Webster defines a democracy as "government by the people; especially: rule of the majority." In a democracy, the majority rules either directly or through its elected representatives. As in a monarchy, the law is whatever the government determines it to be. Laws do not represent reason. They represent force. The restraint is upon the individual instead of government. Unlike that envisioned under a republican form of government, rights are seen as privileges and permissions that are granted by government and can be rescinded by government.

To highlight the offensiveness to liberty that democracy and majority rule is, just ask yourself how many decisions in your life would you like to be made democratically. How about what car you drive, where you live, whom you marry, whether you have turkey or ham for Thanksgiving dinner? If those decisions were made through a democratic process, the average person would see it as tyranny and not personal liberty. Is it no less tyranny for the democratic process to determine whether you purchase health insurance or set aside money for retirement? Both for ourselves, and our fellow man around the globe, we should be advocating liberty, not the democracy that we've become where a roguish Congress does anything upon which they can muster a majority vote.

Continuing Stubborn Ignorance
March 16, 2011

Within the past decade, I've written three columns titled "Deception 101," "Stubborn Ignorance," and "Exploiting Public Ignorance," all explaining which branch of the federal government has taxing and spending authority. How can academics, politicians, news media people, and ordinary citizens get away with statements such as "Reagan's budget deficits," "Clinton's budget surplus," "Bush's budget deficits and tax cut," or "Obama's tax increases"? Which branch of government has taxing and spending authority is not a matter of rocket science, but people continue to make these statements. The only explanation that I come up with is incurable ignorance, willful deception, or just plain stupidity; if there's another answer, I would like to hear it.

Let's look at the facts. Article I, Section 7, of the US Constitution reads: "All bills for raising revenue shall originate in the House of Representatives; but the Senate may propose or concur with amendments as on other Bills." Our Constitution grants the president absolutely no authority to raise or lower taxes. The president is permitted to propose tax measures or veto them. Congress can ignore proposals and override vetoes.

The Constitution grants Congress the final and ultimate say on taxes. The same principle applies to spending. A president cannot spend one dime that Congress does not first appropriate. Therefore, statements such as "Under Barack Obama, government spending has increased 21 percent," and "Under Barack Obama, welfare spending has increased 54 percent" are just plain nonsense, if they are suggesting that Obama has increased spending. Credit or blame, whether it's a balanced budget, budget surplus, budget deficit, or national debt, lies with the US Congress.

Knowing where constitutional authority for taxing and spending lies is vital to our nation. No matter how we feel about President Obama, if we buy into the notion that it's he who's doing the taxing and spending, adding to our debt and deficits, we will focus our attention on trying to restrain the president. That will leave Congress less politically culpable for our deepening quagmire. Of course, if you're a congressman, not being held accountable is what you want.

Adding to the political deception in Washington is the notion that nearly 60 percent of the federal budget is off limits for spending cuts, the so-called nondiscretionary spending such as Social Security, Medicare, and Medicaid. Congress has the constitutional authority, through a simple majority vote, to change whatever laws associated with those "nondiscretionary" spending programs.

As an example, the US Supreme Court held in *Flemming vs. Nestor* (1960) there are no "accrued property rights" to a Social Security check. That means Congress can do anything it wishes with Social Security and that includes means-testing payments, raising eligibility age, reducing payments, increasing "contributions," or eliminating the program altogether. The same applies to any of the other so-called nondiscretionary spending programs.

By the way, thinking about the looming Social Security disaster, I believe that a person who's sixty-five years old and has been forced into Social Security is owed something. But who owes it to him? Congress has spent every penny of what he put into Social Security. Any check he receives comes out of the hide of young workers in the labor force. I think that's unfair. The young worker has no obligation to that senior citizen, but Congress has.

I have a one-time fix to give us some breathing room to make reforms. The federal government has huge quantities of wasting assets—assets that are not producing anything, 650 million acres of land—almost 30 percent of the land area of the United States. It owns 80 percent of the land in Nevada, 70 percent in Alaska, 60 percent in Idaho, and 50 percent in California and Oregon. I would be willing, and I suspect many others, to make a deal with Congress whereby I forsake all Social Security and Medicare benefits for, say, 50 acres of land in Alaska.

Do We Deserve Our Fate?

June 1, 2011

The latest Social Security Trustees Report tells us that the program will be insolvent by the year 2037. The combined unfunded liability of Social Security and Medicare has reached nearly $107 trillion in today's dollars. That is about seven times the size of the US economy and ten times the size of the national debt. Those entitlement programs, along with others, account for nearly 60 percent of federal spending. They are what Congress calls nondiscretionary spending. About half of discretionary spending is for national defense. Each year, nondiscretionary spending consumes a higher and higher percentage of the federal budget.

The language Congress uses to describe their spending is corrupt beyond redemption. Think about the term entitlement. If one American is entitled to something he didn't earn, where in the world does Congress get the money? It's not Santa or the Tooth Fairy. The only way Congress can give one American a dollar is to first take it from another American. Therefore, an entitlement is a congressionally given right for one American to live at the expense of another. In other words, Congress forcibly uses one American to serve the purposes of another American. As such, it differs in degree, but not kind, from that uglier part of our history where black people were forcibly used to serve the purposes of their slave masters.

What about the terms discretionary versus nondiscretionary congressional spending? Nondiscretionary refers to uncontrollable things like sunsets and sunrises, low tides and high tides, and laws of thermodynamics. By contrast, all congressional spending is discretionary and controllable. For political expedience, Congress has written laws to shield certain spending from annual budget scrutiny by calling it nondiscretionary.

The level of congressional spending is unsustainable, but how willing are Americans to do anything about it? A courageous member of

Congress, Paul Ryan, R-Wis., chairman of the House Budget Committee, has put forth a budget plan that would trim the deficit by $4.4 trillion over ten years by reforming Medicare and Medicaid, making defense cuts, and imposing hard spending caps on domestic spending.

Ryan's plan was immediately attacked as trying to balance the budget on the backs of the poor. In the wake of this attack, even some of his Republican backers, including House Speaker John Boehner, have become lukewarm in support.

The president and his supporters call for tax increases as a means to cover the deficit, but higher tax revenues cannot eliminate the deficit. Controlling for inflation, federal tax revenue today is twenty-three times greater than it was in 1960, but congressional spending is forty-two times greater. During the last half-century, except for five years, the nation has faced a federal budget deficit. It's just simple math. If tax revenues soar, but congressional spending soars more, budget deficits cannot be avoided.

People ask what can be done to save our nation from decline. To ask that represents a misunderstanding of history and possibly a bit of arrogance. After all, how different are Americans from the Romans, Spaniards, French, and the English? These were once mighty nations standing at the top of civilization. At the height of these nations' prosperity, no one would have predicted that they'd become third-rate nations, especially England. If during Queen Victoria's Jubilee in 1887 a person had suggested that England would become a third-rate nation and later challenged on the high seas by a sixth-rate nation (Argentina), he would have been declared insane.

One chief causal factor for the decline of these former great nations is what has been described as "bread and circuses," where government spends money for the shallow and immediate wants of the population, and civic virtue all but disappears. For the past half-century, our nation has been doing precisely what brought down other great nations. We might have now reached the point of no return. If so, do we deserve it?

Failing Liberty 101

July 13, 2011

A recent Superman comic book has the hero saying, "I am renouncing my US citizenship" because "truth, justice, and the American way—it's not enough anymore." Though not addressing Superman's statement, Stanford University professor and Hoover Institution senior fellow William Damon explains how such a vision could emerge today but not yesteryear. The explanation is found in his article "American Amnesia," in *Defining Ideas* (July 1, 2011), based upon his most recent book, *Failing Liberty 101: How We Are Leaving Young Americans Unprepared for Citizenship in a Free Society.*

The National Assessment of Educational Progress reports that only one in four high-school seniors scored at least "proficient" in knowledge of US citizenship. Civics and history were American students' worst subjects. Professor Damon said that for the past ten years, his Stanford University research team has interviewed broad cross-sections of American youths about US citizenship. Here are some typical responses: "We just had [American citizenship] the other day in history. I forget what it was." Another said, "Being American is not really special. . . . I don't find being an American citizen very important." Another said, "I don't want to belong to any country. It just feels like you are obligated to this country. I don't like the whole thing of citizen. . . . It's like, citizen, no citizen; it doesn't make sense to me. It's, like, to be a good citizen—I don't know, I don't want to be a citizen. . . . It's stupid to me."

A law professor, whom Damon leaves unnamed, shares this vision in a recent book: "Longstanding notions of democratic citizenship are becoming obsolete. . . . American identity is unsustainable in the face of globalization." Instead of commitment to a nation-state, "loyalties . . . are moving to transnational communities defined by many different ways: by race, ethnicity, gender, religion, age, and sexual orientation." This law professor's vision is shared by many educators who look to "global citizenship" as the proper aim of civics instruction, deemphasizing attachment to any particular country, such as the United States, pointing out that our primary obligation should be to the universal ideals of human rights and justice. To be patriotic to one's own country is seen as suspect because it may turn into a militant chauvinism or a dangerous "my country, right or wrong" vision.

The ignorance about our country is staggering. According to one survey, only 28 percent of students could identify the Constitution as the supreme law of the land. Only 26 percent of students knew that the first ten amendments to the Constitution are called the Bill of Rights. Fewer than one-quarter of students knew that George Washington was the first president of the United States.

Discouraging young Americans from identifying with their country and celebrating our traditional American quest for liberty and equal rights removes the most powerful motivation to learn civics and US history. After all, Damon asks, "why would a student exert any effort to master the rules of a system that the student has no respect for and no interest in being part of? To acquire civic knowledge as well as civic virtue, students need to care about their country." Ignorance and possibly contempt for American values, civics, and history might help explain how someone like Barack Obama could become president of the United States. At no other time in our history could a person with longtime associations with people who hate our country become president. Obama spent twenty years attending the Rev. Jeremiah Wright's hate-filled sermons, which preached that "white folks' greed runs a world in need," called our country the "US of KKK-A" and asked God to "damn America." Obama's other America-hating associates include Weather Underground Pentagon bomber William Ayers and Ayers's wife, Bernardine Dohrn.

The fact that Obama became president and brought openly Marxist people into his administration doesn't say so much about him as it says about the effects of decades of brainwashing of the American people by the education establishment, media and the intellectual elite.

Legal Obedience

August 24, 2011

What laws are we morally obligated to obey? Help with the answer can be found in "Economic Liberty and the Constitution," a sixty-six-page pamphlet by Jacob G. Hornberger, founder and president of The Future of Freedom Foundation.

Hornberger offers a hypothetical whereby Congress enacts a compulsory church attendance law that requires children to attend church service each Sunday. Parents are penalized if their children fail to comply. Would there be any moral or constitutional legitimacy to such a congressional mandate? The law would be a clear violation of one's natural, or God-given, rights to life and liberty. As to whether it would be constitutional, we have to see whether mandating church attendance is one of those enumerated powers of Congress found in Article 1, Section 8, of our Constitution. We'd find no such authority. Our antifederalist founding fathers didn't trust Congress with religious liberty, so they sought to protect it with the First Amendment to explicitly deny Congress the power to mandate religious conduct. Suppose there's widespread popular support for a church-going mandate and the US Supreme Court rules it constitutional; do Americans have a moral obligation to obey the law?

You might say, "Williams, while there are gray areas in the Constitution, the US Supreme Court would never brazenly rule against clear constitutional prohibitions!" That's nonsense. The first clause of Article 1, Section 10, mandates that "No State shall . . . pass any . . . Law impairing the Obligation of Contracts." During the Great Depression, the US Supreme Court upheld a Minnesota law that restricted the ability of banks to foreclose on overdue mortgages, thereby impairing contracts made between lender and borrower. To prevent this kind of contract impairment—routinely done under the Articles of Confederation—was precisely why the framers added the clause.

Another, perhaps more egregious example of the Supreme Court's impairing contracts came during President Franklin Roosevelt's New

Deal, when the government nationalized gold and made it a felony for any American to own gold. Not only was gold ownership made illegal but it nullified all "gold clauses" in private and government contracts. Writing contracts in gold was a way people protected themselves against government theft, namely inflation. The Supreme Court upheld federal nationalization of gold and nullification of gold contracts in the famous Gold Clause Cases. Today many Americans have turned to gold, driving its price to an all-time high, as a safeguard against what they see as pending inflation. Here's my question to you: If Obama and Congress enacted a law demanding that you turn in your gold, would you be morally obligated to obey such a law?

Decent people should not obey immoral laws. What's moral and immoral can be a contentious issue, but there are some broad guides for deciding what laws and government actions are immoral. Lysander S. Spooner, one of America's great nineteenth-century thinkers, said no person or group of people can "authorize government to destroy or take away from men their natural rights; for natural rights are inalienable, and can no more be surrendered to government—which is but an association of individuals—than to a single individual." French economist/philosopher Frederic Bastiat (1801–50) gave a test for immoral government acts: "See if the law benefits one citizen at the expense of another by doing what the citizen himself cannot do without committing a crime." He added in his book *The Law*, "When law and morality contradict each other, the citizen has the cruel alternative of either losing his moral sense or losing his respect for the law."

After reading Hornberger's "Economic Liberty and the Constitution," one cannot avoid the conclusion that the liberties envisioned by the nation's founders have been under siege, trivialized and nullified. Philosopher Johann Wolfgang von Goethe explained that "no one is as hopelessly enslaved as the person who thinks he's free." That's becoming an apt description for Americans who are oblivious to—or ignorant of—the liberties we've lost.

Democracy and Majority Rule
November 21, 2012

President Barack Obama narrowly defeated Gov. Mitt Romney in the popular vote 51 percent to 48 percent. In the all-important Electoral College, the difference was larger, with Obama winning 303 electoral votes and Romney 206. Let's not think so much about the election's outcome but instead ask: What's so good about democracy and majority rule?

How many decisions in our day-to-day lives would we like to be made through majority rule or the democratic process? How about the decision to watch a football game or "Law and Order"? What about whether to purchase a Chevrolet Volt or a Toyota Prius? Would you like the decision of whether to have turkey or ham for Thanksgiving dinner to be made through the democratic process? Were such decisions made in the political arena, most of us would deem it tyranny.

Democracy and majority rule give an aura of legitimacy and decency to acts that would otherwise be deemed tyranny. Most people would agree that having our decisions on what television shows to watch, what kind of car we'll purchase, and what we'll eat for Thanksgiving dinner made through the democratic process is tyranny. Why isn't it also tyranny for the political process to determine decisions such as how much should be put aside out of our paycheck for retirement; whether we purchase health insurance or not; what type of light bulbs we use; or whether we purchase 32- or 16-ounce soda containers?

The founders of our nation held a deep abhorrence for democracy and majority rule. The word democracy appears in neither of our founding documents: our Declaration of Independence and Constitution. In Federalist Paper No. 10, James Madison wrote, "Measures are too often decided, not according to the rules of justice and the rights of the minor party, but by the superior force of an interested and overbearing majority."

John Adams predicted, "Remember, democracy never lasts long. It soon wastes, exhausts, and murders itself. There was never a democracy yet that did not commit suicide."

Edmund Randolph said that "in tracing these evils to their origin every man had found it in the turbulence and follies of democracy."

Chief Justice John Marshall observed, "Between a balanced republic and a democracy, the difference is like that between order and chaos."

In a word or two, the founders knew that a democracy would lead to the same kind of tyranny the colonies suffered under King George III. Our founders intended for us to have a republican form of limited government where political decision-making is kept to the minimum.

Alert to the dangers of majoritarian tyranny, our Constitution's framers inserted several antimajority rules. One such rule is that election of the president is not decided by a majority vote but instead by the Electoral College. Nine states have more than 50 percent of the US population. If a simple majority were the rule, conceivably these nine states could determine the presidency. Fortunately, they can't because they have only 225 Electoral College votes when 270 of the 538 total are needed. Were it not for the Electoral College, presidential candidates could safely ignore less populous states.

Two houses of Congress pose another obstacle to majority rule. Fifty-one senators can block the designs of 435 representatives and 49 senators. The Constitution gives the president a veto that weakens the power of 535 members of both houses of Congress. It takes two-thirds of both houses of Congress to override a presidential veto. To change the Constitution requires not a majority but a two-thirds vote of both Houses to propose an amendment, and to be enacted requires ratification by three-fourths of state legislatures.

Today's Americans think Congress has the constitutional authority to do anything upon which they can get a majority vote. We think whether a measure is a good idea or a bad idea should determine its passage as opposed to whether that measure lies within the enumerated powers granted Congress by the Constitution. Unfortunately, for the future of our nation, Congress has successfully exploited American constitutional ignorance or contempt.

Why the Second Amendment

January 2, 2013

Rep. John Lewis, D-Ga., in the wake of the Newtown, Conn., shootings, said: "The British are not coming. . . . We don't need all these guns to kill people." Lewis's vision, shared by many, represents a gross ignorance of why the framers of the Constitution gave us the Second Amendment. How about a few quotes from the period and you decide whether our founding fathers harbored a fear of foreign tyrants.

Alexander Hamilton: "The best we can hope for concerning the people at large is that they be properly armed," adding later, "If the representatives of the people betray their constituents, there is then no recourse left but in the exertion of that original right of self-defense which is paramount to all positive forms of government." By the way, Hamilton is referring to what institution when he says "the representatives of the people"?

James Madison: "[The Constitution preserves] the advantage of being armed, which the Americans possess over the people of almost every other nation . . . [where] the governments are afraid to trust the people with arms."

Thomas Jefferson: "What country can preserve its liberties if its rulers are not warned from time to time that their people preserve the spirit of resistance? Let them take arms."

George Mason, author of the Virginia Bill of Rights, which inspired our Constitution's Bill of Rights, said, "To disarm the people—that was the best and most effectual way to enslave them."

Rep. John Lewis and like-minded people might dismiss these thoughts by saying the founders were racist anyway. Here's a more recent quote from a card-carrying liberal, the late Vice President Hubert H. Humphrey: "Certainly, one of the chief guarantees of freedom under any government, no matter how popular and respected, is the right of the citizen to keep and bear arms. . . . The right of the citizen to bear arms is just one guarantee against arbitrary government, one more safeguard against the tyranny which now appears remote in America but which historically has proven to be always possible." I have many other Second Amendment references at http://econfaculty. gmu.edu/wew/quotes.html.

How about a couple of quotations with which Rep. Lewis and others might agree? "Armas para que?" (translated: "Guns, for what?") by Fidel Castro. There's a more famous one: "The most foolish mistake we could possibly make would be to allow the subject races to possess arms. History shows that all conquerors who have allowed their subject races to carry arms have prepared their own downfall by so doing." That was Adolf Hitler.

Here's the gun grabbers' slippery-slope agenda, laid out by Nelson T. Shields, founder of Handgun Control Inc.: "We're going to have to take this one step at a time, and the first step is necessarily—given the political realities—going to be very modest. . . . Right now, though, we'd be satisfied not with half a loaf but with a slice. Our ultimate goal—total control of handguns in the United States—is going to take time. . . . The final problem is to make the possession of all handguns and all handgun ammunition—except for the military, police, licensed security guards, licensed sporting clubs and licensed gun collectors—totally illegal" (*The New Yorker*, July 1976).

There have been people who've ridiculed the protections afforded by the Second Amendment, asking what chance would citizens have against the military might of the US government. Military might isn't always the deciding factor. Our 1776 War of Independence was against the mightiest nation on the face of the Earth—Great Britain. In Syria, the rebels are making life uncomfortable for the much better equipped Syrian regime. Today's Americans are vastly better armed than our founders, Warsaw Ghetto Jews, and Syrian rebels.

There are about 300 million privately held firearms owned by Americans. That's nothing to sneeze at. And notice that the people who support gun control are the very people who want to control and dictate our lives.

Is There a Way Out?

October 30, 2013

According to a recent Fox News poll, 73 percent of Americans are dissatisfied with the direction of the country, up 20 points from 2012. Americans sense that there's a lot going wrong in our nation, but most don't have a clue about the true nature of our problem. If they had a clue, most would have little stomach for what would be necessary to arrest our national decline. Let's look at it.

Between two-thirds and three-quarters of federal spending, in contravention of the US Constitution, can be described as Congress taking the earnings or property of one American to give to another, to whom it does not belong. You say, "Williams, what do you mean?" Congress has no resources of its own. Moreover, there's no Santa Claus or Tooth Fairy who gives it resources. The fact that Congress has no resources of its own forces us to recognize that the only way Congress can give one American one dollar is to first—through intimidation, threats, and coercion—confiscate that dollar from some other American through the tax code.

If any American did privately what Congress does publicly, he'd be condemned as an ordinary thief. Taking what belongs to one American to give to another is theft, and the receiver is a recipient of stolen property. Most Americans would suffer considerable anguish and cognitive dissonance seeing themselves as recipients of stolen property, so congressional theft has to be euphemized and given a respectable name. That respectable name is "entitlement." Merriam-Webster defines entitlement as "the condition of having a right to have, do, or get something." For example, I am entitled to walk into the house that I own. I am entitled to drive the car that I own. The challenging question is whether I am also entitled to what you or some other American owns.

Let's look at a few of these entitlements. More than 40 percent of federal spending is for entitlements for the elderly in the forms of Social Security, Medicare, Medicaid, housing, and other assistance programs. The Office of Management and Budget calculates that total entitlement spending comes to about 62 percent of federal spending. Military spending totals 19 percent of federal spending. By the way, putting those two figures into historical perspective demonstrates the success we've had becoming a handout nation. In 1962, military expenditures were almost 50 percent of the federal budget, and entitlement spending was a mere 31 percent. The Congressional Budget Office estimates that entitlement spending will consume all federal tax revenue by 2048.

Entitlement spending is not the only form of legalized theft. The Department of Agriculture gives billions of dollars to farmers. The departments of Energy and Commerce give billions of dollars and subsidized loans to corporations. In fact, every Cabinet-level department in Washington is in charge of handing out at least one kind of subsidy or special privilege. Most federal nondefense "discretionary spending" by Congress is for handouts.

Despite the fact that today's increasing levels of federal government spending are unsustainable, there is little evidence that Americans have the willingness to do anything about it. Any politician who'd even talk about significantly reining in unsustainable entitlement spending would be run out of town. Any politician telling the American people they must pay higher taxes to support handout spending, instead of concealing spending through deficits and running up the national debt and inflation, would also be run out of town. Can you imagine what the American people would do to a presidential candidate who'd declare, as James Madison did in a 1794 speech to the House of Representatives, "Charity is no part of the legislative duty of the government"?

If we are to be able to avoid ultimate collapse, it's going to take a moral reawakening and renewed constitutional respect—not by politicians but by the American people. The prospect of that happening may be whistlin' "Dixie."

Parting Company
January 1, 2014

Here's a question that I've asked in the past that needs to be revisited. Unless one wishes to obfuscate, it has a simple yes or no answer. If one group of people prefers strong government control and management of people's lives while another group prefers liberty and desires to be left alone, should they be required to enter into conflict with one another and risk bloodshed and loss of life in order to impose their preferences on the other group? Yes or no. My answer is no; they should be able to peaceably part company and go their separate ways.

The problem our nation faces is very much like a marriage in which one partner has an established pattern of ignoring and breaking the marital vows. Moreover, the offending partner has no intention to mend his ways. Of course, the marriage can remain intact while one party tries to impose his will on the other and engages in the deviousness of one-upmanship and retaliation. Rather than domination or submission by one party, or domestic violence, a more peaceable alternative is separation.

I believe our nation is at a point where there are enough irreconcilable differences between those Americans who want to control other Americans and those Americans who want to be left alone that separation is the only peaceable alternative. Just as in a marriage where vows are broken, our rights guaranteed by the US Constitution have been grossly violated by a government instituted to protect them. These constitutional violations have increased independent of whether there's been a Democrat-controlled Washington or a Republican-controlled Washington.

There is no evidence that Americans who are responsible for and support constitutional abrogation have any intention of mending their ways. You say, "Williams, what do you mean by constitutional abrogation?" Let's look at the magnitude of the violations.

Article I, Section 8, of our Constitution lists the activities for which Congress is authorized to tax and spend. Nowhere on that list is there authority for Congress to tax and spend for: Medicare, Social Security, public education, farm subsidies, bank and business bailouts, food stamps, and thousands of other activities that account for roughly two-thirds of the federal budget. Neither is there authority for congressional mandates to citizens about what type of health insurance they must purchase, how states and people may use their land, the speed at which they can drive, whether a library has wheelchair ramps, and the gallons of water used per toilet flush. The list of congressional violations of both the letter and spirit of the Constitution is virtually without end. Our derelict Supreme Court has given Congress sanction to do just about anything for which they can muster a majority vote.

James Madison, the acknowledged father of the Constitution, explained in Federalist Paper No. 45: "The powers delegated by the proposed Constitution to the federal government are few and defined. Those which are to remain in the State governments are numerous and indefinite. The former will be exercised principally on external objects, as war, peace, negotiation, and foreign commerce. . . . The powers reserved to the several States will extend to all the objects which in the ordinary course of affairs, concern the lives and liberties, and properties of the people, and the internal order, improvement and prosperity of the State." Our founder's constitutional vision of limited federal government has been consigned to the dustbin of history.

Americans have several options. We can like sheep submit to those who have contempt for liberty and our Constitution. We can resist, fight, and risk bloodshed and death in an attempt to force America's tyrants to respect our liberties and Constitution. A superior alternative is to find a way to peaceably separate into states whose citizens respect liberty and the Constitution. My personal preference is a restoration of the constitutional values of limited government that made us a great nation.

Governed by Rules, Not Men

March 12, 2014

What kind of rules should govern our lives? I'd argue that the best rules are those that we'd be satisfied with if our very worst enemy were in charge of decision-making. The foundation for such rules was laid out by my mother. Let's look at it.

My mother worked as a domestic servant. That meant that my younger sister and I often lunched at home by ourselves during our preteen years. Being bigger and stronger than my sister, I seldom divided the food evenly, especially the desserts. After a tiring day at work, Mom would be greeted by sob stories from my sister about my lunchtime injustices. Mom finally became fed up with the sibling hassles. She didn't admonish me to be more caring, fair, sensitive, and considerate. She just made a rule: Whoever cuts the cake (pie, bread, meat, etc.) allows the other the first selection. With that new rule in place, you can bet that when either my sister or I divided food, it was divided equally.

You say, "That's a nice story, Williams, but what's the point?" The point is that the principle underlying Mom's rule is precisely the kind that is necessary for rules to promote fairness. In general, the rules that we should want are those that promote fairness, whether it's our best friend or it's our worst enemy who's the decision-maker. In the case of Mom's rule, it didn't make any difference whether I hated my sister's guts that day or she hated mine or whether my sister was doing the cutting or I was; there was a just division of the food.

Think for a moment about rules in sports, say basketball. One team loses, and the other wins, but they and their fans leave the stadium peacefully and most often as friends. Why? The game's outcome is seen as fair because there are fixed, known, neutral rules evenly applied by the referees. The referees' job is to apply the rules—not determine the game's outcome. Imagine the chaos and animosity among players and fans if one team paid referees to help it win or the referees were trying to promote some kind of equality among teams.

Billions of dollars and billions of hours are spent campaigning for this or that candidate in our national elections. You can bet that people are not making those expenditures so that politicians will uphold and defend the Constitution; they're looking for favors. The Constitution's framers gave us reasonably fair and neutral rules of the game. If our government acted, as the framers intended, as a referee or night watchman, how much difference would it make to any of us who occupies the White House or Congress? It would make little difference, if any. It would be just like our basketball game example. Any government official who knew and enforced the rules would do. But increasingly, who's in office is making a difference, because government has abandoned its referee and night watchman function and gotten into the business of determining winners and losers. Unfortunately, for our nation, that's what most Americans want.

Thomas Paine said, "Government, even in its best state, is but a necessary evil." Our Bill of Rights is an explicit recognition of the founding fathers' distrust of Congress. Just look at its language, with phrases such as "Congress shall not abridge," "shall not infringe," "shall not deny," "disparage" and "violate." If the framers did not believe that Congress would abuse our God-given, or natural, rights, they would not have used such language. If, after we die, we see anything like the Bill of Rights at our next destination, we'll know that we're in hell. To demand such protections in heaven would be the same as saying we can't trust God.

The Constitution or Good Ideas?

April 30, 2014

Let me run through a few good ideas. I think it's a good idea for children to eat healthful, wholesome foods. In the raising of our daughter, before-dinner treats were fresh vegetables, and after-dinner treats were mostly fruits.

I arrive at my gym sometime between 4 a.m. and 5 a.m., at least four times a week, to lift weights and use the treadmill. During the warmer months, the treadmill is substituted by a weekly total of forty to sixty miles on my bike. My exercise regimen is a good idea. Another good idea is to wear a bike helmet while bike riding and wear a seat belt when driving my car. Among many other good ideas is the enjoyment of two, maybe three, glasses of wine with each evening meal.

You say, "So what, Williams? What's your point?" There's no question that all of those actions, with the possible exception of the last, are indeed good ideas. As evidence that my exercise regimen is a good idea, my doctors tell me that at seventy-eight years of age, I'm in better health and conditioning than most of their male patients many years my junior. My question to you is whether these commonly agreed-upon good ideas should become the law of the land. To be more explicit, should Congress enact a law requiring every able-bodied American to lift weights four times a week and bike forty to sixty miles each week? Just look at all the benefits of such a law. Americans would be healthier, and that would mean lower health care costs. People would have a longer working life. Men would have the strength to protect their women and children folk from thugs. In a word, there would be no downside to the fitter population that would come from a congressional law mandating physical fitness programs. We might title such a law the "Improving American Health Act." The law would impose fines and penalties on any able-bodied person not found to be in compliance. What congressman would have the callousness to vote against such a beneficial measure?

Needless to say, there would be attacks against the Improving American Health Act, launched mostly by libertarians, conservatives, and some Republicans. These people would argue that Congress has no constitutional authority to enact such a liberty-intrusive law. Their arguments would be on weak grounds. Our Constitution's Article 1, Section 8, says, "The Congress shall have Power To . . . provide for the . . . general Welfare of the United States." Our Constitution further empowers Congress to enact the Improving American Health Act by its Article 1, Section 3—sometimes referred to as the commerce clause—which grants Congress the power "To regulate Commerce . . . among the several States." After all, good health lends itself to more efficient interstate commerce and a larger gross domestic product. Sick Americans adversely affect interstate commerce and are a burden on economic activity.

I have no doubt that people who don't want to see a healthier America—again, mostly libertarians, conservatives, and Republicans— will bring suit before the US Supreme Court, arguing that Congress has no such authority under either the general welfare clause or the commerce clause. Would you prefer that Chief Justice John Roberts Jr., speaking for a majority, concur by saying, "This court is guided by the US Constitution, and we find no constitutional authority for the Improving American Health Act, despite Congress's nonsense claims alleging authority under the general welfare and commerce clauses"?

Or would you prefer that Justice Roberts, speaking for the majority, engage in mental contortions in which he agrees that forcing people to exercise exceeds congressional authority under both the commerce clause and the general welfare clause but says the Improving American Health Act is indeed constitutional under Congress's taxing authority?

My bottom line question is: Should we be ruled by what are seen as good ideas or by what's permissible by the US Constitution?

PART II

Politics

My view of our relationship with government, at all levels, has its foundation in the ideas of philosopher John Locke whose ideas of natural rights significantly influenced the founders of our nation. It is the idea that each of us owns ourselves. We are each our own private property. If we establish self-ownership as our initial premise, then what constitutes moral and immoral behavior is more easily delineated. For example, the reason why murder is immoral is that it violates private property. Similarly, rape and theft are immoral for they too violate private property.

Since we own ourselves, each person has a natural right to protect himself against aggressive acts such as murder, rape, theft, and other forms of coercion. As the signers of our Declaration of Independence said, "We hold these truths to be self-evident, that all men are created equal, that they are endowed by their Creator with certain unalienable rights, that among these are life, liberty and the pursuit of happiness. That to secure these rights, governments are instituted among men." Therefore, the fundamental role of government in a free society is to protect private property.

Since individuals have a natural, or God-given, right to protect what is theirs, they can delegate that right. In other words, an organized government might be more efficient at protecting us against international or domestic thugs who would murder, rape, and steal from us. We do not have a natural or God-given right to take from one person to give to another for any reason. That means that we cannot delegate such a right to another person or agent.

Think of it this way. Suppose I saw an elderly woman sleeping on a grate in the dead of winter. She is cold, hungry, and in need of medical care. Wishing to help the woman, I use threats of violence to take $200 dollars from another person. Having stolen that $200, I then purchase shelter, food, and medical attention for the woman. The question is: Would I be guilty of having committed a crime? I am sure that most people will answer yes I have committed theft. The rightful property of one person was taken by force and given to another.

While there would probably be little disagreement with the observation that theft has been committed, there is a question. Would it be theft if I managed to get two or three people to agree to take $200 from another to help the woman out? What if one hundred people agreed? A million? Or 300 million? Alternatively, what if there was a vote taken and a majority agreed to a law whereby money was taken to help the woman? The only difference between an individual taking one person's property to give to another and 300 million people voting in a law doing the same thing is legality. My taking another's money to help the woman is illegal theft and 300 million people using government to do the same thing is legal theft. Both acts are theft and the only difference is legality.

Some might take comfort in an act being legal. However, for moral people legality alone cannot be their moral compass, for history records many acts that were legal but clearly immoral. Slavery in many places was legal but did that status make it moral? Germany's 1935 Nuremberg laws called for the persecution of Jews and led to the genocide of millions. These laws were legal but were they moral? Stalinist and Maoist purges of tens of millions of people were legal but were they moral? Our own country's Fugitive Slave Act of 1850 compelled free states to return escaped slaves to their masters. That was legal but was it moral?

The columns in this section raise a number of issues and arguments about our political lives and relationship with government. They question supposedly settled issues such as the right of states to secede, the con-

tempt that framers of our Constitution had for the ideas of democracy and the ideas of majority rule. At the heart of the columns in this section is my effort to warn my fellow Americans how we are increasingly losing our liberties as the government gains greater and greater control over our everyday lives. One of my sad conclusions is that most Americans have contempt for our Constitution and the limits it places on Congress and White House.

Congress's Financial Mess
January 14, 2009

News media people, often plagued with little understanding, fail miserably in their duty to inform the public. This is particularly evident in their reporting on the current financial meltdown, suggesting it was caused by deregulation and free markets.

Professor David Henderson, research fellow at Stanford's Hoover Institution, writes about regulation in "Are We Ailing from Too Much Deregulation?" in Cato Policy Report (November/December 2008). The *Federal Register*, which lists new regulations, annually averaged 72,844 pages between 1977 and 1980. During the Reagan years, the average fell to 54,335. During the Bush I years, they rose to 59,527, they rose to 71,590 during the Clinton years, and they rose to a record of 75,526 during the Bush II years. Employees in government regulatory agencies grew from 146,139 in 1980 to 238,351 in 2007, a 63 percent increase. In the banking and finance industries, regulatory spending between 1980 and 2007 almost tripled, rising from $725 million to $2.07 billion. So here's my question: What are we to make of congressmen, talking heads, and news media people who tell us the financial meltdown is a result of deregulation and free markets? Are they ignorant, stupid, or venal?

A *New York Times* article, "Fannie Mae Eases Credit to Aid Mortgage Lending" (September 30, 1999), reported, "Fannie Mae, the nation's biggest underwriter of home mortgages, has been under increasing pressure from the Clinton Administration to expand mortgage loans among low and moderate income people." The pressure was the 1977 Community Reinvestment Act that was beefed up during the Clinton administration. It required banks to make high-risk loans they would not have otherwise made. Failure to comply meant fines and difficulty in getting approval for mergers and branch expansion.

When questions began to arise about government policy that intimidated lenders into making high-risk loans, we received congressional assurances. At hearings investigating the solvency of Fannie Mae and Freddie Mac, Rep. Barney Frank said, "The more people exaggerate these problems, the more pressure there is on these companies, the less we will see in terms of affordable housing." In a speech to the Mortgage Bankers Association, Frank advised, "People tend to pay their mortgages. I don't think we are in any remote danger here. This focus on receivership, I think, is intended to create fears that aren't there." Protesting against greater controls against lax mortgage lending, Sen. Harry Reid said, "While I favor improving oversight by our federal housing regulators to ensure safety and soundness, we cannot pass legislation that could limit Americans from owning homes and potentially harm our economy in the process."

One-third of the $15 trillion of mortgages in existence in 2008 are owned, or securitized, by Fannie Mae, Freddie Mac, Ginnie Mae, the Federal Housing, and the Veterans Administration. Wall Street buyers of repackaged loans didn't mind buying risky paper because they assumed that they would be guaranteed by the federal government: read bailout from the taxpayers. Today's housing mess can be laid directly at the feet of Congress and the White House.

Congress and the White House aren't finished with the taxpayers yet. Once a bailout parade gets started, it has a momentum of its own. President Bush, citing danger to the economy, signed a $17 billion bailout for the auto industry. According to the *Wall Street Journal* article "Shovel-Ready on Campus" (December 17, 2008), presidents of 36 state government universities have called for bailouts; they call it a "federal infusion of capital." Soon, if not already, state governors and city mayors will descend on Washington seeking bailouts. California is $15 billion in the hole, Florida $5 billion and things are so bad in Michigan that the governor has shut down one prison to save money.

What kind of assumptions do politicians and news media make about the intelligence of Americans to expect us to buy the idea that our current mess results from deregulation and free markets? I do not find that assumption flattering.

The National Ponzi Scheme
February 4, 2009

The US Securities and Exchange Commission (SEC) was set up to combat fraudulent practices. The SEC's website explains that "Ponzi schemes are a type of illegal pyramid scheme named for Charles Ponzi, who duped thousands of New England residents into investing in a postage stamp speculation scheme back in the 1920s." It goes on to say, "Decades later, the Ponzi scheme continues to work on the 'rob-Peter-to-pay-Paul' principle, as money from new investors is used to pay off earlier investors until the whole scheme collapses." That is how the SEC described the recent Bernard Madoff $50 billion Ponzi scheme, "a stunning fraud that appears to be of epic proportions."

A Ponzi scheme does not generate any wealth whatsoever; that is why it ultimately collapses. As Circuit Judge Anderson said in the 1922 Lowell v. Brown case, the Ponzi scheme was "simply the old fraud of paying the earlier comers out of the contributions of the later comers." So long as the number of late comers—you might call them suckers—grows, the fraudulent scheme has life.

We have a national Ponzi scheme where Congress collects about $785 billion in Social Security taxes from about 163 million workers to send out $585 billion to 50 million Social Security recipients. Social Security's trustees tell us that the surplus goes into a $2.2 trillion trust fund to meet future obligations. The problem is whatever difference between Social Security taxes and benefits paid out is spent by Congress. What the Treasury Department does is give the Social Security Trust Fund nonmarketable "special issue government securities" that are simply bookkeeping entries that are IOUs.

According to Social Security trustee estimates, around 2016 the amount of Social Security benefits paid will exceed taxes collected. That means one of two things, or both, must happen: Congress will raise taxes and/or slash promised Social Security benefits. Each year the situation will get worse since the number of retirees is predicted to increase relative to the number in the workforce paying taxes. In 1940, there were forty-two workers per retiree, in 1950 there were sixteen, today there are three, and in twenty or thirty years there will be two or fewer workers per retiree.

Social Security is unsustainable because it is not meeting the first order condition of a Ponzi scheme, namely expanding the pool of suckers. Social Security has been one congressional lie after another since its inception. Here's what a 1936 Social Security pamphlet said: "After the first 3 years—that is to say, beginning in 1940—you will pay, and your employer will pay, 1.5 cents for each dollar you earn, up to $3,000 a year. . . . [B]eginning in 1943, you will pay 2 cents, and so will your employer, for every dollar you earn for the next 3 years. . . . And finally, beginning in 1949, twelve years from now, you and your employer will each pay 3 cents on each dollar you earn, up to $3,000 a year. That is the most you will ever pay." The pamphlet also said, "Beginning November 24, 1936, the United States government will set up a Social Security account for you. . . . The checks will come to you as a right."

That's another lie. In *Flemming vs Nestor* (1960), the US Supreme court held that you have no "accrued property rights" to a Social Security check. That means Congress can do anything it wishes with Social Security. There is little or nothing that can be done to prevent the economic and political chaos that will result from the collapse of Social Security.

Today's recipients of Social Security, along with their powerful American Association of Retired Persons (AARP) lobby, represent a powerful political force. Few politicians are willing to risk their careers alienating today's senior citizens for the benefit of Americans in 2040. After all what do today's seniors and politicians care about a 2040 calamity? They will be dead by then.

States Rebellion Pending

March 25, 2009

Our Colonial ancestors petitioned and pleaded with King George III to get his boot off their necks. He ignored their pleas, and in 1776, they rightfully declared unilateral independence and went to war. Today it's the same story except Congress is the one usurping the rights of the people and the states, making King George's actions look mild in comparison. Our constitutional ignorance—perhaps contempt, coupled with the fact that we've become a nation of wimps, sissies, and supplicants—has made us easy prey for Washington's tyrannical forces. But that might be changing a bit. There are rumblings of a long-over-due reemergence of Americans' characteristic spirit of rebellion.

Eight state legislatures have introduced resolutions declaring state sovereignty under the Ninth and Tenth amendments to the US Constitution; they include Arizona, Hawaii, Montana, Michigan, Missouri, New Hampshire, Oklahoma, and Washington. There's speculation that they will be joined by Alaska, Alabama, Arkansas, California, Colorado, Georgia, Idaho, Indiana, Kansas, Nevada, Maine, and Pennsylvania.

You might ask, "Isn't the Tenth Amendment that no-good states' rights amendment that Dixie governors, such as George Wallace and Orval Faubus, used to thwart school desegregation and black civil rights?" That's the kind of constitutional disrespect and ignorance that big-government proponents, whether they're liberals or conservatives, want you to have. The reason is that they want Washington to have total control over our lives. The founders tried to limit that power with the Tenth Amendment, which reads: "The powers not delegated to the United States by the Constitution, nor prohibited by it to the States, are reserved to the States respectively, or to the people."

New Hampshire's Tenth Amendment resolution typifies others and, in part, reads: "That the several States composing the United States of America, are not united on the principle of unlimited sub-mission to their General [federal] Government; but that, by a compact under the style and title of a Constitution for the United States, and of amendments thereto, they constituted a General Government for special purposes, delegated to that government certain definite powers, reserving, each State to itself, the residuary mass of right to their own self-government; and that whensoever the General Government assumes undelegated powers, its acts are unauthoritative, void, and of no force." Put simply, these Tenth Amendment resolutions insist that the states and their people are the masters and that Congress and the White House are the servants. Put yet another way, Washington is a creature of the states, not the other way around.

Congress and the White House will laugh off these state resolutions. State legislatures must take measures that put some teeth into their Tenth Amendment resolutions. Congress will simply threaten a state, for example, with a cutoff of highway construction funds if it doesn't obey a congressional mandate, such as those that require seat belt laws or that lower the legal blood-alcohol level to .08 for drivers. States might take a lead explored by Colorado.

In 1994, the Colorado Legislature passed a Tenth Amendment resolution and later introduced a bill titled "State Sovereignty Act." Had the State Sovereignty Act passed both houses of the legislature, it would have required all people liable for any federal tax that's a component of the highway users fund, such as a gasoline tax, to remit those taxes directly to the Colorado Department of Revenue. The money would have been deposited in an escrow account called the "Federal Tax Fund" and remitted monthly to the IRS, along with a list of payees and respective amounts paid. If Congress imposed sanctions on Colorado for failure to obey an unconstitutional mandate and penalized the state by withholding funds due, say $5 million for highway construction, the State Sovereignty Act would have prohibited the state treasurer from remitting any funds in the escrow account to the IRS. Instead, Colorado would have imposed a $5 million surcharge on the Federal Tax Fund account to continue the highway construction.

The eight state legislatures that have enacted Tenth Amendment resolutions deserve our praise, but their next step is to give them teeth.

Government Deception

April 8, 2009

Most Americans accept the continuing attack on tobacco companies and smokers, but how do they feel about the massive government deception? In 1998, forty-six state attorneys general and major tobacco companies signed the Master Settlement Agreement. The major tobacco companies agreed, among other things, to give states $240 billion over twenty-five years to provide for smoking cessation programs and cover the health costs associated with using their product. In return state attorneys general promised tobacco companies that they wouldn't sue them and would use their lawmaking power to protect the major tobacco companies from competition from small tobacco companies. Of the $80 billion extorted so far, states have spent about 30 percent on health, not all tobacco-related, and less than 6 percent on smoking cessation programs. Instead, state legislatures spent the bulk of their tobacco money for items such as museum building, tax relief, rainy-day funds, and other expenditures having nothing to do with tobacco or health.

The US Congress's deception was, and continues to be, a major player in our financial meltdown. In congressional hearings, before the meltdown, on the soundness of Fannie Mae and Freddie Mac, Rep. Maxine Waters said, "Through nearly a dozen hearings, we were frankly trying to fix something that wasn't broke. Mr. Chairman, we do not have a crisis at Freddie Mac, and particularly at Fannie Mae, under the outstanding leadership of Franklin Raines." Rep. Barney Frank, the ranking Democrat on the Financial Services Committee, said, "These two entities—Fannie Mae and Freddie Mac—are not facing any kind of financial crisis. The more people exaggerate these problems, the more pressure there is on these companies, the less we will see in terms of affordable housing." Other congressmen gave similar assurances. Unfortunately for our nation, the forces pushing for "affordable" housing won the day and saddled us with today's unprecedented financial disaster. How stupid is it of us to ask those who brought us "affordable" housing to now turn their attention to bringing us "affordable" health care?

Congressional deception about government finances means today's children will face a financial disaster that will make today's mess seem like a walk in the park. What's called the public debt stands at $11 trillion and growing. That pales in comparison to the federal government's unfunded liability—obligations that are not covered by an asset of equal or greater value.

Mike Whalen, former policy chairman of the Dallas-based National Center for Policy Analysis, commenting on last year's Social Security Trustees annual report on the state of the Social Security and Medicare programs, said, "The report on the state of entitlement programs is rather grim—the combined unfunded liabilities of both programs are $101 trillion." What that means is that in order for government to make good on its promises, Congress would have to put aside tens of trillions of dollars in the bank today. Keep in mind that our GDP is only $14 trillion.

In the absence of massive tax increases or cuts in benefits, in order to meet its promises Congress must cease spending on one in four programs by 2020, such as education and highway construction, and one in two by 2030, and by 2050 or so, all federal revenue will be spent supporting Social Security, Medicare, and prescription drug benefits. Such a scenario is unsustainable. There will be economic and political chaos. Today's politicians are not likely to take measures to avoid the coming chaos because senior citizens, the major beneficiaries of Social Security and Medicare, vote in large numbers and will exact a high political price. Plus, neither today's senior citizens nor today's politicians will be alive in 2050. I'd be more optimistic if my fellow Americans were simply suffering from congressional deception as opposed to their not caring about the economic calamity that awaits tomorrow's Americans. I'd be even more optimistic if today's seniors started putting heat on Congress to allow those Americans who want nothing to do with Social Security to opt out.

Parting Company

April 22, 2009

Texas Gov. Rick Perry rattled cages when he suggested that Texans might at some point become so disgusted with Washington's gross violation of the US Constitution that they would want to secede from the union. Political hustlers, their media allies, and others, who have little understanding, are calling his remarks treasonous. Let's look at it.

When New York delegates met on July 26, 1788, their ratification document read, "That the Powers of Government may be resumed by the People, whensoever it shall become necessary to their Happiness; that every Power, Jurisdiction and right which is not by the said Constitution clearly delegated to the Congress of the United States, or the departments of the government thereof, remains to the People of the several States, or to their respective State Governments to whom they may have granted the same."

On May 29, 1790, the Rhode Island delegates made a similar claim in their ratification document. "That the powers of government may be resumed by the people, whensoever it shall become necessary to their happiness: That the rights of the States respectively to nominate and appoint all State Officers, and every other power, jurisdiction and right, which is not by the said constitution clearly delegated to the Congress of the United States or to the departments of government thereof, remain to the people of the several states, or their respective State Governments to whom they may have granted the same."

On June 26, 1788, Virginia's elected delegates met to ratify the Constitution. In their ratification document, they said, "The People of Virginia declare and make known that the powers granted under the Constitution being derived from the People of the United States may be resumed by them whensoever the same shall be perverted to their injury or oppression and that every power not granted thereby remains with them and at their will."

As demonstrated by the ratification documents of New York, Rhode Island, and Virginia, they made it explicit that if the federal government perverted the delegated rights, they had the right to resume those rights. In fact, when the Union was being formed, where the states created the federal government, every state thought it had a right to secede otherwise there would not have been a Union.

Perry is right when he says that there is no reason for Texas to secede. There are indeed intermediate actions short of secession that states can take. Thomas Jefferson said, "Whensoever the General Government assumes undelegated powers, its acts are unauthoritative, void, and of no force." That suggests that one response to federal encroachment is for state governments to declare federal laws that have no constitutional authority null and void and refuse to enforce them.

While the US Constitution does not provide a specific provision for nullification, the case for nullification is found in the nature of compacts and agreements. Our Constitution represents a compact between the states and the federal government. As with any compact, one party does not have a monopoly over its interpretation, nor can one party change it without the consent of the other. Additionally, no one has a moral obligation to obey unconstitutional laws. That's not to say there is not a compelling case for obedience of unconstitutional laws. That compelling case is the brute force of the federal government to coerce obedience, possibly going as far as using its military might to lay waste to a disobedient state and its peoples.

Finally, here's my secession question for you. Some Americans accept and have respect for the Tenth Amendment, which reads, "The powers not delegated to the United States by the Constitution, nor prohibited by it to the States, are reserved to the States respectively, or to the people." Other Americans, the majority I fear, say to hell with the Tenth Amendment limits on the federal government. Which is a more peaceful solution: one group of Americans seeking to impose their vision on others or simply parting company?

The Housing Boom and Bust

May 27, 2009

Hot off the press is my colleague Dr. Thomas Sowell's forty-third book, *The Housing Boom and Bust*. The book is an eye-opener for anyone interested in the truth about the collapse of the housing market that played a major role in our financial market crisis.

The root of the problem lies in Washington. The Community Reinvestment Act of 1977, later given teeth during the Bush and Clinton administrations, forced financial institutions to make risky mortgage loans they otherwise would not have made. President Clinton's Attorney General Janet Reno threatened legal action against lenders whose racial statistics raised her suspicions. Bank loan qualification standards, in general, came under criticism as being too stringent regarding down payments, credit histories, and income. Fannie Mae and Freddie Mac, two government-sponsored enterprises, by lowering their standards for the kinds of mortgage paper they would purchase from banks and other mortgage lenders, gave financial institutions further incentive to make risky loans.

In 2002, the George W. Bush administration urged Congress to enact the American Dream Down Payment Assistance Act, which subsidized down payments of homebuyers whose income was below a certain level. Bush also urged Congress to pass legislation requiring the Federal Housing Administration to make zero-down-payment loans at low-interest rates to low-income Americans. Between 2005 and 2007, Fannie Mae and Freddie Mac acquired an estimated trillion dollars' worth of subprime loans and guaranteed more than $2 trillion worth of mortgages. That, Sowell points out, is larger than the gross domestic product of all but four nations.

There were numerous warnings that went unheeded. In congressional hearings, US Treasury Secretary John Snow said, regarding the risks assumed by Fannie Mae and Freddie Mac, "The concern is, if something unravels, it could cause systemic risk to the whole financial system." Peter J. Wallison, American Enterprise Institute scholar, warned that if Congress did not rein in Fannie Mae and Freddie Mac, "there will be a massive default with huge losses to the taxpayers and systemic effects on the economy."

There were many other warnings of pending collapse but Congress and the White House in their push for politically popular "affordable housing" ignored them. Congressman Barney Frank, who is now chairman of the House Committee on Financial Services, said critics "exaggerate a threat of safety" and "conjure up the possibility of serious financial losses to the Treasury, which I do not see." Chairman Chris Dodd, of the Senate Banking Committee, called Fannie Mae and Freddie Mac "one of the great success stories of all time" and urged "caution" in restricting their activities, out of fear of "doing great damage to what has been one of the great engines of economic success in the last thirty or forty years."

Sowell provides numerous examples of government actions at both the federal and state levels that created the housing boom and bust and its devastating impact on domestic and foreign financial markets, but here's what I don't get: What can be said about the intelligence of the news media and the American people who buy into congressionally created lies that our problems were caused by Wall Street greed and Bush administration deregulation? In the words of Barney Frank, "We are in a worldwide crisis now because of excessive deregulation" and "mortgages made and sold in the unregulated sector led to the crisis." The fact of the matter is our financial sector is the most heavily regulated sector in our economy. In the banking and finance industries, regulatory spending between 1980 and 2007 almost tripled, rising from $725 million to $2.07 billion. I challenge anyone to come up with one thing banks can do that's not covered by a regulation.

For the Washington politicians to get away with spinning the financial crisis the way they have suggests that American people are either stupid or ignorant. I hope it's ignorance because "The Housing Boom and Bust" is the cure.

Americans Love Government

June 10, 2009

Philosopher Bertrand Russell suggested that "Men are born ignorant, not stupid. They are made stupid by education." And, it was Albert Einstein who explained, "Insanity: doing the same thing over and over again and expecting different results." So which is it—stupidity, ignorance, or insanity—that explains the behavior of my fellow Americans who call for greater government involvement in our lives?

According to latest Rasmussen Reports, 30 percent of Americans believe congressmen are corrupt. Last year, Congress's approval rating fell to 9 percent, its lowest in history. If the average American were asked his opinion of congressmen, among the more polite terms you'll hear are thieves and crooks, liars and manipulators, hustlers and quacks. But what do the same people say when our nation faces a major problem? "Government ought to do something!" When people call for government to do something, it is as if they've been befallen by amnesia and forgotten just who is running government. It's the very people whom they have labeled as thieves and crooks, liars and manipulators, hustlers and quacks.

Aside from the general level of disgust that Americans have for congressmen, there's the question of whether there is anything that Congress does well. What about Social Security and Medicare? Congress has allowed Social Security and Medicare to accumulate an unfunded liability of $101 trillion. That means in order to pay promised elderly entitlement benefits, Congress would have to put trillions in the bank today earning interest. Congressional efforts to create "affordable housing" have created today's financial calamity. Congress props up failed enterprises such as Amtrak and the US Postal Service with huge cash subsidies, and subsidies in the forms of special tax treatment and monopoly rights. I can't think of anything that Congress does well, yet we Americans call for them to take greater control over important areas of our lives.

I don't think that stupidity, ignorance, or insanity explains the love that many Americans hold for government; it's far more sinister and perhaps hopeless. I'll give a few examples to make my case. Many Americans want money they don't personally own to be used for what they see as good causes such as handouts to farmers, poor people, college students, senior citizens, and businesses. If they privately took someone's earnings to give to a farmer, college student, or senior citizen, they would be hunted down as thieves and carted off to jail. However, they get Congress to do the identical thing, through its taxing power, and they are seen as compassionate and caring. In other words, people love government because government, while having neither moral nor constitutional authority, has the legal and physical might to take the property of one American and give it to another.

The unanticipated problem with this agenda is that as Congress uses its might to take what belongs to one American to give to another, what President Obama calls "spreading the wealth around," more and more Americans will want to participate in the looting. It will ultimately produce something none of us wants: absolute control over our lives.

The path we're embarked upon, in the name of good, is a familiar one. The unspeakable horrors of Nazism, Stalinism, and Maoism did not begin in the 1930s and '40s with the men usually associated with those names. Those horrors were simply the end result of a long evolution of ideas leading to consolidation of power in central government in the name of "social justice." In Germany, it led to the Enabling Act of 1933: Law to Remedy the Distress of the People and the Nation and, after all, who could be against a remedy to relieve distress? Decent but misguided Germans, who would have cringed at the thought of what Nazi Germany would become, succumbed to Hitler's charisma.

Today's Americans, enticed, perhaps enchanted, by charismatic speeches, are ceding so much power to Washington, and like yesteryear's Germans are building the Trojan Horse for a future tyrant.

Senate Slavery Apology
July 8, 2009

Last month, the US Senate unanimously passed Senate Resolution 26, "apologizing for the enslavement and racial segregation of African-Americans." The resolution ends with: "Disclaimer.—Nothing in this resolution (a) authorizes or supports any claim against the United States; or (b) serves as a settlement of any claim against the United States." That means Congress apologizes but is not going to pay reparations, at least for now.

Members of the Congressional Black Caucus have expressed concerns about the disclaimer, thinking that it's an attempt to stave off reparations claims from the descendants of slaves. Congressional Black Caucus Chairwoman Barbara Lee, D-Calif., said her organization is studying the language of the resolution and Rep. Bennie Thompson, D-Miss., said, "putting in a disclaimer takes away from the meaning of an apology. A number of us are prepared to vote against it in its present form. There are several members of the Progressive Caucus who feel the same way."

It goes without saying that slavery was a gross violation of human rights. Justice would demand that all the perpetrators—that includes slave owners, and African and Arab slave sellers—make compensatory reparation payments to victims. Since slaves, slave owners and slave sellers are no longer with us, such compensation is beyond our reach and a matter to be settled in the world beyond.

Absent from the reparations debate is: Who pays? Don't say the government because the government doesn't have any money that it doesn't first take from some American. So which Americans owe black people what? Reparations advocates don't want that question asked but let's you and I ask it.

Are the millions of Europeans, Asians, and Latin Americans who immigrated to the United States in the twentieth century responsible for slavery and should they be forced to cough up reparations money?

What about descendants of Northern whites who fought and died in the name of freeing slaves? Should they cough up reparations money for black Americans? What about non-slave-owning Southern whites, a majority of whites; should they be made to pay reparations? And, by the way, would President Obama, whose father is Kenyan and mother white, be eligible for a reparations payment?

On black people's side of the ledger, thorny issues also arise. Some blacks purchased other blacks as a means to free family members. But other blacks owned slaves for the same reason whites owned slaves—to work farms or plantations. Are descendants of these blacks eligible and deserving of reparations? There is no way that Europeans could have captured millions of Africans. They had African and Arab help. Should Congress haul representatives of Ghana, Ivory Coast, Nigeria, and Muslim states before them and demand they compensate American blacks because of their ancestors' involvement in capturing and selling slaves?

Reparations advocates make the foolish unchallenged pronouncement that United States became rich on the backs of free black labor. That's utter nonsense. Slavery has never had a very good record of producing wealth. Think about it. Slavery was all over the South. Buying into the reparations nonsense, you'd have to conclude that the antebellum South was rich and the slave-starved North was poor. The truth of the matter is just the opposite. In fact, the poorest states and regions of our country were places where slavery flourished: Mississippi, Alabama, and Georgia, whereas the richest states and regions were those where slavery was absent: Pennsylvania, New York, and Massachusetts.

The Senate apology is nothing more than political theater but it could be a slick way to get the camel's nose into the tent for future reparations. If the senators are motivated by white guilt, I have the cure. About fifteen years ago I wrote a "Proclamation of Amnesty and Pardon Granted to All Persons of European Descent" that is available at www.gmu.edu/departments/economics/wew/gift.html.

Washington's Lies

September 2, 2009

President Obama and congressional supporters estimate that his health care plan will cost between $50 billion and $65 billion a year. Such cost estimates are lies whether they come from a Democratic president and Congress, or a Republican president and Congress. You say, "Williams, you don't show much trust in the White House and Congress." Let's check out their past dishonesty.

At its start, in 1966, Medicare cost $3 billion. The House Ways and Means Committee, along with President Johnson, estimated that Medicare would cost an inflation-adjusted $12 billion by 1990. In 1990, Medicare topped $107 billion. That's nine times Congress's prediction. Today's Medicare tab comes to $420 billion with no signs of leveling off. How much confidence can we have in any cost estimates by the White House or Congress?

Another part of the Medicare lie is found in Section 1801 of the 1965 Medicare Act that reads: "Nothing in this title shall be construed to authorize any federal officer or employee to exercise any supervision or control over the practice of medicine, or the manner in which medical services are provided, or over the selection, tenure, or compensation of any officer, or employee, or any institution, agency or person providing health care services." Ask your doctor or hospital whether this is true.

Lies and deception are by no means restricted to modern times. During the legislative debate prior to ratification of the Sixteenth Amendment, President Howard Taft and congressional supporters said that only the rich would ever pay federal income taxes. In 1916, only one-half of 1 percent of income earners paid income taxes. Those earning $250,000 a year in today's dollars paid 1 percent, and those earning $6 million in today's dollars paid 7 percent. The lie that only the rich would ever pay income taxes was simply a lie to exploit the politics of envy and dupe Americans into ratifying the Sixteenth Amendment.

The proposed tax increases that the White House and Congress are proposing will probably pass. According to the Washington, D.C.-based Tax Foundation, during 2006, roughly 43.4 million tax returns, representing 91 million individuals, had no federal tax liability. That's out of a total of 136 million federal tax returns. Adding to this figure are 15 million households and individuals who file no tax return at all. Roughly 121 million Americans—or 41 percent of the US population—are completely outside the federal income tax system. These people represent a natural constituency for big-spending politicians. Since they have no federal income tax obligation, what do they care about higher taxes or tax cuts?

Another big congressional lie is Social Security. Here's what a 1936 government pamphlet on Social Security said: "After the first 3 years—that is to say, beginning in 1940—you will pay, and your employer will pay, 1.5 cents for each dollar you earn, up to $3,000 a year . . . beginning in 1943, you will pay 2 cents, and so will your employer, for every dollar you earn for the next 3 years. . . . And finally, beginning in 1949, twelve years from now, you and your employer will each pay 3 cents on each dollar you earn, up to $3,000 a year." Here's Congress's lying promise: "That is the most you will ever pay." Let's repeat that last sentence: "That is the most you will ever pay." Compare that to today's reality, including Medicare, which is 7.65 cents on each dollar that you earn up to nearly $107,000, which comes to $8,185.

The Social Security pamphlet closes with another lie: "Beginning November 24, 1936, the United States government will set up a Social Security account for you. . . . The checks will come to you as a right." First, there's no Social Security account containing your money, but more importantly, the US Supreme Court has ruled on two occasions that Americans have no legal right to Social Security payments.

We can thank public education for American gullibility.

Obama's Nobel Peace Prize

October 28, 2009

According to Alfred Nobel's will, the Peace Prize should be awarded to the person who "during the preceding year, shall have done . . . the most or the best work for fraternity between nations, for the abolition or reduction of standing armies and for the holding and promotion of peace congresses." According to the Norwegian Nobel Committee, appointed by the Norwegian Parliament, 2009 saw a record 205 nominations who competed against President Barack Obama for this year's Nobel Laureate. We don't know the names of other nominees who were passed over because Nobel Foundation statutes do not permit information about nominations, considerations, or investigations relating to awarding the prize to be made public for at least fifty years after a prize has been awarded. Nominations from 1901 to 1955, however, have been released. Past nominees included Adolf Hitler, Joseph Stalin, and Benito Mussolini. Since it takes only one qualified person to nominate someone, these nominations do not necessarily reflect the opinion of Nobel committee members.

When I heard that Obama was selected for this year's Nobel Laureate, I felt a bit embarrassed for him, and given his comment in the Rose Garden, he must have felt a bit embarrassed as well. He said, "To be honest, I do not feel that I deserve to be in the company of so many of the transformative figures who have been honored by this prize, men and women who've inspired me and inspired the entire world through their courageous pursuit of peace."

Typically, the Nobel Prize is awarded to someone, or an organization, that has actually done something, even if that something is controversial or unwise. But what has President Obama accomplished compared to other Nobel Laureates? One might speculate that the Nobel Committee selected Obama because it has started an affirmative action policy and has seen the virtues of racial diversity, which is all the rage these days, particularly among the elite. After all, the committee hasn't seen fit to give the award to a person of African ancestry since it honored Nelson Mandela in 1993 and earlier Desmond Tutu (1984), Martin Luther King (1964), and Ralph Bunche (1950). So as far as people of African ancestry, the Nobel Committee has a ways to go. While people of African ancestry are roughly 14 percent of the world's population, they are only 5 percent of the ninety-eight individuals, since 1901, seen fit to be Nobel Laureates. Having awarded the Peace Prize to only three Asians, while Asians are almost 55 percent of the world's population, suggests that the Nobel Committee's Far Eastern diversity problem is insurmountable.

There might be other reasons why Obama was chosen. He has generated considerable goodwill among Europeans because he shares many of their values. Europeans are a people with little willingness to defend themselves. They are people who believe that peace treaties, appeasement, and disarmament produce peace. As such, Obama has thrown in with their lot not to be a unilateralist and pledging to pursue a world without nuclear weapons. If Europeans had any sense, they should be worried about Obama's vision. Americans pulled their chestnuts out of the fire in World War I, World War II, and prevented them from being gobbled up by the communists during the Cold War. If we become a military weakling, who is going to protect Europe against a future tyrant? In addition to Obama's goodwill among Europeans, shouldn't we be worried about the goodwill and praise our president has received from enemies of liberty such as Fidel Castro, Hugo Chavez, Muammar Qaddafi, and Vladimir Putin?

President Obama could rise several notches in my book if he refused the Nobel Peace Prize, with a nice letter to the Nobel Committee that might read: Since you did not see fit to award Ronald Reagan, the US president who did the most for world peace in this century, by peaceably shutting down the Soviet Union, I respectfully decline your offer.

The Pretense of Knowledge

December 2, 2009

The ultimate constraint that we all face is knowledge—what we know and don't know. The knowledge problem is pervasive and by no means trivial as hinted at by just a few examples. You've purchased a house. Was it the best deal you could have gotten? Was there some other house you could have purchased that ten years later would not have needed extensive repairs or was in a community with more likable neighbors and a better environment for your children? What about the person you married? Was there another person who would have made for a more pleasing spouse? Though these are important questions, the most intelligent answer you can give to all of them is: "I don't know."

Since you don't know the answers, who do you think, here on Earth, is likely to know and whom would you like to make these decisions for you—Nancy Pelosi, Harry Reid, George Bush, a czar appointed by Obama, or a committee of Washington bureaucrats? I bet that if these people were to forcibly make housing or marital decisions for us, most would deem it tyranny.

You say, "Williams, Congress is not making such monumental decisions that affect my life." Try this. You are a twenty-two-year-old healthy person. Instead of spending $3,000 or $4,000 a year for health insurance, you'd prefer investing that money in equipment to start a landscaping business. Which is the best use of that $3,000 or $4,000 a year—purchasing health insurance or starting up a landscaping business—and who should decide that question: Nancy Pelosi, Harry Reid, George Bush, a czar appointed by Obama, or a committee of Washington bureaucrats? How can they possibly know what's the best use of your earnings, particularly in light of the fact that they have no idea of who you are?

Neither you nor the US Congress has the complete knowledge to know exactly what's best for you. The difference is that when individuals make their own tradeoffs, say between purchasing health insurance or investing in a business, they make wiser decisions because it is they who personally bear the costs and benefits of those decisions. You say, "Hold it, Williams, we've got you now! What if that person gets really sick and doesn't have health insurance? Society suffers the burden of taking care of him." To the extent that is a problem, it is not a problem of liberty; it's a problem of congressionally mandated socialism. Let's look at it.

It is not society that bears the burden; it is some flesh-and-blood American worker who finds his earnings taken by Congress to finance the health needs of another person. There is absolutely no moral case, much less constitutional case, for Congress forcibly using one American to serve the purposes of another American, a practice that differs only in degree from slavery, which we all should find morally offensive.

Whether it is health care, education, employment, or most other areas of our lives, I ask you: Who has the capacity to master all the complexity to make choices on behalf of others? Each of us possesses only a tiny percentage of the knowledge that would be necessary to make totally informed decisions in our own lives, much less the lives of others. There is only one reason for the forcible transference of decision-making authority over important areas of our private lives to elite decision-makers in Congress and government bureaucracies. Doing so confers control, power, wealth, and revenue to society's elite. What's in the best interests of individual members of society, such as a person who'd rather launch a landscaping business than purchase a health insurance policy, ranks low on the elite's list of priorities.

Modern Day Lunacy

December 30, 2009

Sen. John Rockefeller, D-W.Va., chairman of the Senate Finance Subcommittee on Health Care, and Rep. Joe Courtney D-Conn., a member of the House Education and Labor Committee, have introduced the Preexisting Condition Patient Protection Act, which would eliminate preexisting condition exclusions in all insurance markets. That's an Obama administration priority. I wonder whether President Obama and his congressional supporters would go a step further and protect not just patients but everyone against preexisting condition exclusions by insurance companies. Let's look at the benefits of such a law.

A person might save quite a bit of money on fire insurance. He could wait until his home is ablaze and then walk into Nationwide and say, "Sell me a fire insurance policy so I can have my house repaired." The Nationwide salesman says, "That's lunacy!" But the person replies, "Congress says you cannot deny me insurance because of a preexisting condition." This mandate against insurance company discrimination would not only apply to home insurance but auto insurance and life insurance as well. Instead of a wife wasting money on costly life insurance premiums, she could spend that money on jewelry, cosmetics, and massages and then wait until her husband kicked the bucket to buy life insurance on him.

Insurance companies don't stay in business and prosper by being stupid. If Congress were to enact a law eliminating preexisting condition exclusions, what might be expected? Say I'm a salesman for Nationwide and you demand that I write you an insurance policy for your house that has already gone up in flames. I send an appraiser out to your house to get an estimate of how much money it would take to make you whole. Let's say it comes to $400,000. Guess how much I'm going to charge you for the policy? If you said somewhere in the neighborhood of $400,000, you'd be pretty close to the right answer. You might say, "Williams, you're right. Forcing fire and auto insurance companies to sell policies for a preexisting fire or auto accident is bizarre and stupid, but it's different with health insurance." Yes, health insurance is different from fire and auto insurance but the insurance principle remains the same.

If Congress and the president are successful in making the Pre-existing Condition Patient Protection Act the law of the land, their treachery won't stop there. Insurance companies will attempt to charge people with preexisting health conditions a higher price to compensate for their higher expected cost. Those people will complain to Congress. Then Congress will enact insurance premium price controls. Insurance companies might try to restrict just what treatments they will cover under such restrictions. That means Congress will play a greater role in managing what insurance companies can and cannot do.

The dilemma Congress always faces, when it messes with the economy, was aptly described in a Negro spiritual play by Marcus Cook Connelly titled "Green Pastures." In it, God laments to the angel Gabriel, "Every time Ah passes a miracle, Ah has to pass fo' or five mo' to ketch up wid it," adding, "Even bein God ain't no bed of roses." When Congress creates a miracle for one American, it creates a non-miracle for another. After that, Congress has to create a compensatory miracle. Many years ago, I used to testify before Congress, something I refuse to do now. At several of the hearings, I urged Congress to get out of the miracle business and leave miracle making up to God.

For a president and congressman to shamelessly propose something like the Preexisting Condition Patient Protection Act demonstrates just how far we've gone down the road to perdition. The most tragic thing is that most Americans have no idea that such an act violates every principle of insurance and it's something that not even yesteryear's lunatics would have thought up.

Conflict or Cooperation

March 31, 2010

Different Americans have different and often intense preferences for all kinds of goods and services. Some of us have strong preferences for beer and distaste for wine while others have the opposite preference—strong preferences for wine and distaste for beer. Some of us hate three-piece suits and love blue jeans while others love three-piece suits and hate blue jeans. When's the last time you heard of beer drinkers in conflict with wine drinkers, or three-piece suit lovers in conflict with lovers of blue jeans? It seldom if ever happens because beer and blue jean lovers get what they want. Wine and three-piece suit lovers get what they want and they all can live in peace with one another.

It would be easy to create conflict among these people. Instead of free choice and private decision-making, clothing and beverage decisions could be made in the political arena. In other words, have a democratic majority-rule process to decide what drinks and clothing that would be allowed. Then we would see wine lovers organized against beer lovers, and blue jean lovers organized against three-piece suit lovers. Conflict would emerge solely because the decision was made in the political arena. Why? The prime feature of political decision-making is that it's a zero-sum game. One person's gain is of necessity another person's loss. That is if wine lovers won, beer lovers lose. As such, political decision-making and allocation of resources is conflict enhancing while market decision-making and allocation is conflict reducing. The greater the number of decisions made in the political arena, the greater the potential for conflict.

Take the issue of prayers in school as an example. I think that everyone, except a maniacal tyrant, would agree that a parent has the right to decide whether his child will recite a morning prayer in school. Similarly, a parent has a right to decide that his child will not recite a morning prayer. Conflict arises because schools are government owned. That means it is a political decision whether prayers will be permitted or not. A win for one parent means a loss for another parent. The losing parent, in order to get what he wants, would have to muster up private school tuition while continuing to pay taxes for a school for which he has no use. If education were only government financed, as opposed to being government financed and produced, say through education vouchers, the conflict would be reduced. Both parents could have their wishes fulfilled by enrolling their child in a private school of their choice and instead of being enemies, they could be friends.

Conflict in education is just one minor example of how government allocation can raise the potential for conflict. Others would include government-backed allocation of jobs and education slots by race and sex, plus the current large conflict over government allocation of health services. Interestingly enough, the very people in our society who protest the loudest against human conflict and violence are the very ones calling for increased government resource allocation. These people fail to recognize or even wonder why our nation, with people of every race, ethnic group and religious group, has managed to live together relatively harmoniously. In their countries of origin, the same ethnic, racial, and religious groups have been trying to slaughter one another for centuries. A good part of the answer is that in the United States, there was little to be gained from being a Frenchman, a German, a Jew, a Protestant, or a Catholic. The reason it did not pay was because for most of our history, government played a small part in our lives. When there's significant government allocation of resources, the most effective means of organizing for the gains are those proven most divisive, such as race, ethnicity, religion, and region.

As our nation forsakes our founders' wisdom of constitutional limitations placed on Washington, we raise the potential for conflict.

Parting Company
April 7, 2010

Here's the question asked in my September 2000 column titled "It's Time to Part Company": "If one group of people prefers government control and management of people's lives and another prefers liberty and a desire to be left alone, should they be required to fight, antagonize one another, risk bloodshed and loss of life in order to impose their preferences or should they be able to peaceably part company and go their separate ways?"

The problem that our nation faces is very much like a marriage where one partner has broken, and has no intention of keeping, the marital vows. Of course, the marriage can remain intact and one party tries to impose his will on the other and engage in the deviousness of one-upmanship. Rather than submission by one party or domestic violence, a more peaceable alternative is separation.

I believe we are nearing a point where there are enough irreconcilable differences between those Americans who want to control other Americans and those Americans who want to be left alone that separation is the only peaceable alternative. Just as in a marriage, where vows are broken, our human rights protections guaranteed by the US Constitution have been grossly violated by a government instituted to protect them. The Democrat-controlled Washington is simply an escalation of a process that has been in full stride for at least two decades. There is no evidence that Americans who are responsible for and support constitutional abrogation have any intention of mending their ways.

You say, "Williams, what do you mean by constitutional abrogation?" Let's look at just some of the magnitude of the violations. Article I, Section 8, of our Constitution lists the activities for which Congress is authorized to tax and spend. Nowhere on that list is authority for Congress to tax and spend for: prescription drugs, Social Security, public education, farm subsidies, bank and business bailouts, food stamps, and other activities that represent roughly two-thirds of the federal budget. Neither is there authority for congressional mandates to the states and people about how they may use their land, the speed at which they can drive, whether a library has wheelchair ramps, and the gallons of water used per toilet flush. The list of congressional violations of both the letter and spirit of the Constitution is virtually without end. Our derelict Supreme Court has given Congress sanction to do anything upon which they can muster a majority vote.

James Madison, the acknowledged father of the Constitution, explained in Federalist Paper No. 45: "The powers delegated by the proposed Constitution to the federal government are few and defined. Those which are to remain in the State governments are numerous and indefinite. The former will be exercised principally on external objects, as war, peace, negotiation, and foreign commerce. . . . The powers reserved to the several States will extend to all the objects which in the ordinary course of affairs, concern the lives and liberties, and properties of the people, and the internal order, improvement and prosperity of the State."

Americans who wish to live free have several options. We can submit to those who have constitutional contempt and want to run our lives. We can resist, fight, and risk bloodshed and death in an attempt to force America's tyrants to respect our liberties and human rights. We can seek a peaceful resolution of our irreconcilable differences by separating. Some independence movements, such as our 1776 war with England and our 1861 War Between the States, have been violent, but they need not be. In 1905, Norway seceded from Sweden; Panama seceded from Columbia (1903), and West Virginia from Virginia (1863). Nonetheless, violent secession can lead to great friendships. England is probably our greatest ally.

The bottom-line question for all of us is: Should we part company or continue trying to forcibly impose our wills on one another? My preference is a restoration of the constitutional values of limited government that made us a great nation.

Will Republicans Save Us?

August 18, 2010

Democrat control of the White House, House of Representatives, and the Senate has produced an unprecedented level of political brazenness and contempt for the limitations placed on the federal government by the US Constitution. As such, it has raised a level of constitutional interest and anger against Washington's interference in our lives that has been dormant for far too long.

Part of this heightened interest and anger is seen in the strength of the tea party movement around the nation. Another is the angry reception that many congressmen receive when they return to their districts and at town hall meetings. According to the most recent Gallup poll, only 20 percent of Americans approve of the job Congress is doing, but that's up from a March 2010 low of 16 percent.

The smart money suggests that there will be a Republican takeover of the House of Representatives and possibly the Senate. The question is what can liberty-minded Americans expect from a Republican majority? Maybe a good starting point for an answer might be to examine how Republicans have handled their majority in the past.

Democrat President Lyndon Johnson's term of office saw massive increases in federal spending. When Johnson was elected into office in 1964, federal spending was $118 billion. When he left office in 1968, federal spending was $178 billion, a 66 percent increase. Worse than the massive increase in federal spending, his administration and Democratic-controlled Congress saddled us with two programs that have helped fuel today's fiscal disaster—Medicare and Medicaid.

The 1994 elections gave Republican control of both the House and Senate. They held a majority for a decade. The 2000 election of George W. Bush as president gave Republicans what the Democrats have now, total control of the legislative and executive branches of government. When Bush came to office, federal spending was $1.788 trillion. When he left office, federal spending was $2.982 trillion. That's a 60 percent increase in federal spending, closely matching the profligacy of Lyndon Johnson's presidency.

During the Republican control, the nation was saddled with massive federal interference in education through No Child Left Behind. Prescription drug handouts became a part of the Republican-controlled Congress's legacy. And it was during this interval that Congress accelerated its interference, assisted by the Federal Reserve Bank, in the housing market in the name of homeownership that produced much of the financial meltdown that the nation suffered in 2008.

During the last two years, Democrats have amassed unprecedented growth of federal government power in the forms of bailouts, corporate takeovers, favors to their political allies, and nationalization of our health care system. My question is how likely is it for Republicans to behave differently if they gain control? Their past behavior doesn't make one confident that they will behave much differently, but I could be wrong.

If Republicans win the House of Representatives, there are measures they should take in their first month of office, and that is to undo most of what the Democratic-controlled Congress has done. If they don't win a veto-proof Senate, they can't undo Obamacare but the House alone can refuse to fund any part of it. There are numerous blocking tactics that a Republican-controlled House can take against those hell-bent on trampling on our Constitution. The question is whether they will have guts and principle to do it. After all, many Americans, including those who are Republicans, have a stake in big government control, special privileges, and handouts.

Ultimately, we Americans must act to ensure that our liberty does not depend on personalities in Washington. Our founders tried to do that with our Constitution. Thomas Jefferson offered us a solution when he said, "The spirit of resistance to government is so valuable on certain occasions, that I wish it to be always kept alive. It will often be exercised when wrong, but better so than not to be exercised at all. I like a little rebellion now and then."

Politicians Exploit Economic Ignorance
October 6, 2010

One of President Obama's campaign promises was not to raise taxes on middle-class Americans. So here's my question: If there's a corporate tax increase either in the form of "cap and trade" or income tax, does it turn out to be a middle-class tax increase? Most people would say no but let's look at it.

There's a whole subject area in economics known as tax incidence— namely, who bears the burden of a tax? The first thing that should be recognized is that the burden of a tax is not necessarily borne by the party upon whom it is levied. That is, for example, if a sales tax is levied on gasoline retailers, they don't bear the full burden of the tax. Part of it is shifted to customers in the form of higher gasoline prices.

Suppose your local politician tells you, as a homeowner, "I'm not going to raise taxes on you! I'm going to raise taxes on your land." You'd probably tell him that he's an idiot because land does not pay taxes; only people pay taxes. That means a tax on your land is a tax on you. You say, "Williams, that's pretty elementary, isn't it?" Not quite.

What about the politician who tells us that he's not going to raise taxes on the middle class; instead, he's going to raise corporate income taxes as means to get rich corporations to pay their rightful share of government? If a tax is levied on a corporation, and if it is to survive, it will have one of three responses, or some combination thereof. One response is to raise the price of its product, so who bears the burden? Another response is to lower dividends; again, who bears the burden? Yet another response is to lay off workers. In each case, it is people, not some legal fiction called a corporation, who bear the burden of the tax.

Because corporations have these responses to the imposition of a tax, they are merely government tax collectors. They collect money from people and send it to Washington. Therefore, you should tell that politician, who promises to tax corporations instead of you, that he's an idiot because corporations, like land, do not pay taxes. Only people pay taxes.

Here's another tax question, even though it doesn't sound like it. Which workers receive higher pay: those on a road construction project moving dirt with shovels and wheelbarrows or those moving dirt atop a giant earthmover? If you said the worker atop the earthmover, go to the head of the class. But why? It's not because he's unionized or that construction contractors have a fondness for earthmover operators. It's because the worker atop the earthmover is working with more capital, thereby making him more productive. Higher productivity means higher wages.

It's not rocket science to conclude that whatever lowers the cost of capital formation, such as lowering the cost of investing in earthmovers, enables contractors to purchase more of them. Workers will have more capital to work with and as a result enjoy higher wages. Policies that raise the cost of capital formation such as capital gains taxes, low depreciation allowances, and corporate taxes, thereby reduce capital formation, and serve neither the interests of workers, investors, nor consumers. It does serve the interests of politicians who get more resources to be able to buy votes.

You might wonder how congressmen can get away with taxes and other measures that reduce our prosperity potential. Part of the answer is ignorance and the antibusiness climate promoted in academia and the news media. The more important reason is that prosperity foregone is invisible. In other words, we can never tell how much richer we would have been without today's level of congressional interference in our lives and therefore don't fight it as much as we should.

Our Contemptible Congress

October 27, 2010

Most people whom we elect to Congress are either ignorant of, have contempt for, or are just plain stupid about the US Constitution. You say: "Whoa, Williams, you're really out of line! You'd better explain." Let's look at it.

Rep. Phil Hare, D-Ill., responding to a question during a town hall meeting, said he's "not worried about the Constitution." That was in response to a question about the constitutionality of Obamacare. He told his constituents that the Constitution guaranteed each of us "life, liberty and the pursuit of happiness." Of course, our Constitution guarantees no such thing. The expression "life, liberty and the pursuit of happiness" is found in our Declaration of Independence.

During a debate, Rep. Jim McGovern, D-Mass., gave his opinion about the US Supreme Court's ruling in Citizens United v. Federal Election Commission, concluding that "the Constitution is wrong." Not to be outdone, at his town hall meeting, Rep. Pete Stark, D-Calif., responded to a constituent's question about Obamacare by saying, "There are very few constitutional limits that would prevent the federal government from [making] rules that can affect your private life." Adding, "Yes, the federal government can do most anything in this country." The questioner responded, "People like you, sir, are destroying this nation." Her comment won shouts of approval from the audience.

Last year, a CNS reporter asked, "Madam Speaker, where specifically does the Constitution grant Congress the authority to enact an individual health insurance mandate?" Speaker Pelosi responded: "Are you serious? Are you serious?" She shares the vision of her fellow Californian Stark that Washington can do most anything.

Congressional ignorance and contempt for our Constitution isn't only on the Democrat side of the aisle. During a town hall meeting, Rep. Frank LoBiondo, R-N.J., was asked by one of his constituents whether he knew what Article I, Section I, of the Constitution mandated. He replied that, "Article I, Section I, is the right to free speech."

Actually, Article I, Section I, reads, "All legislative Powers herein granted shall be vested in a Congress of the United States, which shall consist of a Senate and House of Representatives." LoBiondo was later asked whether he knew the five rights guaranteed by the First Amendment. Fearing further revelation of his ignorance, he replied, "I can't articulate that."

By the way, those five guarantees are: free exercise of religion, freedom of speech, freedom of the press, the right to peaceable assembly, and the right to petition the government for redress of grievances.

Here, in part, is the oath of office that each congressman takes: "I do solemnly swear (or affirm) that I will support and defend the Constitution of the United States against all enemies, foreign and domestic; that I will bear true faith and allegiance to the same. . . ." Here's my question to you: If one takes an oath to uphold and defend, and bear true faith and allegiance to the Constitution, at the minimum, shouldn't he know what he's supposed to uphold, defend, and be faithful to?

If congressmen, judges, the president, and other government officials were merely ignorant of our Constitution, there'd be hope—ignorance is curable through education. These people in Washington see themselves as our betters and rulers. They have contempt for the limits our Constitution places on the federal government envisioned by James Madison, the father of our Constitution, who explained in the Federalist Paper 45: "The powers delegated by the proposed Constitution to the federal government are few and defined. Those which are to remain in the State governments are numerous and indefinite. The former will be exercised principally on external objects, as war, peace, negotiation, and foreign commerce. . . . The powers reserved to the several States will extend to all the objects which in the ordinary course of affairs, concern the lives and liberties, and properties of the people, and the internal order, improvement and prosperity of the State."

How to Control Congress
November 17, 2010

Let's assume that each of our 535 congressmen cares about the destructive impact of deficits and debt on the future of our country. Regardless of party, congressmen face enormous lobbying pressures and awards to spend more and little or no pressure and awards to spend less. The nation's founders would be horrified by today's congressional spending that consumes 25 percent of our GDP. Contrast that to the years 1787 to the 1920s when federal government spending never exceeded 4 percent of our GDP except in wartime. Today, federal, state, and local government consumes 43 percent of what Americans produce each year. The Washington, D.C.-based Tax Foundation computes that the average taxpayer is forced to work from January 1 to mid-April to pay federal, state, and local taxes. If he were taxed enough to pay the $1.5 trillion federal deficit, he'd be forced to work until mid-May.

Tax revenue is not the problem. The federal government has collected just about 20 percent of the nation's GDP almost every year since 1960. Federal spending has exceeded revenue for most of that period and has taken an unprecedented leap since 2008 to produce today's massive deficit. Since federal spending is the problem, that's where our focus should be.

Cutting spending is politically challenging. Every spending constituency sees its handout as vital, whether it's Social Security, Medicare, and Medicaid recipients or farmers, poor people, educators, or the military. It's easy for congressmen to say yes to these spending constituencies because whether it's Democrats or Republicans in control, they face no hard and fast bottom line.

The bottom line is that Americans need a constitutional amendment limiting congressional spending to some fraction, say 20 percent, of the GDP. That limit could be exceeded only if the president declared a state of emergency along with a two-thirds vote of approval in both houses of Congress. Each year of a declared state of emergency would require another two-thirds vote in each house.

During the early 1980s, I was a member of the National Tax Limitation Committee's distinguished blue-ribbon drafting committee that included notables such as Milton Friedman, James Buchanan, Paul McCracken, Bill Niskanen, Craig Stubblebine, Robert Bork, Aaron Wildavsky, Robert Nisbet, Robert Carleson, and others. We drafted a Balanced Budget/Spending Limitation amendment to the US Constitution. The US Senate passed that amendment on August 4, 1982, by a vote of sixty-nine to thirty-one, two more than the two-thirds vote required for approval of a constitutional amendment. The vote was bipartisan: forty-seven Republicans, twenty-one Democrats, and one Independent voted for the amendment.

It was a different story in the House of Representatives. Its leadership, under Tip O'Neill tried to prevent a vote on the amendment; however, a discharge petition forced a vote on it. While the amendment was approved by a majority (236 to 187), it did not meet the two-thirds required by Article V of the Constitution. The vote was again bipartisan: 167 Republicans, 69 Democrats. The amendment can be found in Milton and Rose Friedman's "Tyranny of the Status Quo."

The benefit of a balanced budget/spending limitation amendment is that it would give Congress a bottom line just as we in the private sector have a bottom line. Congress would be forced to play one spending constituency off against another, rather than, as it does today, satisfy most spending constituents and pass the buck to the rest of us and future generations in the forms of federal deficits and debt.

The 1980s discussions settled on giving Congress a spending limit of 18 or 20 percent of our GDP. I thought a 10 percent limit was better. When queried by a reporter as to why 10 percent, I told him that if 10 percent is good enough for the Baptist Church, it ought to be good enough for Congress.

Moral or Immoral Government

December 8, 2010

Immorality in government lies at the heart of our nation's problems. Deficits, debt, and runaway government are merely symptoms. What's moral and immoral conduct can be complicated, but needlessly so. I keep things simple and you tell me where I go wrong.

My initial assumption is that we each own ourselves. I am my private property and you are yours. If we accept the notion that people own themselves, then it's easy to discover what forms of conduct are moral and immoral. Immoral acts are those that violate self-ownership. Murder, rape, assault, and slavery are immoral because those acts violate private property. So is theft, broadly defined as taking the rightful property of one person and giving it to another.

If it is your belief that people do not belong to themselves, they are in whole or in part the property of the US Congress, or people are owned by God, who has placed the US Congress in charge of managing them, then all of my observations are simply nonsense.

Let's look at some congressional actions in light of self-ownership. Do farmers and businessmen have a right to congressional handouts? Does a person have a right to congressional handouts for housing, food, and medical care?

First, let's ask: Where does Congress get handout money? One thing for sure, it's not from the Tooth Fairy or Santa Claus nor is it congressmen reaching into their own pockets. The only way for Congress to give one American one dollar is to first, through the tax code, take that dollar from some other American. It must forcibly use one American to serve another American. Forcibly using one person to serve another is one way to describe slavery. As such, it violates self-ownership.

Government immorality isn't restricted only to forcing one person to serve another. Some regulations such as forcing motorists to wear seatbelts violate self-ownership. If one owns himself, he has the right to take chances with his own life. Some people argue that if you're not wearing a seatbelt, have an accident, and become a vegetable, you'll become a burden on society. That's not a problem of liberty and self-ownership. It's a problem of socialism where through the tax code one person is forcibly used to care for another.

These examples are among thousands of government actions that violate the principles of self-ownership. Some might argue that Congress forcing us to help one another and forcing us to take care of ourselves are good ideas. But my question to you is: When congressmen and presidents take their oaths of office, is that oath to uphold and defend good ideas or the US Constitution?

When the principles of self-ownership are taken into account, two-thirds to three-quarters of what Congress does violates those principles to one degree or another as well as the Constitution to which they've sworn to uphold and defend. In 1794, when Congress appropriated $15,000 to assist some French refugees, James Madison, the father of our Constitution, stood on the floor of the House to object, saying, "I cannot undertake to lay my finger on that article of the Constitution which granted a right to Congress of expending, on objects of benevolence, the money of their constituents." Did James Madison miss something in the Constitution?

You might answer, "He forgot the general welfare clause." No, he had that covered, saying, "If Congress can do whatever in their discretion can be done by money, and will promote the General Welfare, the Government is no longer a limited one, possessing enumerated powers, but an indefinite one."

If we accept the value of self-ownership, it is clear that most of what Congress does is clearly immoral. If this is bothersome, there are two ways around my argument. The first is to deny the implications of self-ownership. The second is to ask, as Speaker Nancy Pelosi did when asked about the constitutionality of Obamacare, "Are you serious? Are you serious?"

Handouts, Morality, and Common Sense
March 9, 2011

Whether Americans realize it or not, the last decade's path of congressional spending is unsustainable. Spending must be reined in, but what spending should be cut? The Republican majority in the House of Representatives fear being booted out of office and are understandably timid. Their rule for whom to cut appears to be: Look around to see who are the politically weak handout recipients.

The problem is that those cuts won't put much of a dent in overall spending. The absolute last thing a Republican or Democrat congressmen wants to do is to cut handouts to, and thereby anger, recipients who vote in large numbers. To spare myself ugly mail, I'm not going to mention that handout group, but members of Congress know of whom I speak.

More than two hundred House members and fifty senators have cosponsored a balanced budget amendment to our Constitution. A balanced budget amendment is no protection against the growth of government and the loss of our liberties. Estimated federal tax revenue for 2011 is $2.2 trillion and federal spending is $3.8 trillion leaving us with a $1.6 trillion deficit. The budget could be balanced simply by taking more of our earnings, making us greater congressional serfs. True protection requires an amendment limiting congressional spending.

You say, "OK, Williams, what would be your rule for getting our fiscal house in order?" We need a rule that combines our Constitution with simple morality and plain common sense. I think it immoral for Congress to forcibly take one American's earnings and give them to another American to whom they do not belong. If a person did the same thing privately, he'd be convicted of theft and jailed. We might ask ourselves whether acts that are clearly immoral and despicable when done privately are any less so when done by Congress. Close to two-thirds of the federal budget, so-called entitlements, represent what thieves do: redistribute income.

Some people might say, "Williams, the programs that you'd cut are vital to the welfare of our nation!" When someone says that, I always ask what did we do before. For example, our nation went from 1787 to 1979 and during that interval produced some of the world's most highly educated people without a Department of Education. Since the department's creation, American primary and secondary education has become a joke among industrialized nations.

What about the Department of Energy; how much energy has it produced?

From our founding in 1787 to 1965, our nation went from a Third World status to building the world's mightiest first-class cities such as New York, Chicago, Los Angeles, Detroit, and Philadelphia without the benefit of Department of Housing and Urban Development (HUD). After HUD was created in 1965, many of our formerly great cities are in decline. No one is saying that HUD is responsible for the decline, but neither was HUD responsible for their rise.

There is a distinct group of Americans who bear a large burden for today's runaway government. You ask, "Who are they?" It's the so-called "greatest generation." When those Americans were born, federal spending as a percentage of GDP was about 3 percent, as it was from 1787 to 1920 except during war. No one denies the sacrifices made and the true greatness of a generation of Americans who suffered through our worst depression, conquered the meanest tyrants during World War II, and later managed to produce a level of wealth and prosperity heretofore unknown to mankind.

But this generation of Americans also laid the political foundation for the greatest betrayal of our nation's core founding principle: limited federal government exercising only constitutionally enumerated powers. It was on their watch that the foundation was laid for today's massive federal spending that tops 25 percent of GDP.

A good part of that generation is still alive. Before they depart, they might do their share to help us have a federal government exercising only constitutionally enumerated powers.

Gov. Perry's Right about Social Security
September 21, 2011

During the recent GOP presidential debate, Texas Gov. Rick Perry said that Social Security is a "monstrous lie" and a "Ponzi scheme." More and more people are coming to see that Social Security is a Ponzi scheme, but is it a lie, as well? Let's look at it.

Here's what the 1936 government pamphlet on Social Security said: "After the first 3 years—that is to say, beginning in 1940—you will pay, and your employer will pay, 1.5 cents for each dollar you earn, up to $3,000 a year. . . . Beginning in 1943, you will pay 2 cents, and so will your employer, for every dollar you earn for the next 3 years. . . . And finally, beginning in 1949, twelve years from now, you and your employer will each pay 3 cents on each dollar you earn, up to $3,000 a year." Here's Congress's lying promise: "That is the most you will ever pay."

Another lie in the Social Security pamphlet is: "Beginning November 24, 1936, the United States government will set up a Social Security account for you. . . . The checks will come to you as a right." Therefore, Americans were sold on the belief that Social Security is like a retirement account and money placed in it is our property. The fact of the matter is you have no property right whatsoever to your Social Security "contributions."

You say, "Williams, you're wrong! We have a right to Social Security payments." In a US Supreme Court case, Helvering v. Davis (1937), the court held that Social Security is not an insurance program, saying, "The proceeds of both (employee and employer) taxes are to be paid into the Treasury like internal revenue taxes generally, and are not earmarked in any way." In a later Supreme Court case, Flemming v. Nestor (1960), the court said, "To engraft upon the Social Security system a concept of 'accrued property rights' would deprive it of the flexibility and boldness in adjustment to ever-changing conditions which it demands."

Belatedly, the Social Security Administration is trying to clean up its history of deception. Its website (http://www.ssa.gov/history/nestor.html) says, "Entitlement to Social Security benefits is not (a) contractual right," adding, "There has been a temptation throughout the program's history for some people to suppose that their FICA payroll taxes entitle them to a benefit in a legal, contractual sense. . . . Congress clearly had no such limitation in mind when crafting the law." That's the SSA's dishonesty. After all, it was the people in that administration who said, in their 1936 pamphlet, that "the checks will come to you as a right."

There's more deceit and dishonesty. In 1950, I was fourteen years old and applied for a work permit for an after-school job. One of the requirements was to obtain a Social Security card. In bold letters on my Social Security card are the words "For Social Security Purposes—Not For Identification." According to the SSA's website, "this legend was removed as part of the design changes for the 18th version of the card, issued beginning in 1972." That's a shameless, unadulterated lie. Because we're idiots, we're asked to believe that the sole purpose for the removal of "Not For Identification" was for design purposes. The fact that our Social Security numbers were going to become a major identification tool had nothing to do with getting rid of the statement.

Aside from these lies, Social Security is a Ponzi scheme. The major difference between Social Security and Bernie Madoff's Ponzi scheme is his was illegal. Three Nobel laureate economists have testified that Social Security is a Ponzi scheme. Dr. Paul Samuelson called it "the greatest Ponzi game ever contrived." Dr. Milton Friedman said it was "the biggest Ponzi scheme on Earth." Dr. Paul Krugman predicted that "the Ponzi game will soon be over."

Three cheers to Gov. Rick Perry for having the guts to tell us that Social Security is a monstrous lie and a Ponzi scheme.

Social Security Disaster

October 5, 2011

Politicians who are principled enough to point out the fraud of Social Security, referring to it as a lie and Ponzi scheme, are under siege. Acknowledgment of Social Security's problems is not the same as calling for the abandonment of its recipients. Instead, it's a call to take actions now, while there's time to avert a disaster. Let's look at it.

The term was derived from the scheme created during the 1920s by Charles Ponzi, a poor but enterprising Italian immigrant. Here's how it works. You persuade some people to give you their money to invest. After a while, you pay them a nice return, but the return doesn't come from investments. What you pay them with comes from the money of other people whom you've persuaded to "invest" in your scheme. The scheme works so long as you can persuade greater and greater numbers of people to "invest" so that you can pay off earlier "investors." After a while, Ponzi couldn't find enough new investors, and his scheme collapsed. He was convicted of fraud and sent to prison.

The very first Social Security check went to Ida May Fuller in 1940. She paid just $24.75 in Social Security taxes but collected a total of $22,888.92 in benefits, getting back all she put into Social Security in a month. According to a Congressional Research Service report titled "Social Security Reform" (October 2002), by Geoffrey Kollmann and Dawn Nuschler, workers who retired in 1980 at age 65 got back all they put into Social Security, plus interest, in 2.8 years. Workers who retired at age 65 in 2002 will have to wait a total of 16.9 years to break even. For those retiring in 2020, it will take 20.9 years. Workers entering the labor force today won't live long enough to get back even half of what they will put into Social Security. Social Security faces Ponzi's problem, not enough new "investors." In 1940, there were 160 workers paying into Social Security per retiree; today there are only 2.9 and falling.

Some politicians claim that Social Security has a huge trust fund and is in good health. An uninformed public and a derelict news media don't challenge that lie. Back in August, politicians were in a tizzy over raising the federal debt limit. In an effort to frighten seniors, President Barack Obama said in a CBS interview, "I cannot guarantee that those checks go out on August 3 if we haven't resolved this issue, because there may simply not be the money in the coffers to do it." Here's how we reveal the trust fund lie: According to the Social Security Administration, it has a trust fund with $2.6 trillion in it. If those were real assets, then the Social Security Administration could have mailed checks out regardless of what Congress did about the debt limit. The reality is that the Social Security trust fund consists of government IOUs that have no real value at all and probably are not even worth the paper upon which they are printed.

I believe that a person who is sixty-five years old and has been forced into Social Security is owed something. But the question is, Who owes it to him? Congress has spent every penny of his Social Security "contribution." Young workers have no obligation to be fleeced in order to make up for the dishonesty and dereliction of Congress. The tragedy is that most seniors just want their money and couldn't care less about whom Congress takes it from.

Here's what might be a temporary fix: The federal government owns huge quantities of wasting assets—assets that are not producing anything—650 million acres of land, almost 30 percent of the land area of the United States. In exchange for those who choose to opt out of Social Security and forsake any future claim, why not pay them off with forty or so acres of land? Doing so would give us breathing room to develop a free choice method to finance retirement.

Devious Taxation

April 25, 2012

The Washington, D.C.-based Tax Foundation does a yeoman's job of keeping track of how much we're paying in taxes and who's paying what. It turns out that American taxpayers worked this year from January 1 to April 17, 107 days, to earn enough money to pay their federal, state, and local tax bills. That statistic requires some clarification, and I ask my readers to help me examine it.

According to the Congressional Budget Office, Congress will spend $3.8 trillion this year, about 24 percent of our $15 trillion gross domestic product. But federal tax revenue will be much less, only $2.5 trillion, or 16 percent of the GDP. That means there's a shortfall of $1.3 trillion. Some people, including economists, say there's a deficit. That's true, but only in an accounting sense, not in any meaningful economic sense. Let's look at it.

If Congress spends $3.8 trillion out of this year's $15 trillion GDP, what must it do to accomplish that goal? If you said it must "find a way to force us not to spend $3.8 trillion privately," go to the head of the class. One way to force us to spend $3.8 trillion less is to tax us that amount, but we're being taxed only $2.5 trillion. Where does the extra $1.3 trillion come from? It surely doesn't come from the Tooth Fairy, Santa Claus, or the Easter Bunny.

The fact of business is that if Congress spends $3.8 trillion of what we produce this year, it necessarily must force us to spend $3.8 trillion less privately this year. The most honest way to force us to do that is through taxation. Another way is to enter the bond market and make interest rates higher than they otherwise would be, thereby forcing us to spend less on private investment in homes and businesses. Then there is debasement of the currency through inflation, which is taxation by stealth.

A common but misleading argument is that future generations of Americans will pay for today's spending. Think about it. Is it possible for someone who has yet to be born to pick up the tab for what we do today? Pose the question another way. When we fought World War II, were the resources used and the sacrifices made to fight the war produced between 1941 and 1945, or were they produced and sacrificed in 1980, 1990, or 2000? Subsequent generations benefited from our fighting the war by being born into a free nation. Congress's profligate spending will burden future generations through making them heirs to less capital and, hence, less wealth.

The bottom line is that whatever Congress consumes this year is produced this year, not in 2020, 2030, or 2040. That means, in the real economic sense, the federal budget is always balanced.

Instead of focusing on how the federal government has grown from 3 or 4 percent of our GDP—as it was from 1787 to 1920—to today's 24 percent, our attention has been diverted to tax fairness demagoguery. Let's look at tax fairness. According to Internal Revenue Service data for 2009, available at http://www.ntu.org/tax-basics/who-pays-income-taxes.html, the top 1 percent of American income earners paid almost 37 percent of federal income taxes. The top 10 percent paid about 70 percent of federal income taxes, and the top 50 percent paid nearly 98 percent. Roughly 47 percent of Americans pay no federal income tax. Here's my fairness question to you: What standard of fairness dictates that the top 10 percent of income earners pay 70 percent of the income tax burden while 47 percent of Americans pay nothing?

The fact that the income tax burden is distributed so unevenly produces great politically borne fiscal problems. People who pay little or no income taxes become natural constituents for big-spending politicians. After all, if you pay no income taxes, what do you care if income taxes are raised? Also, you won't be enthusiastic about tax cuts; you'll see them as a threat to your handouts.

Our Nation's Future

May 30, 2012

Our nation is rapidly approaching a point from which there's little chance to avoid a financial collapse. The heart of our problem can be seen as a tragedy of the commons. That's a set of circumstances when something is commonly owned and individuals acting rationally in their own self-interest produce a set of results that's inimical to everyone's long-term interest. Let's look at an example of the tragedy-of-the-commons phenomenon and then apply it to our national problem.

Imagine there are a hundred cattlemen all having an equal right to graze their herds on one thousand acres of commonly owned grassland. The rational self-interested response of each cattleman is to have the largest herd that he can afford. Each cattleman pursing similar self-interests will produce results not in any of the cattlemen's long-term interest—overgrazing, soil erosion, and destruction of the land's usefulness. Even if they all recognize the dangers, does it pay for any one cattleman to cut the size of his herd? The short answer is no because he would bear the cost of having a smaller herd while the other cattlemen gain at his expense. In the long term, they all lose because the land will be overgrazed and made useless.

We can think of the federal budget as a commons to which each of our 535 congressmen and the president have access. Like the cattlemen, each congressman and the president want to get as much out of the federal budget as possible for their constituents. Political success depends upon "bringing home the bacon." Spending is popular, but taxes to finance the spending are not. The tendency is for spending to rise and its financing to be concealed through borrowing and inflation.

Does it pay for an individual congressman to say, "This spending is unconstitutional and ruining our nation, and I'll have no part of it; I will refuse a $500 million federal grant to my congressional district"? The answer is no because he would gain little or nothing, plus the federal budget wouldn't be reduced by $500 million. Other congressmen would benefit by having $500 million more for their districts.

What about the constituents of a principled congressman? If their congressman refuses unconstitutional spending, it doesn't mean that they pay lower federal income taxes. All that it means is constituents of some other congressmen get the money while the nation spirals toward financial ruin, and they wouldn't be spared from that ruin because their congressman refused to participate in unconstitutional spending.

What we're witnessing in Greece, Italy, Ireland, Portugal, and other parts of Europe is a direct result of their massive spending to accommodate the welfare state. A greater number of people are living off government welfare programs than are paying taxes. Government debt in Greece is 160 percent of gross domestic product. The other percentages of GDP are 120 in Italy, 104 in Ireland, and 106 in Portugal. As a result of this debt and the improbability of their ever paying it, their credit ratings either have reached or are close to reaching junk bond status.

Here's the question for us: Is the United States moving in a direction toward or away from the troubled EU nations? It turns out that our national debt, which was 35 percent of GDP during the 1970s, is now 106 percent of GDP, a level not seen since World War II's 122 percent. That debt, plus our more than $100 trillion in unfunded liabilities, has led Standard & Poor's to downgrade our credit rating from AAA to AA+, and the agency is keeping the outlook at "negative" as a result of its having little confidence that Congress will take on the politically sensitive job of tackling the same type of entitlement that has turned Europe into a basket case.

I am all too afraid that Benjamin Franklin correctly saw our nation's destiny when he said, "When the people find that they can vote themselves money, that will herald the end of the republic."

Duped by Congressional Lies

June 13, 2012

Some of the responses to my column last week, titled "Immoral Beyond Redemption," prove that Americans have been hoodwinked by Congress. Some readers protested my counting Social Security among government handout programs that can be described as Congress's taking what belongs to one American and giving to another, to whom it doesn't belong—legalized theft. They argued that they worked for forty-five years and paid into Social Security and that the money they now receive is theirs. These people have been duped and shouldn't be held totally accountable for such a belief. Let's look at it.

The Social Security pamphlet of 1936 read, "Beginning November 24, 1936, the United States Government will set up a Social Security account for you. . . . The checks will come to you as a right" (http://www.ssa.gov/history/ssb36.html). Americans were led to believe that Social Security was like a retirement account and that money placed in it was, in fact, their property. Shortly after the Social Security Act's passage, it was challenged in the US Supreme Court, in Helvering v. Davis (1937). The court held that Social Security was not an insurance program, saying, "The proceeds of both employee and employer taxes are to be paid into the Treasury like any other internal revenue generally, and are not earmarked in any way." In a 1960 case, Flemming v. Nestor, the Supreme Court said, "To engraft upon Social Security system a concept of 'accrued property rights' would deprive it of the flexibility and boldness in adjustment to ever-changing conditions which it demands."

Decades after Americans were duped into thinking that the money taken from them was theirs, the Social Security Administration belatedly and quietly tried to clean up its history of deception. Its website (http://www.ssa.gov/history/nestor.html) explains, "Entitlement to Social Security benefits is not (a) contractual right." It adds: "There has been a temptation throughout the program's history for some people to suppose that their FICA payroll taxes entitle them to a benefit in a legal, contractual sense. . . . Congress clearly had no such limitation in mind when crafting the law." The Social Security Administration's explanation fails to mention that it was the SSA itself that created the lie that "the checks will come to you as a right."

Here's my question to those who protest that their Social Security checks are not handouts: Seeing as Congress has not "set up a Social Security account for you" containing your forty-five years' worth of Social Security contributions, where does the money you receive come from? I promise you it is not Santa Claus or the Tooth Fairy. The only way Congress can give one American a dollar is to first take it from some other American. Congress takes the earnings of a person who's currently in the workforce to give to a Social Security recipient. The sad fact of business is that Social Security recipients want their monthly check and couldn't care less about who has to pay. That's a vision shared by thieves who want something; the heck with who has to pay for it.

Then there's the fairness issue that we're so enamored with today. It turns out that half the federal budget is spent on programs primarily serving senior citizens, such as Social Security, Medicare, and Medicaid. But let's look at a few comparisons between younger Americans and older Americans. More than 80 percent of those older than sixty-five are homeowners, and 66 percent of them have no mortgage. Home-ownership is at 40 percent for those younger than thirty-five, and only 12 percent own their home free and clear of a mortgage. The average net worth of people older than sixty-five is about $230,000, whereas that of those younger than thirty-five is $10,000. There's nothing complicated about this; older people have been around longer. But what standard of fairness justifies taxing the earnings of workers who are less wealthy in order to pass them on to retirees who are far wealthier? There's no justi-fication, but there's an explanation. Those older than sixty-five vote in greater numbers and have the ear of congressmen.

Who May Tax and Spend?

September 12, 2012

Within the past decade, I've written columns titled "Deception 101," "Stubborn Ignorance," and "Exploiting Public Ignorance," all explaining which branch of the federal government has taxing and spending authority. So here it is again: The first clause of Article 1, Section 7, of the US Constitution, generally known as the "origination clause," reads: "All Bills for raising Revenue shall originate in the House of Representatives; but the Senate may propose or concur with Amendments as on other Bills." Constitutionally and by precedent, the House of Representatives has the exclusive prerogative to originate bills to appropriate money, as well as to raise revenues. The president is constitutionally permitted to propose tax and spending measures or veto them. Congress has the authority to ignore the president's proposals and override his vetoes.

There is little intellectually challenging about the fact that the Constitution gave Congress ultimate taxing and spending authority. My question is this: How can academics, politicians, news media people and ordinary citizens continually make and get away with statements such as "Reagan's budget deficits," "Clinton's budget surplus," "Bush's tax cut," and "Obama's spending binge"? I know that the nation's law schools teach little about Framer intent, but I wonder whether they tell students that it's the executive branch of government that holds taxing and spending authority. Maybe it's simply incurable ignorance, willful deception, sloppy thinking, or just plain stupidity. If there's an explanation that I've missed, I'd surely like to hear it.

Seeing as a president cannot spend one dime that Congress does not first appropriate, what meaning can we attach to statements such as "under Barack Obama, government spending has increased 21 percent" and "under Barack Obama, welfare spending has increased 54 percent"? You ask, "Williams, are you saying Obama is without fault?" Let's look at it.

Knowing which branch of government has the ultimate taxing and spending authority is vital. No matter how Obama's presidency is viewed, if we buy into the notion that it's he whose spending binge is crippling our nation through massive debt and deficits, we will naturally focus our attention on the White House. The fact of the matter is that Washington has been on a spending binge no matter who has occupied the White House. In 1970, federal spending was $926 billion. Today it's $3.8 trillion. In inflation-adjusted dollars that's about a 300 percent increase. Believing that presidents have taxing and spending powers leaves Congress less politically accountable for our deepening economic quagmire. Of course, if you're a congressman, not being held accountable is what you want.

Let's look at a minor case that demonstrates Congress's appropriation powers. The California Navel Orange Commission is a government-sanctioned grower collusion that establishes production quotas so as to restrict supply in order to keep orange prices high. In 1980, the Federal Trade Commission was going to study such agriculture collusions, euphemistically called marketing orders, as a result of increasing criticism from economists, reformers in federal agencies, consumer groups, and some orange growers. Big growers descended on Congress to protest the threat to their collusive behavior that an FTC study might create. Congress, as a part of its FTC appropriation, prohibited the agency from monitoring marketing orders. In November 1983, Congress started using a legislative rider to prohibit the Office of Management and Budget from spending any money to review marketing orders.

This example demonstrates that Congress has ultimate spending power and that when it suits favored interest groups, it will use it. Most members of our Republican-controlled House of Representatives say they're against Obamacare. If they really were, they surely would attach a legislative rider or some other legislative device to the

Department of Health and Human Services' appropriation bill to ban spending any money on Obamacare; they have the power to. But they don't have the political courage to do so, and their lives are made easier by the pretense that it's the president controlling the spending. And we fall for it.

Parting Company

November 28, 2012

For decades, it has been obvious that there are irreconcilable differences between Americans who want to control the lives of others and those who wish to be left alone. Which is the more peaceful solution: Americans using the brute force of government to beat liberty-minded people into submission or simply parting company? In a marriage, where vows are ignored and broken, divorce is the most peaceful solution. Similarly, our constitutional and human rights have been increasingly violated by a government instituted to protect them. Americans who support constitutional abrogation have no intention of mending their ways.

Since Barack Obama's reelection, hundreds of thousands of petitions for secession have reached the White House. Some people have argued that secession is unconstitutional, but there's absolutely nothing in the Constitution that prohibits it. What stops secession is the prospect of brute force by a mighty federal government, as witnessed by the costly War of 1861. Let's look at the secession issue.

At the 1787 constitutional convention, a proposal was made to allow the federal government to suppress a seceding state. James Madison, the acknowledged father of our Constitution, rejected it, saying: "A Union of the States containing such an ingredient seemed to provide for its own destruction. The use of force against a State would look more like a declaration of war than an infliction of punishment and would probably be considered by the party attacked as a dissolution of all previous compacts by which it might be bound."

On March 2, 1861, after seven states had seceded and two days before Abraham Lincoln's inauguration, Sen. James R. Doolittle of Wisconsin proposed a constitutional amendment that said, "No State or any part thereof, heretofore admitted or hereafter admitted into the Union, shall have the power to withdraw from the jurisdiction of the United States."

Several months earlier, Reps. Daniel E. Sickles of New York, Thomas B. Florence of Pennsylvania, and Otis S. Ferry of Connecticut proposed a constitutional amendment to prohibit secession. Here's my no-brainer question: Would there have been any point to offering these amendments if secession were already unconstitutional?

On the eve of the War of 1861, even unionist politicians saw secession as a right of states. Rep. Jacob M. Kunkel of Maryland said, "Any attempt to preserve the Union between the States of this Confederacy by force would be impractical, and destructive of republican liberty."

The Northern Democratic and Republican parties favored allowing the South to secede in peace. Just about every major Northern newspaper editorialized in favor of the South's right to secede. *New York Tribune* (February 5, 1860): "If tyranny and despotism justified the Revolution of 1776, then we do not see why it would not justify the secession of Five Millions of Southrons from the Federal Union in 1861." *Detroit Free Press* (February 19, 1861): "An attempt to subjugate the seceded States, even if successful, could produce nothing but evil—evil unmitigated in character and appalling in content." *The New York Times* (March 21, 1861): "There is growing sentiment throughout the North in favor of letting the Gulf States go."

There's more evidence seen at the time our Constitution was ratified. The ratification documents of Virginia, New York, and Rhode Island explicitly said that they held the right to resume powers delegated, should the federal government become abusive of those powers. The Constitution would have never been ratified if states thought that they could not maintain their sovereignty.

The War of 1861 settled the issue of secession through brute force that cost 600,000 American lives. Americans celebrate Abraham Lincoln's Gettysburg Address, but H. L. Mencken correctly evaluated the speech: "It is poetry, not logic; beauty, not sense." Lincoln said that the soldiers sacrificed their lives "to the cause of self-determination—that government of the people, by the people, for the people should not perish from the earth." Mencken says: "It is difficult to imagine anything more untrue. The Union soldiers in the battle actually fought against self-determination; it was the Confederates who fought for the right of people to govern themselves."

Our Government-Created Financial Crisis

December 12, 2012

Suppose you saw a building on fire. Would you seek counsel from the arsonist who set it ablaze for advice on how to put it out? You say, "Williams, you'd have to be a lunatic to do that!" But that's precisely what we've done: turned to the people who created our fiscal crisis to fix it. I have never read a better account of our doing just that than in John A. Allison's new book, *The Financial Crisis and the Free Market Cure.*

Allison is the former CEO of Branch Banking and Trust, the nation's tenth-largest bank. He assembles evidence that shows that our financial crisis, followed by the Great Recession, was caused by Congress, the Federal Reserve, Freddie Mac, and Fannie Mae and was helped along by the Bill Clinton, George W. Bush, and Barack Obama White Houses.

The Federal Reserve, under the chairmanship of Alan Greenspan, created the massive housing bubble by over-expanding the money supply. President Bush and members of Congress, through the Community Reinvestment Act, intimidated banks and other financial institutions into making home loans to people ineligible for loans under traditional lending criteria. They became subprime lenders. Lending institutions made these loans, now often demeaned as predator loans, because they knew they'd be sold to government-sponsored enterprises (GSEs) Freddie and Fannie.

The GSEs had no problem taking this risky path, because they knew that Congress would force taxpayers to bail them out. Current Fed Chairman Ben Bernanke is following in the footsteps of his predecessor by massively expanding the money supply by purchasing Treasury debt. He is creating prime conditions for a calamity by the end of this decade.

Then there were the crony capitalists, among whom are Goldman Sachs, Citigroup, Countrywide, Bear Stearns, JPMorgan Chase,

General Motors, and Chrysler. These and many other companies, through the thousands of Washington lobbyists they hire, are able to get Congress to shortcut market forces. Free market capitalism is unforgiving. In order to earn a profit and stay in business, producers must please customers and wisely use resources to do so. If they fail to do this, they face losses or go bankrupt.

It's this market discipline of profits and losses that many businesses seek to avoid. That's why they descend upon Washington calling for government bailouts, subsidies, and special privileges. Many businessmen wish not to be held strictly accountable to consumers and stockholders, who hold little sympathy for economic blunders and will give them the ax on a moment's notice. With a campaign contribution here and a gift there, they get Congress and the White House to act against the best interests of consumers and investors. Allison suggests that if our country had a separation of "business and state" as it does a separation of "church and state," crony capitalism or crony socialism could not exist.

Allison says that crony capitalism should not be our only concern. The foundation for economic collapse twenty to twenty-five years from now has already been set. Social Security and Medicare deficits, unfunded state and local pension liabilities, government operating deficits, baby boomer retirement, and a failed K-12 education system have eaten out our substance.

What I take away from Allison's highly readable book is that our biggest problem lies in the Federal Reserve's ability to manipulate our monetary system to accommodate big government and use inflation to rob Americans. That's why politicians and government leaders everywhere hate a monetary system based on gold. They can manipulate the quantity of paper money, but they can't manipulate the quantity of gold.

Here's a tidbit of information about John Allison, now president of the Washington-based Cato Institute, that speaks to this man's morality as BB&T's CEO, which can't be praised highly enough. His company refused to lend money to developers who acquired land by having the government take it from private owners, euphemistically called eminent domain. That's putting his money where his mouth is, not sacrificing principle for the sake of earnings.

Official Lies

January 30, 2013

Let's expose presidential prevarication. Earlier this year, President Barack Obama warned that Social Security checks will be delayed if Congress fails to increase the government's borrowing authority by raising the debt ceiling. However, there's an issue with this warning. According to the 2012 Social Security trustees report, assets in Social Security's trust funds totaled $2.7 trillion, and Social Security expenditures totaled $773 billion. Therefore, regardless of what Congress does about the debt limit, Social Security recipients are guaranteed their checks. Just take the money from the $2.7 trillion assets held in trust.

Which is the lie: Social Security checks must be delayed if the debt ceiling is not raised, or there's $2.7 trillion in the Social Security trust funds? The fact of the matter is that they are both lies. The Social Security trust funds contain nothing more than IOUs, bonds that have absolutely no market value. In other words, they are worthless bookkeeping entries. Social Security is a pay-as-you-go system, meaning that the taxes paid by today's workers are immediately sent out as payment to today's retirees. Social Security is just another federal program funded out of general revenues.

If the congressional Republicans had one ounce of brains, they could easily thwart the president and his leftist allies' attempt to frighten older Americans about not receiving their Social Security checks and thwart their attempt to frighten other Americans by saying "we are not a deadbeat nation" and suggesting the possibility of default if the debt ceiling is not raised. In 2012, monthly federal tax revenue was about $200 billion. Monthly Social Security expenditures were about $65 billion per month, and the monthly interest payment on our $16 trillion national debt was about $30 billion. The House could simply enact a bill prioritizing how federal tax revenues will be spent. It could mandate that Social Security recipients and interest payments on the national debt be the first priorities and then send the measure to the Senate and the president for concurrence. It might not be a matter of brains as to why the Republican House wouldn't enact such a measure; it likes spending just as the Democrats.

I believe our nation is rapidly approaching our last chance to do something about runaway government before we face the type of economic turmoil seen in Greece and other European nations. Tax revenue has remained constant for the past fifty years, averaging about 18 percent of gross domestic product. During that interval, federal spending has risen from less than 20 percent to more than 25 percent of GDP. What accounts for this growth in federal spending? The liberals like to blame national defense, but in 1962, national defense expenditures were 50 percent of the federal budget; today they are 19 percent. What accounts for most federal spending is the set of programs euphemistically called entitlements. In 1962, entitlement spending was 31 percent of the federal budget; today it is 62 percent. Medicare, Medicaid, and Social Security alone take up 44 percent of the federal budget, and worse than that, it's those expenditures that are the most rapidly growing spending areas.

Our federal debt and deficits are unsustainable and are driven by programs under which Congress takes the earnings of one American to give to another, or entitlements. How long can Congress take in $200 billion in revenue per month and spend $360 billion per month? That means roughly 40 cents of every federal dollar spent has to be borrowed. The undeniable fact of business is that a greater number of people are living off government welfare programs than are paying taxes. That's what's driving Europe's economic problems, and it's what's driving ours. The true tragedy is that just to acknowledge that fact is political suicide, as presidential contender Mitt Romney found out. We can't blame politicians. It's the American people who will crucify a politician who even talks about cutting their favorite handout.

Abraham Lincoln

February 20, 2013

Steven Spielberg's "Lincoln" has been a box-office hit and nominated for twelve Academy Awards, including best picture, best director, and best actor for Daniel Day-Lewis, who portrayed our sixteenth president. I haven't seen the movie; therefore, this column is not about the movie but about a man deified by many. My colleague Thomas DiLorenzo, economics professor at Loyola University Maryland, exposed some of the Lincoln myth in his 2006 book, *Lincoln Unmasked*. Now comes Joseph Fallon, cultural intelligence analyst and former US Army Intelligence Center instructor, with his new e-book, *Lincoln Uncensored*. Fallon's book examines ten volumes of collected writings and speeches of Lincoln's, which include passages on slavery, secession, equality of blacks, and emancipation. We don't have to rely upon anyone's interpretation. Just read his words to see what you make of them.

In an 1858 letter, Lincoln said, "I have declared a thousand times, and now repeat that, in my opinion neither the General Government, nor any other power outside of the slave states, can constitutionally or rightfully interfere with slaves or slavery where it already exists." In a Springfield, Illinois, speech, he explained, "My declarations upon this subject of negro slavery may be misrepresented, but can not be misunderstood. I have said that I do not understand the Declaration [of Independence] to mean that all men were created equal in all respects." Debating with Sen. Stephen Douglas, Lincoln said, "I am not, nor ever have been, in favor of . . . making voters or jurors of Negroes nor of qualifying them to hold office nor to intermarry with white people; and I will say in addition to this that there is a physical difference between the white and black races, which I believe will forever forbid the two races living together on terms of social and political equality."

You say, "His Emancipation Proclamation freed the slaves! That proves he was against slavery." Lincoln's words: "I view the matter

[Emancipation Proclamation] as a practical war measure, to be decided upon according to the advantages or disadvantages it may offer to the suppression of the rebellion." He also wrote: "I will also concede that emancipation would help us in Europe, and convince them that we are incited by something more than ambition." At the time Lincoln wrote the proclamation, war was going badly for the Union. London and Paris were considering recognizing the Confederacy and considering assisting it in its war effort.

The Emancipation Proclamation was not a universal declaration. It detailed where slaves were freed, only in those states "in rebellion against the United States." Slaves remained slaves in states not in rebellion—such as Kentucky, Maryland, and Delaware. The hypocrisy of the Emancipation Proclamation came in for heavy criticism. Lincoln's own secretary of state, William Seward, said, "We show our sympathy with slavery by emancipating slaves where we cannot reach them and holding them in bondage where we can set them free."

Lincoln did articulate a view of secession that would have been welcomed in 1776: "Any people anywhere, being inclined and having the power, have the right to rise up and shake off the existing government and form a new one that suits them better. . . . Nor is this right confined to cases in which the whole people of an existing government may choose to exercise it. Any portion of such people that can may revolutionize and make their own of so much of the territory as they inhabit." But that was Lincoln's 1848 speech in the US House of Representatives regarding the war with Mexico and the secession of Texas.

Why didn't Lincoln feel the same about Southern secession? Following the money might help with an answer. Throughout most of our history, the only sources of federal revenue were excise taxes and tariffs. During the 1850s, tariffs amounted to 90 percent of federal revenue. Southern ports paid 75 percent of tariffs in 1859. What "responsible" politician would let that much revenue go?

Americans Deserve the IRS
May 29, 2013

Individually, Americans do not deserve to be subservient to such a fear-mongering, intimidating, and powerful agency as the Internal Revenue Service; but collectively, we do. Let's look at it.

Since the 1791 ratification of our Constitution, until well into the 1920s, federal spending as a percentage of gross domestic product never exceeded 5 percent, except during war. Today federal spending is 25 percent of our GDP. State and local government spending is about 15 percent of the GDP. That means government spends more than 40 cents of each dollar we earn. If we add government's regulatory burden, which is simply a disguised form of taxation, the government take is more than 50 percent of what we produce.

In order to squeeze out of us half of what we produce, a government tax collection agency must be ruthless and able to put the fear of God into its citizens. The IRS has mastered that task. Congress has given it powers that would be deemed criminal if used by others. For example, the Constitution's Fifth Amendment protects Americans against self-incrimination and being forced to bear witness against oneself. That's precisely what one does when he is compelled to sign his income tax form. However, a Fifth Amendment argument can't be used as a defense in a court of law. The IRS will counter that you voluntarily provided the information on your tax return.

If you're in debt to Bank of America, Wells Fargo, or any other private creditor, in order for it to garnish your wages as a means of collecting debt, it must first get a court order. By contrast, the IRS can garnish your wages without having to get a court order first. If your employer doesn't obey the IRS and send it a portion of your wages, he will be held accountable for what you owe. At the minimum, some IRS collection procedures violate one of the basic tenets of the rule of law—namely, the law of the land applies equally to individuals (and other private entities) and the government (and its officials and agents).

Our founding fathers feared the emergence of an agency such as the IRS and its potential for abuse. That's why they gave us Article 1, Section 9, of the Constitution, which reads: "No Capitation, or other direct, Tax shall be laid, unless in Proportion to the Census or Enumeration herein before directed to be taken." A capitation is a tax placed directly on an individual. That's what an income tax is. The founders feared the abuse and the government power inherent in a direct tax. In Section 8 of Article 1, they added, "But all Duties, Imposts and Excises shall be uniform throughout the United States." These protections the founders gave us were undone by the Progressive era's Sixteenth Amendment, which reads, "The Congress shall have power to lay and collect taxes on incomes, from whatever source derived, without apportionment among the several States, and without regard to any census or enumeration."

If federal spending were only 5 percent of our GDP ($750 billion)—instead of 25 percent ($3.8 trillion)—there would be no need for today's oppressive and complicated tax system. You might ask, "How could we be a great nation without all the government spending?" When our Constitution was ratified in 1791, we were a weak and poor nation. One hundred forty years later, with federal spending a mere pittance of what it is today, we became the world's richest and most powerful nation. No small part of this miracle was limited and unintrusive government.

The bottom line is that members of Congress need such a ruthless tax collection agency as the IRS because of the charge we Americans have given them. We want what the IRS does—namely, to take the earnings of one American so Congress can create a benefit for some other American. Don't get angry with IRS agents. They are just following orders.

Distrusting Government
July 3, 2013

Recent opinion polls demonstrate a deepening distrust of the federal government. That's not an altogether bad thing. Our nation's founders recognized that most human abuses are the result of government. As Thomas Paine said, "government, even in its best state, is but a necessary evil." Because of their fear of abuse, the Constitution's framers sought to keep the federal government limited in its power. Their distrust of Congress is seen in the governing rules and language used throughout our Constitution. The Bill of Rights is explicit in that distrust, using language such as Congress shall not abridge, shall not infringe and shall not deny and other shall-nots, such as disparage, violate, and deny. If the framers did not believe that Congress would abuse our God-given, or natural, rights, they would not have provided those protections. I've always suggested that if we see anything like the Bill of Rights at our next destination after we die, we'll know that we're in hell. A perceived need for such protection in heaven would be an affront to God. It would be the same as saying we can't trust him.

Other framer protections from government are found in the Constitution's separation of powers, checks and balances, and several antimajoritarian provisions, such as the Electoral College, the two-thirds vote to override a veto, and that two-thirds of state legislatures can call for reconvening the constitutional convention, with the requirement that three-quarters of state legislatures ratify changes to the Constitution.

The heartening news for us is that state legislatures are beginning to awaken to their duty to protect their citizens from unconstitutional acts by the Congress, the White House and a derelict Supreme Court. According to an Associated Press story, about four-fifths of the states now have local laws that reject or ignore federal laws on marijuana use, gun control, health insurance requirements, and identification standards for driver's licenses. Kansas Gov. Sam Brownback recently signed a measure threatening felony charges against federal agents who enforce certain firearms laws in his state.

Missouri legislators recently enacted the Second Amendment Preservation Act, which in part reads that not only is it the right of the state legislature to check federal overreaching but that "the Missouri general assembly is duty-bound to watch over and oppose every infraction of those principles which constitute the basis of the Union of the States, because only a faithful observance of those principles can secure the nation's existence and the public happiness." The bill further declares that the Missouri General Assembly is "firmly resolved to support and defend the United States Constitution against every aggression, either foreign or domestic." The legislation awaits Gov. Jay Nixon's signature or veto.

Both lower houses of the South Carolina and Oklahoma legislatures enacted measures nullifying Obamacare on the grounds that it is an unconstitutional intrusion and violation of the Tenth Amendment. You might say, "Williams, the US Supreme Court has ruled Obamacare constitutional, and that settles it. Federal law is supreme." It's worth heeding this warning from Thomas Jefferson: "To consider the judges as the ultimate arbiters of all constitutional questions [is] a very dangerous doctrine indeed, and one which would place us under the despotism of an oligarchy." Jefferson and James Madison, in 1798 and 1799 in the Kentucky and Virginia Resolutions, said, "Resolved, That the several States composing, the United States of America, are not united on the principle of unlimited submission to their general government . . . and whensoever the general government assumes undelegated powers, its acts are unauthoritative, void, and of no force." In other words, heed the Tenth Amendment to our Constitution, which reads, "The powers not delegated to the United States by the Constitution, nor prohibited by it to the States, are reserved to the States respectively, or to the people." That's the message state legislatures should send to Washington during this year's celebration of our Declaration of Independence.

Congressionally Duped Americans
November 6, 2013

Last week's column, "Is There a Way Out?," generated quite a few responses, some a bit angry. Some people were offended by my reference to Social Security and Medicare as entitlements or handouts. They said that they worked for forty-five years and paid into Social Security and Medicare and how dare I refer to the money they now receive as an entitlement. These people have been duped by Congress and shouldn't be held totally accountable for such a belief. Let's examine the plethora of congressional Social Security lies. I'll leave the Medicare lies for another column.

The Social Security pamphlet of 1936 read, "Beginning November 24, 1936, the United States Government will set up a Social Security account for you. . . . The checks will come to you as a right" (http://tinyurl.com/maskyul). Therefore, Americans have been led to believe that Social Security is like a retirement account and money placed in it is their property. The fact of the matter belies that belief.

A year after the Social Security Act's passage, it was challenged in the US Supreme Court, in Helvering v. Davis. The court held that Social Security is not an insurance program, saying, "The proceeds of both employee and employer taxes are to be paid into the Treasury like any other internal revenue generally, and are not earmarked in any way." In a 1960 case, Flemming v. Nestor, the Supreme Court held, "To engraft upon the Social Security system a concept of 'accrued property rights' would deprive it of the flexibility and boldness in adjustment to ever-changing conditions which it demands."

Decades after Americans had been duped into thinking that the money taken from them was theirs, the Social Security Administration belatedly—and very quietly—tried to clean up its history of deception. Its website explains, "Entitlement to Social Security benefits is not (a) contractual right." It adds: "There has been a temptation throughout the program's history for some people to suppose that their FICA payroll taxes entitle them to a benefit in a legal, contractual sense. . . . Congress clearly had no such limitation in mind when crafting the law" (http://tinyurl.com/49p8fl2). The Social Security Administration failed to mention that it was the SSA itself, along with Congress, that created the lie that "the checks will come to you as a right."

Here's my question to those who protest that their Social Security checks are not an entitlement or handouts: Seeing as Congress has not "set up a Social Security account for you" containing your Social Security and Medicare "contributions," where does the money you receive come from? I promise you it's neither Santa Claus nor the Tooth Fairy. The only way Congress can send checks to Social Security and Medicare recipients is to take the earnings of a person currently in the workforce. The way Congress conceals its Ponzi scheme is to dupe Social Security and Medicare recipients into thinking that it's their money that is put away and invested. Therefore, Social Security recipients want their monthly check and are oblivious about who has to pay and the pending economic calamity that awaits future generations because of the federal government's $100 trillion-plus unfunded liability, of which Social Security and Medicare are the major parts.

Pointing to the congressional lies and future economic chaos is not the same as calling for a cessation of checks going out to recipients. Instead, it's a call for the recognition that we've made a mistake that needs to be corrected while there's time to avoid a calamity. It's also a call for us to recognize that we all share in the blame and hence the burden to make it right. Politicians have little interest in doing something about an economic calamity that will happen in 2030 or 2040; they only care about the next election. Older Americans, who own most of the political clout, must lead the fight to get Congress to do something about entitlement programs. Of course, the alternative is continued belief in the Social Security and Medicare myth and the heck with future generations.

Does Washington Know Best?

November 13, 2013

According to some estimates, there are more than 100 million traffic signals in the United States, but whatever the number, how many of us would like Washington, in the name of public health and safety, to be in sole charge of their operation? Congress or a committee it authorizes would determine the position of traffic signals at intersections, the length of time the lights stay red, yellow, and green, and what hours of the day they can be flashing red.

While you ponder that, how many Americans would like Washington to be in charge of managing the delivery of food and other items to the nation's supermarkets? Today's average well-stocked US supermarket stocks 60,000 to 65,000 different items from all over the United States and the world. Congress or some congressionally created committee could organize the choice of products and their prices. Maybe there'd be some cost savings. After all, what says that we should have so many items from which to choose? Why wouldn't 10,000 do?

You say, "Williams, those are ludicrous ideas whose implementation would spell disaster!" You're right. Nobel laureate Friedrich Hayek, one of the greatest economists of the twentieth century, said it is a fatal conceit for anyone to think that a single mind or group of minds, no matter how intelligent and well-meaning, could manage to do things better than the spontaneous, unstructured, complex, and creative forces of the market. The biggest challenges in any system, whether it's an economic, biological, or ecological system, are information, communication, and control. Congressmen's taking over control of the nation's traffic signals would require a massive amount of information that they are incapable of possessing, such as traffic flows at intersections, accident experiences, terrain patterns, and peak and off-peak traffic flows.

The same information problem exists at supermarkets. Consider the challenge in organizing inputs in order to get 65,000 different items to a supermarket. Also, consider how uncompromising supermarket customers are. We don't tell the supermarket manager in advance when we're going to shop or what we're going to buy and in what quantity, but if the store doesn't have what we want when we want it, we'll fire the manager by taking our business elsewhere. The supermarket manager does a fairly good job doing what's necessary to meet that challenge.

You say, "C'mon, Williams, nobody's proposing that Congress take over the nation's traffic signals and supermarkets!" You're right, at least for now, but Congress and the president are taking over an area of our lives infinitely more challenging and complex than the management of traffic signals and supermarkets, namely our health care system. Oblivious to the huge information problem in the allocation of resources, the people in Washington have great confidence that they can run our health care system better than we, our physicians, and hospitals. Charles Darwin wisely noted more than a century and a half ago that "ignorance more frequently begets confidence than does knowledge." Congress exudes confidence.

Suggesting that Congress and the president are ignorant of the fact that knowledge is highly dispersed and decisions made locally produce the best outcomes might be overly generous. It could be that they know they really don't know what they're doing but just don't give a hoot because it's in their political interest to centralize health care decision-making. Just as one example, how can Congress know whether buying a $4,000 annual health insurance policy would be the best use of healthy twenty-five-year-old Joe Sanders's earnings? Would he be better off purchasing a cheaper catastrophic health insurance policy and saving the rest of the money to put toward a business investment? Politicians really don't care about what Joe thinks is best, because they arrogantly think they know what's best and have the power to coerce.

Hayek said, "The curious task of economics is to illustrate to men how little they really know about what they imagine they can design." We economists have failed miserably in that task.

Do Americans Prefer Deception?

November 20, 2013

There's more to the deceit and dishonesty about Social Security and Medicare discussed in my recent columns. Congress tells us that one-half (6.2 percent) of the Social Security tax is paid by employees and that the other half is paid by employers, for a total of 12.4 percent. Similarly, we are told that a Medicare tax of 1.45 percent is levied on employees and that another 1.45 percent is levied on employers. The truth of the matter is that the burden of both taxes is borne by employees. In other words, we pay both the employee and the so-called employer share. You say, "Williams, that's nonsense! Just look at what it says on my pay stub." OK, let's look at it.

Pretend you are my employer and agree to pay me $50,000 a year, out of which you're going to send $3,100 to Washington as my share of Social Security tax (6.2 percent of $50,000), as well as $725 for my share of Medicare (1.45 percent of $50,000), a total of $3,825 for the year. To this you must add your half of Social Security and Medicare taxes, which is also $3,825 for the year. Your cost to hire me is $53,825.

If it costs you $53,825 a year to hire me, how much value must I produce for it to be profitable for you to keep me? Is it our agreed salary of $50,000 or $53,825? If you said $53,825, you'd be absolutely right. Then who pays all of the Social Security and Medicare taxes? If you said that I do, you're right again. The Social Security and Medicare fiction was created because Americans would not be so passive if they knew that the tax they are paying is double what is on their pay stubs—not to mention federal income taxes.

The economics specialty that reveals this is known as the incidence of taxation. The burden of a tax is not necessarily borne by the party upon whom it is levied. The Joint Committee on Taxation held that "both the employee's and employer's share of the payroll tax is borne by the employee." The Congressional Budget Office "assumes—as do most economists—that employers' share of payroll taxes is passed on to employees in the form of lower wages than would otherwise be paid." Health insurance is not an employer gift, either. It is paid for by employees in the form of lower wages.

Another part of Social Security and Medicare deception is that the taxes are officially called FICA, which stands for Federal Insurance Contributions Act. First, it's not an insurance program. More importantly, the word "contribution" implies something voluntary. Its synonyms are alms, benefaction, beneficence, charity, donation, and philanthropy. Which one of those synonyms comes close to describing how Congress gets Social Security and Medicare money from us?

There's more deceit and dishonesty. In 1950, I was fourteen years old and applied for a work permit for an after-school job. One of the requirements was to obtain a Social Security card. In bold letters on my Social Security card, which I still possess, are the words "For Social Security Purposes—Not For Identification." That's because earlier Americans feared that their Social Security number would become an identity number. According to the Social Security Administration website, "this legend was removed as part of the design changes for the 18th version of the card, issued beginning in 1972." That statement assumes we're idiots. We're asked to believe that the sole purpose of the removal was for design purposes. Apparently, the fact that our Social Security number had become a major identification tool, to be used in every aspect of our lives, had nothing to do with the SSA's getting rid of the legend saying "For Social Security Purposes—Not For Identification."

I wonder whether political satirist H. L. Mencken was right when he said, "Nobody ever went broke underestimating the intelligence of the American public."

Dumb Politicians Won't Get Elected
December 25, 2013

Politicians can be progressives, liberals, conservatives, Democrats or Republicans, and right-wingers. They just can't be dumb. The American people will never elect them to office. Let's look at it.

For years, I used to blame politicians for our economic and social mess. That changed during the 1980s as a result of several lunches with Sen. Jesse Helms, R-N.C., which produced an epiphany of sorts.

At the time, I had written several columns highly critical of farm subsidies and handouts. Helms agreed, saying something should be done. Then he asked me whether I could tell him how he could vote against them and remain a senator from North Carolina. He said that if he voted against them, North Carolinians would vote him out of office and replace him with somebody probably worse. My epiphany came when I asked myself whether it was reasonable to expect a politician to commit what he considered to be political suicide—in a word, be dumb.

The Office of Management and Budget calculates that more than 40 percent of federal spending is for entitlements for the elderly in the forms of Social Security, Medicare, Medicaid, housing, and other assistance programs. Total entitlement spending comes to about 62 percent of federal spending. The Congressional Budget Office estimates that entitlement spending will consume all federal tax revenue by 2048.

Only a dumb politician would argue that something must be done immediately about the main components of entitlement spending: Social Security, Medicare, and Medicaid. Senior citizens indignantly would tell him that what they're receiving are not entitlements. It's their money that Congress put aside for them. They would attack any politician who told them that the only way they get Social Security and Medicare money is through taxes levied on current workers. The smart politician would go along with these people's vision that Social Security and Medicare are their money that the government was holding for them. The dumb politician, who is truthful about Social Security and Medicare and their devastating impact on our nation's future, would be run out of office.

Social Security and Medicare are by no means the only sources of unsustainable congressional spending. There are billions upon billions in handouts going to farmers, corporations, poor people, and thousands of federal programs that have no constitutional basis whatsoever. But a smart politician reasons that if Congress enables one group of Americans to live at the expense of another American, then in fairness, what possible argument can be made for not giving that same right to other groups of Americans? Making a constitutional and moral argument against the growth of handouts would qualify as dumb.

Let's examine some statements of past Americans whom we've mistakenly called great but would be deemed both heartless and dumb if they were around today. In 1794, James Madison, the father of our Constitution, irate over a $15,000 congressional appropriation to assist some French refugees, said, "I cannot undertake to lay my finger on that article of the Constitution which granted a right to Congress of expending, on objects of benevolence, the money of their constituents." He added, "Charity is no part of the legislative duty of the government."

In 1854, President Franklin Pierce vetoed a bill intended to help the mentally ill, saying, "I cannot find any authority in the Constitution for public charity" and to approve such spending "would be contrary to the letter and the spirit of the Constitution and subversive to the whole theory upon which the Union of these States is founded."

Grover Cleveland vetoed hundreds of congressional spending bills during his two terms as president in the late 1800s. His often stated veto message was, "I can find no warrant for such an appropriation in the Constitution."

If these men were around today, making similar statements, Americans would hold them in contempt and disqualify them from office. That's a sad commentary on how we've trashed our Constitution.

Politics and Minimum Wage

January 8, 2014

There's little debate among academic economists about the effect of minimum wages. University of California, Irvine economist David Neumark has examined more than a hundred major academic studies on the minimum wage. He reports that 85 percent of the studies "find a negative employment effect on low-skilled workers." A 1976 American Economic Association survey found that 90 percent of its members agreed that increasing the minimum wage raises unemployment among young and unskilled workers. A 1990 survey reported in the *American Economic Review* (1992) found that 80 percent of economists agreed with the statement that increases in the minimum wage cause unemployment among the youth and low-skilled. If you're searching for a consensus in a field of study, most of the time you can examine the field's introductory and intermediate college textbooks. Economics textbooks that mention the minimum wage say that it increases unemployment for the least skilled worker. The only significant debate about the minimum wage is the magnitude of its effect. Some studies argue that a 10 percent increase in the minimum wage will cause a 1 percent increase in unemployment, whereas others predict a higher increase.

How about the politics of the minimum wage? In the political arena, one dumps on people who can't dump back on him. Minimum wages have their greatest unemployment impact on the least skilled worker. After all, who's going to pay a worker an hourly wage of $10 if that worker is so unfortunate as to have skills that enable him to produce only $5 worth of value per hour? Who are these workers? For the most part, they are low-skilled teens or young adults, most of whom are poorly educated blacks and Latinos. The unemployment statistics in our urban areas confirm this prediction, with teen unemployment rates as high as 50 percent.

The politics of the minimum wage are simple. No congressman or president owes his office to the poorly educated black and Latino youth vote. Moreover, the victims of the minimum wage do not know why they suffer high unemployment, and neither do most of their "benefactors." Minimum wage beneficiaries are highly organized, and they do have the necessary political clout to get Congress to price their low-skilled competition out of the market so they can demand higher wages. Concerned about the devastating unemployment effects of the minimum wage, Republican politicians have long resisted increases in the minimum wage, but that makes no political sense. The reason is the beneficiaries of preventing increases in the minimum wage don't vote Republican no matter what; where's the political quid pro quo?

Higher-skilled and union workers are not the only beneficiaries of higher minimum wages. Among other beneficiaries are manufacturers who produce substitutes for workers. A recent example of this is Wawa's experiment with customers using touch screens as substitutes for counter clerks. A customer at the convenience store selects his order from a touch screen. He takes a printed slip to the cashier to pay for it while it's being filled. I imagine that soon the customer's interaction with the cashier will be eliminated with a swipe of a credit card. Raising the minimum wage and other employment costs speeds up the automation process. I'm old enough to remember attendants at gasoline stations and theater ushers, who are virtually absent today. It's not because today's Americans like to smell gasoline fumes and stumble down the aisles in the dark to find their seat. The minimum wage law has eliminated such jobs.

Finally, there's a nastier side to support for minimum wage laws, documented in my book *Race and Economics: How Much Can Be Blamed on Discrimination?* During South Africa's apartheid era, racist labor unions were the country's major supporters of minimum wage laws for blacks. Their stated intention was to protect white workers from having to compete with lower-wage black workers. Our nation's first minimum wage law, the Davis-Bacon Act of 1931, had racist motivation. Among the widespread racist sentiment was that of American Federation of Labor President William Green, who complained, "Colored labor is being sought to demoralize wage rates."

Concealing Evil

February 19, 2014

Evil acts are given an aura of moral legitimacy by noble-sounding socialistic expressions, such as spreading the wealth, income redistribution, caring for the less fortunate, and the will of the majority. Let's have a thought experiment to consider just how much Americans sanction evil.

Imagine there are several elderly widows in your neighborhood. They have neither the strength to mow their lawns, clean their windows, and perform other household tasks nor the financial means to hire someone to help them. Here's a question that I'm almost afraid to ask: Would you support a government mandate that forces you or one of your neighbors to mow these elderly widows' lawns, clean their windows, and perform other household tasks? Moreover, if the person so ordered failed to obey the government mandate, would you approve of some sort of sanction, such as fines, property confiscation, or imprisonment? I'm hoping, and I believe, that most of my fellow Americans would condemn such a mandate. They'd agree that it would be a form of slavery—namely, the forcible use of one person to serve the purposes of another.

Would there be the same condemnation if, instead of forcing you or your neighbor to actually perform weekly household tasks for the elderly widows, the government forced you or your neighbor to give one of the widows $50 of your weekly earnings? That way, she could hire someone to mow her lawn or clean her windows. Would such a mandate differ from one under which you are forced to actually perform the household task? I'd answer that there is little difference between the two mandates except the mechanism for the servitude. In either case, one person is being forcibly used to serve the purposes of another.

I'm guessing that most Americans would want to help these elderly ladies in need but they'd find anything that openly smacks of servitude or slavery deeply offensive. They might have a clearer conscience if all the neighbors were forced (taxed) to put money into a government pot. A government agency would then send the widows $50 to hire someone to mow their lawns and perform other household tasks. This collective mechanism makes the particular victim invisible, but it doesn't change the fact that a person is being forcibly used to serve the purposes of others. Putting the money into a government pot simply conceals an act that would otherwise be deemed morally depraved.

This is why socialism is evil. It employs evil means, confiscation and intimidation, to accomplish what are often seen as noble goals—namely, helping one's fellow man. Helping one's fellow man in need by reaching into one's own pockets to do so is laudable and praiseworthy. Helping one's fellow man through coercion and reaching into another's pockets is evil and worthy of condemnation. Tragically, most teachings, from the church on down, support government use of one person to serve the purposes of another; the advocates cringe from calling it such and prefer to call it charity or duty.

Some might argue that we are a democracy, in which the majority rules. But does a majority consensus make moral acts that would otherwise be deemed immoral? In other words, if the neighbors got a majority vote to force one of their number—under pain of punishment—to perform household tasks for the elderly widows, would that make it moral?

The bottom line is that we've betrayed much of the moral vision of our Founding Fathers. In 1794, when Congress appropriated $15,000 for relief of French refugees who had fled from insurrection in San Domingo to Baltimore and Philadelphia, James Madison rose on the floor of the House of Representatives to object, saying, "I cannot undertake to lay my finger on that article of the Constitution which granted a right to Congress of expending, on objects of benevolence, the money of their constituents." Tragically, today's Americans—Democrat or Republican, liberal or conservative—would hold such a position in contempt and run a politician like Madison out of town on a rail.

Bizarre Arguments and Behavior
March 26, 2014

Some statements and arguments are so asinine that you'd have to be an academic or a leftist to take them seriously. Take the accusation that Republicans and conservatives are conducting a war on women. Does that mean they're waging war on their daughters, wives, mothers, and other female members of their families? If so, do they abide by the Geneva Conventions' bans on torture, or do they engage in enhanced interrogation and intimidation methods, such as waterboarding, with female family members? You might say that leftists don't mean actual war. Then why do they say it?

What would you think of a white conservative mayor's trying to defund charter schools where blacks are succeeding? While most of New York's black students could not pass a citywide math proficiency exam, there was a charter school where 82 percent of its students passed. New York's left-wing mayor, Bill de Blasio, is trying to shut it down, and so far, I've heard not one peep from the Big Apple's civil rights hustlers, including Al Sharpton and Charles Rangel. According to columnist Thomas Sowell, the attack on successful charter schools is happening in other cities, too (http://tinyurl.com/nxulxc).

US Attorney General Eric Holder recently stated that we must revisit the laws that ban convicted felons from voting. Why? According to a recent study by two professors, Marc Meredith of the University of Pennsylvania and Michael Morse of Stanford, published in *The Annals of the American Academy of Political and Social Science* (http://tinyurl.com/pgolu8x), three-fourths of America's convicted murderers, rapists, and thieves are Democrats. Many states restrict felons from voting; however, there's a movement afoot to eliminate any restriction on their voting. If successful, we might see Democratic candidates campaigning in prisons, seeking the support of some of America's worst people.

Decades ago, I warned my fellow Americans that the tobacco zealots' agenda was not about the supposed health hazards of secondhand smoke. It was really about control. The fact that tobacco smoke is unpleasant gained them the support of most Americans. By the way, to reach its secondhand smoke conclusions, the Environmental Protection Agency employed statistical techniques that were grossly dishonest. Some years ago, I had the opportunity to ask a Food and Drug Administration official whether his agency would accept pharmaceutical companies using similar statistical techniques in their drug approval procedures. He just looked at me.

Seeing as Americans are timid and compliant, why not dictate other aspects of our lives—such as the size of soda we may buy, as former Mayor Michael Bloomberg tried in New York? Former US Department of Agriculture spokesman John Webster said: "Right now, this anti-obesity campaign is in its infancy. . . . We want to turn people around and give them assistance in eating nutritious foods." The city of Calabasas, Calif., adopted an ordinance that bans smoking in virtually all outdoor areas. The stated justification is not the desire to fight against secondhand smoke but the desire to protect children from bad influences—seeing adults smoking. Most Americans don't know that years ago, if someone tried to stop a person from smoking on a beach or sidewalk or buying a 16-ounce cup of soda or tried to throw away his kid's homemade lunch, it might have led to a severe beating. On a very famous radio talk show, I suggested to an anti-obesity busybody who was calling for laws to restrict restaurants' serving sizes that he not be a coward and rely on government. He should just come up, I told him, and take the food he thought I shouldn't have from my plate.

The late H. L. Mencken's description of health care professionals in his day is just as appropriate today: "A certain section of medical opinion, in late years, has succumbed to the messianic delusion. Its spokesmen are not content to deal with the patients who come to them for advice; they conceive it to be their duty to force their advice upon everyone, including especially those who don't want it. That duty is purely imaginary. It is born of vanity, not of public spirit. The impulse behind it is not altruism, but a mere yearning to run things."

Spending and Morality

July 9, 2014

During last year's budget negotiation meetings, President Barack Obama told House Speaker John Boehner, "We don't have a spending problem." When Boehner responded with "But, Mr. President, we have a very serious spending problem," Obama replied, "I'm getting tired of hearing you say that." In one sense, the president is right. What's being called a spending problem is really a symptom of an unappreciated deep-seated national moral rot. Let's examine it with a few questions.

Is it moral for Congress to forcibly use one person to serve the purposes of another? I believe that most Americans would pretend that to do so is offensive. Think about it this way. Suppose I saw a homeless, hungry elderly woman huddled on a heating grate in the dead of winter. To help the woman, I ask somebody for a $200 donation to help her out. If the person refuses, I then use intimidation, threats, and coercion to take the person's money. I then purchase food and shelter for the needy woman. My question to you: Have I committed a crime? I hope that most people would answer yes. It's theft to take the property of one person to give to another.

Now comes the hard part. Would it be theft if I managed to get three people to agree that I should take the person's money to help the woman? What if I got 100, 1 million, or 300 million people to agree to take the person's $200? Would it be theft then? What if instead of personally taking the person's $200, I got together with other Americans and asked Congress to use Internal Revenue Service agents to take the person's $200? The bottom-line question is: Does an act that's clearly immoral when done privately become moral when it is done collectively and under the color of law? Put another way, does legality establish morality?

For most of our history, Congress did a far better job of limiting its activities to what was both moral and constitutional. As a result, federal spending was only 3 to 5 percent of the gross domestic product from our founding until the 1920s, in contrast with today's 25 percent. Close to three-quarters of today's federal spending can be described as Congress taking the earnings of one American to give to another through thousands of handout programs, such as farm subsidies, business bailouts, and welfare.

During earlier times, such spending was deemed unconstitutional and immoral. James Madison, the acknowledged father of our Constitution, said, "Charity is no part of the legislative duty of the government." In 1794, when Congress appropriated $15,000 to assist some French refugees, Madison stood on the floor of the House of Representatives to object, saying, "I cannot undertake to lay my finger on that article of the Constitution which granted a right to Congress of expending, on objects of benevolence, the money of their constituents." Today's Americans would crucify a politician expressing similar statements.

There may be nitwits out there who'd assert, "That James Madison guy forgot about the Constitution's general welfare clause." Madison had that covered, explaining in a letter, "If Congress can do whatever in their discretion can be done by money, and will promote the general welfare, the Government is no longer a limited one possessing enumerated powers, but an indefinite one." Thomas Jefferson agreed, writing: Members of Congress "are not to do anything they please to provide for the general welfare. . . . It would reduce the [Constitution] to a single phrase, that of instituting a Congress with power to do whatever would be for the good of the United States; and, as they would be the sole judges of the good or evil, it would be also a power to do whatever evil they please."

The bottom line is that spending is not our basic problem. We've become an immoral people demanding that Congress forcibly use one American to serve the purposes of another. Deficits and runaway national debt are merely symptoms of that larger problem.

Favors and Loot for Sale

September 10, 2014

At a July fundraising event in Chicago, Michelle Obama remarked, "So, yeah, there's too much money in politics. There's (sic) special interests that have too much influence." Sen. John McCain has been complaining for years that "there is too much money washing around political campaigns today." According to a 2012 Reuters poll, "Seventy-five percent of Americans feel there is too much money in politics." Let's think about money in politics, but first a few facts.

During the 2012 presidential campaign, Barack Obama raised a little over $1 billion, while Mitt Romney raised a little under $1 billion. Congressional candidates raised over $3.5 billion. In 2013, there were 12,341 registered lobbyists and $3.2 billion was spent on lobbying. During the years the Clintons have been in national politics, they've received at least $1.4 billion in contributions, according to *Time* magazine and the Center for Responsive Politics, making them "The First Family of Fundraising."

Here are my questions to you: Why do people and organizations cough up billions of dollars to line political coffers? One might answer that these groups and individuals are simply extraordinarily civic-minded Americans who have a deep and abiding interest in encouraging elected officials to live up to their oath of office to uphold and defend the US Constitution. Another possible answer is that the people who spend these billions of dollars on politicians just love participating in the political process. If you believe either of these explanations for coughing up billions for politicians, you're probably a candidate for psychiatric attention, a straitjacket, and a padded cell.

A far better explanation for the billions going to the campaign coffers of Washington politicians and lobbyists lies in the awesome government power and control over business, property, employment, and other areas of our lives. Having such power, Washington politicians are in the position to grant special privileges, extend favors, change laws, and do other things that if done by a private person would land him in jail. The major component of congressional power is the use of the IRS to take the earnings of one American to give to another.

The Dow Chemical Co. posted record lobbying expenditures last year, spending over $12 million. Joined by Alcoa, who spent $3.5 million, Dow supports the campaigns of congressmen who support natural gas export restrictions. Natural gas is a raw material for both companies. They fear natural gas prices would rise if export restrictions were lifted. Dow and other big users of natural gas make charitable contributions to environmentalists who seek to limit natural gas exploration. Natural gas export restrictions empower Russia's Vladimir Putin by making Europeans more dependent on Russian natural gas.

General Electric spends tens of millions of dollars lobbying. Part of their agenda was to help get Congress to outlaw incandescent light bulbs so that they could sell their more expensive compact fluorescent bulbs. It should come as no surprise that General Electric is a contributor to global warmers who helped convince Congress that incandescent bulbs were destroying the planet.

These are just two examples, among thousands, of the role of money in politics. Most concerns about money in politics tend to focus on relatively trivial matters such as the costs of running for office and interest-group influence on Congress and the White House. The bedrock problem is the awesome power of Congress. We Americans have asked, demanded, and allowed congressmen to ignore their oaths of office and ignore the constitutional limitations imposed on them. The greater the congressional power to give handouts and grant favors and make special privileges, the greater the value of being able to influence congressional decision-making. There's no better influence than money.

You say, "Williams, you've explained the problem. What's your solution?" Maybe we should think about enacting a law mandating that Congress cannot do for one American what it does not do for all Americans. For example, if Congress creates a monopoly for one American, it should create a monopoly for all Americans. Of course, a better solution is for Congress to obey our Constitution.

PART III

Race

The most common vision on race portrays black Americans as poor, down-trodden, and unequipped to compete without special privileges. That vision is an insult of major proportions. As a group, black Americans have made the greatest gains, over some of the highest hurdles, in the shortest span of time than any other racial group in mankind's history.

This unprecedented progress can be seen through several measures. If one were to total black earnings, and consider black Americans a separate nation, he would have found that in 2008 black Americans earned $726 billion, making them the world's eighteenth-richest nation. Black Americans are, and have been, chief executives of some of the world's largest and richest cities such as New York, Chicago, Los Angeles, Philadelphia, and Washington, D.C. It was a black American, Gen. Colin Powell, appointed Joint Chief of Staff in October 1989, who headed the world's mightiest military and later became US secretary of state, and was succeeded by Condoleezza Rice, another black American. Black Americans are among the world's most famous personalities and a few black Americans are among the richest. Most blacks are not poor but middle class.

The significance of such achievement is that at the end of the Civil War, neither an ex-slave nor an ex-slave owner would have believed these gains possible in less than a mere century and a half, if indeed ever. As such, that progress speaks well not only of the sacrifices and intestinal fortitude of a people; it just as importantly speaks well of a nation in which these gains were possible. These gains would not have been possible anywhere on Earth other than the United States of America.

The question before us is how can these gains be extended to the 30 percent or so of the black population for whom these gains appear to be elusive. I think that a good start is to abandon the civil rights vision that holds that the major problem for blacks is racial discrimination. I do not argue that racial discrimination is nonexistent and that it has no effect but the policy-relevant question is how much of what we see can be attributed to racial discrimination.

The fact that most black children are raised in single-parent families is a devastating handicap but it has little to do with racial discrimination, particularly in light of the fact during earlier periods, as early as the late 1800s, the black family structure didn't differ significantly from that of other groups.

Over 70 percent of black children are born out of wedlock and often to teenage mothers. That is a devastating handicap but it has nothing to do with racial discrimination, particularly in light of the fact that as late as the 1940s black illegitimacy was around 14 percent.

Each year, roughly 7,000 blacks are murdered. Ninety-four percent of the time, the murderer is another black person. According to the Bureau of Justice Statistics, between 1976 and 2011, there were 279,384 black murder victims. Though blacks are 13 percent of the nation's population, they account for more than 50 percent of homicide victims. This is a devastating problem but it has little or nothing to do with racial discrimination.

The magnitude of this problem can be seen in another light. According to a Tuskegee Institute study, between the years 1882 and 1968, 3,446 blacks were lynched at the hands of whites. Black fatalities during the Korean War (3,075), Vietnam War (7,243), and all wars since 1980 (8,197) total 18,515, a number that pales in comparison with black loss of life at home. It's a tragic commentary to be able to say that young black males have a greater chance of reaching maturity on the battlefields of Iraq and Afghanistan than on the streets of Philadelphia, Chicago, Detroit, Oakland, Newark, and other cities.

Unemployment is a major problem particularly among black youth that is often blamed on employer discrimination. But that hypothesis comes into question if we look at unemployment in earlier periods. For example, in 1948, black teen unemployment was less than 10 percent and less than their white counterparts. Black teens had a labor force participation rate higher than whites (that is, black teens were more active in the labor market). I do not think that anyone would attribute this more favorable employment situation in earlier periods by saying there was less racial discrimination during the forties.

My columns in this section will argue that many problems of black Americans are a result of ostensibly well-intentioned public policy such as labor laws and self-destructive behavior that few people have the courage to talk about lest they be accused of racism or "blaming the victim."

The Racism of Diversity

July 22, 2009

The US Naval Academy's PowerPoint display explains diversity by saying, "Diversity is all the different characteristics and attributes of individual sailors and civilians which enhance the mission readiness of the Navy," adding, "Diversity is more than equal opportunity, race, gender or religion. Diversity is the understanding of how each of us brings different skills, talents and experiences to the fight—and valuing those differences. Leveraging diversity creates an environment of excellence and continuous improvement to remove artificial achievement barriers and value the contribution of all participants." Adm. Gary Roughead, chief of naval operations, says that "diversity is the No. 1 priority" at the academy.

Diversity at the Naval Academy, as at most academic institutions, is not about equal opportunity but a race and sex spoils system to achieve what the Navy brass see as a pleasing race and sex mix. They accomplish that vision by the removal of "artificial achievement barriers." Let's go over what the Naval Academy sees as an artificial achievement barrier. A black candidate with B and C grades, with no particular leadership qualities, and 500 on both portions of the SAT, is virtually guaranteed admittance. A white student, who's not an athlete, with such scores is deemed not qualified.

Many black students are admitted to the Naval Academy through remedial training at the Naval Academy Preparatory School (NAPS) in Newport, R.I., which is a one-year postsecondary school. Finishing the year with a 2.0 GPA, a C average, almost guarantees admission to the academy. A C average for remedial work is nothing to write home about. Occasionally, when students don't make the 2.0 GPA target, the target is renegotiated downward. Minority applicants with SAT scores down to the 300s and with C and D grades (and no particular leadership or athletics) are also admitted after a remedial year at the Naval Academy Preparatory School.

Bruce Fleming, an English professor at the academy for twenty-two years, teaches a remedial English class and finds that in his spring 2009 class, most of NAPS's students earn Cs and Ds and many are on probation. About seven years ago, Professor Fleming was on the admissions board, where the standing instruction is not to write anything down because "everything is 'FOIable'"—meaning it can be demanded under the Freedom of Information Act. Such an instruction highlights the dishonesty of race preferences. The dishonesty doesn't stop there. The academy will go to great lengths to retain black students. When Professor Fleming charged a black student with plagiarism, he was not properly informed of the hearing and subsequently the student's peer group found him not guilty. Honor violations by black students are usually "remediated."

I suspected that the Naval Academy's diversity agenda would give rise to resentments so I asked Professor Fleming about it. He said there are two levels of resentment. Some black students, who were admitted to the academy meritoriously on the same basis as white students, resent the idea of being seen as having the same academic qualities as blacks who were given preferential treatment, in other words being dumb. Another level of resentment comes from white students who see blacks as being admitted and retained at lower levels of academic performance and being treated with kid gloves. If these whites openly complained about the unequal treatment, they would run the risk of being labeled as racists. This is one of the unappreciated aspects of preferential treatment. It runs the risk of creating racist attitudes, and possibly feelings of racial superiority, among whites and others who were formerly racially neutral.

Colleges and universities with racially preferential admittance policies are doing a great disservice to blacks in another, mostly ignored, way. By admitting poorly prepared blacks, they are helping to conceal the grossly fraudulent education the blacks receive at the K through 12 grades.

Black Opportunity Destruction
February 10, 2010

"Do you mean he is taller than me am?," sarcastically barked Dr. Martin Rosenberg, my high school English teacher, to one of the students in our class. The student actually said, "He is taller than me," but Rosenberg was ridiculing the student's grammar. The subject of the elliptical (or understood) verb "am" must be in the subjective case. Thus, the correct form of the sentence is: He is taller than I.

This correction or dressing down of a student, that occasionally included me, occurred during my attendance at North Philadelphia's Benjamin Franklin High School in the early 1950s. Franklin was predominantly black; its students were poor or low middle class. On top of that, Franklin had just about the lowest academic standing in the city. All of our teachers, except two or three, were white. Despite the fact that we were poor, most of Franklin's teachers held fairly high standards and expectations.

Today, high standards and expectations, at some schools, would mean trouble for a teacher. Teachers, as pointed out in one teaching program, are encouraged to "Recognize and understand the cultural differences among students from diverse backgrounds, and treat such differences with respect. Intervene immediately, should a fellow student disparage a Black student's culture or language." That means if a black student says, "I be wiff him" or "He axed me a question," teachers shouldn't bother to correct the student's language. What's more, should anyone disparage or laugh at the way the student speaks, the teacher should intervene in his defense. Correcting the student's speech might be deemed as insensitive to diversity at best and racism at worst, leading possibly to a teacher's reprimand, termination, and possibly assault.

A teacher's job is to teach and failure to correct a student's speech, just as failure to correct a math error, is a dereliction of duty. You might say, "Williams, Ebonics or black English is part of the cultural roots of black people and to disparage it is racism." That's utter nonsense.

During the 1940s and 1950s, I lived in North Philadelphia's Richard Allen housing project, along with its most famous resident, Bill Cosby. We all were poor or low-middle class but no one spoke black English. My wife was the youngest of ten children. Listening to her brothers and sisters speak, compared to many of her nieces and nephews, you wouldn't believe they were in the same family. The difference has nothing to do with cultural roots of black people. The difference is that parents, teachers, and others in authority over youngsters have become less judgmental, politically correct, and lazy; therefore, speaking poorly is accepted.

Language is our tool of communication. If a person has poor oral language skills, he's likely to have poor writing, reading, and comprehension skills. To my knowledge, there are no books in any field of study written in Ebonics or black English. It is very likely that a person with poor language skills will suffer significant deficits in other areas of academic competence such as mathematics and the sciences. It doesn't mean that the person is unintelligent; it means that he doesn't have all the tools of intelligence. That is what's so insidious about the state of black education today; so many blacks do not have a chance to develop the tools of intelligence. Many might have high native intelligence but come off sounding like a moron.

Black Americans should thank God that nonjudgmental, politically correct people weren't around during the early civil rights movement when blacks began breaking discriminatory barriers. Discriminatory employers would have had ready-made excuses not to hire a black as a trolley car motorman, cashier, or department store sales clerk.

There are some significant challenges to being judgmental and politically incorrect and insisting on proper language. A professor or teacher can get cursed out by students or parents. A black student who speaks well, carries books, and studies can be accused of "acting white" and find himself shunned and assaulted by other students.

I would be interested in hearing the teaching establishment's defense of permitting poor language.

Black Americans and Liberty

May 5, 2010

Having recently reached seventy-four years of age, if one were to ask me what's my greatest disappointment in life, a top contender would surely be the level of misunderstanding, perhaps contempt that black Americans have for the principles of personal liberty and their abiding faith in government. Contempt or misunderstanding of the principles of personal liberty and faith in government by no means make blacks unique among Americans, but the unique history of black Americans should make us, above all other Americans, most suspicious of any encroachment on personal liberty and most distrustful of government. Let's look at it.

The most serious injustices suffered by blacks came at the hands of government, at different levels, failure to protect personal liberty. Slavery was only the most egregious example of that failure. Congress and the courts supported the injustice of slavery through the 1850 Fugitive Slave Act and the Dred Scott decision. After emancipation, there were government-enforced Jim Crow laws denying blacks basic liberties and court decisions such as Plessy v. Ferguson that reinforced and gave sanction to private acts that abridged black people's liberties.

The heroic civil rights movement, culminating with the 1964 Civil Rights Act, put an end to the grossest abuses of personal liberties, but government evolved into a subtler enemy. Visit any major city and one would find that the overwhelmingly law-abiding members of the black community are living in constant fear of robbery, assault, and murder. In fact, 52 percent of US homicides are committed by blacks, 49 percent of homicide victims are black, and 93 percent of them were murdered by fellow blacks. The level of crime in black communities is the result of government's failure to perform its most basic function, namely the protection of its citizens. The level of criminal activity not only puts residents in physical jeopardy but represents a heavy tax on people least able to bear it. That tax is paid in the forms of higher prices for goods and services and fewer shopping opportunities because supermarkets and other large retailers are reluctant to bear the costs of doing business in high-crime areas. This government failure has the full effect of a law prohibiting economic development in many black communities.

Then there's the grossly fraudulent education delivered by the government schools that serve most black communities. The average black high school senior has a sixth- or seventh-grade achievement level and most of those who manage to graduate have what's no less than a fraudulent diploma, one that certifies a twelfth-grade level of achievement when in fact the youngster might not have half that. If the Grand Dragon of the Ku Klux Klan wanted to sabotage black academic excellence, he could not find a more effective means to do so than the government school system in most cities.

Tragically, most Americans, including black people whose ancestors have suffered from gross injustices of slavery, think it quite proper for government to forcibly use one person to serve the purposes of another. That's precisely what income redistribution is: the practice of forcibly taking the fruits of one person's labor for the benefit of another. That's also what theft is and the practice differs from slavery only in degree but not kind.

What about blacks who cherish liberty and limited government and joined in the tea party movement, or blacks who are members of organizations such as the Lincoln Institute, Frederick Douglass Foundation, and Project 21? They've been maligned as Oreos, Uncle Toms, and traitors to their race. To make such a charge borders on stupidity, possibly racism. After all, when President Reagan disagreed with Tip O'Neill, did either charge the other with being a traitor to his race? Then why is it deemed traitorous when one black disagrees with another, unless you think that all blacks must think alike?

I hope it's misunderstanding, rather than contempt, that explains black hostility toward the principles of liberty.

The Right to Discriminate

June 2, 2010

Rand Paul of Kentucky, US Senate hopeful, is caught up in a swirl of controversy in response to his comments on MSNBC's "Rachel Maddow Show." He has been dishonestly accused of saying he thinks that private businesses have a right to discriminate against black people. Here's a partial transcript of the pertinent question in the interview:

Maddow: "Do you think that a private business has a right to say, 'We don't serve black people'?" To which Paul answered, "I'm not, I'm not, I'm not in . . . yeah . . . I'm not in favor of any discrimination of any form."

The "yeah" was spun in the media as "yes" to the question whether private businesses had a right to refuse service to black people. Paul had told Maddow that while he supported the 1964 Civil Rights Act in general, he thought that provisions banning private discrimination might have gone too far.

Democrats launched an attack on Paul accusing him of being a racist. Republicans criticized and in the words of Republican National Committee Chairman Michael Steele, Paul's "philosophy is misplaced in these times." He added that Paul has a libertarian perspective and "[has] a very, very strong view about the limitation of government intrusion into the private sector."

Should people have the right to discriminate by race, sex, religion, and other attributes? In a free society, I say yes. Let's look at it. When I was selecting a marriage partner, I systematically discriminated against white women, Asian women, and women of other ethnicities that I found less preferable. The Nation of Islam discriminates against white members. The Aryan Brotherhood discriminates against having black members. The Ku Klux Klan discriminates against having Catholic and Jewish members. The NFL discriminates against hiring female quarterbacks. The NAACP National Board of Directors, at least according to the photo on their Web page, has no white members.

You say, Williams, that's different. It's not like public transportation, restaurants, and hotel service in which Title II of the 1964 Civil Rights Act "prohibits discrimination because of race, color, religion, or national origin in certain places of public accommodation, such as hotels, restaurants, and places of entertainment." While there are many places that serve the public, it doesn't change the fact that they are privately owned, and who is admitted, under what conditions, should be up to the owner.

If places of public accommodation were free to racially discriminate, how much racial discrimination would there be? In answering that question, we should acknowledge that just because a person is free to do something, it doesn't follow that he will find it in his interest to do so. An interesting example is found in an article by Dr. Jennifer Roback titled "The Political Economy of Segregation: The Case of Segregated Streetcars," in the *Journal of Economic History* (1986). During the late 1800s, private streetcar companies in Augusta, Houston, Jacksonville, Mobile, Montgomery, and Memphis were not segregated, but by the early 1900s, they were. Why? City ordinances forced them to segregate black and white passengers. Numerous Jim Crow laws ruled the day throughout the South mandating segregation in public accommodations.

When one sees a law on the books, he should suspect that the law is there because not everyone would voluntarily comply with the law's specifications. Extralegal measures, that included violence, backed up Jim Crow laws. When white solidarity is confronted by the specter of higher profits by serving blacks, it's likely that profits will win. Thus, Title II of the 1964 Civil Rights Act represented government countering government-backed Jim Crow laws.

One does not have to be a racist to recognize that the federal government has no constitutional authority to prohibit racial or any other kind of discrimination by private parties. Moreover, the true test of one's commitment to freedom of association doesn't come when he permits people to associate in ways he deems appropriate. It comes when he permits people to voluntarily associate in ways he deems offensive.

Can Black Americans Afford Obama?

June 9, 2010

My March 2008 column "Is Obama Ready for America?" started out: "Some pundits ask whether America is ready for Obama. The much more important question is whether Obama is ready for America and even more important is whether black people can afford Obama." Let's look at this.

In 1947, Jackie Robinson, in signing a contract with the Brooklyn Dodgers, broke the color bar in Major League Baseball. In 1950, three blacks broke the color bar in the National Basketball Association (NBA): Earl Lloyd (Washington Capitals), Chuck Cooper (Boston Celtics), and Nat "Sweetwater" Clifton (New York Knicks). Their highly successful performances opened the way for other blacks to follow—peaking at 27 percent in Major League Baseball and 80 percent in the NBA.

Without a question, the first blacks, relative to their white peers, in professional sports were exceptional. There's no sense of justice that should require that these players be as good as they were in order to get a job. But the fact of business, in order to deal with racial hostility and stereotypes of incompetence, they had to be first rate and possess character beyond question. It was not only important for their careers, it was important for their fellow blacks. At the time the sports color bar was being broken, black people could ill afford stumblebums. Today, black people can afford stumblebums in several sports. In fact, black people can afford for the Philadelphia Sixers to put Williams in their starting lineup. Any person watching me mess up royally would have to be a lunatic to say, "Those blacks can't play basketball." The bottom line is that whether we like it or not, whether for good reason or bad reason, whether it's fair or unfair, people make stereotypes, and stereotypes can have effects.

In that March 2008 column, I said, "For the nation and for black people, the first black president should be the caliber of a

Jackie Robinson and Barack Obama is not. Barack Obama has charisma and charm but in terms of character, values, and understanding, he is no Jackie Robinson." Obama's electoral success was truly remarkable. It's a testament to the essential goodness of the American people. A June 6–9, 2008, NBC News/*Wall Street Journal* poll reported "that 17 percent were enthusiastic about Obama being the first African American President, 70 percent were comfortable or indifferent, and 13 percent had reservations or were uncomfortable."

President Obama, with the assistance of devious House and Senate leadership, has gotten a health care law enacted that the majority of American voters are against. According to a recent Rasmussen poll, 58 percent of voters support repeal of the health care law. Under the president's leadership, the 2010 budget deficit will reach more than $1.5 trillion, about 10 percent of gross domestic product, the largest deficit since the end of World War II. We're not that far behind the troubled nation of Greece, which has a current budget deficit of nearly 13 percent of GDP. Our national debt at $13 trillion is about 90 percent of GDP and budgeted to grow by $9 trillion over the next decade. On the diplomatic front, the Obama team is not doing much better, showing every sign of permitting a terrorist nation like Iran to acquire nuclear weapons.

Early indications suggest that the Barack Obama presidency might turn out to be similar to the failed presidency of Jimmy Carter. That's bad news for the nation but especially bad news for black Americans. No white presidential candidate had to live down the disgraced presidency of Carter but I'm all too fearful that a future black presidential candidate will find himself carrying the heavy baggage of a failed black president. That's not a problem for white liberals who voted for Obama who received their one-time guilt-relieving dose from voting for a black man to be president, but it is a problem for future generations of black Americans.

Racism or Stupidity
July 28, 2010

A black or white person, now dead, who lived during the civil rights struggles of the 1930s, '40s, or '50s, might very well be appalled and disgusted by black behavior accepted today. Yesteryear, it was the Klan or White Citizens Council who showed up at polling places to intimidate black voters. During the 2008 elections, it was the New Black Panthers who showed up at a Philadelphia polling place to intimidate white voters and tell them, "You are about to be ruled by the black man, cracker." What's worse is the US Department of Justice has decided not to prosecute.

Black intimidation of voters, to my knowledge, is rare, but black intimidation of Asians is not. Recent reports out of Philadelphia and San Francisco tell of black students beating up Asian students. The Asian American Legal Defense and Education Fund, in the wake of serious black-on-Asian violence at South Philadelphia High School, charged the district with "deliberate indifference" to the harassment of Asian students and with "intentional disregard" for their welfare.

The violence is not restricted to Asian youngsters. Asian adults are included, such as the recent bludgeoning to death of an eighty-three-year-old Chinese man in San Francisco and the pushing of a fifty-seven-year-old Asian lady onto Muni subway tracks.

A white Charleston, S.C., teacher frequently complained of black students calling her: white b———, white m———f———, white c———, and white ho. Most people would judge that to be racism and demand it to end. Charleston school officials told the teacher this racially charged profanity was simply part of the students' culture, and if she couldn't handle it, she was in the wrong school. The teacher brought a harassment suit and the school district settled out of court for $200,000.

What about black youngsters who hit the books and study after school instead of hitting the streets? Sometimes they are ridiculed as being incog-negro or acting white and the ridicule is often accompanied with life-threatening physical violence. Many blacks, particularly black males, have arrived at the devastating conclusion that academic excellence is a betrayal of their black identity.

The pathology seen among a large segment of the black population is not likely to change because it's not seen for what it is. It has little to do with slavery, poverty, and racial discrimination. Let's look at it. Today's black illegitimacy rate is about 70 percent. When I was a youngster, during the 1940s, illegitimacy was around 15 percent. In the same period, about 80 percent of black children were born inside marriage. In fact, historian Herbert Gutman, in "Persistent Myths about the Afro-American Family" in the *Journal of Interdisciplinary History* (Autumn 1975), reports the percentage of black two-parent families, depending on the city, ranged 75 to 90 percent. Today, only 35 percent of black children are raised in two-parent households. The importance of these and other statistics showing greater stability and less pathology among blacks in earlier periods is that they put a lie to today's excuses. Namely, at a time when blacks were closer to slavery, faced far more discrimination, more poverty, and had fewer opportunities, there was not the kind of chaos, violence, family breakdown, and black racism that we see today.

Intellectuals and political hustlers who blame the plight of so many blacks on poverty, discrimination, and the "legacy of slavery" are complicit in the socioeconomic and moral decay. But as Booker T. Washington suggested, "There is another class of colored people who make a business of keeping the troubles, the wrongs, and the hardships of the Negro race before the public. Having learned that they are able to make a living out of their troubles, they have grown into the settled habit of advertising their wrongs—partly because they want sympathy and partly because it pays. Some of these people do not want the Negro to lose his grievances, because they do not want to lose their jobs."

Is Profiling Racist?

August 4, 2010

We live in a world of imperfect and costly information, and people seek to economize on information costs in a variety of ways. If we don't take that fact into account, we risk misidentifying and confusing one type of human behavior with another. Let's look at it.

Pima Indians of Arizona have the world's highest diabetes rates. With knowledge that his patient is a Pima Indian, it would probably be a best practice for a physician to order more thorough blood glucose tests to screen for diabetes. Prostate cancer is nearly twice as common among black men as white men. It would also be a best practice for a physician to be attentive to—even risk false positive PSAs—prostate cancer among his black patients. What about physicians who order routine mammograms for their forty-year and older female patients but not their male patients? The American Cancer Society predicts that about four hundred men will die of breast cancer this year.

Because of a correlation between race, sex, and disease, the physician is using a cheap-to-observe characteristic, such as race or sex, as an estimate for a more costly-to-observe characteristic, the presence of a disease. The physician is practicing both race and sex profiling. Does that make the physician a racist or sexist? Should he be brought up on charges of racial discrimination because he's guessing that his black patients are more likely to suffer from prostate cancer? Should sex discrimination or malpractice suits be brought against physicians who prescribe routine mammograms for their female patients but not their male patients? You say, "Williams, that would be lunacy!"

Is an individual's race or sex useful for guessing about other unseen characteristics? Suppose gambling becomes legal for an Olympic event such as the 100-meter sprint. I wouldn't place a bet on an Asian or white runner. Why? Blacks who trace their ancestry to West Africa, including black Americans, hold more than 95 percent of the top times in sprinting. That's not to say an Asian or white can never win but I know the correlations and I'm playing the odds. If women were permitted to be in the sprint event with men, I'd still put my money on a black male. Does that make me a sexist as well as a racist?

What about when a black hails a taxicab and the driver passes him up and picks up a white passenger down the street? Is that racism? Many people assume that it is but it might not be any different from a physician using race and sex as an estimator for some other characteristic. Ten years ago, a black D.C. commissioner warned cabbies, most of whom are black, against picking up dangerous-looking passengers. She described dangerous-looking as a "young black guy . . . with shirttail hanging down longer than his coat, baggy pants, unlaced tennis shoes." She also warned cabbies to stay away from low-income black neighborhoods. Cabbies themselves have developed other profiling criteria.

There is no sense of justice or decency that a law-abiding black person should suffer the indignity of being passed up. At the same time, a taxicab driver has a right to earn a living without being robbed, assaulted, and possibly murdered. One of the methods to avoid victimization is to refuse to pick up certain passengers in certain neighborhoods or passengers thought to be destined for certain neighborhoods. Again, a black person is justifiably angered when refused service but that anger should be directed toward the criminals who prey on cabbies.

Not every choice based on race represents racism and if you think so, you risk misidentifying and confusing human behavior. The Rev. Jesse Jackson once said, "There is nothing more painful for me at this stage in my life than to walk down the street and hear footsteps and start thinking about robbery—then look around and see somebody white and feel relieved."

Racial Stupidity and Malevolence
September 8, 2010

The white liberal's agenda, coupled with that of black race hustlers, has had and continues to have a devastating impact on ordinary black people. Perhaps the most debilitating aspect of this liberal malevolence is in the area of education.

Recently, I spoke with a Midwestern university engineering professor who was trying to help an inner-city black student who was admitted to the university's electrical engineering program. The student was sure that he was well prepared for an engineering curriculum; his high school had convinced him of that and the university recruiters supported that notion. His poor performance on the university's math placement exam required that he take remedial math courses. He's failed them and is now on academic probation after two semesters of earning less than a 2.0 grade point average.

The young man and his parents were sure of his preparedness. After all, he had good high school grades, but those grades only meant that he was well behaved. The college recruiters probably knew this youngster didn't have the academic preparation for an electrical engineering curriculum. They were more concerned with racial diversity.

This young man's background is far from unique. Public schools give most black students fraudulent diplomas that certify a twelfth-grade achievement level. According to a report by Abigail Thernstrom, "The Racial Gap in Academic Achievement," black students in twelfth grade dealt with scientific problems at the level of whites in the sixth grade; they wrote about as well as whites in the eighth grade. The average black high school senior had math skills on a par with a typical white student in the middle of ninth grade. The average seventeen-year-old black student could only read as well as the typical white child who had not yet reached age thirteen.

Black youngsters who take the SAT exam earn an average score that's 70 to 80 percent of the score of white students, and keep in mind, the achievement level of white students is nothing to write home about. Under misguided diversity pressures, colleges recruit many black students who are academically ill equipped. Very often, these students become quickly disillusioned, embarrassed, and flunk out, or they're steered into curricula that have little or no academic content, or professors practice affirmative-action grading. In any case, the twelve years of poor academic preparation is not repaired in four or five years of college. This is seen by the huge performance gap between blacks and whites on exams for graduate school admittance such as the GRE, MCAT, and LSAT.

Is poor academic performance among blacks something immutable or preordained? There is no evidence for such a claim. Let's sample some evidence from earlier periods. In "Assumptions Versus History in Ethnic Education," in *Teachers College Record* (1981), Dr. Thomas Sowell reports on academic achievement in some of New York City's public schools. He compares test scores for sixth-graders in Harlem schools with those in the predominantly white Lower East Side for April 1941 and December 1941.

In paragraph and word meaning, Harlem students, compared to Lower East Side students, scored equally or higher. In 1947 and 1951, Harlem third-graders in paragraph and word meaning, and arithmetic reasoning and computation, scored about the same as—and in some cases, slightly higher, and in others, slightly lower than—their white Lower East Side counterparts.

Going back to an earlier era, Washington, D.C.'s Dunbar High School's black students scored higher in citywide tests than any of the city's white schools. In fact, from its founding in 1870 to 1955, most of Dunbar's graduates went off to college.

Let's return to the tale of the youngster at the Midwestern college. Recruiting this youngster to be a failure is cruel, psychologically damaging, and an embarrassment for his family. But the campus hustlers might come to the aid of the student by convincing him that his academic failure is a result of white racism and Eurocentric values.

America's New Racists
June 22, 2011

The late South African economist William Hutt, in his 1964 book, *The Economics of the Colour Bar*, said that one of the supreme tragedies of the human condition is that those who have been the victims of injustices and oppression "can often be observed to be inflicting not dissimilar injustices upon other races."

Born in 1936, I've lived through some of our openly racist history, which has included racist insults, beatings, and lynchings. Tuskegee Institute records show that between the years 1880 and 1951, 3,437 blacks and 1,293 whites were lynched. I recall my cousin's and my being chased out of Fishtown and Grays Ferry, two predominantly Irish Philadelphia neighborhoods, in the 1940s, not stopping until we reached a predominantly black North or South Philly neighborhood.

Today all that has changed. Most racist assaults are committed by blacks. What's worse is there are blacks, still alive, who lived through the times of lynching, Jim Crow laws and open racism who remain silent in the face of it.

Last year, four black Skidmore College students yelled racial slurs while they beat up a white man because he was dining with a black man. Skidmore College's first response was to offer counseling to one of the black students charged with the crime. In 2009, a black Columbia University professor assaulted a white woman during a heated argument about race relations. According to interviews and court records obtained and reported by Denver's ABC affiliate (December 4, 2009), black gangs roamed downtown Denver verbally venting their hatred for white victims before assaulting and robbing them during a four-month crime wave. Earlier this year, four black girls beat a white girl at a McDonald's, and the victim suffered a seizure. Chicago Mayor Rahm Emanuel ordered an emergency shutdown of the beaches in Chicago because mobs of blacks were terrorizing families. According to the NBC affiliate there (June 8, 2011), a gang of black teens stormed a city bus, attacked white victims, and ran off with their belongings.

Racist black attacks are not only against whites but also against Asians. In San Francisco, five blacks beat an eighty-three-year-old Chinese man to death. They threw a fifty-seven-year-old woman off a train platform. Two black Oakland teenagers assaulted a fifty-nine-year-old Chinese man; the punching knocked him to the ground, killing him. At Philly's South Philadelphia High School, Asian students report that black students routinely pelt them with food and beat, punch, and kick them in school hallways and bathrooms as they hurl racial epithets such as "Hey, Chinese!" and "Yo, Dragon Ball!" The Asian American Legal Defense and Education Fund charged the School District of Philadelphia with "deliberate indifference" toward black victimization of Asian students.

In many of these brutal attacks, the news media make no mention of the race of the perpetrators. If it were white racist gangs randomly attacking blacks, the mainstream media would have no hesitation reporting the race of the perps. Editors for the *Los Angeles Times*, *The New York Times*, and the *Chicago Tribune* admitted to deliberately censoring information about black crime for political reasons. *Chicago Tribune* Editor Gerould Kern recently said that the paper's reason for censorship was to "guard against subjecting an entire group of people to suspicion."

These racist attacks can, at least in part, be attributed to the black elite, who have a vested interest in racial paranoia. And that includes a president who has spent years aligned with people who have promoted racial grievance and polarization and appointed an attorney general who's accused us of being "a nation of cowards" on matters of race and has refused to prosecute black thugs who gathered at a Philadelphia voting site in blatant violation of federal voter intimidation laws. Tragically, black youngsters—who are seething with resentments, refusing to accept educational and other opportunities unknown to blacks yesteryear—will turn out to be the larger victims in the long run.

Black silence in the face of black racism has to be one of the biggest betrayals of the civil rights struggle that included black and white Americans.

Race and Economics

August 31, 2011

Overall US unemployment is 9.1 percent. For white adults, it's 8 percent, and for white teens, 23 percent. Black adult unemployment stands at 17 percent, and for black teens, it's 40 percent, more than 50 percent in some cities, for example, Washington.

Chapter 3 of *Race and Economics*, my most recent book, starts out, "Some might find it puzzling that during times of gross racial discrimination, black unemployment was lower and blacks were more active in the labor force than they are today." Up until the late 1950s, the labor force participation rate of black teens and adults was equal to or greater than their white counterparts. In fact, in 1910, 71 percent of black males older than nine were employed, compared with 51 percent for whites. As early as 1890, the duration of unemployment among blacks was shorter than it was among whites, whereas today unemployment is both higher and longer lasting among blacks than among whites.

How might one explain yesteryear's lower black unemployment and greater labor force participation? The usual academic, civil rights, or media racial discrimination explanation for black/white socioeconomic differences just wouldn't hold up. I can't imagine even the most harebrained professor, civil rights leader, or media "expert" arguing that there was less discrimination a century ago and that explains why there was greater black labor market participation. Racial discrimination or low skills can explain low wages but not unemployment.

During the 1930s, there were a number of federal government interventions that changed the black employment picture. The first was the Davis-Bacon Act of 1931, which mandated minimum wages on federally financed or assisted construction projects. During the bill's legislative debate, the racial objectives were clear. Rep. John Cochran, D-Mo., said he had "received numerous complaints ... about Southern contractors employing low-paid colored mechanics getting work and bringing the employees from the South." Rep. Clayton

Allgood, D-Ala., complained: "Reference has been made to a contractor from Alabama who went to New York with bootleg labor. . . . That contractor has cheap colored labor that he transports, and he puts them in cabins, and it is labor of that sort that is in competition with white labor throughout the country." Rep. William Upshaw, D-Ga., spoke of the "superabundance or large aggregation of Negro labor." American Federation of Labor President William Green said, "Colored labor is being sought to demoralize wage rates." For decades after Davis-Bacon enactment, black workers on federally financed or assisted construction projects virtually disappeared. The Davis-Bacon Act is still on the books, and tragically today's black congressmen, doing the bidding of their labor union allies, vote against any effort to modify or eliminate its restrictions.

The National Industrial Recovery Act of 1933 and the Fair Labor Standards Act of 1938 broadened the number of workers covered by minimum wages, with negative consequences for black employment across a much wider range of industries. Good intentions motivate most Americans in their support for minimum wage laws, but for compassionate public policy, one should examine the laws' effect. That's seen by putting oneself in the place of an employer and asking, "If I must pay $7.25 an hour to no matter whom I hire, does it pay me to hire a worker who's so unfortunate as to have skills that enable him to produce, say, only $4 worth of value an hour?" Most employers would view hiring such a worker as a losing economic proposition; therefore, a minimum wage law discriminates against low-skilled workers by reducing employment opportunity.

Being unemployed has significant negative social consequences, one of them noted in the 1960s by Sen. Daniel Patrick Moynihan, who raised the alarm about the link between joblessness and the decline of the black family, saying that men without work become less attractive as marriage partners. Between 1890 and 1940, a slightly higher percentage of black adults had married than white adults. Today black marriage rates have fallen precipitously, where 72 percent of black children are born to unwed mothers.

Blacks and Politics

September 7, 2011

At one of last month's Congressional Black Caucus-sponsored "job fairs," Rep. Andre Carson, D-Ind., told the audience: "This is the effort that we're seeing of Jim Crow. Some of these folks in Congress right now would love to see us as second-class citizens. Some of them in Congress right now with this tea party movement would love to see you and me—I'm sorry, Tamron—hanging on a tree." Carson's reference to Tamron was acknowledgment of the presence of MSNBC's black reporter Tamron Hall, who didn't deem it fit to report the congressman's statement. Another black attacker of the tea party movement is Rep. Maxine Waters, who told her constituents: "This is a tough game. You can't be intimidated. You can't be frightened. And as far as I'm concerned, the tea party can go straight to hell." "Let us all remember who the real enemy is. And the real enemy is the tea party," reminded Rep. Frederica Wilson, D-Fla. The Rev. Jesse Jackson said the tea party should be called the "Fort Sumter tea party that sought to maintain states' rights and slavery." Rep. Alcee Hastings, D-Fla., in telling a job fair audience to register to vote, said, "Turn the tea party upside down!"

What about Hastings's call for blacks to register to vote? What has it meant? For several decades, blacks have held significant political power, in the form of being mayors and dominant forces on city councils in our major cities, including Philadelphia, Detroit, Washington, Memphis, Atlanta, Baltimore, New Orleans, Oakland, Newark, Cincinnati, and many others. In most of these cities, blacks have served as school superintendents, school principals, and chiefs of police. Plus, there's precedent setting black political power at the national level, with thirty-nine black congressmen and a black president.

Here's my question: What would you think of someone who claimed that black political power has yielded great results? In these cities where blacks dominate the political machinery, black academic proficiency is on a par with the rest of the nation. Black families are more stable and illegitimacy and welfare dependency are much lower than they were when whites dominated the political machinery of these cities. Also, since blacks have replaced white mayors and city councils, black citizens are murdered less and are far safer on the streets and in their homes. Even more noticeable is the fall in unemployment, particularly since the nation elected a black president. You say, "Williams, anyone making such statements suffers from a special kind of lunacy and ought to be put into an insane asylum!"

It doesn't demean black political achievement to ask what black political power means for the lives of ordinary black people. Put another way, is political power a necessary condition for economic power? Let's look around.

Japanese- and Chinese-Americans faced gross discrimination in our country, but when's the last time you heard them worrying about how many mayors and congressmen they have? Are they in a tizzy over the tea party's call for constitutional government, reduced spending, and a balanced budget? By the way, Japanese- and Chinese-Americans have median family incomes higher than white Americans despite having no political power, even in areas where they are most numerous.

Let me be clear. I am not stating a causal link between the fact of black political power and the poor living conditions of so many blacks in our urban centers. I'm simply offering evidence that the expectation that black political power will translate into socioeconomic well-being for the ordinary black citizen is apt to be disappointing. Political power empowers—and even enriches—the political elite; for them, getting out their constituent vote is the be-all and end-all. It's the economic arena, featured by personal liberty, that best serves the ordinary person.

As long as black politicians can successfully run a rope-a-dope on their constituents by keeping them focused on allegations of white racism and telling them that salvation lies in voting for them, little good will come to their poorest constituency.

It's Hard to Be a Racist

October 12, 2011

Years ago it was easy to be a racist. All you had to be was a white person using some of the racial epithets that are routinely used in song and everyday speech by many of today's blacks. Or you had to chant "two, four, six, eight, we don't want to integrate" when a black student showed up for admission to your high school or college. Of course, there was that dressing up in a hooded white gown. In any case, you didn't have to be sophisticated to be a racist.

Today all that has changed. Rep. Charles Rangel, D-N.Y., pointed that out back in 1994 when the Republican-led Congress pushed for tax relief. Rangel denounced Republicans' plan as a form of modern-day racism, saying, "It's not 'spic' or 'nigger' anymore. [Instead,] they say, 'Let's cut taxes.'" That means the simple use of the N-word is not enough to make one a racist. If it were, blacks would be the nation's premier racists. Today it's the call for tax cuts that makes you a racist. That's why the "tea" party, short for "taxed enough already," is nothing more than organized racists. What makes tea partyers even more racist is their constant call for the White House and Congress to return to the confines of the Constitution.

Racism has other guises. Say that you're a believer in Martin Luther King's wish, expressed in his "I Have a Dream" speech, that our "children will one day live in a nation where they will not be judged by the color of their skin, but by the content of their character." The call to judge people by the content of their character rather than the color of their skin is really code for racism. There's no question about one's racial antipathy if he voted for measures such as California's Proposition 209, Michigan's Proposal 2, Washington state's Initiative 200, or Nebraska's Civil Rights Initiative 424. These measures outlaw judging people by the color of their skin for admission to college, awarding of government contracts, and employment. The call for equal treatment is simply racism by stealth and is far more insidious than name-calling and hood-donning.

One might think that seeing as America elected its first black president, it would usher in the end of racism; but it's all a racist plot that's easily uncovered simply by asking: "Who really elected Obama to the presidency?" It surely wasn't black people. Of the 67 million votes that Obama received in the 2008 election, I doubt whether even 7 million or 8 million came from blacks. That means white people put Obama in office, and that means he is beholden to white people, not black people.

You say, "Williams, that's preposterous! What's your evidence?" Just look at the unemployment statistics. White unemployment is 8 percent, and black unemployment is double that, at 17 percent, and in some cities, black unemployment is near 30 percent. It's gotten so bad under Obama's presidency that New York's Urban Justice Center has appealed to the United Nations Human Rights Council for help. But Obama's tired of black complaints. Obama told the Congressional Black Caucus to "Stop whining!" "Take off your bedroom slippers; put on your marching shoes. Shake it off. Stop complaining; stop grumbling; stop crying." This kind of talk is unprecedented. Just ask yourself: "When have I ever heard a Democratic or a Republican leader talk this way to his party's strongest supporters? Would Obama tell Jews to stop whining about Israel? Would he tell unions to stop grumbling about card check? Would he tell feminists, if they were complaining about sex discrimination, to shake it off?"

This kind of political treatment of blacks should not be surprising, because black people are a one-party people in a two-party system. That means Democratic politicians have learned to take the black vote for granted, and Republicans make little effort to get it. That's not smart for blacks to set themselves up that way.

Obama's Racial Politics

February 1, 2012

There's been a heap of criticism placed upon President Barack Obama's domestic policies that have promoted government intrusion and prolonged our fiscal crisis and his foreign policies that have emboldened our enemies. Any criticism of Obama pales in comparison with what might be said about the American people who voted him in to the nation's highest office.

Obama's presidency represents the first time in our history that a person could have been elected to that office who had long-standing close associations with people who hate our nation. I'm speaking of the Rev. Jeremiah Wright, Obama's pastor for twenty years, who preached that blacks should sing not "God Bless America," but "God damn America." Then there's William Ayers, now professor of education at the University of Illinois at Chicago but formerly a member of the Weather Underground, an anti-US group that bombed the Pentagon, US Capitol, and other government buildings. Although Ayers was never convicted of any crime, he told a *New York Times* reporter, in the wake of the September 2001 terrorist attack, "I don't regret setting bombs. . . . I feel we didn't do enough." Obama has served on a foundation board, appeared on panels, and even held campaign events in Ayers's home, joined by Ayers's former-fugitive wife, Bernardine Dohrn. Bill Ayers's close association with Obama is reflected by his admission that he helped write Obama's memoirs, *Dreams from My Father*.

Many Americans thought that with Obama's presidency, we were moving to a "post-racial society." Little can be further from the truth. Victor Davis Hanson, senior fellow at the Hoover Institution, in a *National Review* (January 18, 2012) article titled "Obama's Racial Politics," says that Obama's message about race and his charges of racial bigotry are "usually coded and subtle." Criticizing Republicans, before a Mexican-American audience, Obama said that he ran for office because "America should be a place where you can always make it if you try—a place where every child, no matter what they look like [or] where they come from, should have a chance to succeed." If you don't get it, "no matter what they look like" is code for nonwhite. Hanson says that Obama's attorney general, Eric Holder, has "found race a convenient refuge from criticism—most recently accusing his congressional auditors of racism, for their grilling him over government sales of firearms to Mexican cartel hitmen."

Obama's racial politics are aided and abetted by a dishonest news media. When Republican candidate Texas Gov. Rick Perry referred to "a big black cloud that hangs over America, that debt that is so monstrous," he was dishonestly accused of racism by MSNBC's Ed Schultz, who said, "That black cloud Perry is talking about is President Barack Obama." Schultz omitted the second half of Perry's quote. Chris Matthews referred to Perry's vision of federalism as "Bull Connor with a smile."

The media have help from black congressmen in stirring up racial dissent. Rep. Emanuel Cleaver, D-Mo., said white presidents must be "pushed a great deal more" to address black unemployment than would a black president. Rep. Sheila Jackson Lee, D-Texas, said that argument over the debt ceiling is proof of racial animosity toward Obama. Rep. Barbara Lee, D-Calif., said that Republicans are trying to deny blacks the vote. Rep. Andre Carson, D-Ind., said the tea party wishes to lynch blacks and hang them from trees. Rep. Charles Rangel, D-N.Y., said Perry's job creation in Texas is "one stage away from slavery."

All of this places a heavy burden on people who care about our nation. We must ensure that the 2012 elections are the most open and honest elections in US history. Should Obama lose, I wouldn't put it past leftists, progressives, the news media, and their race-hustling allies, as well as the president, to fan the fires of hate and dissention by charging that racists somehow stole the election, thereby giving support and excuses for the kind of violence and lawlessness that we've witnessed in flash mobs and Occupy Wall Street riots.

Rising Black Social Pathology
February 15, 2012

The *Philadelphia Inquirer*'s big story February 4 was about how a budget crunch at the Philadelphia School District had caused the district to lay off ninety-one school police officers. Over the years, there's been no discussion of what has happened to our youth that makes a school police force necessary in the first place. The *Inquirer*'s series "Assault on Learning" (March 2011) reported that in the 2010 school year, "690 teachers were assaulted; in the last five years, 4,000 were." The newspaper reported that in Philadelphia's 268 schools, "on an average day 25 students, teachers, or other staff members were beaten, robbed, sexually assaulted, or victims of other violent crimes. That doesn't even include thousands more who are extorted, threatened, or bullied in a school year."

I graduated from Philadelphia's Benjamin Franklin High School in 1954. Franklin's students were from the poorest North Philadelphia neighborhoods—such as the Richard Allen housing project, where I lived—but there were no policemen patrolling the hallways. There were occasional after-school fights—rumbles, we called them—but within the school, there was order. Students didn't use foul language to teachers, much less assault them.

How might one explain the greater civility of Philadelphia and other big-city, predominantly black schools during earlier periods compared with today? Would anyone argue that during the '40s and '50s, back when Williams attended Philadelphia schools, there was less racial discrimination and poverty and there were greater opportunities for blacks and that's why academic performance was higher and there was greater civility? Or how about "in earlier periods, there was more funding for predominantly black schools"? Or how about "in earlier periods, black students had more black role models in the forms of black principals, teachers, and guidance counselors"? If such arguments were to be made, it would be sheer lunacy. If white and black liberals and civil rights leaders want to make such arguments, they'd best wait until those of us who lived during the '40s and '50s have departed the scene.

Over the past couple of decades, I've attended neighborhood reunions. I've asked whether any of us recall classmates who couldn't read, write, or perform simple calculations, and none of us does. Back in those days, most Philadelphia school principals, teachers, and counselors were white. At Stoddart-Fleisher junior high school, where I attended, I recall that only one teacher was black, and at Benjamin Franklin, there might have been two. What does that say about the role model theory? By the way, Asian-Americans are at the top of the academic ladder, and, at least historically, they rarely experience an Asian-American teacher during their K-through-12 schooling.

Many black students are alien and hostile to the education process. They are permitted to make education impossible for other students. Their misbehavior and violence require schools to divert resources away from education and spend them on security, such as hiring school police and purchasing metal detectors, all of which does little for school safety. The violent school climate discourages the highest-skilled teachers from teaching at schools where they risk assaults, intimidation and theft. At a bare minimum, part of the solution to school violence and poor academic performance should be the expulsion of students who engage in assaults and disrespectful behavior. You say, "What's to be done for these students?" Even if we don't know what to do with them, how compassionate and intelligent is it to permit them to make education impossible for other students?

The fact that black parents, teachers, politicians, and civil rights organizations tolerate and make excuses for the despicable and destructive behavior of so many young blacks is a gross betrayal of the memory, struggle, sacrifice, sweat, and blood of our ancestors. The sorry and tragic state of black education is not going to be turned around until there's a change in what's acceptable and unacceptable behavior by young people. That change has to come from within the black community.

Leftist Race-baiters

May 9, 2012

MSNBC's Chris Matthews, in a recent debate with former Republican National Chairman Michael Steele, called the Republican Party the "grand wizard crowd." Grand wizard is the title given to the leader of the Ku Klux Klan. It is truly misinformed to call Republicans the party of the Klan. Throughout our history, most Klansmen and most racists have been Democrats. Here are a few racist quotes from major Democratic figures.

The late Sen. Robert Byrd, D-W.Va., a former Klansman, wrote during World War II: "I shall never fight in the armed forces with a Negro by my side. . . . Rather I should die a thousand times, and see Old Glory trampled in the dirt never to rise again, than to see this beloved land of ours become degraded by race mongrels, a throwback to the blackest specimen from the wilds."

When Lyndon B. Johnson was in the House of Representatives, he said that President Harry Truman's civil rights program was "a farce and a sham—an effort to set up a police state in the guise of liberty." He continued: "I am opposed to that program. I have voted against the so-called poll tax repeal bill. . . . I have voted against the so-called anti-lynching bill." When Johnson had become senator, he observed, "These Negroes, they're getting pretty uppity these days, and that's a problem for us since they've got something now they never had before, the political pull to back up their uppityness."

Chris Matthews is by no means unique among NBC's race-baiters. After NBC was caught red-handed doctoring George Zimmerman's 911 call to a police dispatcher, in an effort to make him out to be a racist, Steve Capus, president of NBC's news division, said it was "a mistake and not a deliberate act to misrepresent the phone call." That's a baldfaced lie, for it's almost impossible to make such a mistake. Furthermore, the producer who allegedly was fired remains a secret.

When Texas Gov. Rick Perry referred to our national debt as a "big black cloud that hangs over America, (a) debt that is so monstrous," MSNBC's Ed Schultz said, "That black cloud Perry is talking about is President Barack Obama." Matthews chimed in to say that Perry's vision of federalism is "Bull Connor with a smile."

In August 2009, MSNBC's Contessa Brewer was discussing a tea party rally in Arizona, where it's legal to carry an unconcealed weapon. She said: "A man at a pro-health care reform rally . . . wore a semiautomatic assault rifle on his shoulder and a pistol on his hip. . . . There are questions about whether this has racial overtones. I mean, here you have a man of color in the presidency and white people showing up with guns." All that her audience was shown were a rifle and pistol strapped to a man's back. MSNBC concealed the fact that the armed man was black and did not show the interview he gave to the reporter. Brewer knowingly deceived her audience because an armed black man didn't fit the racial narrative.

It's not just white liberals in the media who are stirring up racial animosity; they have help from black politicians. During last year's debate on the debt ceiling, Rep. Sheila Jackson Lee, D-Texas, said that argument over the debt ceiling was proof of racial animosity toward Obama. Rep. Andre Carson, D-Ind., said the tea party wishes to lynch blacks and hang them from trees. Rep. Charles Rangel, D-N.Y., said Perry's job creation in Texas is "one stage away from slavery." While appearing on MSNBC, Philadelphia Mayor Michael Nutter referred to Trayvon Martin's death as an "assassination." Nutter had better worry about the 118 "assassinations" in Philadelphia so far this year.

To their own detriment—and that of the nation—black people are being used to further the liberal big-government agenda. Black people have been misled to think that their problems are with white people and government and that black politicians are the solution. There's not a speck of evidence supporting either vision—despite the election of a white African as president.

Should Black People Tolerate This?
May 23, 2012

Each year, roughly 7,000 blacks are murdered. Ninety-four percent of the time, the murderer is another black person. According to the Bureau of Justice Statistics, between 1976 and 2011, there were 279,384 black murder victims. Using the 94 percent figure means that 262,621 were murdered by other blacks. Though blacks are 13 percent of the nation's population, they account for more than 50 percent of homicide victims. Nationally, black homicide victimization rate is six times that of whites, and in some cities, it's twenty-two times that of whites. Coupled with being most of the nation's homicide victims, blacks are most of the victims of violent personal crimes, such as assault and robbery.

The magnitude of this tragic mayhem can be viewed in another light. According to a Tuskegee Institute study, between the years 1882 and 1968, 3,446 blacks were lynched at the hands of whites. Black fatalities during the Korean War (3,075), Vietnam War (7,243), and all wars since 1980 (8,197) come to 18,515, a number that pales in comparison with black loss of life at home. It's a tragic commentary to be able to say that young black males have a greater chance of reaching maturity on the battlefields of Iraq and Afghanistan than on the streets of Philadelphia, Chicago, Detroit, Oakland, Newark, and other cities.

A much larger issue is how might we interpret the deafening silence about the day-to-day murder in black communities compared with the national uproar over the killing of Trayvon Martin. Such a response by politicians, civil rights organizations, and the mainstream news media could easily be interpreted as "blacks killing other blacks is of little concern, but it's unacceptable for a white to kill a black person."

There are a few civil rights leaders with a different vision. When President Barack Obama commented about the Trayvon Martin case, T. Willard Fair, president of the Urban League of Greater Miami, told

The Daily Caller that "the outrage should be about us killing each other, about black-on-black crime." He asked rhetorically, "Wouldn't you think to have 41 people shot [in Chicago] between Friday morning and Monday morning would be much more newsworthy and deserve much more outrage?" Former NAACP leader Pastor C. L. Bryant said the rallies organized by Al Sharpton and Jesse Jackson suggest there is an epidemic of "white men killing black young men," adding: "The epidemic is truly black-on-black crime. The greatest danger to the lives of young black men are young black men."

Not only is there silence about black-on-black crime; there's silence and concealment about black racist attacks on whites—for example, the recent attacks on two *Virginian-Pilot* newspaper reporters set upon and beaten by a mob of young blacks. The story wasn't even covered by their own newspaper. In March, a black mob assaulted, knocked unconscious, disrobed, and robbed a white tourist in downtown Baltimore. Black mobs have roamed the streets of Denver, Chicago, Philadelphia, New York, Cleveland, Washington, Los Angeles, and other cities, making unprovoked attacks on whites and running off with their belongings.

Racist attacks have been against not only whites but also Asians. Such attacks include the San Francisco beating death of an eighty-three-year-old Chinese man, the pushing of a fifty-seven-year-old woman off a train platform, and the knocking of a fifty-nine-year-old Chinese man to the ground, which killed him. For years, Asian school students in New York and Philadelphia have been beaten up by their black classmates and called racist epithets—for example, "Hey, Chinese!" and "Yo, dragon ball!" But that kind of bullying, unlike the bullying of homosexuals, goes unreported and unpunished.

Racial demagoguery from the president on down is not in our nation's best interests, plus it's dangerous. As my colleague Thomas Sowell recently put it, "if there is anything worse than a one-sided race war, it is a two-sided race war, especially when one of the races outnumbers the other several times over."

Racial Double Standards

June 20, 2012

Back in 2009, US Attorney General Eric Holder said we were "a nation of cowards" on matters of race. Permit me to be brave and run a few assertions by you just to see whether we're on the same page. There should be two standards for civilized conduct: one for whites, which is higher, and another for blacks, which is lower. In other words, in the name of justice and fair play, blacks should not be held accountable to the same standards that whites are and should not be criticized for conduct that we'd deem disgusting and racist if said or done by whites.

You say, "Williams, what in the world are you talking about?" Mitt Romney hasn't revealed all of his fall campaign strategy yet, but what if he launched a "White Americans for Romney" movement in an effort to get out the white vote? If the Romney campaign did that, there'd be a media-led outcry across the land, with charges ranging from racial insensitivity to outright racism. When President Barack Obama announced his 2012 launch of "African Americans for Obama" (http://www.youtube.com/watch?v=BdjoHA5ocwU), the silence was deafening. Should the same standards be applied to Obama as would be applied to Romney? The answer turns out to be no, because Obama is not held to the same standards as Romney.

Liberals won't actually come out and say that criticism of Obama is in and of itself racist, but they come pretty close. Former President Jimmy Carter said that criticism of Obama shows that there is an "inherent feeling" in America that a black man should not be president. Chris Matthews, host of MSNBC's "Hardball," said that critics of Obama are crackers. Morgan Freeman said that the campaign to see that Obama serves one term is a "racist thing." Former Obama czar Van Jones said that Romney's campaign sign "Obama Isn't Working" implies Obama is a "lazy, incompetent affirmative action baby."

Racial double standards also apply to how crime is reported. I'm betting that if mobs of white youths were going about severely beating and robbing blacks at random and preying on black businesses, it would be major news. News anchors might open, "Tonight we report on the most recent wave of racist whites organizing unprovoked attacks on innocent black people and their businesses." If white thugs were actually doing that, politicians would be demanding answers. Such random attacks do happen, but it's blacks preying on whites.

On St. Patrick's Day in Baltimore, a nineteen-year-old white man was viciously attacked by a mob of black thugs. He broke loose, but a second mob of black thugs attacked him, taking all of his belongings. Baltimore County Delegate Pat McDonough demanded the governor send in the Maryland State Police to control "roving mobs of black youths" at Baltimore's Inner Harbor. Maryland Gov. Martin O'Malley and other activists demanded that McDonough apologize for talking about "black youth mobs."

Similar episodes of unprovoked violence by black thugs against white people chosen at random on beaches, in shopping malls, and at other public places have occurred in Philadelphia, New York, Denver, Chicago, Cleveland, Washington, Los Angeles, and other cities. Most of the time, the race of the attackers, euphemistically called flash mobs, is not reported, even though media leftists and their allies are experts in reporting racial disparities in prison sentencing and the alleged injustice of the criminal justice system.

Racial double standards are not restricted to the political arena and crime reporting; we see it on college campuses and in the workplace. Black people ought to be offended by the idea that we are held accountable to lower standards of conduct and achievement. White people ought to be ashamed for permitting and fostering racial double standards that have effects that are in some ways worse than the cruel racism of yesteryear.

Black and White Standards
October 31, 2012

The *Washington Post* (October 25, 2012), in giving President Barack Obama an endorsement for another four years, wrote, "Much of the 2012 presidential campaign has dwelt on the past, but the key questions are who could better lead the country during the next four years—and, most urgently, who is likelier to put the government on a more sound financial footing." The suggestion appears to be that a president is not to be held accountable to his promises and past record and that his past record is no indication of his future behavior. Possibly, the *Washington Post* people believe that a black president shouldn't be held accountable to his record and campaign promises. Let's look at it.

What about Obama's pledge to cut the deficit in half during his first term in office? Instead, we saw the first trillion-dollar deficit ever, under any president of the United States. Plus, it has been followed by trillion-dollar deficits in every year of his administration. What about Obama's pledge of transparency, in which his legislative proposals would be placed on the internet days before Congress voted on them so that Americans could inspect them? Obama's major legislative proposal, Obamacare, was enacted in such secrecy and with such speed that even members of Congress did not have time to read it. Remember that it was Rep. Nancy Pelosi who told us, "But we have to pass the [health care] bill so that you can find out what is in it." What about Obama's stimulus packages and promises to get unemployment under control? The Current Employment Statistics program shows that in 2008, the total number of US jobs was more than 138 million, compared with 133.5 million today. As Stanford University economics professor Edward Lazear summed it up, "there hasn't been one day during the entire Obama presidency when as many Americans were working as on the day President Bush left office."

While Obama's national job approval rating is a little less than 50 percent, among blacks his job approval is a whopping 88 percent. I'd like to ask people who approve of Obama's performance, "What has President Obama done during the past four years that you'd like to see more of in the next four years?"

Black support of politicians who have done little or nothing for their ordinary constituents is by no means unusual. Blacks are chief executives of major cities, such as Philadelphia, Detroit, Washington, Memphis, Atlanta, Baltimore, New Orleans, Oakland, Newark, Cleveland, and Cincinnati. In most of these cities, the chief of police, the superintendent of schools and other high executives are black. But in these cities, black people, like no other sector of our population, suffer from the highest rates of homicides, assaults, robberies and shootings. Black high-school dropout rates in these cities are the highest in the nation. Even if a black youngster manages to graduate from high school, his reading, writing, and computational proficiency is likely to be equivalent to that of a white seventh- or eighth-grader. That's even with school budgets per student being among the highest in the nation.

Last year, in reference to President Obama's failed employment policies and high unemployment among blacks, Rep. Emanuel Cleaver, D-Mo., who is chairman of the Congressional Black Caucus, said, "If Bill Clinton had been in the White House and had failed to address this problem, we probably would be marching on the White House." That's a vision that seems to explain black tolerance for failed politicians—namely, if it's a black politician whose policies are ineffectual and possibly harmful to the masses of the black community, it's tolerable, but it's entirely unacceptable if the politician is white.

Black people would not accept excuses upon excuses and vote to reelect decade after decade any white politician, especially a Republican politician, to office who had the failed records of our big-city mayors. What that suggests about black people is not very flattering.

Black Self-Sabotage

July 31, 2013

If we put ourselves into the shoes of racists who seek to sabotage black upward mobility, we couldn't develop a more effective agenda than that followed by civil rights organizations, black politicians, academics, liberals, and the news media. Let's look at it.

First, weaken the black family, but don't blame it on individual choices. You have to preach that today's weak black family is a legacy of slavery, Jim Crow, and racism. The truth is that black female-headed households were just 18 percent of households in 1950, as opposed to about 68 percent today. In fact, from 1890 to 1940, the black marriage rate was slightly higher than that of whites. Even during slavery, when marriage was forbidden for blacks, most black children lived in biological two-parent families. In New York City, in 1925, 85 percent of black households were two-parent households. A study of 1880 family structure in Philadelphia shows that three-quarters of black families were two-parent households.

During the 1960s, devastating nonsense emerged, exemplified by a Johns Hopkins University sociology professor who argued, "It has yet to be shown that the absence of a father was directly responsible for any of the supposed deficiencies of broken homes." The real issue, he went on to say, "is not the lack of male presence but the lack of male income." That suggests marriage and fatherhood can be replaced by a welfare check.

The poverty rate among blacks is 36 percent. Most black poverty is found in female-headed households. The poverty rate among black married couples has been in single digits since 1994 and is about 8 percent today. The black illegitimacy rate is 75 percent, and in some cities, it's 90 percent. But if that's a legacy of slavery, it must have skipped several generations, because in the 1940s, unwed births hovered around 14 percent.

Along with the decline of the black family comes antisocial behavior, manifested by high crime rates. Each year, roughly 7,000 blacks are murdered. Ninety-four percent of the time, the murderer is another black person. According to the Bureau of Justice Statistics, between 1976 and 2011, there were 279,384 black murder victims. Using the 94 percent figure means that 262,621 were murdered by other blacks. Though blacks are 13 percent of the nation's population, they account for more than 50 percent of homicide victims. Nationally, the black homicide victimization rate is six times that of whites, and in some cities, it's twenty-two times that of whites. I'd like for the president, the civil rights establishment, white liberals, and the news media, who spent massive resources protesting the George Zimmerman trial's verdict, to tell the nation whether they believe that the major murder problem blacks face is murder by whites. There are no such protests against the thousands of black murders.

There's an organization called Neighborhood Scout. Using 2011 population data from the US Census Bureau, 2011 crime statistics from the FBI, and information from 17,000 local law enforcement agencies in the country, it came up with a report titled "Top 25 Most Dangerous Neighborhoods in America" (http://tinyurl.com/cdqrev4). They include neighborhoods in Detroit, Chicago, Houston, St. Louis, and other major cities. What's common to all twenty-five neighborhoods is that their makeup is described as "Black" or "Mostly Black." The high crime rates have several outcomes that are not in the best interests of the overwhelmingly law-abiding people in these neighborhoods. There can't be much economic development. Property has a lower value, but worst of all, people can't live with the kind of personal security that most Americans enjoy.

Disgustingly, black politicians, civil rights leaders, liberals, and the president are talking nonsense about "having a conversation about race." That's beyond useless. Tell me how a conversation with white people is going to stop black predators from preying on blacks. How is such a conversation going to eliminate the 75 percent illegitimacy rate? What will such a conversation do about the breakdown of the black family (though "breakdown" is not the correct word, as the family doesn't form in the first place)? Only black people can solve our problems.

Would They Be Proud?

August 7, 2013

One can't imagine the fear in the hearts of the parents of those nine black students who walked past shouting placard-carrying mobs as they entered Little Rock Central High School in 1957. Each day, they were greeted with angry shouts of "Two, four, six, eight, we don't want to integrate." In some rural and urban areas, during the school desegregation era, parents escorted their five- and six-year-old children past crowds shouting threats and screaming racial epithets. Often there were Ku Klux Klan marches and cross burnings. Much of this protest was in the South, but Northern cities were by no means exempt from the turmoil and violence of school desegregation.

Most of the parents and civil rights leaders whose sacrifices and courage made today's educational opportunities possible are no longer with us. My question is: If they could know what many of today's black youngsters have done with the fruits of their sacrifice, would they be proud? Most schools identified as "persistently dangerous" are predominantly black schools. To have a modicum of safety, many schools are equipped with walkthrough metal detectors, security cameras, and conveyor belt X-ray machines that scan book bags and purses. Nationally, the black four-year high-school graduation rate is 52 percent. In some cities, such as Detroit and Philadelphia, it's considerably lower—20 percent and 24 percent, respectively. In Rochester, N.Y., it's 9 percent.

What black politicians, parents, teachers, and students have created is nothing less than a gross betrayal and squandering of the struggle paid in blood, sweat, and tears by previous generations to make possible the educational opportunities that were denied to blacks for so long.

Born in 1936, I've lived during some of our racially discriminatory history. I recall being chased out of Fishtown and Grays Ferry, two predominantly Irish Philadelphia neighborhoods, with my cousin in the 1940s and not stopping until we reached a predominantly black North Philly or South Philly neighborhood. Today that might be different. A black person seeking safety might run from a black neighborhood to a white neighborhood.

On top of that, today whites are likely to be victims of blacks. According to the Bureau of Justice Statistics' 2008 National Crime Victimization Survey, in instances of interracial crimes of violence, 83 percent of the time, a black person was the perpetrator and a white person was the victim. Most interracial assaults are committed by blacks. What's worse is there are blacks still alive—such as older members of the Congressional Black Caucus, NAACP, and National Urban League—who lived through the times of lynching, Jim Crow, and open racism and who remain silent in the face of the current situation.

After the George Zimmerman trial, in cities such as Baltimore, Los Angeles, Milwaukee, Chicago, and New York, there have been a number of brutal revenge attacks on whites in the name of "justice for Trayvon." Over the past few years, there have been many episodes of unprovoked attacks by black gangs against white people at beaches, in shopping malls, on public conveyances, and in other public places in cities such as Denver, Chicago, Philadelphia, New York, Washington, and Los Angeles. There's no widespread condemnation, plus most of the time, the race of the attackers was not reported, even though media leftists and their allies are experts in reporting racial differences in everything else.

Would those black Americans who fought tooth and nail against Jim Crow, segregation, lynching, and racism be proud of the findings of a recent Rasmussen poll in which 31 percent of blacks think that most blacks are racists and 24 percent of blacks think that most whites are racists? Among whites, in the same Rasmussen poll, 38 percent consider most blacks racist, and 10 percent consider most whites racist.

Black people don't need to have a conversation with white people on matters of race. One first step would be to develop a zero tolerance for criminal and disruptive school behavior, as well as a zero tolerance for criminal behavior in neighborhoods. If city authorities cannot or will not provide protection, then law-abiding black people should find a way to provide that protection themselves.

Progressives and Blacks
August 21, 2013

Sometimes I wonder when black people will reject the patronizing insults of white progressives and their black handmaidens. After CNN's Piers Morgan's interview with the key witness in the George Zimmerman trial, he said: "Rachel Jeantel is not uneducated. She's a smart cookie." That's a remarkable conclusion. Here's a nineteen-year-old young lady, still in high school, who cannot read cursive and appears to be barely literate. Morgan may have meant Jeantel is smart—for a black person.

Progressives treat blacks as victims in need of kid glove treatment and special favors, such as racial quotas and preferences. This approach has been tried in education for decades and has revealed itself a failure. I say it's time we explore other approaches. One approach is suggested by sports. Blacks excel—perhaps dominate is a better word—in sports such as basketball, football, and boxing to such an extent that blacks are 80 percent of professional basketball players, are 66 percent of professional football players, and, for decades, have dominated most professional boxing categories.

These outcomes should raise several questions. In sports, when have you heard a coach explain or excuse a black player's poor performance by blaming it on a "legacy of slavery" or on that player's being raised in a single-parent household? When have you heard sports standards called racist or culturally biased? I have yet to hear a player, much less a coach, speak such nonsense. In fact, the standards of performance in sports are just about the most ruthless anywhere. Excuses are not tolerated. Think about it. What happens to a player, black or white, who doesn't come up to a college basketball or football coach's standards? He's off the team. Players know this, and they make every effort to excel. They do so even more if they have aspirations to be a professional player. By the way, blacks also excel in the entertainment industry— another industry in which there's ruthless dog-eat-dog competition.

Seeing as blacks have demonstrated an ability to thrive in an environment of ruthless competition and demanding standards, there might be some gains from a similar school environment. Maybe we ought to have some schools in which youngsters are loaded up with homework, frequent tests, and demanding, top-notch teachers. In such schools, there would be no excuses for anything. Youngsters cut the mustard, or they're kicked out and put into some other school. I'm betting that a significant number of black youngsters would prosper in such an environment, just as they prosper in the highly competitive sports and entertainment environments.

Progressives' agenda calls for not only excuse-making but also dependency. Nowhere is this more obvious than it is in their efforts to get as many Americans as they can to be dependent on food stamps; however, in this part of their agenda, they offer racial equal opportunity. During President Barack Obama's years in office, the number of people receiving food stamps has skyrocketed by 39 percent. Professor Edward Lazear, chairman of the president's Council of Economic Advisers from 2006–09, wrote in a *Wall Street Journal* article titled "The Hidden Jobless Disaster" (June 5, 2013) that research done by University of Chicago's Casey Mulligan suggests "that because government benefits are lost when income rises, some people forgo poor jobs in lieu of government benefits—unemployment insurance, food stamps and disability benefits among the most obvious." Government handouts probably go a long way toward explaining the unprecedented number of Americans, close to 90 million, who are no longer looking for work.

This is all a part of the progressive agenda to hook Americans, particularly black Americans, on government handouts. In future elections, they will be able to claim that anyone who campaigns on cutting taxing and spending is a racist. That's what Rep. Charles Rangel, D-N.Y., said in denouncing the Republican 1994 call for tax cuts. He said, "It's not 'spic' or 'nigger' anymore. [Instead,] they say, 'Let's cut taxes.'"

When black Americans finally recognize the harm of the progressive agenda, I'm betting they will be the nation's most conservative people, for who else has been harmed by progressivism as much?

Racial Tradeoffs

October 9, 2013

Tradeoffs apply to our economic lives, as well as our political lives. That means getting more of one thing requires giving up something else. Let's look at some examples.

Black congressmen and black public officials in general, including Barack Obama, always side with teachers unions in their opposition to educational vouchers, tuition tax credits, charter schools, and other measures that would allow black parents to take their children out of failing public schools. Most black politicians and many black professionals take the position of the Rev. Jesse Jackson, who is on record as saying, "We shouldn't abandon the public schools."

Taking such a political stance is understandable because black congressmen and other black elected officials are part of a coalition. As such, they are expected to vote for things that other coalition members want in order that those coalition members vote for things that black politicians want. There's no question that these black public officials are getting something in return for their support of teachers unions and others who benefit from the educational status quo. The question not addressed by black people is whether what black politicians are getting for their support of a failed educational system is worth the sacrifice of whole generations of black youngsters, educationally handicapping them and making many virtually useless in the high-tech world of the twenty-first century.

Though many black politicians mouth that we should fix, not abandon, public schools, they themselves have abandoned public schools. They see their children as too precious to be sacrificed in the name of public education. While living in Chicago, Barack Obama sent his daughters to the prestigious University of Chicago Laboratory Schools. When he moved to Washington, President Obama enrolled his daughters in the prestigious Sidwell Friends School. According to a report by The Heritage Foundation, "exactly 52 percent of Congressional Black

Caucus members and 38 percent of Congressional Hispanic Caucus members sent at least one child to private school." Overall, only 6 percent of black students attend private school.

It's not just black politicians who fight tooth and nail against parental school choice and have their children in private schools. When President Obama's White House chief of staff Rahm Emanuel resigned and became mayor of Chicago, he did not enroll his children in the Windy City's public schools. He enrolled his son and two daughters in the University of Chicago Lab Schools. And members of Congress, regardless of race, are three to four times likelier than the public to send their children to private schools.

According to a 2004 Thomas B. Fordham Institute study, more than one in five public school teachers sent their children to private schools. In some cities, the figure is much higher. In Philadelphia, 44 percent of the teachers put their children in private schools; in Cincinnati, it's 41 percent, and Chicago (39 percent) and Rochester, N.Y. (38 percent), also have high figures. In the San Francisco-Oakland area, 34 percent of public school teachers enroll their children in private schools, and in New York City, it's 33 percent.

Only 11 percent of all parents enroll their children in private schools. The fact that so many public school teachers enroll their own children in private schools ought to raise questions. After all, what would you think, after having accepted a dinner invitation, if you discovered that the owner, chef, waiters, and busboys at the restaurant to which you were being taken don't eat there? That would suggest they have some inside information from which you might benefit.

I don't think anything that black politicians get from the National Education Association, the American Federation of Teachers, the NAACP (many members are teachers), the National Urban League, or others who have a vested financial interest in a failed educational system is worth committing whole generations of black youngsters to educational mediocrity. The prospects for a change are not good, particularly in light of the new fact that the NAACP is being wooed to join the AFL-CIO.

Racial Tradeoffs: Part II
October 16, 2013

Last week's column discussed the political tradeoffs made by black politicians and civil rights organizations that condemn whole generations of black youngsters to failing schools (http://tinyurl.com/6mmlsf). Similar political tradeoffs in labor markets condemn many blacks, particularly black youths, to high rates of unemployment and reduced economic opportunities. Let's look at this, starting with a few historical facts.

Today white teen unemployment is about 20 percent, while that for blacks is about 40 percent and more than 50 percent in some cities. In 1948, the unemployment rate of black sixteen-year-old and seventeen-year-old males was 9.4 percent, whereas that of whites was 10.2 percent. Up until the late 1950s, both black teens and black adults were more active in the labor market than their white counterparts. In fact, in 1910, 71 percent of black males older than nine were employed, compared with 51 percent for whites. As early as 1890, the duration of unemployment among blacks was shorter than it was among whites, whereas today unemployment is both higher and longer lasting among blacks than among whites.

It would be sheer lunacy to attempt to explain these more favorable employment statistics by suggesting that during earlier periods, blacks faced less racial discrimination. What best explains the loss of teenage employment opportunities is increases in minimum wage laws. There's little dispute within the economics profession that higher minimum wages discriminate against the employment of the least skilled worker. Such a demographic is disproportionately represented by black teenagers.

Despite these devastating effects, the entire Congressional Black Caucus and President Barack Obama support increases in minimum wages. At the state and local levels of government, there is similar black political support for higher state and local minimum wages, sometimes called "living wages." It's not just minimum wages to which black politicians give support; they give support to the Davis-Bacon Act, a Depression-era mega minimum wage law with racist origins. The Davis-Bacon Act mandates that "prevailing wages" be paid on all federally financed or assisted construction projects. It's a pro-union law that discriminates against both nonunionized black construction contractors and black workers.

During the 1931 Davis-Bacon Act legislative debates, quite a few congressmen expressed their racist intentions, such as Rep. Miles Allgood, D-Ala., who said: "Reference has been made to a contractor from Alabama who went to New York with bootleg labor. This is a fact. That contractor has cheap colored labor that he transports, and he puts them in cabins, and it is labor of that sort that is in competition with white labor throughout the country." Rep. John Cochran, D-Mo., said he had "received numerous complaints . . . about Southern contractors employing low-paid colored mechanics getting work and bringing the employees from the South." Rep. William Upshaw, D-Ga., spoke of the "superabundance or large aggregation of Negro labor." American Federation of Labor President William Green complained, "Colored labor is being sought to demoralize wage rates." Though today's Davis-Bacon supporters don't use the same language, the racially discriminatory effects are the same.

President Obama, the Congressional Black Caucus, black state and local politicians, and civil rights organizations are neither naive nor stupid. They have been made aware of the unemployment effects of the labor laws they support; however, they are part of a political coalition. In order to get labor unions, environmental groups, business groups, and other vested interests to support their handout agenda and make campaign contributions, they must give political support to what these groups want. They must support minimum wage increases even though the increases condemn generations of black youths to high unemployment rates. They must support Davis-Bacon Act restrictions even though those restrictions handicap black contractors and nonunion construction workers.

I can't imagine what black politicians and civil rights groups are getting that's worth condemning black youths to a high rate of unemployment and its devastating effects on upward economic mobility, but then again, I'm not a politician.

Blacks and Obama

December 4, 2013

In a March 2008 column, I criticized pundits' concerns about whether America was ready for Barack Obama, suggesting that the more important issue was whether black people could afford Obama. I proposed that we look at it in the context of a historical tidbit.

In 1947, Jackie Robinson, after signing a contract with the Brooklyn Dodgers organization, broke the color barrier in Major League Baseball. He encountered open racist taunts and slurs from fans, opposing team players, and even some members of his own team. Despite that, his batting average was nearly .300 in his first year. He led the National League in stolen bases and won the first Rookie of the Year award. There's no sense of justice that requires a player to be as good as Robinson in order to have a chance in the major leagues, but the hard fact of the matter is that as the first black player, he had to be.

In 1947, black people could not afford an incompetent black baseball player. Today we can. The simple reason is that as a result of the excellence of Robinson—and many others who followed him, such as Satchel Paige, Don Newcombe, Larry Doby, and Roy Campanella—today no one in his right mind, watching the incompetence of a particular black player, could say, "Those blacks can't play baseball."

In that March 2008 column, I argued that for the nation—but more importantly, for black people—the first black president should be the caliber of a Jackie Robinson, and Barack Obama is not. Obama has charisma and charm, but in terms of character, values, experience, and understanding, he is no Jackie Robinson. In addition to those deficiencies, Obama became the first person in US history to be elected to the highest office in the land while having a long history of associations with people who hate our nation, such as the Rev. Jeremiah Wright, Obama's pastor for twenty years, who preached that blacks should sing not "God bless America" but "God damn America." Then there's Obama's association with William Ayers, formerly a member of the

Weather Underground, an anti-US group that bombed the Pentagon, US Capitol, and other government buildings. Ayers, in the wake of the 9/11 terrorist attack, told a *New York Times* reporter, "I don't regret setting bombs.... I feel we didn't do enough."

Obama's electoral success is truly a remarkable commentary on the goodness of the American people. A 2008 NBC News/*Wall Street Journal* poll reported "that 17 percent were enthusiastic about Obama being the first African American President, 70 percent were comfortable or indifferent, and 13 percent had reservations or were uncomfortable." I'm seventy-seven years old. For almost all of my life, a black's becoming the president of the United States was at best a pipe dream. Obama's electoral success further confirms what I've often held: The civil rights struggle in America is over, and it's won. At one time, black Americans did not have the constitutional guarantees enjoyed by white Americans; now we do. The fact that the civil rights struggle is over and won does not mean that there are not major problems confronting many members of the black community, but they are not civil rights problems and have little or nothing to do with racial discrimination.

There is every indication to suggest that Obama's presidency will be seen as a failure similar to that of Jimmy Carter's. That's bad news for the nation but especially bad news for black Americans. No white presidential candidate had to live down the disgraced presidency of Carter, but I'm all too fearful that a future black presidential candidate will find himself carrying the heavy baggage of a failed black president. That's not a problem for white liberals who voted for Obama—they received their one-time guilt-relieving dose from voting for a black man to be president—but it is a problem for future generations of black Americans. But there's one excuse black people can make; we can claim that Obama is not an authentic black person but, as *The New York Times* might call him, a white black person.

Black People Duped

March 5, 2014

People in the media and academia are mostly leftists hellbent on growing government and controlling our lives. Black people, their politicians, and civil rights organizations have become unwitting accomplices. The leftist pretense of concern for the well-being of black people confers upon them an aura of moral superiority and, as such, gives more credibility to their calls for increasing government control over our lives.

Ordinary black people have been sold on the importance of electing blacks to high public office. After centuries of black people having been barred from high elected office, no decent American can have anything against their wider participation in our political system. For several decades, blacks have held significant political power, in the form of being mayors and dominant forces on city councils in major cities such as Philadelphia, Detroit, Washington, Memphis, Tennessee, Atlanta, Baltimore, New Orleans, Oakland, California, Newark, New Jersey, and Cincinnati. In these cities, blacks have held administrative offices such as school superintendent, school principal, and chief of police. Plus, there's the precedent-setting fact of there being forty-four black members of Congress and a black president.

What has this political power meant for the significant socioeconomic problems faced by a large segment of the black community? Clearly, it has done little or nothing for academic achievement; the number of black students scoring proficient is far below the national average. It is a disgrace—and ought to be a source of shame—to know that the average white seventh- or eighth-grader can run circles around the average black twelfth-grader in most academic subjects. The political and education establishment tells us that the solution lies in higher budgets, but the fact of business is that some of the worst public school districts have the highest spending per student. Washington, D.C., for example, spends more than $29,000 per student and scores at nearly the bottom in academic achievement.

Each year, roughly 7,000—and as high as 9,000—blacks are murdered. Ninety-four percent of the time, the murderer is another black person. According to the Bureau of Justice Statistics, between 1976 and 2011, there were 279,384 black murder victims. Contrast this with the fact that black fatalities during the Korean War (3,075), Vietnam War (7,243), and wars since 1980 (about 8,200) total about 18,500. Young black males have a greater chance of reaching maturity on the battlefields than on the streets of Philadelphia, Chicago, Detroit, Oakland, Newark, and other cities. Black political power and massive city budgets have done absolutely nothing to ameliorate this problem of black insecurity.

Most of the problems faced by the black community have their roots in a black culture that differs significantly from the black culture of yesteryear. Today only 35 percent of black children are raised in two-parent households, but as far back as 1880, in Philadelphia, 75 percent of black children were raised in two-parent households—and it was as high as 85 percent in other places. Even during slavery, in which marriage was forbidden, most black children were raised with two biological parents. The black family managed to survive several centuries of slavery and generations of the harshest racism and Jim Crow, to ultimately become destroyed by the welfare state. The black family has fallen victim to the vision fostered by some intellectuals that, in the words of a sociology professor in the 1960s, "it has yet to be shown that the absence of a father was directly responsible for any of the supposed deficiencies of broken homes." The real issue to these intellectuals "is not the lack of male presence but the lack of male income." That suggests that fathers can be replaced by a welfare check. The weakened black family gives rise to problems such has high crime, predation, and other forms of antisocial behavior.

The cultural problems that affect many black people are challenging and not pleasant to talk about, but incorrectly attributing those problems to racism and racial discrimination, a need for more political power, and a need for greater public spending condemns millions of blacks to the degradation and despair of the welfare state.

Sex and Race Equality
April 2, 2014

There are several race and sex issues that need addressing. Let's look at a few of them with an ear to these questions: Should we insist upon equal treatment of people by race and sex or tolerate differences in treatment? And just how equal are people by race and sex in the first place?

According to the National Institutes of Health, male infants one to three months old should be fed 472 to 572 calories per day, whereas their female counterparts should receive 438 to 521 calories per day (http://tinyurl.com/nj35qvh). That's an official sex-based caloric 10 percent ripoff of baby females. In addition to this government-sanctioned war on women, one wonders whether the NIH has a race-based caloric ripoff where they recommend that black newborns receive fewer calories than white newborns.

Anyone who watches "Lockdown" on television will see gross racial segregation in California prisons—such as Pelican Bay, Corcoran, and San Quentin—where prisoners are housed by race. Colored signs have hung above living quarters—for example, blue for black inmates, white for white, red, green, or pink for Hispanic, and yellow for others (http://tinyurl.com/m7n4df8). Sometimes inmate yard times are racially segregated. Being seventy-eight years old and having lived through an era in which I saw signs for white and colored water fountains, waiting rooms, and toilets, I find California's racial segregation practices offensive. Prison Law Office, a public interest law firm that seeks justice for prisoners, criticizes such flagrant racial segregation policy, but I question its sincerity. Criticizing racial segregation while not uttering one word about flagrant prison sex segregation is at the minimum two-faced. In my book, if the all-male military bastion is being eliminated, it stands to reason that prison segregation by sex should be eliminated. No decent American would accept the idea of a prison for blacks and another one for whites. If we value equality, we shouldn't accept one prison for men and another for women. There should be integration.

Speaking of sex segregation, there have been recent calls to end the ban on women in combat units, but there's no mention of the Army's sexist physical fitness test. For a male seventeen to twenty-one years of age to pass, he must do thirty-five pushups, do forty-seven situps, and run two miles in sixteen minutes, thirty-six seconds. His female counterpart, who receives the same pay, can pass the fitness test by doing a mere thirteen pushups, doing forty-seven situps, and running two miles in nineteen minutes, forty-two seconds (http://tinyurl.com/yaphmzl). How can anyone who values equality and self-respect tolerate this gross discrimination? You say, "Williams, what's your solution?" I say we should either force women to come up to the physical fitness standards for men or pass men who meet the female standards of fitness. Maybe we should ask our adversaries which is better—raising female fitness standards or lowering those of males.

There are a couple of other inequalities that cannot be justified, much less tolerated, in a society that values equality. Jews are only 3 percent of the US population, but they take 39 percent of US Nobel laureates. That's a gross disparity, for which there is no moral justification. Ask any academic, intellectual, or civil rights leader and he'll tell you that equality and diversity means that people are to be represented across socioeconomic lines according to their numerical representation in the population. The fact that Jews are 39 percent of US Nobel laureates can mean only one thing—they are taking the rightful Nobel laureates of other racial groups.

Jews are not the only people taking more than their fair share of things. Blacks are 13 percent of the population but have taken nearly 80 percent of the player jobs in the National Basketball Association. Compounding that injustice, they are highest-paid NBA players. Blacks are also guilty of taking 66 percent, an unfair share, of professional football jobs.

Any American sharing the value of race and sex equality and diversity should find these and other differences offensive and demand that the liberal and progressive elements in society eliminate them.

Coming End to Racial Preferences

May 7, 2014

Last week's US Supreme Court 6–2 ruling in Schuette v. Coalition to Defend Affirmative Action et al. upheld Michigan's constitutional amendment that bans racial preferences in admission to its public universities. Justice Sonia Sotomayor lashed out at her colleagues in a bitter dissent, calling them "out of touch with reality." She went on to make the incredible argument that the amendment, which explicitly forbids racial discrimination, itself amounts to racial discrimination. Her argument was that permissible "race-sensitive admissions policies," the new name for racial preferences, both serve the compelling interest of obtaining the educational benefits that flow from a diverse student body and inure people to the benefit of racial minorities. By the way, no one has come up with hard evidence of the supposed "educational benefits" that come from a racially mixed student body, and there's mounting evidence of harm done to minorities through academic mismatching.

Far more important than the legal battles over racial preferences in college admissions is the question of why they are being called for in the first place. The SAT's purpose is to predict how well a student will perform in college classes. Blacks score at least a hundred points lower than whites in each of the assessment areas—critical reading, math, and writing. Asians score higher than whites in math and writing. SAT scores are also reported for Mexican-Americans, Puerto Ricans, Indians, and others. Blacks score lower than these minorities, who themselves score lower than whites and Asians.

If we reject the racist notion of mental inferiority of blacks, holding that blacks can never compete academically and that "racially sensitive" college admissions are needed in perpetuity, we must seek an explanation for their relatively poor academic performance. My long-time colleague and friend Dr. Thomas Sowell offers some evidence in a recent column, "Will Dunbar Rise Again?" (http://tinyurl.com/ mjt39ks). Paul Laurence Dunbar High School was founded in 1870 as the first public high school in the nation for black students. As far back as 1899, when tests were given in Washington's four academic high schools, Dunbar students scored higher than students in two of the three white high schools. Over the first several decades of the twentieth century, about 80 percent of Dunbar graduates went on to college, a percentage far greater than that of high-school graduates of any race in the country at large at the time. Most blacks went to inexpensive local colleges, but among those who went on to Ivy League and other elite colleges, a significant number graduated Phi Beta Kappa. At one time, Dunbar graduates were admitted to Dartmouth or Harvard without having to take an entrance exam. One would have to be a lunatic to chalk up this academic success, in the early to mid-1900s, to Sotomayor's "race-sensitive admissions policies."

The shame of the nation is that poor black children are trapped in terrible schools. But worse than that is that white liberals, black politicians, and civil rights leaders, perhaps unwittingly, have taken steps to ensure that black children remain trapped. Sowell says, "Of all the cynical frauds of the Obama administration, few are so despicable as sacrificing the education of poor and minority children to the interests of the teachers' unions." Attorney General Eric Holder's hostility, along with that of the teachers unions, toward the spread of charter schools is just one of the signs of that cynicism. Holder's threats against schools that discipline more black students than he thinks they should add official support to a hostile learning environment.

The weakening of racial preferences in college admissions can be beneficial if it can focus our attention on the causes of the huge gap in academic achievement between blacks and whites and Asians. Worrying about what happens when blacks are trying to get in to college is too late—as a matter of fact, twelve years late.

A Lesson on Racial Discrimination

May 14, 2014

Donald Sterling, Los Angeles Clippers owner, was recorded by his mistress making some crude racist remarks. Since then, Sterling's racist comments have dominated the news, from talk radio to late-night shows. A few politicians have weighed in, with President Barack Obama congratulating the NBA for its sanctions against Sterling. There's little defense for Sterling, save his constitutional right to make racist remarks. But in a sea of self-righteous indignation, I think we're missing the most valuable lesson that we can learn from this affair—a lesson that's particularly important for black Americans.

Though Sterling might be a racist, there's an important "so what?" Does he act in ways commonly attributed to racists? Let's look at his employment policy. This season, Sterling paid his top three players salaries totaling over $46 million. His twenty-person roster payroll totaled over $73 million. Here are a couple of questions for you: What race are the players whom racist Sterling paid the highest salaries? What race dominated the twenty-man roster? The fact of business is that Sterling's highest-paid players are black, and 85 percent of Clippers players are black. Down through the years, hundreds of US corporations have faced charges of racism, and many have been subjects of Equal Employment Opportunity Commission investigations, but none of them had such a favorable employment and wage policy as Sterling. How does one explain this? People with limited thinking ability might conclude that Sterling is a racist in his private life but a nice card-carrying liberal in his public life, manifested by his hiring so many blacks, not to mention paying Doc Rivers, the Clippers' black head coach, a healthy $7 million a year. The likelier explanation is given no attention at all.

Let's use a bit of simple economics to analyze the contrast in Sterling's private and public behavior. First, professional basketball is featured by considerable market competition. There's an open opportunity in the acquisition of basketball playing skills. Youngsters just buy a basketball and shoot hoops. There's open competition in joining both high school and college teams. You just sign up for tryouts in high school and get noticed by college scouts. Then there's considerable competition among the NBA teams in the acquisition of the best college players. Minorities and less preferred people always do better when there are open markets instead of regulated markets.

Recently deceased Nobel Prize-winning economist Gary Becker pointed this phenomenon out some years ago in his path-breaking study "The Economics of Discrimination." Many people think that it takes government to eliminate racial discrimination, but economic theory predicts the opposite. Market competition imposes inescapable profit penalties on for-profit enterprises when they make employment decisions on any basis other than worker productivity. Professor Becker's study of racial discrimination upended the view that discriminatory bias benefits those who discriminate. He demonstrated that racial discrimination is less likely in the most competitive industries, which need to hire the best workers.

According to *Forbes* magazine, the Los Angeles Clippers would sell for $575 million. Ask yourself what the Clippers would sell for if Sterling were a racist in his public life and hired only white players. All the evidence suggests that would be a grossly losing proposition on at least two counts. Percentage-wise, blacks more so than whites excel in basketball. That's not to say that it is impossible to recruit a team of first-rate, excellent white players. However, because there is a smaller number of top-tier white players relative to black players, the recruitment costs would be prohibitive. In other words, a team of excellent white players would be far costlier to field than a team of excellent black players. It's simply a matter of supply and demand.

The takeaway from the Sterling affair is that we should mount not a moral crusade but an economic liberty crusade. In other words, eliminate union restrictions, wage controls, occupational and business licensure, and other anti-free market restrictions. Make opportunity depend on one's productivity.

White Privilege

May 28, 2014

What would you think if your eight-year-old came home and told you that "white privilege is something that white people have, meaning they have an advantage in a lot of things and they can get a job more easily"? You would have heard that at the recent fifteenth annual White Privilege Conference in Madison, Wisconsin, attended by 2,500 public-school teachers, administrators, and students from across the nation (http://tinyurl.com/lkoqj9b).

The average parent has no idea of the devious indoctrination going on in classrooms in many public schools. What follows are some of the lessons of the conference.

In one of the workshops, "Examining White Privilege and Building Foundations for Social Justice Thinking in the Elementary Classroom," educators Rosemary Colt and Diana Reeves told how teachers can "insert social justice, anti-racist information" into their lessons that "even little kids" can understand.

Kim Radersma, a former high school English teacher, hosted a session titled "Stories from the front lines of education: Confessions of a white, high school English teacher." She said that teaching is a purely political act and that neutral people should "get the f—— out of education" (http://tinyurl.com/q5adt2d). She also explained: "Being a white person who does anti-racist work is like being an alcoholic. I will never be recovered by my alcoholism, to use the metaphor. I have to every day wake up and acknowledge that I am so deeply embedded with racist thoughts and notions and actions in my body that I have to choose every day to do anti-racist work and think in an anti-racist way" (http://tinyurl.com/q4z969q).

But the propaganda and lunacy go even deeper. Jacqueline Battalora, professor of sociology and criminal justice at Saint Xavier University, informed conference participants that "white people did not exist before 1681. Again, white people did not exist on planet Earth until 1681" (http://tinyurl.com/lkoqj9b). That's truly incredible. If Professor Battalora is correct, how are we to identify William Shakespeare (1564), Sir Isaac Newton (1642), John Locke (1632), Leonardo da Vinci (1452), and especially dear Plato (428 B.C.)? Were these men people of color, or did they not exist?

John A. Powell, a University of California, Berkeley law professor, told his audience, "And right now, I'm going to suggest to you that race is driving almost everything that's happening in the country." He explained the Hurricane Katrina disaster in New Orleans by saying, "They took money away from protecting the levees because the levees were protecting black people."

Stephanie Baran's message to conference participants was that capitalism is the cause of racism in the world today. This adjunct professor at Kankakee Community College, who calls herself a vulgar Marxist, added that racism was invented in Colonial America by white capitalists as a tool to divide labor and keep the working class in their place.

Educator Paul Kivel explained what he sees as Christian hegemony, saying, "Very simply, I define it as the everyday pervasive, deep-seated, and institutionalized dominance of Christian values, Christian institutions, leaders, and Christians as a group, primarily for the benefit of Christian ruling elites."

Speaker Leonard Zeskind—according to the MacIver Institute, which covered the event—explained that "the longer you are in the tea party the more racist you become." He added, "Parents put their kids in private schools because they're racist."

University of Iowa Professor Adrien Wing gave some of her observations about white privilege, asking, "Does having a black president change that? Has it changed that? Unfortunately, it hasn't. . . . [President Obama] ends up being the front man for the system. . . . He works for the master of the system of white privilege."

I can't imagine people being stupid enough to believe all that was said at the White Privilege Conference. There's something else at work. I think it's white guilt. That's why, for almost three decades, there has appeared on my website a certificate of amnesty and pardon that I've granted to Americans of European ancestry in the hope that they stop feeling guilty and stop acting like fools (http://tinyurl .com/opd8vgd).

Slavery Reparations

June 18, 2014

Calls for slavery reparations have returned with the publication of Ta-Nehisi Coates's "The Case for Reparations" in *The Atlantic* magazine (May 21, 2014). In making his argument, Coates goes through the horrors of slavery, Reconstruction, Jim Crow, and gross racial discrimination.

First off, let me say that I agree with reparations advocates that slavery was a horrible, despicable violation of basic human rights. The gross discrimination that followed emancipation made a mockery of the guarantees of the US Constitution. I also agree that slave owners and slave traders should make reparations to those whom they enslaved. The problem, of course, is that slaves, slave owners, and slave traders are all dead. Thus, punishing perpetrators and compensating victims is out of the hands of the living.

Punishing perpetrators and compensating victims is not what reparations advocates want. They want government to compensate today's blacks for the bondage suffered by our ancestors. But there's a problem. Government has no resources of its very own. The only way for government to give one American a dollar is to first—through intimidation, threats, and coercion—confiscate that dollar from some other American. Therefore, if anybody cares, a moral question arises. What moral principle justifies punishing a white of today to compensate a black of today for what a white of yesterday did to a black of yesterday?

There's another moral or fairness issue. A large percentage, if not most, of today's Americans—be they of European, Asian, African, or Latin ancestry don't even go back three or four generations as American citizens. Their ancestors arrived on our shores long after slavery. What standard of justice justifies their being taxed to compensate blacks for slavery? For example, in 1956, thousands of Hungarians fled the brutality of the USSR to settle in the United States. What do Hungarians owe blacks for slavery?

There's another thorny issue. During slavery, some free blacks purchased other blacks as a means to free family members. But other blacks owned slaves for the same reason whites owned slaves—to work farms or plantations. Are descendants of these slaveholding blacks eligible for and deserving of reparations?

When African slavery began, there was no way Europeans could have enslaved millions of Africans. They had no immunity from diseases that flourished in tropical Africa. Capturing Africans to sell into slavery was done by Arabs and black Africans. Would reparations advocates demand that citizens of Ghana, Ivory Coast, Nigeria, Kenya, and several Muslim states tax themselves to make reparation payments to progeny of people whom their ancestors helped to enslave?

Reparations advocates make the foolish unchallenged argument that the United States became rich on the backs of free black labor. That's nonsense that cannot be supported by fact. Slavery doesn't have a very good record of producing wealth. Slavery was all over the South, and it was outlawed in most of the North. Buying into the reparations argument about the riches of slavery, one would conclude that the antebellum South was rich and the slave-starved North was poor. The truth of the matter is just the opposite. In fact, the poorest states and regions of our nation were places where slavery flourished—Mississippi, Alabama, and Georgia—whereas the richest states and regions were those where slavery was absent: Pennsylvania, New York, and Massachusetts.

One of the most ignored facts about slavery's tragic history—and it's virtually a secret today—is that slavery was a worldwide institution for thousands of years. It did not become a moral issue until the eighteenth century. Plus, the moral crusade against slavery started in the West, most notably England.

I think the call for slavery reparations is simply another hustle. Advocates are not demanding that government send checks to individual black people. They want taxpayer money to be put into some kind of reparations fund from which black leaders decide who receives how much and for what purpose.

Do Blacks Need Favors?
July 23, 2014

Earlier this month, the fiftieth anniversary of the Civil Rights Act was celebrated. During the act's legislative debate, then-Sen. Hubert Humphrey, responding to predictions, promised, "I'll eat my hat if this leads to racial quotas." I don't know whether Humphrey got around to keeping his promise, but here's my question: Is it within the capacity of black Americans to make it in this society without the special favors variously called racial preferences, quotas, affirmative action, and race-sensitive policies? What might a "yes" answer to that question assume and imply about blacks? Likewise, what would a "no" answer assume and imply? Let's look at it.

There are some areas of black life in which excellence can be found without the slightest hint of racial preferences. Young blacks dominate basketball, football, and some track-and-field events despite the fact that there has been a history of gross racial discrimination in those activities. Blacks are also prominent in several areas of the entertainment industry. Those observations mean that racial discrimination alone is not an insurmountable barrier to success. By the way, I can't think of any two fields with more ruthless competition.

You say, "OK, Williams, everyone knows about the success of blacks in sports and entertainment, but what about the intellectual arena?" A few inner-city junior high and high schools have produced black champion chess players, schools such as Philadelphia's Roberts Vaux High School and New York's Edward R. Murrow High School. Last year, two black teens—from Intermediate School 318 Eugenio Maria de Hostos in Brooklyn, New York—won the national high school chess championship. All of this is in addition to quite a few black international masters and grandmasters in chess. Moreover, there's a long list of former and current black inventors and scientists. So there's no question that black people have the capacity to compete intellectually.

Civil rights organizations and their progressive allies, who all but suggest that blacks cannot achieve unless they are given special privileges, grossly insult and demean black people. But worse than that, when civil rights organizations and their progressive allies pursue special privileges for blacks in college admissions and when they attack academic performance standards as racially discriminatory, they are aiding and abetting an education establishment that delivers fraudulent education. They let educators off the hook, thereby enabling them to continue to produce educational fraud.

You say, "What do you mean by educational fraud, Williams?" There are many inputs to education that are beyond the control of educators, such as poor home environment, derelict parental oversight, and students with minds alien and hostile to the education process. But there's one thing entirely within the control of the education establishment. That is the conferral of a high school diploma. When a school confers a diploma upon a student, it attests that the student has mastered the twelfth-grade levels of reading, writing, and arithmetic. If, in fact, the student cannot perform at the seventh- or eighth-grade levels, the school has committed gross fraud. Even worse is the fact that black people, including those holding fraudulent diplomas, are completely unaware. It has absolutely nothing to do with racial discrimination. In fact, black education is the worst in cities where blacks have been the mayor, chief of police, and superintendent of schools and where most of the teachers and principals are black.

Racial preferences in college admissions give elementary schools, middle schools, and high schools a free hand to continue their destructive educational policy. If colleges did not have special admissions practices for black students, there would be far fewer blacks in colleges, and the fraud would be more apparent to parents. They might begin to ask why so many blacks with high school diplomas could not get into college.

If the civil rights establishment and the progressives have their way, blacks will have to rely on special privileges in perpetuity.

Please Stop Helping Us
July 30, 2014

While reading the first chapter of Jason Riley's new book, *Please Stop Helping Us*, I thought about Will Rogers's Prohibition-era observation that "Oklahomans vote dry as long as they can stagger to the polls." Demonstrative of similar dedication, one member of Congress told Vanderbilt University political scientist Carol Swain that "one of the advantages and disadvantages of representing blacks is their shameless loyalty.... You can almost get away with raping babies and be forgiven. You don't have any vigilance about your performance." In my opinion, there appear to be no standards of performance low enough for blacks to lose their loyalty to their black political representatives.

Riley says that between 1970 and 2001, the number of black elected officials skyrocketed from fewer than 1,500 to more than 9,000, but black poverty has remained roughly the same. Between 1940 and 1960, when black political power was virtually nonexistent, the black poverty rate fell from 87 percent to 47 percent. Riley points out that there has been significant achievement among the black middle class but that wide black-white gaps remain with respect to income, educational achievement, unemployment, labor force participation, incarceration rates, and other measures. Despite political gains, there have been dramatic reversals in teen unemployment, crime, out-of-wedlock births, and family stability. Political power is neither a necessary nor a sufficient condition for socioeconomic progress.

Riley lays out the devastating deal black political leaders and civil rights leaders have made with labor unions, in his aptly named chapter "Mandating Unemployment." Black leaders of the past recognized that labor unions were hostile to the interests of ordinary blacks. Frederick Douglass, in his 1874 essay "The Folly, Tyranny, and Wickedness of Labor Unions," argued that unions were not friends of blacks. W. E. B. Du Bois called unions "the greatest enemy of the black working man." Booker T. Washington also opposed unions because of their adverse impact on blacks.

Today's black leaders have little reservation about giving their support to union policies that harm their constituents. They support minimum wage increases, which have had a devastating impact on black employment, particularly that of teenagers. Recently, black teen unemployment reached 44 percent, but few people realize that during the late 1940s, before rapid minimum wage escalation, it was less than 10 percent and lower than white teen unemployment. Black leaders also give their support to a super-minimum wage law known as the Davis-Bacon Act of 1931. The legislative history of Davis-Bacon makes clear that its union and congressional supporters sought to eliminate black employment in the construction trades.

Riley's "Educational Freedom" chapter details the sorry story of black education. Between 1970 and today, educational spending has tripled and the school workforce has doubled, far outpacing student enrollment. Despite these massive increases in resources, black academic achievement is a national disgrace. According to the National Assessment of Educational Progress, known as the nation's report card, black seventeen-year-olds score at the same level as white thirteen-year-olds in reading and math. White thirteen-year-olds score higher than black seventeen-year-olds in science.

A number of studies show that black students who attend private and charter schools do far better than their peers in public schools. If there were greater parental choice, through educational vouchers, black achievement would be higher. However, teachers unions see school choice as a threat to their monopoly, and virtually every black politician, including the president, backs the teachers unions.

At an 1865 gathering of the Massachusetts Anti-Slavery Society, Douglass said everybody had asked, "What should we do with the Negro?" Douglass said: "I have had but one answer from the beginning. Do nothing with us! Your doing with us has already played the mischief with us." Later on, Washington explained, "It is important and right that all privileges of the law be ours, but it is vastly more important that we be prepared for the exercise of these privileges." It's the abandonment of these visions that accounts for the many problems of today that Riley's book does a masterful job of explaining.

Blacks Must Confront Reality

August 27, 2014

Though racial discrimination exists, it is nowhere near the barrier it once was. The relevant question is: How much of what we see today can be explained by racial discrimination? This is an important question because if we conclude that racial discrimination is the major cause of black problems when it isn't, then effective solutions will be elusive forever. To begin to get a handle on the answer, let's pull up a few historical facts about black Americans.

In 1950, female-headed households were 18 percent of the black population. Today it's close to 70 percent. One study of nineteenth-century slave families found that in up to three-fourths of the families, all the children lived with the biological mother and father. In 1925 New York City, 85 percent of black households were two-parent households. Herbert Gutman, author of *The Black Family in Slavery and Freedom, 1750–1925*, reports, "Five in six children under the age of six lived with both parents." Also, both during slavery and as late as 1920, a teenage girl raising a child without a man present was rare among blacks.

A study of 1880 family structure in Philadelphia found that three-quarters of black families were nuclear families (composed of two parents and children). What is significant, given today's arguments that slavery and discrimination decimated the black family structure, is the fact that years ago, there were only slight differences in family structure among racial groups.

Coupled with the dramatic breakdown in the black family structure has been an astonishing growth in the rate of illegitimacy. The black illegitimacy rate in 1940 was about 14 percent; black illegitimacy today is over 70 percent, and in some cities, it is over 80 percent.

The point of bringing up these historical facts is to ask this question, with a bit of sarcasm: Is the reason the black family was far healthier in the late 1800s and 1900s that back then there was far less racial discrimination and there were greater opportunities? Or did what experts call the "legacy of slavery" wait several generations to victimize today's blacks?

The Census Bureau pegs the poverty rate among blacks at 28.1 percent. A statistic that one never hears about is that the poverty rate among intact married black families has been in the single digits for more than two decades, currently at 8.4 percent. Weak family structures not only spell poverty and dependency but also contribute to the social pathology seen in many black communities—for example, violence and predatory sex. Each year, roughly 7,000 blacks are murdered. Ninety-four percent of the time, the murderer is another black person. Though blacks are 13 percent of the nation's population, they account for more than 50 percent of homicide victims. Nationally, the black homicide victimization rate is six times that of whites, and in some cities, it's twenty-two times that of whites. According to the Bureau of Justice Statistics, between 1976 and 2011, there were 279,384 black murder victims. Coupled with being most of the nation's homicide victims, blacks are also major victims of violent personal crimes, such as assault, rape, and robbery.

To put this violence in perspective, black fatalities during the Korean War (3,075), Vietnam War (7,243), and all wars since 1980 (about 8,200) come to about 18,500, a number that pales in comparison with black loss of life at home. Young black males had a greater chance of reaching maturity on the battlefields of Iraq and Afghanistan than on the streets of Philadelphia, Chicago, Detroit, Oakland, Newark, and other cities.

The black academic achievement gap is a disaster. Often, black twelfth-graders can read, write, and deal with scientific and math problems at only the level of white sixth-graders. This doesn't bode well for success in college or passing civil service exams.

If it is assumed that problems that have a devastating impact on black well-being are a result of racial discrimination and a "legacy of slavery" when they are not, resources spent pursuing a civil rights strategy will yield disappointing results.

PART IV

Education

Primary and secondary education in our country is in shambles. Education spending in the United States has more than doubled since 1970. The total inflation-adjusted cost of sending a pupil from kindergarten through high school in 1970 was $57,600. Today, that cost is $164,400. Over that interval academic proficiency has either declined or remained stagnant. It turns out that over 50 percent of incoming college freshmen are not college ready and must enroll in remedial courses in English and mathematics.

I do not think that it is unreasonable to conclude that high schools confer fraudulent diplomas to a very large percentage of their students. Some might consider fraud too strong a term. A high school diploma attests that the bearer has a twelfth-grade level of educational preparedness in reading, writing, and arithmetic. If the student's academic performance is well below that level the diploma is fraudulent.

The education establishment will attempt to excuse their performance saying that the poor educational outcomes are because of factors far beyond their control. They are absolutely correct in pointing out that many parents do not take an active role in their children's education. Many students are alien and hostile to the education process. However, the decision to confer a high school diploma is entirely within the power of educators. And, is it not dishonest to confer a high school diploma on a youngster who has not mastered the high school curricula?

Recently, there has been an exposure of another kind of dishonesty within the education establishment. In a number of big cities, such as Philadelphia, Atlanta, Detroit, and Washington, D.C., widespread teacher cheating has been discovered. Teachers have gone as far as to have weekend pizza parties to correct student answers on standard tests before turning them in. In at least one case, teachers who refused to cheat were punished and forced out. Several state attorneys generals have filed criminal charges against cheating teachers.

The primary and secondary education received by white students is nothing to write home about but that received by black students is nothing less than a disaster. The National Assessment of Educational Progress, published by the US Department of Education's National Center for Education Statistics, sometimes referred to as the Nation's Report Card, measures student performance in the fourth, eighth, and twelfth grades. The NAEP academic achievement score earned by the average black students aged seventeen means that he cannot read, write, do math, and science with any greater facility than whites who are four years younger and still in junior high school.

To highlight some of the disaster, only 7 percent of Detroit's students scored high enough on the National Assessment of Educational Progress test in 2011 to be rated "proficient" or better in reading, and only 4 percent scored high enough to be rated "proficient" or better in math. In 2013, 46 percent of Philadelphia eighth-graders scored below basic, and 35 percent scored basic in math. Below basic is a score meaning that a student is unable to demonstrate even partial mastery of knowledge and skills fundamental for proficient work at his grade level. Basic indicates only partial mastery. It's a similar story in reading, with 42 percent below basic and 41 percent basic. Educators say that more money is needed. However, Washington, D.C., spends $29,409 per pupil, near the top nationwide, and in terms of academic achievement, its students are nearly the nation's worst.

What makes the education outcome so tragic for blacks is that neither the student nor his parents are aware that he has a grossly fraudulent diploma. When a black person is not admitted to college, flunks out of *college, can't pass a civil service test, or doesn't get job promotions, he is more likely to blame racial discrimination than his poor education. Politicians, civil rights organizations, and the education establishment will do nothing about the fraud. In fact, they give their full allegiance to the perpetrators and mislead the education victims into thinking that it is racial discrimination that explains their plight.*

Between 1950 and 2010, the number of school districts in the United States fell from about 84,000 to 14,000. That suggests considerable educational monopolization. Along with education monopoly has come a decline in education quality and an increase in education cost. This observation suggests that part of the solution to our education problems is to reduce education monopoly and introduce competition and increase the number of decisions made at the local level and by parents.

One way to do this is to recognize that to publicly finance education, through our tax dollars, does not also require that we publicly produce education. We publicly finance many things such as food, pharmaceuticals, and fighter jets but we leave their production up to the private sector. A way to accomplish this in education is through tuition tax credits or educational vouchers. A tuition tax credit system would be where parents, some other adult, or business would get a credit against their tax obligation in the amount of tuition paid. Alternatively, an educational voucher system would be where the locality or state would issue a voucher to each parent and the parent decides the school to enroll their children. My preference would be a tuition tax credit system because it would avoid government involvement, such as a department of vouchers.

Fraud in Academia
May 6, 2009

Soon college students will come home and present parents with their grades. To avoid delusion, parents should do some serious discounting because of rampant grade inflation. If grade inflation continues, a college bachelor's degree will have just as much credibility as a high school diploma.

Writing for the National Association of Scholars, Professor Thomas C. Reeves documents what is no less than academic fraud in his article "The Happy Classroom: Grade Inflation Works." From 1991 to 2007, in public institutions, the average grade point average (GPA) rose, on a four-point scale, from 2.93 to 3.11. In private schools, the average GPA climbed from 3.09 to 3.30. Put within a historical perspective, in the 1930s, the average GPA was 2.35 (about a C-plus); whereby now it's a B-plus.

Academic fraud is rife at many of the nation's most prestigious and costliest universities. At Brown University, two-thirds of all letter grades given are an A. At Harvard, 50 percent of all grades were either A or A- (up from 22 percent in 1966); 91 percent of seniors graduated with honors. The *Boston Globe* called Harvard's grading practices "the laughing stock of the Ivy League." Eighty percent of the grades given at the University of Illinois are As and Bs. Fifty percent of students at Columbia University are on the Dean's list. At Stanford University, where F grades used to be banned, only 6 percent of student grades were as low as a C.

Some college administrators will tell us that the higher grades merely reflect higher-quality students. Balderdash! SAT scores have been in decline for four decades and at least a third of entering freshmen must enroll in a remedial course either in math, writing, or reading, which indicates academic fraud at the high school level. A recent survey of more than 30,000 first-year students revealed that nearly half spent more hours drinking than studying. Another survey found that a third of students expected Bs just for attending class, and 40 percent said they deserved a B for completing the assigned reading.

Last year, the Delaware-based Intercollegiate Studies Institute (ISI) published results of their national survey titled "Our Fading Heritage: Americans Fail a Basic Test on Their History and Institutions." The survey questions were not rocket science. Only 21 percent of survey respondents knew that the phrase "government of the people, by the people, for the people" comes from President Abraham Lincoln's Gettysburg Address. Almost 40 percent incorrectly believe the Constitution gives the president the power to declare war. Only 27 percent knew that the Bill of Rights expressly prohibits establishing an official religion for the United States. Remarkably, close to 25 percent of Americans believe that Congress shares its foreign policy powers with the United Nations. Other questions asked included: "Who is the commander-in-chief of the U S. military?" "Name two countries that were our enemies during World War II." "Under our Constitution, some powers belong to the federal government. What is one power of the federal government?" Of the 2,508 nationwide sample of Americans taking ISI's civic literacy test, 71 percent failed; the average score on the test was 49 percent.

Possessing a college degree often does not mean much in terms of basic skills. According to a 2006 Pew Charitable Trusts study, 50 percent of college seniors failed a test that required them to interpret a table about exercise and blood pressure, understand the arguments of newspaper editorials, and compare credit card offers. About 20 percent of college seniors did not have the quantitative skills to estimate if their car had enough gas to get to the gas station. According a recent National Assessment of Adult Literacy, the percentage of college graduates proficient in prose literacy has declined from 40 percent to 31 percent within the past decade. Employers report that many college graduates lack the basic skills of critical thinking, writing, and problem-solving.

The bottom line: To approach truth in grading, parents and employers should lower the average student's grade by one letter, and interpret a C grade as an F.

Vicious Academic Liberals

June 24, 2009

Ward Connerly, former University of California Regent, has an article, "Study, Study, Study—A Bad Career Move," in the June 2, 2009, edition of *Minding the Campus* (www.mindingthecampus.com) that should raise any decent American's level of disgust for what's routinely practiced at most of our universities. Mr. Connerly tells of a conversation he had with a high-ranking UC administrator about a proposal that the administrator was developing to increase campus diversity. Connerly asked the administrator why he considered it important to tinker with admissions instead of just letting the chips fall where they may. His response was that that unless the university took steps to "guide" admissions decisions, the University of California campuses would be dominated by Asians. When Connerly asked, "What would be wrong with that?," the UC administrator told him that Asians are "too dull—they study, study, study." Then he said to Connerly, "If you ever say I said this, I will have to deny it." Connerly did not reveal the administrator's name. It would not have done any good because it's part of a diversity vision shared by most college administrators.

With the enactment of California's Proposition 209 in 1996, outlawing racial discrimination in college admissions, Asian enrollment at UC campuses has skyrocketed. The UC Berkeley student body is 42 percent Asian students; UC Irvine 55 percent; UC Riverside 43 percent; and UCLA 38 percent. Asian student enrollment on all nine UC campuses is over 40 percent. That's in a state where the Asian population is about 13 percent. When there are policies that emphasize and reward academic achievement, Asians excel. College officials and others who are proponents of "diversity" and equal representation find that outcome offensive.

To deal with the Asian "menace," the UC Regents have proposed, starting in 2010, that no longer will the top 12.5 percent of students based on statewide performance be automatically admitted. Students won't have to take SAT subject-matter tests. Grades and test scores will no longer weigh so heavily in admission decisions. This is simply gross racial discrimination against those "dull" Asian students who "study, study, study" in favor of "interesting" black, white, and Hispanic students who don't "study, study, study."

This is truly evil and would be readily condemned as such if applied to other areas lacking in diversity. With blacks making up about 80 percent of professional basketball players, there is little or no diversity in professional basketball. Even at college-level basketball, it is not at all unusual to watch two teams playing and there not being a single white player on the court, much less a Chinese or Japanese player. I can think of several rule changes that might increase racial diversity in professional and college basketball. How about eliminating slam dunks and disallowing three-point shots? Restrict dribbling? Lower the basket's height? These and other rule changes would take away the "unfair" advantage that black players appear to have and create greater basketball diversity. But wouldn't diversity so achieved be despicable? If you answer yes, why would it be any less so when it's used to fulfill somebody's vision of college diversity?

Ward Connerly ends his article saying, "There is one truth that is universally applicable in the era of 'diversity,' especially in American universities: an absolute unwillingness to accept the verdict of color-blind policies." Hypocrisy is part and parcel of the liberal academic elite. But the American people, who fund universities either as parents, donors, or taxpayers, should not accept this evilness and there's a good way to stop it—cut off the funding to racially discriminating colleges and universities.

Education

September 16, 2009

Instead of President Obama addressing school students across the nation, he might have accomplished more by focusing his attention on the educational rot in schools in the nation's capital. The American Legislative Exchange Council recently came out with their fifteenth edition of "Report Card on American Education: A State-by-State Analysis." Academic achievement in no state is much to write home about but in Washington, D.C., by any measure, it approaches criminal fraud. Let's look at the numbers.

Only 14 percent of Washington's fourth-graders score at or above proficiency in the reading and math portions of the National Assessment of Educational Progress (NAEP) test. Their national rank of fifty-one makes them the nation's worst. Eighth-graders are even further behind with only 12 percent scoring at or above proficiency in reading and 8 percent in math and again the worst performance in the nation. One shouldn't be surprised by Washington student performance on college admissions tests. They have an average composite SAT score of 925 and ACT score of 19.1, compared to the national average respectively of 1017 and 21.1. In terms of national ranking, their SAT and ACT rankings are identical to their fourth- and eighth-grade rankings—dead last.

Washington's political and education establishment might excuse these outcomes by arguing that because most students are black, the schools are underfunded and overcrowded. Let's look at such a claim. During the 2006–07 academic year, expenditures per pupil averaged $13,848 compared to a national average of $9,389. That made Washington's per-pupil expenditures the third highest in the nation, coming in behind New Jersey ($14,998) and New York ($14,747). Washington's teacher-student ratio is 13.9 compared with the national average of 15.3 students per teacher, ranking eighteenth in the nation. What about teacher salaries? Washington's teachers are the highest paid in the nation, having an average annual salary of $61,195 compared with the nation's average $46,593. Despite the academic performance of Washington's students, they have a graduation rate of 61 percent compared to the national average of 70 percent. That suggests the issuance of fraudulent high school diplomas.

Currently, Washington, D.C., has an Opportunity Scholarship Program, which allows qualified low-income families to claim up to $7,500 per student toward a private education of their choice. Obama's Democratic Congress, acting on the behalf of the education establishment, has killed the program and there's the possibility that the 1,700 students currently enrolled will have to return to D.C. public schools.

The staunchest opponents of school choice are hypocrites. They want, demand, and can afford school choice for themselves but for others not so affluent school choice it is a different matter. President and Mrs. Barack Obama enrolled their two daughters in Washington's most prestigious Sidwell Friends School, forking over $28,000 a year for each girl. While senator from Illinois, the Obamas enrolled their girls in the University of Chicago's Laboratory School, a private school in Chicago charging almost $20,000 for each girl. A Heritage Foundation survey found that 37 percent of the members of the House of Representatives and 45 percent of senators in the 110th Congress sent their children to private schools. Public school teachers enroll their own children in nonpublic schools to a much greater extent than the general public, in some cases four and five times greater. In Cincinnati, about 41 percent of public school teachers send their children to nonpublic schools. In Chicago it is 38 percent, Los Angeles 24 percent, New York 32 percent, and Philadelphia 44 percent. The behavior of public school teachers is quite suggestive. It's like my offering to take you to a restaurant and you find out that neither the chef nor the waiters eat there. That suggests they have some inside information from which you might benefit.

For people in power to tolerate the Washington, D.C., school system is despicable. For a black president to do so might qualify as betrayal.

Academic Dishonesty
October 14, 2009

College education is a costly proposition with tuition, room, and board at some colleges topping $50,000 a year. Is it worth it? Increasing evidence suggests that it's not. Since the 1960s, academic achievement scores have plummeted, but student college grade point averages (GPA) have skyrocketed. In October 2001, the *Boston Globe* published an article entitled "Harvard's Quiet Secret: Rampant Grade Inflation." The article reported that a record 91 percent of Harvard University students were awarded honors during the spring graduation. The newspaper called Harvard's grading practices "the laughing stock of the Ivy League." Harvard is by no means unique. For example, 80 percent of the grades given at the University of Illinois are As and Bs. Fifty percent of students at Columbia University are on the Dean's list. At Stanford University, where F grades used to be banned, only 6 percent of student grades were as low as a C. In the 1930s, the average GPA at American colleges and universities was 2.35, about a C plus; today the national average GPA is 3.2, more than a B.

Today's college students are generally dumber than their predecessors. An article in the *Wall Street Journal* (January 30, 1997) reported that a "bachelor of arts degree in 1997 may not be the equal of a graduation certificate from an academic high school in 1947." The American Council on Education found that only 15 percent of universities require tests for general knowledge; only 17 percent for critical thinking; and only 19 percent for minimum competency. According a recent National Assessment of Adult Literacy, the percentage of college graduates proficient in prose literacy has declined from 40 percent to 31 percent within the past decade. Employers report that many college graduates lack the basic skills of critical thinking, writing, and problem-solving and some employers find they must hire English and math teachers to teach them how to write memos and perform simple computations.

What is being labeled grade inflation is simply a euphemism for academic dishonesty. After all, it's dishonesty when a professor assigns a grade the student did not earn. When a university or college confers a degree upon a student who has not mastered critical thinking skills, writing, and problem-solving, it's academic dishonesty. Of course, I might be in error calling it dishonesty. Perhaps academic standards have been set so low that idiots could earn As and Bs.

Academic dishonesty and deception go beyond fraudulent grades. "Minding the Campus" is a newsletter published by the Manhattan Institute. Edward Fiske tells a chilling tale of deception titled "Gaming the College Rankings" (September 17, 2009). The *U.S. News & World Report* college rankings are worshiped by some college administrators, and they go to great lengths to strengthen their rankings. Some years ago, University of Miami omitted scores of athletes and special admission students so as to boost SAT scores of incoming freshmen. At least one college mailed dollar bills to alumni with a request that they send them back to the annual fund thereby inflating the number of alumni donors.

"Gaming the College Rankings" contains an insert by John Leo, who is the editor of "Minding the Campus," reporting that in the mid-1990s, Boston University raised its SAT scores by excluding the verbal scores of foreign students while including their math scores. Monmouth University simply added 200 SAT points to its group scores. University of California reported that thirty-four of its professors were members of a prestigious engineering association when in fact only seventeen of their current faculty were. Baylor University offered students, who were already admitted to the university, $300 in bookstore credits to take the SAT again in the hopes of boosting Baylor's SAT averages.

Academic dishonesty, coupled with incompetency, particularly at the undergraduate level, doesn't bode well for the future of our nation. And who's to blame? Most of the blame lies at the feet of the boards of trustees, who bear ultimate responsibility for the management of our colleges and universities.

Black Education

December 23, 2009

Detroit's (predominantly black) public schools are the worst in the nation and it takes some doing to be worse than Washington, D.C. Only 3 percent of Detroit's fourth-graders scored proficient on the most recent National Assessment of Education Progress (NAEP) test, sometimes called "The Nation's Report Card." Twenty-eight percent scored basic and 69 percent below basic. "Below basic" is the NAEP category when students are unable to demonstrate even partial mastery of knowledge and skills fundamental for proficient work at their grade level. It's the same story for Detroit's eighth-graders. Four percent scored proficient, 18 percent basic, and 77 percent below basic.

Michael Casserly, executive director of the D.C.-based Council on Great City Schools, in an article appearing in *Crain's Detroit Business* (December 8, 2009), titled "Detroit's Public Schools Post Worst Scores on Record in National Assessment," said, "There is no jurisdiction of any kind, at any level, at any time in the 30-year history of NAEP that has ever registered such low numbers." The academic performance of black students in other large cities such as Philadelphia, Chicago, New York, and Los Angeles is not much better than Detroit and Washington.

What's to be done about this tragic state of black education? The education establishment and politicians tell us that we need to spend more for higher teacher pay and smaller class size. The fact of business is higher teacher salaries and smaller class sizes mean little or nothing in terms of academic achievement. Washington, D.C., for example, spends over $15,000 per student, has class sizes smaller than the nation's average, and with an average annual salary of $61,195, its teachers are the most highly paid in the nation.

What about role models? Standard psychobabble asserts a positive relationship between the race of teachers and administrators and student performance. That's nonsense. Black academic performance is the worst in the very cities where large percentages of teachers and administrators are black, and often the school superintendent is black, the mayor is black, most of the city council is black, and very often the chief of police is black.

Black people have accepted hare-brained ideas that have made large percentages of black youngsters virtually useless in an increasingly technological economy. This destruction will continue until the day comes when black people are willing to turn their backs on liberals and the education establishment's agenda and confront issues that are both embarrassing and uncomfortable. To a lesser extent, this also applies to whites because the educational performance of many white kids is nothing to write home about; it's just not the disaster that black education is.

Many black students are alien and hostile to the education process. They have parents with little interest in their education. These students not only sabotage the education process, but make schools unsafe as well. These students should not be permitted to destroy the education chances of others. They should be removed or those students who want to learn should be provided with a mechanism to go to another school.

Another issue deemed too delicate to discuss is the overall quality of people teaching our children. Students who have chosen education as their major have the lowest SAT scores of any other major. Students who have an education degree earn lower scores than any other major on graduate school admission tests such as the GRE, MCAT, or LSAT. Schools of education, either graduate or undergraduate, represent the academic slums of most any university. They are home to the least able students and professors. Schools of education should be shut down.

Yet another issue is the academic fraud committed by teachers and administrators. After all, what is it when a student is granted a diploma certifying a twelfth-grade level of achievement when in fact he can't perform at the sixth- or seventh-grade level?

Prospects for improvement in black education are not likely given the cozy relationship between black politicians, civil rights organizations, and teachers' unions.

Black Education Disaster

December 22, 2010

Harvard University Professor Stephan Thernstrom's recent essay, "Minorities in College—Good News, But . . . ," in Minding the Campus (November 4, 2010), a website sponsored by the New York-based Manhattan Institute, commented on the results of the most recent National Assessment of Education Progress test: The scores "mean that black students aged 17 do not read with any greater facility than whites who are four years younger and still in junior high. . . . Exactly the same glaring gaps appear in NAEP's [National Assessment of Educational Progress] tests of basic mathematics skills."

Thernstrom asks, "If we put a randomly selected group of 100 eighth-graders and another of 100 twelfth-graders in a typical college, would we expect the first group to perform as well as the second?" In other words, is it reasonable to expect a college freshman of any race with the equivalent of an eighth-grade education to compete successfully with those having a twelfth-grade education?

SAT scores confirm the poor education received by blacks. In 2009, average SAT reading test scores were: whites (528), Asians (516), and blacks (429). In math, it was whites (536), Asians (587), and blacks (426). Twelve years of fraudulent primary and secondary education received by most blacks are not erased by four or five years of college.

This is evidenced by examination scores taken for admission to graduate schools. In 2007, Graduate Record Examination verbal scores were: whites (493), Asians (485), and blacks (395). The math portion scores were: whites (562), Asians (617), and blacks (419). Scores on the LSAT in 2006, for admission to law school, were: whites (152), Asians (152), and blacks (142). In 2010, MCAT scores for admission to medical schools were: whites (26), Asians (26), and blacks (21).

What's some of the response of the black community to efforts to do something about fraudulent primary and secondary education?

Voters in Washington, D.C., might provide a partial answer. Mayor Adrian Fenty appointed and backed Michelle Rhee as chancellor of D.C. Public Schools.

She fired large numbers of ineffective teachers, most of whom were black, and fought the teachers' union. During her tenure, there were small gains made in student test scores.

How did all of this go over with Washington voters? Washington's teachers' union, as well as D.C.'s public-employee unions, spent massive amounts of money campaigning against Fenty. Voters unseated him in the November elections and with him went Chancellor Rhee. Fenty had other "faults"; he didn't play the racial patronage game that has become a part of D.C.'s political landscape. The clear message given by D.C. voters and teachers' union is that any politician who's willing to play hardball in an effort to improve black education will be run out of town.

The education establishment's solution is always more money; however, according to a *Washington Post* article (April 6, 2008), "The Real Cost of Public Schools," written by Andrew J. Coulson, if we include its total operating budget, teacher retirement, capital budget, and federal funding, the D.C. public schools spend $24,600 per student.

Washington's fraudulent black education is by no means unique; it's duplicated in one degree or another in most of our major cities. However, there is a glimmer of hope in the increasing demand for charter schools and educational vouchers. This movement is being fought tooth and nail by an education establishment that fears the competition and subsequent threats to their employment. The charter school and the educational vouchers movement will help prevent parents and children who care about education from being held hostage in an environment hostile to the learning process. And there's plenty of evidence that children do better and parents are more pleased when they have a measure of school choice.

The fact that black youngsters trail their white counterparts by three or four years becomes even more grim when we recognize that the education white youngsters receive is nothing to write home about.

According to the recently released Program for International Student Assessment exam, our fifteen-year-olds rank twenty-fifth among thirty-four industrialized nations in math and fourteenth in reading.

Black Education

February 2, 2011

In my "Black Education Disaster" column (December 22, 2010), I presented National Assessment of Educational Progress test data that demonstrated that an average black high school graduate had a level of reading, writing, and math proficiency of a white seventh- or eighth-grader. The public education establishment bears part of the responsibility for this disaster, but a greater portion is borne by black students and their parents, many of whom who are alien and hostile to the education process.

Let's look at the education environment in many schools and ask how conducive it is to the education process. According to the National Center for Education Statistics, nationally during 2007–2008, more than 145,000 teachers were physically attacked. Six percent of big-city schools report verbal abuse of teachers and 18 percent report nonverbal disrespect for teachers.

An earlier NCES study found that 18 percent of the nation's schools accounted for 75 percent of the reported incidents of violence, and 6.6 percent accounted for 50 percent. So far as serious violence, murder, and rapes, 1.9 percent of schools reported 50 percent of the incidents. The preponderance of school violence occurs in big-city schools attended by black students.

What's the solution? Violence, weapons-carrying, gang activity, and student or teacher intimidation should not be tolerated. Students engaging in such activity should be summarily expelled.

Some might worry about the plight of expelled students. I think we should have greater concern for those students whose education is made impossible by thugs and the impossible learning environment they create.

Another part of the black education disaster has to do with the home environment. More than 70 percent of black children are born to unwedded mothers, who are often themselves born to unwedded mothers. Today's level of female-headed households is new in black history. Until the 1950s, almost 80 percent of black children lived in two-parent households, as opposed to today's 35 percent.

Often, these unwedded mothers have poor parenting skills and are indifferent, and sometimes hostile, to their children's education. The resulting poorly behaving students should not be permitted to sabotage the education of students whose parents are supportive of the education process.

At the minimum, a mechanism such as tuition tax credit or educational voucher ought to be available to allow parents and children who care to opt out of failing schools. Some people take the position that we should repair not abandon failing schools. That's a vision that differs little from one that says that no black child's education should be improved unless we can improve the education of all black children.

What needs to be done is not rocket science. Our black ancestors, just two, three, four generations out of slavery, would not have tolerated school behavior that's all but routine today. The fact that the behavior of many black students has become acceptable and made excuses for is no less than a gross betrayal of sacrifices our ancestors made to create today's opportunities.

Some of today's black political leadership is around my age, seventy-five, such as Reps. Maxine Waters, Charles Rangel, John Conyers, former Virginia governor Douglas Wilder, Jesse Jackson, and many others. Forget that they are liberal Democrats but ask them whether their parents, kin, or neighbors would have tolerated children cursing to, or in the presence of, teachers and other adults. Ask them what their parents would have done had they assaulted an adult or teacher. Ask whether their parents would have accepted the grossly disrespectful behavior seen among many black youngsters on the streets and other public places using foul language and racial epithets. Then ask why should today's blacks tolerate something our ancestors would not.

The sorry and tragic state of black education is not going to be turned around until there's a change in what's acceptable and unacceptable behavior by young people. The bulk of that change has to come from within the black community.

Diversity Perversity

April 6, 2011

The terms affirmative action, equal representation, preferential treatment, and quotas just don't sell well. The intellectual elite and their media, government, and corporate enthusiasts have come up with diversity, a seemingly benign term that's a cover for racially discriminatory policy. They call for college campuses, corporate offices, and government agencies to "look like America."

Part of looking like America means if blacks are 13 percent of the population, they should be 13 percent of college students and professors, corporate managers, and government employees. Behind this vision of justice is the silly notion that but for the fact of discrimination, we'd be distributed equally by race across incomes, education, occupations, and other outcomes. There is absolutely no evidence that statistical proportionality is the norm anywhere on Earth; however, much of our thinking, laws, and public policy is based upon proportionality being the norm. Let's look at some racial differences while thinking about their causes and possible remedies.

While 13 percent of our population, blacks are 80 percent of professional basketball players and 65 percent of professional football players and are the highest-paid players in both sports. By contrast, blacks are only 2 percent of NHL's professional ice hockey players. There is no racial diversity in basketball, football, and ice hockey. They come nowhere close to "looking like America."

Even in terms of sports achievement, racial diversity is absent. Four out of the five highest career home-run hitters were black. Since blacks entered the major leagues, of the eight times more than a hundred bases were stolen in a season, all were by blacks.

The US Department of Justice recently ordered Dayton, Ohio's police department to lower its written exam passing scores so as to have more blacks on its police force. What should Attorney General Eric Holder do about the lack of diversity in sports? Why don't the intellectual elite protest? Could it be that the owners of these multibillion-dollar professional basketball, football, and baseball teams are pro-black while those of the NHL and major industries are racists unwilling to put blacks in highly paid positions?

There's one ethnic diversity issue completely swept under the rug. Jewish Americans are less than 3 percent of our population and only two-tenths of 1 percent of the world's population. Yet between 1901 and 2010, Jews were 35 percent of American Nobel Laureate winners and 22 percent of the world's.

If the diversity gang sees underrepresentation as "probative" of racial discrimination, what do they propose we do about overrepresentation? Because if one race is overrepresented, it might mean they're taking away what rightfully belongs to another race.

There are other representation issues to which we might give some attention with an eye to corrective public policy. Asians routinely get the highest scores on the math portion of the SAT whereas blacks get the lowest. Men are 50 percent of the population and so are women; yet men are struck by lightning six times as often as women. The population statistics for South Dakota, Iowa, Maine, Montana, and Vermont show that not even 1 percent of their populations is black. On the other hand, in states such as Georgia, Alabama, and Mississippi, blacks are overrepresented in terms of their percentages in the general population.

There are many international examples of disproportionality. For example, during the 1960s, the Chinese minority in Malaysia received more university degrees than the Malay majority—including four hundred engineering degrees compared with four for the Malays, even though Malays dominate the country politically. In Brazil's state of Sao Paulo, more than two-thirds of the potatoes and 90 percent of the tomatoes produced were produced by people of Japanese ancestry.

The bottom line is that there is no evidence anywhere that but for discrimination, people would be divided according to their percentages in the population in any activity. Diversity is an elitist term used to give respectability to acts and policy that would otherwise be deemed as racism.

Academic Rot

April 20, 2011

The average American, as parent, student, and taxpayer, has little idea of the academic rot at so many of our colleges. Save for a tiny handful of the nation's colleges, what distinguishes one college from another is the magnitude of that rot.

One of the best sources of information about our colleges is the New York City–based Manhattan Institute's quarterly Web magazine, Minding the Campus, edited by John Leo, former columnist for *U.S. News & World Report*.

The magazine's Winter 2010 edition contains an article by Dr. Candace de Russy, former member of the board of trustees of the State University of New York (SUNY), titled "Hate-America Sociology." De Russy's colleague sent her a copy of a student's exam from an introductory sociology class found lying in a room at an East Coast public college. The professor had given it a perfect score of 100. Here are some of the questions asked and the student's written response:

"Question: How does the United States 'steal' the resources of other (third world) countries?

"Answer: We steal through exploitation. Our multinationals are aware that indigenous people in developing nations have been coaxed off their plots and forced into slums. Because it is lucrative, our multinationals offer them extremely low wage labor that cannot be turned down.

"Question: Why is the US on shaky moral ground when it comes to preventing illegal immigration?

"Answer: Some say that it is wrong of the United States to prevent illegal immigration because the same people we are denying entry to, we have exploited for the purpose of keeping the American wheel spinning.

"Question: What is the interactionist approach to gender?

"Answer: The majority of multi-gender encounters are male-dominated. [F]or example, while involved in conversation, the male is much more likely to interrupt. Most likely because the male believes the female's expressed thoughts are inferior to his own.

"Question: Please briefly explain the matrix of domination.

"Answer: The belief that domination has more than one dimension. For example, males are dominant over females, whites over blacks, and affluent over impoverished."

Out of retaliation fears, de Russy withheld the name and university of her colleague who sent the exam. Teaching students hate-America indoctrination is widespread, as I've documented in the past.

A few years ago, according to UCLA's *Bruin Standard*, Mary Corey, UCLA history professor, instructed her class, "Capitalism isn't a lie on purpose. It's just a lie." She continued, "[Capitalists] are swine. . . . They're bastard people."

Rod Swanson, a UCLA economics professor, told his class, "The United States of America, backed by facts, is the greediest and most selfish country in the world."

Professor Andrew Hewitt, chairman of UCLA's Department of Germanic Languages, told his class, "Bush is a moron, a simpleton and an idiot." The professor's opinion of the rest of us: "American consumerism is a very unique thing; I don't think anyone else lusts after money in such a greedy fashion."

An English professor at Montclair State University in New Jersey tells his students, "Conservatism champions racism, exploitation, and imperialist war."

University officials are aware of this kind of academic rot, but not university trustees who bear the ultimate responsibility for the university's welfare. Trustees are mostly yes-men for the president. Legislators and charitable foundations that pour billions into colleges are unaware as well. Most tragically, parents who cough up thousands in tuition to send their youngsters off to be educated, rather than indoctrinated, are unaware of the academic rot as well.

You say, "Williams, what can be done?" Students should record classroom professorial propaganda and give it wide distribution over the internet. I've taught for more than forty years and have routinely invited students to record my lectures so they don't have to be stenographers during class. I have no idea of where those recordings have wound up, but if you find them, you'll hear zero proselytization or discussion of my political and other personal preferences. To do otherwise, I consider academic dishonesty.

Education Is Worse Than We Thought
July 20, 2011

Last December, I reported on Harvard University professor Stephan Thernstrom's essay "Minorities in College—Good News, But. . . . ," on Minding the Campus, a website sponsored by the New York-based Manhattan Institute. He was commenting on the results of the most recent National Assessment of Educational Progress, saying that the scores "mean that black students aged 17 do not read with any greater facility than whites who are four years younger and still in junior high. . . . Exactly the same glaring gaps appear in NAEP's tests of basic mathematics skills." Thernstrom asked, "If we put a randomly selected group of 100 eighth-graders and another of 100 twelfth-graders in a typical college, would we expect the first group to perform as well as the second?" In other words, is it reasonable to expect a college freshman of any race who has the equivalent of an eighth-grade education to compete successfully with those having a twelfth-grade education?

Maybe this huge gap in black/white academic achievement was in the paternalistic minds of the 6th US Circuit Court of Appeals justices who recently struck down Michigan's ban on the use of race and sex as criteria for college admissions. The court said that it burdens minorities and violates the US Constitution. Given the black education disaster, racial preferences in college admissions will become a permanent feature, because given the status quo, blacks as a group will never make it into top colleges based upon academic merit.

The situation is worse than we thought. *U.S. News & World Report* (July 7, 2011) came out with a story titled "Educators Implicated in Atlanta Cheating Scandal," saying that "for 10 years, hundreds of Atlanta public school teachers and principals changed answers on state tests in one of the largest cheating scandals in US history, according to a scathing 413-page investigative report released Tuesday by Georgia Gov. Nathan Deal." The report says that more than three-quarters of the fifty-six Atlanta schools investigated cheated on the 2009 standardized National Assessment of Educational Progress. Eighty-two teachers have confessed to erasing students' answers. A total of 178 educators, including 38 principals, many of whom are black, systematically fabricated test scores of struggling black students to cover up academic failure. The governor's report says that cheating orders came from the top and that widespread cheating has occurred since at least 2001. So far, no Atlanta educator has been criminally charged, even though some of the cheating was brazen, such as teachers pointing to correct answers while students were taking the tests, reading answers aloud during testing and seating low-achieving students next to high-achieving students to make cheating easier.

Teacher and principal exam cheating is not restricted to Atlanta; it's widespread. The *Detroit Free Press* and *USA Today* (March 8, 2011) released an investigative report that found higher-than-average erasure rates on tests taken by students at thirty-four schools in and around Detroit in 2008 and 2009. Overall, their report "found 304 schools where experts say the gains on standardized tests in 2009–10 are so statistically improbable, they merit further investigation. Besides Michigan, the other states [where suspected cheating was found] were Ohio, Arizona, Colorado, Florida and California." A *Dallas Morning News* investigation reported finding high rates of test erasures in Texas. Six teachers and two principals were dismissed after cheating was uncovered.

In 2007, Baltimore's George Washington Elementary School was named a Blue Ribbon School after the number of students who passed state reading tests shot from 32 percent to nearly 100 percent in just four years. Last year, *The Baltimore Sun* reported thousands of erasures on those tests. Susan Burgess, the school's principal, had her professional license revoked after an investigation by state and city school board officials.

Why is there widespread cheating by America's educators? According to Diane Ravitch, who is the research professor of education at New York University, it's not teachers and principals who are to blame; it's the mandates of the No Child Left Behind law, enacted during the George W. Bush administration. In other words, the devil made them do it.

Too Much Higher Education
September 14, 2011

Too much of anything is just as much a misallocation of resources as it is too little, and that applies to higher education just as it applies to everything else. A recent study from The Center for College Affordability and Productivity titled "From Wall Street to Wal-Mart," by Richard Vedder, Christopher Denhart, Matthew Denhart, Christopher Matgouranis, and Jonathan Robe, explains that college education for many is a waste of time and money. More than one-third of currently working college graduates are in jobs that do not require a degree. An essay by Vedder that complements the CCAP study reports that there are "one-third of a million waiters and waitresses with college degrees." The study says Vedder—distinguished professor of economics at Ohio University, an adjunct scholar at the American Enterprise Institute and director of CCAP—"was startled a year ago when the person he hired to cut down a tree had a master's degree in history, the fellow who fixed his furnace was a mathematics graduate, and, more recently, a TSA airport inspector (whose job it was to ensure that we took our shoes off while going through security) was a recent college graduate."

The nation's college problem is far deeper than the fact that people simply are overqualified for particular jobs. Citing the research of American Enterprise Institute scholar Charles Murray's book *Real Education* (2008), Vedder says: "The number going to college exceeds the number capable of mastering higher levels of intellectual inquiry. This leads colleges to alter their mission, watering down the intellectual content of what they do." In other words, colleges dumb down courses so that the students they admit can pass them. Murray argues that only a modest proportion of our population has the cognitive skills, work discipline, drive, maturity, and integrity to master truly higher education. He says that educated people should be able to read and understand classic works, such as John Locke's "Essay Concerning Human Understanding" or William Shakespeare's "King Lear." These works are "insightful in many ways," he says, but a person of average intelligence "typically lacks both the motivation and ability to do so." Mastering complex forms of mathematics is challenging but necessary to develop rigorous thinking and is critical in some areas of science and engineering.

Richard Arum and Josipa Roksa, authors of *Academically Adrift: Limited Learning on College Campuses* (2011), report on their analysis of more than 2,300 undergraduates at 24 institutions. Forty-five percent of these students demonstrated no significant improvement in a range of skills—including critical thinking, complex reasoning, and writing—during their first two years of college. According to an August 2006 issue brief by the Alliance for Excellent Education, student "lack of preparation is also apparent in multiple subject areas; of college freshmen taking remedial courses, 35 percent were enrolled in math, 23 percent in writing, and 20 percent in reading." Declining college admissions standards have contributed to the deterioration of the academic quality of our secondary schools. Colleges show high schools that they do not have to teach much in order for youngsters to be admitted.

According to *Education Next*, an August Harvard University study titled "Globally Challenged: Are US Students Ready to Compete?," found that only 32 percent of US students achieved proficiency in math, compared with "75 percent of students in Shanghai, 58 percent in Korea, and 56 percent in Finland. Countries in which a majority—or near majority—of students performed at or above the proficiency level in math include Switzerland, Japan, Canada, and the Netherlands." Results from the 2009 Program for International Student Assessment international test show that US students rank thirty-second among industrialized nations in proficiency in math and seventeenth in reading.

Much of American education is in shambles. Part of a solution is for colleges to refuse to admit students who are unprepared to do real college work. That would help to reveal the shoddy education provided at the primary and secondary school levels. Here, I'm whistlin' "Dixie," because college administrators are more interested in numbers of students, which equal more money.

Schools of Education
January 25, 2012

Larry Sand's article "No Wonder Johnny (Still) Can't Read"—written for The John William Pope Center for Higher Education Policy, based in Raleigh, N.C.—blames schools of education for the decline in America's education. Education professors drum into students that they should not "drill and kill" or be the "sage on the stage" but instead be the "guide on the side" who "facilitates student discovery." This kind of harebrained thinking, coupled with multicultural nonsense, explains today's education. During his teacher education, Sand says, "teachers-to-be were forced to learn about this ethnic group, that impoverished group, this sexually anomalous group, that under-represented group, etc.—all under the rubric of 'Culturally Responsive Education.'"

Education majors are woefully lacking in academic skills. Here are some sample test questions for you to answer. Question 1: Which of the following is equal to a quarter-million? a) 40,000, b) 250,000, c) 2,500,000, d) 1/4,000,000, or e) 4/1,000,000. Question 2: Martin Luther King Jr. (insert the correct choice) for the poor of all races. a) spoke out passionately, b) spoke out passionate, c) did spoke out passionately, d) has spoke out passionately or e) had spoken out passionate. Question 3: What would you do if your student sprained an ankle? a) Put a Band-Aid on it, b) Ice it, or c) Rinse it with water.

Guess whether these questions were on a sixth-grade, ninth-grade, or twelfth-grade test. I bet the average reader would guess that it's a sixth-grade test. Wrong. How about ninth-grade? Wrong again. You say, "OK, Williams, so they're twelfth-grade test questions!" Still wrong. According to a Heartland Institute-published *School Reform News* (September 2001) article titled "Who Tells Teachers They Can Teach?," those test questions came from prospective teacher tests. The first two questions are samples from the Praxis I test for teachers, and the third is from the 1999 teacher certification test in Illinois. According to the *Chicago Sun-Times* (September 6, 2001), 5,243 Illinois teachers failed their teacher certification tests. The *Chicago Sun-Times* also reported, "One teacher failed 24 of 25 teacher tests—including 11 of 12 Basic Skills tests and all 12 tests on teaching learning-disabled children." Yet that teacher was assigned to teach learning-disabled children in Chicago. Departments of education have solved the problem of teacher test failure. According to a *New York Post* story (November 14, 2011) titled "City teacher tests turn into E-ZPass," more than 99 percent of teachers pass.

Textbooks used in schools of education advocate sheer nonsense. A passage in Enid Lee et al.'s *Beyond Heroes and Holidays* reads: "We cannot afford to become so bogged down in grammar and spelling that we forget the whole story. . . . The onslaught of antihuman practices that this nation and other nations are facing today: racism, and sexism, and the greed for money and human labor that disguises itself as 'globalization.'" Marilyn Burns's text *About Teaching Mathematics* reads, "There is no place for requiring students to practice tedious calculations that are more efficiently and accurately done by using calculators." *New Designs for Teaching and Learning*, by Dennis Adams and Mary Hamm, says: "Content knowledge is not seen to be as important as possessing teaching skills and knowledge about the students being taught. . . . Successful teachers understand the outside context of community, personal abilities, and feelings, while they establish an inside context or environment conducive to learning." That means it's no problem if a teacher can't figure out that a quarter-million is the same as 250,000. Harvey Daniels and Marilyn Bizar's text *Methods That Matter* reads, "Students can no longer be viewed as cognitive living rooms into which the furniture of knowledge is moved in and arranged by teachers, and teachers cannot invariably act as subject-matter experts." The authors add, "The main use of standardized tests in America is to justify the distribution of certain goodies to certain people."

Schools of education represent the academic slums of most any college. American education can benefit from slum removal.

Math Matters

February 22, 2012

If one manages to graduate from high school without the rudiments of algebra, geometry, and trigonometry, there are certain relatively high-paying careers probably off-limits for life—such as careers in architecture, chemistry, computer programming, engineering, medicine, and certain technical fields. For example, one might meet all of the physical requirements to be a fighter pilot, but he's grounded if he doesn't have enough math to understand physics, aerodynamics, and navigation. Mathematical ability helps provide the disciplined structure that helps people to think, speak, and write more clearly. In general, mathematics is an excellent foundation and prerequisite for study in all areas of science and engineering. So where do US youngsters stand in math?

Drs. Eric Hanushek and Paul Peterson, senior fellows at the Hoover Institution, looked at the performance of our youngsters compared with their counterparts in other nations, in their *Newsweek* article, "Why Can't American Students Compete?" (August 28, 2011), reprinted under the title "Math Matters" in the *Hoover Digest* (2012). In the latest international tests administered by the Organization for Economic Cooperation and Development, only 32 percent of US students ranked proficient in math—coming in between Portugal and Italy but far behind South Korea, Finland, Canada, and the Netherlands. US students couldn't hold a finger to the 75 percent of Shanghai students who tested proficient.

What about our brightest? It turns out that only 7 percent of US students perform at the advanced level in math. Forty-five percent of the students in Shanghai are advanced in math, compared with 20 percent in South Korea and Switzerland and 15 percent of students in Japan, Belgium, Finland, the Netherlands, New Zealand, and Canada.

Hanushek and Peterson find one bright spot among our young people. That's Asian-American students, 52 percent of whom perform at the proficient level or higher. Among white students, only 42 percent perform math at a proficient level. The math performance of black and Hispanic students is a disaster, with only 11 and 15 percent, respectively, performing math at the proficient level or higher.

The National Center for Education Statistics revealed some of the results of American innumeracy. Among advanced degrees in engineering awarded at US universities during the 2007–08 academic year, 28 percent went to whites; 2 percent went to blacks; 2 percent went to Hispanics; and 61 percent went to foreigners. Of the advanced degrees in mathematics, 40 percent went to whites; 2 percent went to blacks; 5 percent went to Hispanics; and 50 percent went to foreigners. For advanced degrees in education, 65 percent went to whites; 17 percent went to blacks; 5 percent went to Hispanics; and 8 percent went to foreigners. The pattern is apparent. The more rigorous a subject area, the higher the percentage of foreigners—and the lower the percentage of Americans—earning advanced degrees. In subject areas such as education, which have little or no rigor, Americans are likelier—and foreigners are less likely—to earn advanced degrees.

In a *New York Times* article—"Do We Need Foreign Technology Workers?" (April 8, 2009)—Dr. Vivek Wadhwa of the Pratt School of Engineering at Duke University said "that 47 percent of all US science and engineering workers with doctorates are immigrants as were 67 percent of the additions to the US science and engineering work force between 1995 to 2006. And roughly 60 percent of engineering PhD students and 40 percent of master's students are foreign nationals."

American mathematic proficiency levels leave a lot to be desired if we're to maintain competitiveness. For blacks and Hispanics, it's a tragedy with little prospect for change, but the solution is not rocket science. During my tenure as a member of Temple University's faculty in the 1970s, I tutored black students in math. When they complained that math was too difficult, I told them that if they spent as much time practicing math as they did practicing jump shots, they'd be just as good at math as they were at basketball. The same message of hard work and discipline applies to all students, but someone must demand it.

Too Much College

June 27, 2012

In President Barack Obama's 2012 State of the Union address, he said that "higher education can't be a luxury. It is an economic imperative that every family in America should be able to afford." Such talk makes for political points, but there's no evidence that a college education is an economic imperative. A good part of our higher education problem, explaining its spiraling cost, is that a large percentage of students currently attending college are ill-equipped and incapable of doing real college work. They shouldn't be there wasting their own resources and those of their families and taxpayers. Let's look at it.

Robert Samuelson, in his *Washington Post* article "It's time to drop the college-for-all crusade" (May 27, 2012), said that "the college-for-all crusade has outlived its usefulness. Time to ditch it. Like the crusade to make all Americans homeowners, it's now doing more harm than good." Richard Vedder—professor of economics at Ohio University, adjunct scholar at the American Enterprise Institute, and director of The Center for College Affordability & Productivity, or CCAP—in his article "Ditch . . . the College-for-All Crusade," published on *The Chronicle of Higher Education*'s blog, "Innovations" (June 7, 2012), points out that the "US Labor Department says the majority of new American jobs over the next decade do not need a college degree. We have a six-digit number of college-educated janitors in the US." Another CCAP essay by Vedder and his colleagues, titled "From Wall Street to Wal-Mart," reports that there are "one-third of a million waiters and waitresses with college degrees." More than one-third of currently working college graduates are in jobs that do not require a degree, such as flight attendants, taxi drivers, and salesmen. Was college attendance a wise use of these students' time and the resources of their parents and taxpayers?

There's a recent study published by the Raleigh, N.C.-based Pope Center titled "Pell Grants: Where Does All the Money Go?" Authors Jenna Ashley Robinson and Duke Cheston report that about 60 percent of undergraduate students in the country are Pell Grant recipients, and at some schools, upward of 80 percent are. Pell Grants are the biggest expenditure of the Department of Education, totaling nearly $42 billion in 2012.

The original focus of Pell Grants was to facilitate college access for low-income students. Since 1972, when the program began, the number of students from the lowest income quartile going to college has increased by more than 50 percent. However, Robinson and Cheston report that the percentage of low-income students who completed college by age twenty-four decreased from 21.9 percent in 1972 to 19.9 percent today.

Richard Arum and Josipa Roksa, authors of *Academically Adrift: Limited Learning on College Campuses* (2011), report on their analysis of more than 2,300 undergraduates at twenty-four institutions. Forty-five percent of these students demonstrated no significant improvement in a range of skills—including critical thinking, complex reasoning, and writing—during their first two years of college.

Citing the research of AEI scholar Charles Murray's book *Real Education* (2008), Professor Vedder says: "The number going to college exceeds the number capable of mastering higher levels of intellectual inquiry. This leads colleges to alter their mission, watering down the intellectual content of what they do." Up to 45 percent of incoming freshmen require remedial courses in math, writing, or reading. That's despite the fact that colleges have dumbed down courses so that the students they admit can pass them. Let's face it; as Murray argues, only a modest proportion of our population has the cognitive skills, work discipline, drive, maturity, and integrity to truly master higher education.

Primary and secondary school education is in shambles. Colleges are increasingly in academic decline as they endeavor to make comfortable environments for the educationally incompetent. Colleges should refuse admission to students who are unprepared to do real college work. That would not only help reveal shoddy primary and secondary education but also reduce the number of young people making unwise career choices. Sadly, that won't happen. College administrators want warm bodies to bring in money.

Obama's Educational Excellence Initiative
August 15, 2012

President Barack Obama recently wrote an executive order that established a White House initiative on educational excellence for black Americans that will be housed in the Department of Education. It proposes "to identify evidence-based best practices" to improve black achievement in school and college. Though black education is in desperate straits, the president's executive order will accomplish absolutely nothing to improve black education. The reason is that it does not address the root causes of educational rot among black Americans. It's not rocket science; let's look at it.

The president's initiative contains not one word about rampant inner-city school violence, which makes educational excellence impossible. During the past five years, Philadelphia's 268 schools had 30,000 serious criminal incidents, including assaults—4,000 of which were on teachers—robberies and rapes. Prior to recent layoffs, Philadelphia's school district employed about 500 police officers. In Chicago last year, 700 young people were gunfire victims, and dozens of them lost their lives. Similar stories of street and school violence can be told in other large, predominantly black cities, such as Baltimore, Detroit, Cleveland, Oakland, and Newark.

If rampant school crime is not eliminated, academic excellence will be unachievable. If anything, the president's initiative will help undermine school discipline, because it advocates "promoting a positive school climate that does not rely on methods that result in disparate use of disciplinary tools." That means, for example, if black students are suspended or expelled at greater rates than, say, Asian students, it's a "disparate use of disciplinary tools." Thus, even if blacks are causing a disproportionate part of disciplinary problems, they cannot be disciplined disproportionately.

Whether a student is black, white, orange, or polka dot and whether he's poor or rich, there are some minimum requirements that must be met in order to do well in school. Someone must make the student do his homework, see to it that he gets a good night's rest, fix a breakfast, make sure he gets to school on time, and make sure he respects and obeys his teachers. Here's my question: Which one of those requirements can be accomplished by a presidential executive order, a congressional mandate or the edict of a mayor? If those minimal requirements aren't met, whatever else is done is for naught.

Spending more money on education cannot replace poor parenting. If it could, black academic achievement wouldn't be a problem. Washington, D.C., for example, spends $18,667 per student per year, more than any state, but comes in dead last in terms of student achievement. Paul Laurence Dunbar High School was established in 1870 in Washington, D.C., as the nation's first black public high school. From 1870 to 1955, most of its graduates went off to college, earning degrees from Harvard, Princeton, Williams, Wesleyan, and others. As early as 1899, Dunbar students scored higher on citywide tests than students at any of the district's white schools. Its attendance and tardiness records were generally better than those of white schools. During this era of high achievement, there was no school violence. It wasn't racially integrated. It didn't have a big budget. It didn't even have a lunchroom or all those other things that today's education establishment says are necessary for black academic achievement.

Numerous studies show that children raised in stable two-parent households do far better educationally and otherwise than those raised in single-parent households. Historically, black families have been relatively stable. From 1880 to 1960, the proportion of black children raised in two-parent families held steady at about 70 percent; in 1925 Harlem, it was 85 percent. Today only 33 percent of black children benefit from two-parent families. In 1940, black illegitimacy was 19 percent; today it's 72 percent.

Too many young blacks have become virtually useless in an increasingly high-tech economy. The only bright outlook is the trickle of more and more black parents realizing this and taking their children out of public schools. The president's initiative will help enrich the education establishment but do nothing for black youngsters in desperate educational need.

Educational Lunacy

August 22, 2012

If I were a Klansman, wanting to sabotage black education, I couldn't find better allies than education establishment liberals and officials in the Obama administration, especially Secretary of Education Arne Duncan, who in March 2010 announced that his department was "going to reinvigorate civil rights enforcement."

For Duncan, the civil rights issue was that black elementary and high school students are disciplined at a higher rate than whites. His evidence for discrimination is that blacks are three and a half times more likely to be suspended or expelled than their white peers. Duncan and his Obama administration supporters conveniently ignored school "racial discrimination" against whites, who are more than two times as likely to be suspended as Asians and Pacific Islanders.

Heather Mac Donald reports on all of this in "Undisciplined," appearing in *City Journal* (Summer 2012). She writes that between September 2011 and February 2012, twenty-five times more black Chicago students than white students were arrested at school, mostly for battery. In Chicago schools, black students outnumber whites by four to one.

Mac Donald adds, "Nationally, the picture is no better. The homicide rate among males between the ages of 14 and 17 is nearly ten times higher for blacks than for whites and Hispanics combined. Such data make no impact on the Obama administration and its orbiting advocates, who apparently believe that the lack of self-control and socialization that results in this disproportionate criminal violence does not manifest itself in classroom comportment as well."

According to the National Center for Education Statistics, nationally during 2007–2008, more than 145,000 teachers were physically attacked. Six percent of big-city schools report verbal abuse of teachers, and 18 percent report nonverbal disrespect for teachers. An earlier NCES study found that 18 percent of the nation's schools accounted for 75 percent of the reported incidents of violence, and 6.6 percent accounted for 50 percent. So far as serious violence, murder, and rapes, 1.9 percent of schools reported 50 percent of the incidents. The preponderance of school violence occurs in big-city schools attended by black students.

Educators might not see classroom comportment as a priority. According to a recent hire, a Baltimore high school now asks prospective teachers: "How do you respond to being mistreated? What do you do if someone cusses you out?" The proper answer is: "Nothing." That vision might explain why a thirty-four-year veteran of the school had to be taken from the premises in an ambulance after a student shattered the glass in a classroom display case.

Mac Donald reports that a fifth-grade teacher in St. Paul, Minn., scoffs at the notion that minority students are being unfairly targeted for discipline, saying "Anyone in his right mind knows that these [disciplined] students are extremely disruptive."

In response to the higher disciplinary rates for minority students, the St. Paul school district has spent $350,000 for teacher "cultural-proficiency" training sessions where they learn about "whiteness." At one of these sessions, an Asian teacher asked: "How do I help the student who blurts out answers and disrupts the class?" The black facilitator said: "That's what black culture is." If a white person made such a remark, I'm sure it would be deemed racist.

Some of today's black political leaders are around my age, seventy-six, such as Reps. Maxine Waters, Charles Rangel, John Conyers, former Virginia Gov. Douglas Wilder, Jesse Jackson, and many others. Ask them what their parents would have done had they cursed, assaulted a teacher, or engaged in disruptive behavior that's become routine in far too many schools. Would their parents have accepted the grossly disrespectful public behavior that includes foul language and racial epithets? Their silence and support of the status quo represent a betrayal of epic proportions to the blood, sweat and tears of our ancestors in their struggle to make today's education opportunities available.

Academic Dishonesty
September 19, 2012

Many of the nation's colleges and universities have become cesspools of indoctrination, intolerance, academic dishonesty, and an "enlightened" form of racism. This is a decades-old trend. In a 1991 speech, Yale President Benno Schmidt warned: "The most serious problems of freedom of expression in our society today exist on our campuses. The assumption seems to be that the purpose of education is to induce correct opinion rather than to search for wisdom and to liberate the mind."

Unfortunately, parents, taxpayers, and donors have little knowledge of the extent of the dishonesty and indoctrination. There are several clues for telling whether there's academic dishonesty and indoctrination. One is to see whether a college spends millions for diversity and multiculturalism centers and hires directors of diversity and inclusion, managers of diversity recruitment, associate deans for diversity, and vice presidents of diversity. See whether colleges spend money to indoctrinate incoming freshmen with programs such as "The Tunnel of Oppression," in which, among other things, students call one another vile racial and sexual names in order to develop "oppression awareness."

An American Council of Trustees and Alumni survey in 2004 of fifty selective colleges found that 49 percent of students complained of professors frequently injecting political comments into their courses even if they had nothing to do with the subject, while 46 percent reported that professors used their classrooms to promote their own political views. One English professor told his students that "conservatism champions racism, exploitation and imperialist war." The "critical race studies" program at UCLA School of Law says that its aim is to "transform racial justice advocacy." At an East Coast college, an exam was found with questions such as, "How does the United States 'steal' the resources of other (third world) countries?" The answer marked correct was, "We steal through exploitation." An economics professor told his class, "The United States of America, backed by facts, is the greediest and most selfish country in the world." A Germanic languages professor told his class, "Bush is a moron, a simpleton and an idiot."

A recent National Association of Scholars report, "A Crisis of Competence," reported that the UCLA Higher Education Research Institute found that "more faculty now believe that they should teach their students to be agents of social change than believe that it is important to teach them the classics of Western civilization." Use of public funds for private advocacy not only is academic dishonesty but also borders on criminality.

In today's college climate, we shouldn't be surprised by the outcomes. A survey conducted by the Center for Survey Research and Analysis at the University of Connecticut gave 81 percent of the seniors a D or an F in their knowledge of American history. Many students could not identify Valley Forge, words from the Gettysburg Address, or even the basic principles of the US Constitution. The National Center for Education Statistics reported that only 31 percent of college graduates can read and understand a complex book.

A 2007 national survey titled "Our Fading Heritage: Americans Fail a Basic Test on Their History and Institutions," by the Intercollegiate Studies Institute, found that earning a college degree does little to increase knowledge of America's history. Among the questions asked were: "Who is the commander in chief of the U S. military?" "Name two countries that were our enemies during World War II." The average score among college graduates was 57 percent, or an F. Only 24 percent of college graduates knew the First Amendment prohibits establishing an official religion for the United States.

A 2006 survey conducted by The Conference Board, Corporate Voices for Working Families, the Partnership for 21st Century Skills, and the Society for Human Resource Management found that only 24 percent of employers thought graduates of four-year colleges were "excellently prepared" for entry-level positions.

Our sad state of college education proves what my grandmother admonished: "If you're doing something you're not supposed to be doing, you can't do what you're supposed to do."

Dishonest Educators

January 9, 2013

Nearly two years ago, *U.S. News & World Report* came out with a story titled "Educators Implicated in Atlanta Cheating Scandal." It reported that "for 10 years, hundreds of Atlanta public school teachers and principals changed answers on state tests in one of the largest cheating scandals in US history." More than three-quarters of the fifty-six Atlanta schools investigated had cheated on the National Assessment of Educational Progress test, sometimes called the national report card. Cheating orders came from school administrators and included brazen acts such as teachers reading answers aloud during the test and erasing incorrect answers. One teacher told a colleague, "I had to give your kids, or your students, the answers because they're dumb as hell." Atlanta's not alone. There have been investigations, reports, and charges of teacher-assisted cheating in other cities, such as Philadelphia, Houston, New York, Detroit, Baltimore, Los Angeles, and Washington.

Recently, *The Atlanta Journal-Constitution*'s blog carried a story titled "A new cheating scandal: Aspiring teachers hiring ringers." According to the story, for at least fifteen years, teachers in Arkansas, Mississippi, and Tennessee paid Clarence Mumford, who's now under indictment, between $1,500 and $3,000 to send someone else to take their Praxis exam, which is used for K-12 teacher certification in forty states. Sandra Stotsky, an education professor at the University of Arkansas, said, "[Praxis I] is an easy test for anyone who has completed high school but has nothing to do with college-level ability or scores." She added, "The test is far too undemanding for a prospective teacher. . . . The fact that these people hired somebody to take an easy test of their skills suggests that these prospective teachers were probably so academically weak it is questionable whether they would have been suitable teachers."

Here's a practice Praxis I math question: Which of the following is equal to a quarter-million—40,000, 250,000, 2,500,000, 1/4,000,000, or 4/1,000,000? The test taker is asked to click on the correct answer. A practice writing skills question is to identify the error in the following sentence: "The club members agreed that each would contribute ten days of voluntary work annually each year at the local hospital." The test taker is supposed to point out that "annually each year" is redundant.

CNN broke this cheating story last July, but the story hasn't gotten much national press since then. In an article for *NewsBusters*, titled "Months-Old, Three-State Teacher Certification Test Cheating Scandal Gets Major AP Story—on a Slow News Weekend" (November 25, 2012), Tom Blumer quotes speculation by the blog "educationrealist": "I will be extremely surprised if it does not turn out that most if not all of the teachers who bought themselves a test grade are black. (I am also betting that the actual testers are white, but am not as certain. It just seems that if black people were taking the test and guaranteeing passage, the fees would be higher.)"

There's some basis in fact for the speculation that it's mostly black teachers buying grades, and that includes former Steelers wide receiver Cedrick Wilson, who's been indicted for fraud. According to a study titled "Differences in Passing Rates on Praxis I Tests by Race/Ethnicity Group" (March 2011), the percentages of blacks who passed the Praxis I reading, writing and mathematics tests on their first try were 41, 44, and 37, respectively. For white test takers, the respective percentages were 82, 80 and 78.

This test-taking fraud is merely the tip of a much larger iceberg. It highlights the educational fraud being perpetrated on blacks during their K-12 education. Four or five years of college—even majoring in education, an undemanding subject—cannot make up for those 13 years of rotten education. Then they're given a college degree that is fraudulent, seeing as some have difficulty passing a test that shouldn't be challenging to even a twelfth-grader. Here's my question: If they manage to get through the mockery of teacher certification, at what schools do you think they will teach?

Minority Student Needs

April 3, 2013

Professor Craig Frisby is on the faculty of University of Missouri's Department of Educational, School and Counseling Psychology. His most recent book is *Meeting the Psychoeducational Needs of Minority Students*. It's a 662-page textbook covering a range of topics from multiculturalism and home and family influences to student testing and school discipline. There's no way full justice can be given to this excellent work in the space of this column, so I'll highlight a few valuable insights he makes that would help educators do a better job with minority students.

Quack multiculturalism is the name Frisby gives to the vision of multiculturalism that promotes the falsehoods and distortions that dominate today's college agenda, sold under various names such as "valuing diversity," "being sensitive to cultural differences," and "cultural competence." He identifies different brands of multiculturalism such as boutique, Kumbayah, light-and-fluffy, and bean-counting multiculturalism. Insider language used to promote multiculturalism includes terms such as "practice tolerance," "celebrate diversity," "equity with excellence," and "differences are not deficits." Escalating costs and budget crunches don't stop colleges from hiring vice presidents, deans and directors of diversity.

Multiculturalism teaches that one set of cultural values is equal to another. That means if black students talk, dress and comport themselves in a certain way, to criticize them is merely cultural imperialism. Frisby cites college textbooks that teach: "Racism is what people do, regardless of what they think or feel" and "Institutional racism is characterized by practices or policies that systematically limit opportunities for people who historically have been characterized as psychologically, intellectually, or physically deficient," and "One can view the clock as a tool of racism that the monochromic dominant society uses to regulate subordinate groups."

All of this boils down to teaching undergraduate and graduate students and professionals in the fields of psychology and education to be noncritical and feel sympathy for blacks and other minorities. I might add that such sympathy doesn't extend to Japanese, Chinese, and Jews, who are even more of a minority.

Frisby gives many examples of multicultural lunacy. One particularly egregious one was the twelfth annual White Privilege Conference (WPC) held in 2011 in Minneapolis, Minn., and sponsored by the University of Colorado's Matrix Center for the Advancement of Social Equity. The WPC is "built on the premise that the US was started by white people, for white people." Among the 150 workshops offered during the conference were "Making Your School or Classroom a Force for Eliminating Racism," "Helping Non-White Students Survive Academia—The Pinnacle of White Dominance," and "Uprooting Christian Hegemony." This vision of the mission of education might help to explain why students, particularly minority students, emerge from high school and college with little reading, writing, and thinking ability.

Frisby turns his attention to school discipline and criminal behavior. He discusses the atmosphere at one New York school, which is by no means unique among schools. Teachers experience being pushed, shoved, and spit upon by students. A male teacher transferred to another school after a student threatened to rape his wife. In this kind of atmosphere, should anyone be surprised that only 3 percent of the students were at grade level in English and only 9 percent in math?

The fundamental problem crippling low-income minority students is school behavioral disorder. Its visible manifestations are graffiti, broken and vandalized furniture, fights, sexual activity, drug use in the bathrooms, and rowdy behavior. Frisby says we should tell students exactly how to behave and tolerate no disorder. That's not rocket science, except for today's liberal establishment who run our schools and colleges.

You say, "Williams, what Frisby says simply reflects the insensitivity of privileged white people." But what if I told you that Professor

Craig Frisby is a black professor at the University of Missouri who has a record of fine scholarship? My read of his book is that it supplies more evidence that the actions of soft-minded, guilty white liberals have done far more harm to black people than racists of the past could have ever done.

Academic Cesspools

April 24, 2013

Over the past ten years, I have written columns variously titled "Academic Cesspools," "Academic Dishonesty," "The Shame of Higher Education," "Academic Rot," and "Indoctrination of Our Youth." Therefore, I was not surprised by David Feith's April 5 *Wall Street Journal* article, "The Golf Shot Heard Round the Academic World." In it, Feith tells of a golf course conversation between Barry Mills, the president of Bowdoin College, in Brunswick, Maine, and philanthropist Thomas Klingenstein. Klingenstein voiced disapproval of campus celebration of diversity and ethnic differences while there's "not enough celebration of our common American identity."

Because Klingenstein wouldn't help finance the college's diversity craze, Mills insinuated, in remarks to the student body, that Klingenstein is a racist. Mills also told students: "We must be willing to entertain diverse perspectives throughout our community. . . . Diversity of ideas at all levels of the college is crucial for our credibility and for our educational mission."

Klingenstein decided to check out Mills's commitment to diverse perspectives by commissioning the National Association of Scholars to examine Bowdoin's intellectual diversity, rigorous academics, and civic identity. Its report—"What Does Bowdoin Teach?"—isn't pretty. There are "no curricular requirements that center on the American founding or the history of the nation." Even history majors aren't required to take a single course in American history. In the history department, no course is devoted to American political, military, diplomatic, or intellectual history; the only ones available are organized around some aspect of race, class, gender, or sexuality.

Some of the thirty-seven seminars designated for freshmen are "Affirmative Action and US Society," "Fictions of Freedom," "Racism,"

"Queer Gardens," "Sexual Life of Colonialism," and "Modern Western Prostitutes." As for political diversity, the report estimates that "four or five out of approximately 182 full-time faculty members might be described as politically conservative." During the 2012 presidential campaign, 100 percent of faculty donations went to President Barack Obama. Despite political bias and mediocrity, in 2012, Bowdoin was ranked sixth among the nation's liberal arts colleges in *U.S. News & World Report* and was ranked fourteenth on *Forbes* magazine's list of America's top colleges. That ought to tell us how much faith should be put in college rankings.

I applaud Klingenstein for not making a contribution to a college agenda that is so common today. Wealthy donors are generous but tend to be lazy and uninformed in their giving. They give large sums of money that winds up supporting college agendas that are contemptuous of donors' values, such as enlightened racism, anticapitalism, and Marxism. A rough rule of thumb to discover modern-day racism is to search a college's website to see whether it has vice presidents or deans of diversity and diversity programs. If so, keep your money.

Recent evidence has emerged that some colleges have become bold enough to hire former terrorists to teach and possibly indoctrinate our young people. That's the case with Columbia University in the hiring of convicted Weather Underground terrorist Kathy Boudin, who spent twenty-two years in prison for the murder of two policemen and a Brink's guard. She now holds a professorship at Columbia's School of Social Work. Her Weather Underground comrade William Ayers is a professor of education on the faculty of the University of Illinois at Chicago. Unrepentant, in the wake of 9/11, Ayers told us: "I don't regret setting bombs. I feel we didn't do enough." Bernardine Dohrn, his wife, is a professor at Northwestern University School of Law. Her stated mission is to overthrow capitalism. Ayers and Dohrn, as well as the Rev. Jeremiah Wright, are people who hate our nation and are longtime associates of President Obama's. That might help in explaining our president's vision.

What we see on college campuses represents a dereliction of duty by boards of trustees, which bear the ultimate responsibility. Wealthy donors who care about the fraud of higher education should recognize that there's nothing like the sound of pocketbooks snapping shut to open the closed minds of college administrators.

Black Education Tragedy

July 10, 2013

As if more evidence were needed about the tragedy of black education, Rachel Jeantel, a witness for the prosecution in the George Zimmerman murder trial, put a face on it for the nation to see. Some of that evidence unfolded when Zimmerman's defense attorney asked nineteen-year-old Jeantel to read a letter that she allegedly had written to Trayvon Martin's mother. She responded that she doesn't read cursive, and that's in addition to her poor grammar, syntax, and communication skills.

Jeantel is a senior at Miami Norland Senior High School. How in the world did she manage to become a twelfth-grader without being able to read cursive writing? That's a skill one would expect from a fourth-grader. Jeantel is by no means an exception at her school. Here are a few achievement scores from her school: Thirty-nine percent of the students score basic for reading, and 38 percent score below basic. In math, 37 percent score basic, and 50 percent score below basic. Below basic is the score when a student is unable to demonstrate even partial mastery of knowledge and skills fundamental for proficient work at his grade level. Basic indicates only partial mastery.

Few Americans, particularly black Americans, have any idea of the true magnitude of the black education tragedy. The education establishment might claim that it's not their fault. They're not responsible for the devastation caused by female-headed families, drugs, violence, and the culture of dependency. But they are totally responsible for committing gross educational fraud. It's educators who graduated Jeantel from elementary and middle school and continued to pass her along in high school. It's educators who will, in June 2014, confer upon her a high school diploma.

It's not just Florida's schools. According to the National Assessment of Educational Progress, nationally most black twelfth-graders test either basic or below basic in reading, writing, math, and science. Drs. Abigail and Stephan Thernstrom wrote in their 2004 book, *No*

Excuses: Closing the Racial Gap in Learning, "Blacks nearing the end of their high school education perform a little worse than white eighth-graders in both reading and US history, and a lot worse in math and geography." Little has changed since the book's publication.

Drexel University history and political science professor George Ciccariello-Maher disapprovingly says that the reaction to Jeantel's court performance "has been in terms of aesthetics, of disregarding a witness on the basis of how she talks, how good she is at reading and writing." Harking back to Jim Crow days, he adds: "These are subtle things that echo literacy testing at the polls, echo the question of whether black Americans can testify against white people, of being always suspect in their testimony. It's the same old dynamics emerging in a very different guise." Then there's Morgan Polikoff, assistant professor of education at the University of Southern California, who says: "Cursive should be allowed to die. In fact, it's already dying, despite having been taught for decades." That's the kind of educational philosophy that accounts for much of our nation's educational decline.

The educational system and black family structure and culture have combined to make increasing numbers of young black people virtually useless in the increasingly high-tech world of the twenty-first century. Too many people believe that pouring more money into schools will help. That's whistlin' "Dixie." Whether a student is black or white, poor or rich, there are some minimum requirements that must be met in order to do well in school. Someone must make the student do his homework, see to it that he gets a good night's sleep, fix a breakfast, make sure he gets to school on time, and make sure he respects and obeys his teachers. Here are my questions: Which one of those requirements can be achieved through a higher school budget? Which can be achieved by politicians? If those minimal requirements aren't met, whatever else is done is mostly for naught.

I hope Rachel Jeantel's court performance is a wake-up call for black Americans about the devastation wrought by our educational system.

Reeducation at George Mason

August 28, 2013

This week begins my thirty-fourth year serving on George Mason University's distinguished economics faculty. You might imagine my surprise when I received a letter from its Office of Equity and Diversity Services notifying me that I was required to "complete the in-person Equal Opportunity and Prevention of Sexual Harassment Policies and Procedures training." This is a leftist agenda for indoctrination, thought control, and free speech suppression to which I shall refuse to submit. Let's look at it.

Ideas such as equity and equal opportunity, while having high emotional value, are vacuous analytical concepts. For example, I've asked students whether they plan to give every employer an equal opportunity to hire them when they graduate. To a person, they always answer no. If they aren't going to give every employer an equal opportunity to hire them, what's fair about forcing employers to give them an equal opportunity to be hired?

I'm guilty of gross violation of equality of opportunity, racism, and possibly sexism. Back in 1960, when interviewing people to establish a marital contract, every woman wasn't given an equal opportunity. I discriminated against not only white, Indian, Asian, Mexican, and handicapped women but men of any race. My choices were confined to good-looking black women. You say, "Williams, that kind of discrimination doesn't harm anyone!" Nonsense! When I married Mrs. Williams, other women were harmed by having a reduced opportunity set.

George Mason's Office of Equity and Diversity Services has far more challenging equity and diversity work than worrying about the reeducation of Professor Williams. They must know that courts have long held that gross racial disparities are probative of a pattern and practice of discrimination. The most notable gross racial disparity on campus, and hence probative of discrimination, can be found on GMU's fabulous men's basketball team. Blacks are less than 9 percent of student enrollment but are 85 percent of our varsity basketball team and dominate its starting five. It's not just GMU. Watch any Saturday afternoon college basketball game and ask yourself the question fixated in the minds of equity, diversity, and inclusion hunters: Does this look like America? Among the ten players on the court, at best there might be two white players. In 2010, 61 percent of Division I basketball players were black, and only 31 percent were white.

Allied with the purveyors of equity, diversity, and inclusion are the multiculturalists, who call for the celebration of cultures. For them, all cultures are morally equivalent and to deem otherwise is Eurocentrism. That's unbridled nonsense. Ask your multiculturalist: Is forcible female genital mutilation, as practiced in nearly thirty sub-Saharan Africa and Middle Eastern countries, a morally equivalent cultural value? Slavery is practiced in Sudan and Niger; is that a cultural equivalent? In most of the Middle East, there are numerous limits on women—such as prohibitions on driving, employment, voting, and education. Under Islamic law, in some countries, female adulterers face death by stoning, and thieves face the punishment of having their hand severed. Are these cultural values morally equivalent, superior, or inferior to those of the West?

Western values are superior to all others. Why? The greatest achievement of the West was the concept of individual rights. The Western transition from barbarism to civility didn't happen overnight. It emerged feebly—mainly in England, starting with the Magna Carta of 1215—and took centuries to get where it is today.

One need not be a Westerner to hold Western values. A person can be Chinese, Japanese, Jewish, African, or Arab and hold Western values. It's no accident that Western values of reason and individual rights have produced unprecedented health, life expectancy, wealth, and comfort for the ordinary person.

Western values are under ruthless attack by the academic elite on college campuses across America. They want to replace personal liberty with government control and replace equality before the law with entitlement. The multiculturalism and diversity agenda is a cancer on our society, and our tax dollars and charitable donations are supporting it.

Student Indoctrination

September 18, 2013

The new college academic year has begun, and unfortunately, so has student indoctrination. Let's look at some of it.

William Penn, Michigan State University professor of creative writing, greeted his first day of class with an anti-Republican rant. Campus Reform, a project of the Arlington, Va.-based Leadership Institute, has a video featuring the professor telling his students that Republicans want to prevent "black people" from voting. He added that "this country still is full of closet racists" and described Republicans as "a bunch of dead white people—or dying white people" (http://tinyurl.com/lve4te7). To a student who had apparently displayed displeasure with those comments, Professor Penn barked, "You can frown if you want." He gesticulated toward the student and added, "You look like you're frowning. Are you frowning?" When the professor's conduct was brought to the attention of campus authorities, MSU spokesman Kent Cassella said, "At MSU it is important the classroom environment is conducive to a free exchange of ideas and is respectful of the opinions of others."

That mealy-mouthed response is typical of university administrators. Professor Penn was using his classroom to proselytize students. That is academic dishonesty and warrants disciplinary or dismissal proceedings. But that's not likely. Professor Penn's vision is probably shared by his colleagues, seeing as he was the recipient of MSU's Distinguished Faculty Award in 2003. University of Southern California professor Darry Sragow shares Penn's opinion. Last fall, he went on a rant telling his students that Republicans are "stupid and racist" and "the last vestige of angry old white people" (http://tinyurl.com/l85khtk).

UCLA's new academic year saw its undergraduate student government fighting for constitutional rights by unanimously passing a resolution calling for the end of the use of the phrase "illegal immigrant." The resolution states, "The racially derogatory I-word endangers basic human rights including the presumption of innocence and the right to due process guaranteed under the US Constitution." No doubt some UCLA administrators and professors bereft of thinking skills helped them craft the resolution.

The *New York Post* (August 25, 2011) carried a story about a student in training to become dorm supervisor at DePauw University in Indiana. She said: "We were told that 'human' was not a suitable identity, but that instead we were first 'black,' 'white,' or 'Asian'; 'male' or 'female'; . . . 'heterosexual' or 'queer.' We were forced to act like bigots and spout off stereotypes while being told that that was what we were really thinking deep down." At many universities, part of the freshman orientation includes what's called the "tunnel of oppression." They are taught the evils of "white privilege" and how they are part of a "rape culture." Sometimes they are forced to discuss their sexual identities with complete strangers. The *New York Post* story said: "DePauw is no rare case. At least 96 colleges across the country have run similar 'tunnel of oppression' programs in the last few years."

University officials are aware of this kind of academic dishonesty and indoctrination; university trustees are not. For the most part, trustees are yes men for the president. Legislators and charitable foundations that pour billions into colleges are unaware, as well. Most tragically, parents who pay tens of thousands of dollars for tuition and pile up large debt to send their youngsters off to be educated are unaware of the academic rot, as well.

You ask, "Williams, what can be done?" Students should record classroom professorial propaganda and give it wide distribution over the internet. I've taught for more than forty-five years and routinely invited students to record my lectures so they don't have to be stenographers during class. I have no idea of where those recordings have wound up, but if you find them, you'll hear zero proselytization or discussion of my political and personal preferences. To use a classroom to propagate one's personal beliefs is academic dishonesty.

Vladimir Lenin said, "Give me four years to teach the children and the seed I have sown will never be uprooted." That's the goal of the leftist teaching agenda.

Schoolteacher Cheating

February 5, 2014

Philadelphia's public school system has joined several other big-city school systems, such as those in Atlanta, Detroit, and Washington, D.C., in widespread teacher-led cheating on standardized academic achievement tests. So far, the city has fired three school principals, and *The Wall Street Journal* reports, "Nearly 140 teachers and administrators in Philadelphia public schools have been implicated in one of the nation's largest cheating scandals" (January 23, 2014) (http://tinyurl.com/q5makm3). Investigators found that teachers got together after tests to erase the students' incorrect answers and replace them with correct answers. In some cases, they went as far as to give or show students answers during the test.

Jerry Jordan, president of the Philadelphia Federation of Teachers, identifies the problem as district officials focusing too heavily on test scores to judge teacher performance, and they've converted low-performing schools to charters run by independent groups that typically hire nonunion teachers. But William Hite, superintendent of the School District of Philadelphia, said cheating by adults harms students because schools use test scores to determine which students need remedial help, saying, "There is no circumstance, no matter how pressured the cooker, that adults should be cheating students."

While there's widespread teacher test cheating to conceal education failure, most notably among black children, it's just the tip of the iceberg. The National Assessment of Educational Progress, published by the US Department of Education's National Center for Education Statistics and sometimes referred to as the Nation's Report Card, measures student performance in the fourth and eighth grades. In 2013, 46 percent of Philadelphia eighth-graders scored below basic, and 35 percent scored basic. Below basic is a score meaning that a student is unable to demonstrate even partial mastery of knowledge and skills fundamental for proficient work at his grade level. Basic indicates only partial mastery. It's a similar story in reading, with 42 percent below basic and 41 percent basic. With this kind of performance, no one should be surprised that of the state of Pennsylvania's twenty-seven most poorly performing schools on the SAT, twenty-five are in Philadelphia.

Philadelphia's four-year high-school graduation rate in 2012 was 64 percent, well below the national rate of 78 percent. Even if a student graduates from high school, what does it mean? What a high-school diploma means for white students is nothing to write home about, as suggested by the fact that every year, nearly 60 percent of first-year college students must take remedial courses in English or mathematics. What a high school diploma means for black students is nothing less than a disaster, as pointed out by Drs. Abigail and Stephan Thernstrom in their 2009 book, *No Excuses: Closing the Racial Gap in Learning.* They state that "blacks nearing the end of their high school education perform a little worse than white eighth-graders in both reading and US history, and a lot worse in math and geography." Little has changed since the book's publication.

Hite rightfully said that test cheating by adults harms students, but that harm pales in comparison with the harm done by teachers awarding fraudulent grades and conferring fraudulent high school diplomas, particularly to black students. You say, "Williams, what do you mean by fraudulent diplomas?" When a student is given a high school diploma, that attests that he can read, write, and compute at a twelfth-grade level, and when he can't do so at the eighth-grade level, that diploma is fraudulent. What makes it so tragic is that neither the student nor his parents are aware that he has a fraudulent diploma. When a black person is not admitted to college, flunks out of college, can't pass a civil service test, or doesn't get job promotions, he is likelier to blame racial discrimination than his poor education.

Politicians, civil rights organizations, and the education establishment will do nothing about the fraud. In fact, they give their full allegiance to the perpetrators.

Solutions to Black Education
February 26, 2014

A fortnight ago, my column focused on how Philadelphia's school-teachers have joined public-school teachers in cities such as Atlanta, Detroit, Los Angeles, Columbus, New York, and Washington in changing student scores on academic achievement tests. Teachers have held grade-fixing parties, sometimes wearing rubber gloves to hide fingerprints. In some cases, poorly performing students were excused from taking exams to prevent them from dragging down averages. As a result of investigations, a number of schoolteachers and administrators have been suspended, fired, or indicted by states attorneys general.

Most of these cheating scandals have occurred in predominantly black schools across the nation. At one level, it's easy to understand—but by no means condone—the motivation teachers have to cheat. Teachers have families to raise, mortgages, car payments, and other financial obligations. Their pay, retention and promotions depend on how well their students perform on standardized tests.

Very often, teachers must deal with an impossible classroom atmosphere in which many, if not most, of the students are disorderly, disobedient, and alien and hostile to the education process. Many students pose a significant safety threat. The latest statistics available, published by the Department of Education's National Center for Education Statistics, in a report titled "Indicators of School Crime and Safety: 2012," tell us that nationwide between 2007 and 2008, about 145,100 public-school teachers were physically attacked by students, and another 276,700 were threatened with injury.

Should any of this criminal behavior be tolerated? Should unruly students be able to halt the education process? And, a question particularly for black people: Are we in such good educational shape that we can afford to allow some students to make education impossible? A report supported in part by the Congressional Black Caucus Foundation, titled "Reducing Suspension among Academically Disengaged

Black Males" (http://tinyurl.com/my95jh3), suggests a tolerance for disruptive students.

There are some members of the Congressional Black Caucus, the NAACP, and the National Urban League who attended school during the years I attended (1942–54). During those days, no youngster would have even cursed a teacher, much less assaulted one. One has to wonder why black leaders accept behavior that never would have been tolerated by their parents and teachers. Back then, to use foul language or assault a teacher or any other adult would have resulted in some form of corporal punishment in school or at home or both. Today such discipline would have a teacher or parent jailed. That, in turn, means there is little or no meaningful sanction against unruly or criminal behavior.

No one argues that yesteryear's students were angels. In Philadelphia, where I grew up, students who posed severe disciplinary problems were removed. Daniel Boone School was for unruly boys, and Carmen was for girls. Some people might respond: But what are we going to do with the students kicked out? Whether or not there are resources to help them is not the issue. The critical issue is whether they should be permitted to make education impossible for students who are capable of learning. It's a policy question similar to: What do you do when you have both drunken drivers and sober drivers on the road? The first order of business is to get the drunken drivers off the road. Whether there are resources available to help the drunks is, at best, a secondary issue.

There is little that the political and education establishment will do about the grossly fraudulent education received by many black youngsters, and more money is not the answer. For example, according to findings by Cato Institute's Andrew J. Coulson, Washington, D.C., spends $29,409 per pupil (http://tinyurl.com/mpc82dq). In terms of academic achievement, its students are nearly the nation's worst. The average tuition for a K-12 Catholic school is $9,000, and for a nonsectarian private K-12 school, it is $16,000. A voucher system would empower black parents to remove their children from high-cost and low-quality public schools and enroll them in lower-cost and higher-quality nonpublic schools.

The Education Establishment's Success
June 25, 2014

Many view America's education as a failure, but in at least one important way, it's been a success—a success in dumbing down the nation so that we fall easy prey to charlatans, hustlers, and quacks. You say, "Williams, that's insulting! Explain yourself." OK, let's start with a question or two.

Are you for or against global warming, later renamed climate change and more recently renamed climate disruption? Environmentalists have renamed it because they don't want to look silly in the face of cooling temperatures. About 650 million years ago, the Earth was frozen from pole to pole, a period scientists call Snowball Earth. The Earth is no longer frozen from pole to pole. There must have been global warming, and it cannot be blamed on humans. Throughout the Earth's history, we've had both ice ages and higher temperatures when CO_2 emissions were ten times higher than they are today. There's one immutable fact about climate. It changes, and mankind can't do anything about it. Only idiocy would conclude that mankind's capacity to change the climate is more powerful than the forces of nature.

During Barack Obama's 2008 presidential campaign, his slogans were about hope and change. At the time, I asked people whether they were for or against change. Most often, I received a blank stare, whereupon I reminded them that change is a fact of life. Nonetheless, when candidate Obama uttered "hope and change," it was received with thunderous applause. There was also thunderous applause when Obama promised, "This was the moment when the rise of the oceans began to slow and our planet began to heal." Only a deranged environmental wacko and duped people could believe that a non-god can change ocean depths.

Americans fall easy prey to charlatans of all stripes because of the education establishment's success in dumbing down the nation. Nowhere has this dumbing down been more successful than it has in creating a historical amnesia. Historian Arthur M. Schlesinger Jr. wrote in *The Disuniting of America*: "History is to the nation . . . as memory is to the individual. As an individual deprived of memory becomes disoriented and lost, not knowing where he has been or where he is going, so a nation denied a conception of its past will be disabled in dealing with its present and its future."

The National Assessment of Educational Progress tests students in grades four, eight, and twelve on several broad subject areas every few years. Just 20 percent of fourth-graders, 17 percent of eighth-graders, and 12 percent of twelfth-graders were at grade-level proficiency in American history in the 2010 exams. Because students don't learn American history, they learn little about our founding principles and they fail to learn why America is an exceptional nation. But that's a part of the progressive/liberal agenda. If Americans knew and understood our founding principles and values, special interest groups and politicians couldn't run roughshod over our liberties.

But it's not just K-12 students who are ignorant of our history. In a 1990 survey—and there's been no improvement since—almost half of college seniors couldn't locate the Civil War within the correct half-century. More recently, 60 percent of American adults couldn't name the president who ordered the dropping of the first atomic bomb, and over 20 percent didn't know where—or even whether—the atomic bomb had been used. The same people didn't know who America's enemies were during World War II (Germany, Japan, and Italy). In a civics survey, more American teenagers were able to name The Three Stooges (Larry, Moe, and Curly) than the three branches of the federal government (executive, legislative, and judicial). A third of the people who were asked the origin of the statement "From each according to his ability, to each according to his need" responded by saying it's from our Bill of Rights, when it's actually from "The Communist Manifesto."

I'd say that the education establishment has been successful beyond its wildest dreams in reducing Americans' ability to think and therefore causing them to have little knowledge of or love for our founding principles.

Tuition Pays for This

August 20, 2014

According to the College Board, average tuition and fees for the 2013–14 school year totaled $30,094 at private colleges, $8,893 for in-state residents at public colleges, and $22,203 for out-of-state residents. Many schools, such as Columbia University and George Washington University, charge yearly tuition and fees close to $50,000. Faced with the increasing costs of higher education, parents and taxpayers might like to know what they're getting for their money.

Campus Reform documents outrageous behavior at some colleges. Mark Landis, a former accounting professor at San Francisco State University, frequently entertained students at this home. He now faces fifteen charges of invasion of privacy. Police say he was discovered with dozens of graphic videos he had made of students using his bathroom.

Mireille Miller-Young—professor of feminist studies at the University of California, Santa Barbara—recently pleaded no contest to charges of theft of banners and assault on a pro-life protester last March.

Every so often, colleges get it right, as the University of Illinois at Urbana-Champaign did when it withdrew its teaching offer to Steven G. Salaita. He had used his Twitter account to tell followers they are awful human beings if they support Israel, saying he supports the complete destruction of Israel, as well as calling for the decolonization of North America.

Then there are some strange college courses. At Georgetown University, there's a course called Philosophy and Star Trek, where professor Linda Wetzel explores questions such as "Can persons survive death?" and "Is time travel possible? Could we go back and kill our grandmothers?"

At Columbia College Chicago, there's a class called Zombies in Popular Media. The course description reads, "Daily assignments focus on reflection and commentary, while final projects foster thoughtful connections between student disciplines and the figure of the zombie."

West Coast colleges refuse to be left behind the times. University of California, Irvine physics professor Michael Dennin teaches The Science of Superheroes, in which he explores questions such as "Have you ever wondered if Superman could really bend steel bars?" and "Would a 'gamma ray' accident turn you into the Hulk?," and "What is a 'spidey-sense'?"

The average person would think that the major task of colleges is to educate and advance human knowledge. The best way to do that is to have competition in the marketplace of ideas. But Michael Yaki, head of the US Commission on Civil Rights, disagrees. During a July 5 briefing on sexual harassment law in education, Yaki explained that college free speech restrictions are necessary because adolescent and young adult brains process information differently than adult brains.

Fortunately, the Foundation for Individual Rights in Education (FIRE) has waged a successful campaign against college restrictions on free speech. Some of its past victories include eliminating restrictions such as Bowdoin College's ban on jokes and stories "experienced by others as harassing"; Brown University's ban on "verbal behavior" that produced "feelings of impotence, anger or disenfranchisement," whether "unintentional or intentional"; the University of Connecticut's absurd ban of "inappropriately directed laughter"; and Colby College's ban on any speech that could lead to a loss of self-esteem. Some colleges sought to protect female students. Bryn Mawr College banned "suggestive looks," and "unwelcome flirtations" were not allowed at Haverford College.

Greg Lukianoff, president of FIRE and author of *Unlearning Liberty*, argues that campus censorship is contributing to an atmosphere of stifled discourse. In 2010, an Association of American Colleges and Universities study found that only 17 percent of professors strongly agreed with the statement that it is "safe to hold unpopular positions on campus." Only 30 percent of college seniors strongly agreed with that statement. The First Amendment Center's annual survey found that a startling 47 percent of young people believe that the First Amendment "goes too far."

The bottom line is that many colleges have lost sight of their basic educational mission of teaching young people critical thinking skills, and they're failing at that mission at higher and higher costs to parents and taxpayers.

PART V:

Environment and Health

If one listens to the global warming rhetoric of environmentalists, one would think that there is a certain temperature that the Earth should be. Of course, they will not tell us just what that temperature is. But that is just a small part of the dishonesty of much of the environmental movement. More of that dishonesty is seen in their abandoning of the term global warming. They have been embarrassed by the fact that world temperatures have not gotten warmer as they have been predicting. To deal with that embarrassment, they no longer use the term global warming. Now they call it climate change. That way they see themselves as maintaining a modicum of respectability because whatever happens to climate they are "right." That is, if there is an above-average warm spell they are right in their predictions and if temperatures are well below average they are right. Some environmentalists play it even safer by calling it climate disruption. That means if temperature rises, falls, or remains the same, they cannot be criticized for erroneous predictions.

Some environmentalist arguments are beyond reason. Here are some: "The world that we live in is beautiful but fragile." "The third rock from the sun is a fragile oasis." "Remember that Earth needs to be saved every single day." These statements are the stock in trade of environmentalists and are held to be beyond question. I question them.

The 1883 eruption of the Krakatoa volcano, in present-day Indonesia, had the force of 200 megatons of TNT. That's the equivalent of 13,300 15-kiloton atomic bombs of the kind that destroyed Hiroshima in

1945. Preceding the 1883 eruption was the 1815 Tambora eruption, also in present-day Indonesia. It holds the record as the largest known volcanic eruption. It spewed so much debris into the atmosphere, blocking sunlight, that 1816 became known as the "Year Without a Summer" or "Summer That Never Was." It led to crop failures and livestock death in much of the Northern Hemisphere and caused the worst famine of the nineteenth century. Then there was the 535 A.D. Krakatoa eruption that had such force that it blotted out much of the light and heat of the sun for eighteen months and is said to have led to the Dark Ages. Despite these cataclysmic events, that would make anything done by mankind's activity look like child's play, somehow the "fragile" Earth survived and so did mankind. So how fragile is the Earth when it survived these and many other cataclysmic events?

Most Americans have no knowledge of the disregard of and contempt for human life held by environmentalists. One need go no further than their own statements, such as those cited in Chris Horner's article "In Gaia We Trust," a 2003 newsletter published by the Competitive Enterprise Institute. Ecologist Lamont Cole said, "To feed a starving child is to exacerbate the world population problem." Regarding the deaths of millions of people because of a worldwide prohibition on DDT spraying, Charles Wursta of the Environmental Defense Fund said, "This is as good a way to get rid of them as any." Paul Watson, founder of Greenpeace, said, "I got the impression that instead of going out to shoot birds, I should go out and shoot the kids who shoot birds."

Then there are statements like these: David Brower, founder of Friends of the Earth, and former executive director of Sierra Club, said, "While the death of young men in war is unfortunate, it is no more serious than the touching of mountains and wilderness areas by humankind." David M. Graber, research biologist with the National Park Service said, "Human happiness, and certainly human fecundity, are not as important as a wild and healthy planet." John Davis, editor of Earth First Journal said, "Human beings, as a species, have no more value than slugs." He added, "I suspect that eradicating smallpox was wrong. It played an important part in balancing ecosystems." These are simply a few samples of statements of some environmentalists that stand as proof of their abiding contempt for humankind.

During the debate over Obamacare, Speaker Nancy Pelosi was asked by a news reporter, "Madam Speaker, where specifically does the Constitution grant Congress the authority to enact an individual health insurance mandate?" Speaker Pelosi responded, "Are you serious? Are you serious?" The reporter said, "Yes, yes, I am." Speaker Pelosi refused to respond but her press spokesman said about the reporter's question regarding what constitutional authority gave Congress the power to mandate that individual Americans buy health insurance, "You can put this on the record. That is not a serious question. That is not a serious question."

Speaker Pelosi's contempt for the constitutional limits imposed on Congress is widely shared by most members of Congress, be they Republicans or Democrats. But the true tragedy is that contempt is shared by most Americans. Whether congressional acts are good ideas or bad ideas is irrelevant. The relevant question that should be asked about any congressional act is: Is it permissible by the US Constitution?

Even if constitutionality is ignored, there is the question whether socialized or government-controlled medicine works. The columns in this section offer abundant evidence that socialized medicine falls wide of its promise to deliver better medical care to the ordinary person.

Sweden's Government Health Care
March 4, 2009

Government health care advocates used to sing the praises of Britain's National Health Service (NHS). That's until its poor delivery of health care services became known. A recent study by David Green and Laura Casper, "Delay, Denial and Dilution," written for the London-based Institute of Economic Affairs, concludes that the NHS health care services are just about the worst in the developed world. The head of the World Health Organization calculated that Britain has as many as 25,000 unnecessary cancer deaths a year because of under-provision of care. Twelve percent of specialists surveyed admitted refusing kidney dialysis to patients suffering from kidney failure because of limits on cash. Waiting lists for medical treatment have become so long that there are now "waiting lists" for the waiting list.

Government health care advocates sing the praises of Canada's single-payer system. Canada's government system isn't that different from Britain's. For example, after a Canadian has been referred to a specialist, the waiting list for gynecological surgery is four to twelve weeks, cataract removal twelve to eighteen weeks, tonsillectomy three to thirty-six weeks, and neurosurgery five to thirty weeks. Toronto-area hospitals, concerned about lawsuits, ask patients to sign a legal release accepting that while delays in treatment may jeopardize their health, they nevertheless hold the hospital blameless. Canadians have an option the British don't: close proximity of American hospitals. In fact, the Canadian government spends over $1 billion each year for Canadians to receive medical treatment in our country. I wonder how much money the US government spends for Americans to be treated in Canada.

"OK, Williams," you say, "Sweden is the world's socialist wonder." Sven R. Larson tells about some of Sweden's problems in "Lesson from Sweden's Universal Health System: Tales from the Health-care Crypt," published in the *Journal of American Physicians and Surgeons* (Spring 2008). Mr. D., a Gothenburg multiple sclerosis patient, was prescribed a new drug. His doctor's request was denied because the drug was

33 percent more expensive than the older medicine. Mr. D. offered to pay for the medicine himself but was prevented from doing so. The bureaucrats said it would set a bad precedent and lead to unequal access to medicine.

Malmo, with its 280,000 residents, is Sweden's third-largest city. To see a physician, a patient must go to one of two local clinics before they can see a specialist. The clinics have security guards to keep patients from getting unruly as they wait hours to see a doctor. The guards also prevent new patients from entering the clinic when the waiting room is considered full. Uppsala, a city with 200,000 people, has only one specialist in mammography. Sweden's National Cancer Foundation reports that in a few years most Swedish women will not have access to mammography.

Dr. Olle Stendahl, a professor of medicine at Linkoping University, pointed out a side effect of government-run medicine: its impact on innovation. He said, "In our budget-government health care there is no room for curious, young physicians and other professionals to challenge established views. New knowledge is not attractive but typically considered a problem [that brings] increased costs and disturbances in today's slimmed-down health care."

These are just a few of the problems of Sweden's single-payer government-run health care system. I wonder how many Americans would like a system that would, as in the case of Mr. D. of Gothenburg, prohibit private purchase of your own medicine if the government refused paying. We have problems in our health care system but most of them are a result of too much government. Over 50 percent of health care expenditures in our country are made by government. Government health care advocates might say that they will avoid the horrors of other government-run systems. Don't believe them.

The American Association of Physicians and Surgeons, who published Sven Larson's paper, is a group of liberty-oriented doctors and health care practitioners who haven't sold their members down the socialist river as have other medical associations. They deserve our thanks for being a major player in the '90s defeat of "Hillary care."

EPA Cover-up

July 15, 2009

Here's what I wrote in last year's column titled "Global Warming Rope-a-Dope" (December 24, 2008): "Once laws are written, they are very difficult, if not impossible, to repeal. If a time would ever come when the permafrost returns to northern US, as far south as New Jersey as it once did, it's not inconceivable that Congress, caught in the grip of the global warming zealots, would keep all the laws on the books they wrote in the name of fighting global warming. Personally, I would not put it past them to write more." On June 28, 2009, the House of Representatives, by a narrow margin (219–212), passed the Waxman-Markey bill. The so-called "cap and trade" bill has been sold as a system for cutting greenhouse gas emissions in the struggle against global warming. There's a full-court press on the US Senate to pass its version of "cap and trade."

"Cap and trade" is first a massive indirect tax on the American people and hence another source of revenue for Congress. More importantly "cap and trade" is just about the most effective tool for controlling most economic activity short of openly declaring ourselves a communist nation and it's a radical environmentalist's dream come true.

So why the rush and the press on the Senate? Increasing evidence is emerging that far from there being global warming, the Earth has been cooling and has been doing so for ten years. Prominent atmospheric scientists have recently sent a letter to Congress saying, "You are being deceived about global warming. . . . The Earth has been cooling for ten years. . . . The present cooling was not predicted by the alarmists' computer models." Last March, more than 700 international scientists went on record dissenting over manmade global warming claims. About 31,500 American scientists, including 9,029 with PhDs, have signed a petition, that in part reads, "There is no convincing scientific evidence that human release of carbon dioxide, methane or other greenhouse gases is causing or will, in the foreseeable future, cause catastrophic heating of the Earth's atmosphere and disruption of the Earth's climate."

The Obama administration's EPA sees the increasing evidence against global warming as a threat to their agenda and has taken desperate measures. About a week before the House vote on "cap and trade," the Washington, D.C.-based Competitive Enterprise Institute (CEI) released some EPA e-mails, demonstrating that an internal report by Alan Carlin, a thirty-five-year career EPA analyst, criticizing EPA's position on global warming, had been squelched for political reasons (http://bit.ly/11XwoC). One of the e-mails, from Dr. Al McGartland, director of the EPA's National Center for Environmental Economics, reads, "The administrator and administration has decided to move forward on endangerment, and your comments do not help the legal or policy case for this decision. . . . I can see only one impact of your comments given where we are in the process, and that would be a very negative impact on our office."

The Competitive Enterprise Institute summarizes Dr. Carlin's report, saying, "[T]hat EPA, by adopting the United Nations' 2007 'Fourth Assessment' report, is relying on outdated research and is ignoring major new developments. Those developments include a continued decline in global temperatures, a new consensus that future hurricanes will not be more frequent or intense, and new findings that water vapor will moderate, rather than exacerbate, temperature. New data also indicate that ocean cycles are probably the most important single factor in explaining temperature fluctuations, though solar cycles may play a role as well, and that reliable satellite data undercut the likelihood of endangerment from greenhouse gases."

Geologist Dr. David Gee, chairman of the science committee of the 2008 International Geological Congress, currently at Uppsala University in Sweden asks, "For how many years must the planet cool before we begin to understand that the planet is not warming? For how many years must cooling go on?" Obviously, ten years is not enough.

Who May Harm Whom?

August 5, 2009

"No one has a right to harm another." Just a little thought, along with a few examples, would demonstrate that blanket statement as pure nonsense. Suppose there is a beautiful lady that both Jim and Bob are pursuing. If Jim wins her hand, Bob is harmed. By the same token, if Bob wins her hand, Jim is harmed. Whose harm is more important and should the beautiful lady be permitted to harm either Bob or Jim are nonsense questions.

During the 1970s, when Hewlett-Packard and Texas Instruments came out with scientific calculators, great harm was suffered by slide rule manufacturers such as Keuffel & Esser, and Pickett. Slide rulers have since gone the way of the dodo but the question is: Should Hewlett-Packard and Texas Instruments have been permitted to inflict such grievous harm on slide rule manufacturers? In 1927, General Electric successfully began marketing the refrigerator. The ice industry, a major industry and the livelihoods of thousands of workers, was destroyed virtually overnight. Should such harm have been permitted and what should Congress have done to save jobs in the slide rule and ice industries?

The first thing we should acknowledge is that we live in a world of harms. Harm is reciprocal. For example, if the government stopped Hewlett-Packard and Texas Instruments from harming Keuffel & Esser and Pickett, or stopped General Electric from harming ice producers, by denying them the right to manufacture calculators and refrigerators, they would have been harmed, plus the billions of consumers who benefited from calculators and refrigerators. There is no scientific or intelligent way to determine which person's harm is more important than the other. That means things are more complicated than saying that one person has no rights to harm another. We must ask which harms are to be permitted in a free society and are not to be permitted. For example, it's generally deemed acceptable for me to harm you by momentarily disturbing your peace and quiet by driving a motorcycle past your house. It's deemed unacceptable for me to harm you by tossing a brick through your window.

In a free society, many conflicting harms are settled through the institution of private property rights. Private property rights have to do with rights belonging to the person deemed owner of property to keep, acquire, use, and dispose of property as he deems fit so long as he does not violate similar rights of another. Let's say that you are offended, possibly harmed, by bars that play vulgar rap music and permit smoking. If you could use government to outlaw rap music and smoking in bars, you would be benefited and people who enjoyed rap music and smoking would be harmed. Again, there is no scientific or intelligent way to determine whose harm is more important. In a free society, the question of who has the right to harm whom, by permitting rap music and smoking, is answered by the property rights question: Who owns the bar? In a socialistic society, such conflicting harms are resolved through government intimidation and coercion.

What about the right to harm oneself, such as the potential harm that can come from not wearing a seatbelt. That, too, is a property rights question. If you own yourself, you have the right to take chances with your own life. Some might argue that if you're not wearing a seatbelt and wind up a vegetable, society has to take care of you; therefore, the fascist threat "click it or ticket." Becoming a burden on society is not a problem of liberty and private property. It's a problem of socialism where one person is forced to take care of someone else. That being the case, the government, in the name of reducing health care costs, assumes part ownership of you and as such assumes a right to control many aspects of your life. That Americans have joyfully given up self-ownership is both tragic and sad.

Global Warming Is a Religion

January 13, 2010

Manmade global warming, for many, is an Earth-worshipping religion. The essential feature of any religion is that its pronouncements are to be accepted on the basis of faith as opposed to hard evidence. Questioning those pronouncements makes one a sinner. No one denies that the Earth's temperature changes. Millions of years ago, much of our planet was covered by ice, at some places up to a mile thick, a period some scientists call "Snowball Earth." Today, the Earth is not covered by a mile of ice; a safe conclusion is that there must have been a bit of global warming. I don't know the cause of that warming, but I'd wager everything I own that it was not caused by coal-fired electric generation plants, incandescent light bulbs, and SUVs tooling up and down the highways.

The very idea that mankind can make significant parametric changes to the Earth has to be the height of arrogance. How about a few questions, because temperature is just one characteristic of the Earth? The Earth's orbit is another. If all 6.5 billion of us, all at once, started jumping up and down for a little while, do you think we'd change the Earth's orbit or rotation? Do you think mankind could change the direction and timing of the ocean's tides? Is there anything that mankind can do to stop or start a tsunami or hurricane? You say, "Williams, it's stupid to suggest that mankind could change the Earth's orbit or rotation, ocean tides, or cause or stop a tsunami or hurricane!" You're right and it's also stupid to think that mankind's activities can make globalized changes in the Earth's temperature.

Nonetheless, there is much at stake in getting people to subscribe to the global warming religion. There is so much at stake that some scientists, using government grants, are fraudulently manipulating climate data and engaging in criminal activity, as revealed in what has been called "Climate gate." One of the most dangerous features of the global warming religion is its level of intimidation of heretics or would-be heretics.

A few years back, Dr. Heidi Cullen, the Weather Channel's climatologist, advocated that the American Meteorological Society (AMS) strip their seal of approval from any TV weatherman expressing skepticism about the predictions of manmade global warming. Scott Pelley, CBS News "60 Minutes" correspondent, compared skeptics of global warming to "Holocaust deniers." Former Vice President Al Gore called skeptics "global warming deniers." But it gets worse. On one of her shows, Dr. Cullen featured columnist Dave Roberts, who, in his September 19, 2006, online publication, said, "When we've finally gotten serious about global warming, when the impacts are really hitting us and we're in a full worldwide scramble to minimize the damage, we should have war crimes trials for these bastards—some sort of climate Nuremberg."

As a result, many climatologists have been intimidated into silence. That means the public is not informed about counter-alarmists facts such as: Over long periods of time, there is absolutely no close relationship between CO_2 levels and temperature. Humans contribute approximately 3.4 percent of annual CO_2 levels compared to 96.6 percent by nature. There was an explosion of life forms 550 million years ago (Cambrian Period) when CO_2 levels were eighteen times higher than today. During the Jurassic Period, when dinosaurs roamed the Earth, CO_2 levels were as much as nine times higher than today. Contrary to what educators are brainwashing our children with, polar bear numbers increased dramatically from around 5,000 in 1950 to as many as 25,000 today, higher than any time in the twentieth century.

Political commentator Henry Louis Mencken (1880–1956) warned that "The whole aim of practical politics is to keep the populace alarmed—and hence clamorous to be led to safety—by menacing it with an endless series of hobgoblins, all of them imaginary." That's the political goal of the global warmers.

Global Warming Update
February 24, 2010

Private industry and governments around the world have spent trillions of dollars in the name of saving our planet from manmade global warming. Academic institutions, think tanks, and schools have altered their curricula and agenda to accommodate what was seen as the global warming "consensus."

Mounting evidence suggests that claims of manmade global warming might turn out to be the greatest hoax in mankind's history. Immune and hostile to the evidence, President Barack Obama's administration and most of the US Congress sides with Climate Czar Carol Browner, who says, "I'm sticking with the 2,500 scientists. These people have been studying this issue for a very long time and agree this problem is real."

The scientists whom Browner references are associated with the U.N.'s Intergovernmental Panel on Climate Change (IPCC). Let's look some of what they told us. The 2007 IPCC report, which won them a Nobel Peace Prize, said that the probability of Himalayan glaciers "disappearing by the year 2035 and perhaps sooner is very high" as a result of manmade global warming. Recently, the IPCC was forced to retract their glacier-disappearance claim, which was made on the basis of a nonscientific magazine article. When critics initially questioned the prediction, Rajendra Pachauri, IPCC's chairman, dismissed them as "voodoo scientists."

The IPCC also had to retract its claim that up to 40 percent of the Amazonian forests were at risk from global warming and would likely be replaced by "tropical savannas" if temperatures continued to rise. The IPCC claim was based on a paper coauthored by the World Wildlife Fund (WWF) and the International Union for Conservation of Nature (IUCN), two environmental activist groups.

England's now-disgraced University of East Anglia's Climatic Research Unit (CRU) has been a leader in climate research data. Their data, collected and analyzed by them, have been used for years to bolster IPCC efforts to press governments to cut carbon dioxide emissions. Climatologists, including CRU's disgraced former director Professor Phil Jones, have been accused of manipulating data and criminally withholding scientific information to prevent its disclosure under the Freedom of Information Act.

Professor Jones, considered to be the high priest of the manmade global warming movement, has been in the spotlight since he was forced to step down as CRU's director after the leaking of e-mails that skeptics claim show scientists were manipulating data. In a recent interview with the BBC, he admitted that he did not believe that "the debate on climate change is over" and that he didn't "believe the vast majority of climate scientists think this."

Long denied by the warmers, Professor Jones admitted that the Medieval Warm Period (800 A.D. to 1300 A.D.) might well have been as warm as the Current Warm Period (1975–present), or warmer, and that if it was, "then obviously the late-20th century warmth would not be unprecedented." That suggests global warming may not be a manmade phenomenon. In any case, Professor Jones said that for the past fifteen years, there has been no "statistically significant" global warming.

During the BBC interview, Professor Jones dodged several questions: why he had asked a colleague to delete e-mails relating to the IPCC's Fourth Assessment Report and ask others to do likewise; whether some of his handling of data had crossed the line of acceptable scientific practice; and what about his letter saying that he had used a "trick" to "hide the decline" in tree-ring temperature data?

Given all the false claims and evidence pointing to scientific fraud, I don't think it wise to continue spending billions of dollars and enacting economically crippling regulations in the name of fighting global warming. At the minimum, we should stop the Environmental Protection Agency from going on with their plans to regulate carbon emissions. Companies should resign from the United States Climate

Action Partnership (USCAP), a lobbying group of businesses and radical environmentalists. Dr. Tom Borelli, who is director of the National Center for Public Policy Research's Free Enterprise Project, says that BP, Caterpillar, Conoco Phillips, Marsh Inc., and Xerox had the common sense to do so already.

Is Health Care a Right?

March 10, 2010

Most politicians, and probably most Americans, see health care as a right. Thus, whether a person has the means to pay for medical services or not, he is nonetheless entitled to them. Let's ask ourselves a few questions about this vision.

Say a person, let's call him Harry, suffers from diabetes and he has no means to pay a laboratory for blood work, a doctor for treatment, and a pharmacy for medication. Does Harry have a right to XYZ lab's and Dr. Jones's services and a prescription from a pharmacist? And, if those services are not provided without charge, should Harry be able to call for criminal sanctions against those persons for violating his rights to health care?

You say, "Williams, that would come very close to slavery if one person had the right to force someone to serve him without pay." You're right. Suppose instead of Harry being able to force a lab, doctor, and pharmacy to provide services without pay, Congress uses its taxing power to take a couple of hundred dollars out of the paycheck of some American to give to Harry so that he could pay the lab, doctor, and pharmacist. Would there be any difference in principle, namely forcibly using one person to serve the purposes of another? There would be one important strategic difference, that of concealment. Most Americans, I would hope, would be offended by the notion of directly and visibly forcing one person to serve the purposes of another. Congress's use of the tax system to invisibly accomplish the same end is more palatable to the average American.

True rights, such as those in our Constitution, or those considered to be natural or human rights, exist simultaneously among people. That means exercise of a right by one person does not diminish those held by another. In other words, my rights to speech or travel impose no obligations on another except those of noninterference. If we apply ideas behind rights to health care to my rights to speech or travel, my free speech rights would require government-imposed obligations on others to provide me with an auditorium, television studio, or radio station. My right to travel freely would require government-imposed obligations on others to provide me with airfare and hotel accommodations.

For Congress to guarantee a right to health care, or any other good or service, whether a person can afford it or not, it must diminish someone else's rights, namely their rights to their earnings. The reason is that Congress has no resources of its very own. Moreover, there is no Santa Claus, Easter Bunny, or Tooth Fairy giving them those resources. The fact that government has no resources of its very own forces one to recognize that in order for government to give one American citizen a dollar, it must first, through intimidation, threats, and coercion, confiscate that dollar from some other American. If one person has a right to something he did not earn, of necessity it requires that another person not have a right to something that he did earn.

To argue that people have a right that imposes obligations on another is an absurd concept. A better term for new-fangled rights to health care, decent housing, and food is wishes. If we called them wishes, I would be in agreement with most other Americans for I, too, wish that everyone had adequate health care, decent housing, and nutritious meals. However, if we called them human wishes, instead of human rights, there would be confusion and cognitive dissonance. The average American would cringe at the thought of government punishing one person because he refused to be pressed into making someone else's wish come true.

None of my argument is to argue against charity. Reaching into one's own pockets to assist his fellow man in need is praiseworthy and laudable. Reaching into someone else's pockets to do so is despicable and deserves condemnation.

Salt Tyrants

April 28, 2010

Here's how my June 14, 2006, column started: "Down through the years, I've attempted to warn my fellow Americans about the tyrannical precedent and template for further tyranny set by anti-tobacco zealots. . . . In the early stages of the anti-tobacco campaign, there were calls for 'reasonable' measures such as non-smoking sections on airplanes and health warnings on cigarette packs. In the 1970s, no one would have ever believed such measures would have evolved into today's level of attack on smokers, which includes confiscatory cigarette taxes and bans on outdoor smoking. The door was opened, and the zealots took over."

What the anti-tobacco zealots established is that government had the right to forcibly control our lives if it was done in the name of protecting our health. In the Foundation for Economic Education's Freeman publication, I wrote a column titled "Nazi Tactics" (January 2003): "These people who want to control our lives are almost finished with smokers; but never in history has a tyrant arisen one day and decided to tyrannize no more. The nation's tyrants have now turned their attention to the vilification of fast food chains such as McDonald's, Burger King, Wendy's, and Kentucky Fried Chicken, charging them with having created an addiction to fatty foods. . . . In their campaign against fast food chains, restaurants, and soda and candy manufacturers the nation's food Nazis always refer to the anti-tobacco campaign as the model for their agenda."

America's tyrants have now turned their attention to salt, as reported in the *Washington Post*'s article "FDA plans to limit amount of salt allowed in processed foods for health reasons" (April 19, 2010). Why do food processors put a certain quantity of salt in their products? The answer is the people who buy their product like it and they earn profits by pleasing customers. The Food and Drug Administration has taken the position that what the American buying public wants is irrelevant. They know what's best and if you disagree, they will fine, jail, or put you out of business.

Tyranny knows no bounds. Let's say that the FDA orders Stouffer's to no longer put 970 mg of sodium in their roasted turkey dinner; they mandate a maximum of 400 mg. Suppose Stouffer's customers, assuming they continue buying the product, add more salt—what will the FDA do? The answer is easy. They will copy the successful anti-tobacco zealot template. They might start out with warning labels on salt. Congress will levy confiscatory taxes on salt. Maybe lawsuits will be brought against salt companies. State and local agencies might deny child-adoption rights to couples found using too much salt. Before a couple can adopt a baby, they would have to take a blood test to determine their dietary habits. Teachers might ask schoolchildren to report their parents for adding salt to their meals. You might say, "Williams, they'd never go that far in the name of health." In 1960, you might have said the same thing about tobacco zealots but yet they've done the same and more.

The late H. L. Mencken's description of health care professionals in his day is just as appropriate for many of today's: "A certain section of medical opinion, in late years, has succumbed to the messianic delusion. Its spokesmen are not content to deal with the patients who come to them for advice; they conceive it to be their duty to force their advice upon everyone, including especially those who don't want it. That duty is purely imaginary. It is born of vanity, not of public spirit. The impulse behind it is not altruism, but a mere yearning to run things."

Thomas Jefferson put it simpler in his Notes on Religion in 1776, "Laws provide against injury from others, but not from ourselves."

Making Americans Sick

July 21, 2010

Health and Human Services Secretary Kathleen Sebelius promised, "The US government plans to increase funding to battle obesity and views healthcare reform as an opportunity to encourage better eating habits." Rather than spending money and attacking the food industry, the secretary and others concerned with the health of Americans ought to go after the US Congress. Let's look at it.

According to a study by researchers at the University of California, Davis, published in the *Journal of Clinical Investigation* (May 2009), widespread use of fructose may be directly responsible for some of the ongoing increase in rates of childhood diabetes and obesity. Consuming fructose-sweetened, not glucose-sweetened, beverages increases abdominal fat and decreases insulin sensitivity in overweight/obese people. The participants in the study who consumed fructose-sweetened food showed an increase of fat cells around major organs including their hearts and livers, and also underwent metabolic changes that are precursors to heart disease and diabetes.

Other studies have linked diets rich in high-fructose corn syrup to elevated risks of high triglycerides (a type of blood fat), fat buildup in the liver and insulin resistance, notes Dr. Gerald Shulman and his colleagues at Yale University School of Medicine.

"This is the first evidence we have that fructose increases diabetes and heart disease independently from causing simple weight gain," said Kimber Stanhope, a molecular biologist who led the UC Davis study, adding, "We didn't see any of these changes in the people eating glucose."

You say, "Williams, glucose, fructose—what's the fuss?" Sucrose is the sugar sold in five- or ten-pound bags at your supermarket that Americans have used as a sweetener throughout most of our history. Fructose is a sweetener that has more recently come into heavy use by beverage manufacturers and food processors. You ask, "How come all the fructose use now?"

Enter the US Congress. The Fanjul family of Palm Beach, Fla., a politically connected family, has given more than $1.8 million to both Democratic and Republican parties over the years. They and others in the sugar industry give millions to congressmen to keep high tariffs on foreign sugar so the US sugar industry can charge us higher prices. According to one study, the Fanjul family alone earns about $65 million a year from congressional protectionism.

Chairman Emeritus of Archer Daniels Midland Company, Dwayne Andreas, has given politicians millions of dollars to help him enrich ADM at our expense. For that money, congressmen vote to restrict sugar imports that in turn drive up sugar prices. Higher sugar prices benefit ADM, who produces corn syrup (fructose), which is a sugar substitute. When sugar prices are high, sugar users (soda, candy, and food processors) turn to corn syrup as a cheaper substitute sweetener. Early on, some sugar-using companies found out they could import products like ice tea, distill out its sugar content, and still beat the high prices caused by Congress's protectionist sugar policy, but to do so was eventually made illegal.

Congress's sugar policy not only reduces the health of American people, it reduces American jobs as well. Chicago used to be America's candy manufacturing capital. In 1970, employment by Chicago's candy manufacturers totaled 15,000 and now it's 8,000 and falling. Brach's used to employ about 2,300 people; now most of its jobs are in Mexico. Ferrara Pan Candy has also moved much of its production to Mexico. Yes, wages are lower in Mexico, but wages aren't the only factor in candy manufacturers' flight from America. Sugar is a major cost and in Mexico, they pay one-third to one-half what they pay in the United States. Life Savers, which for ninety years was manufactured in America, has moved to Canada, where wages are comparable to ours, but their yearly sugar cost is $10 million less.

Working in the favor of Congress with these and other life-threatening and health-reducing schemes is American unawareness and the fact that most often, their victims are invisible.

Health Tyrants
November 24, 2010

Do federal, state, and local governments have a right to intervene in our lives when it comes to choices affecting our health? Recently, the San Francisco Board of Supervisors voted to forbid restaurants from giving gifts with meals that contain too much fat and sugar, a measure aimed at McDonald's Happy Meals. The reasoning of these tyrants is to prevent McDonald's from using toys to lure children into liking foods the board deems non-nutritious. Fortunately, San Francisco's mayor, Gavin Newsom, by no means a libertarian, has threatened to veto the measure saying, "Despite its good intentions, I cannot support this unwise and unprecedented governmental intrusion into parental responsibilities and private choices."

If the board of supervisors gets away with this intrusion into parental responsibilities and choices, we can bet the rent money that they will not stop with McDonald's Happy Meals. The reason is that Happy Meals are not the only contributors to child obesity.

What and how much they eat at home, what time they eat, and how much they exercise play a role. When San Francisco's Board of Supervisors see that their Happy Meal ban has not produced the desired results, they'll seek to widen their reach. That might include laws that set purchase limits on non-nutritious items in the city's grocery stores. Depending on family size, there would be a limit on the purchases of delights such as Twinkies, Pop Tarts, lard, salt, and other threats to good health. Maybe the Board of Supervisors would issue ration stamps that a person would need in order to purchase foods that threaten obesity.

There will be other challenges for San Francisco's Board of Supervisors. Not every California city has banned Happy Meals. Happy Meals lovers can just go across the Bay Bridge into Oakland or the Golden Gate Bridge into Sausalito to dine on Happy Meals or smuggle them into San Francisco. Maybe a Happy Meal black market would emerge. That means the Board of Supervisors might make random stops of cars coming into the city and have its police make Happy Meal arrests.

You say, "Williams, you're really stretching it; they'd never go to those extremes!" There's no limit to what do-gooder zealots will do to accomplish their mission. Think back to the 1964, the time of the "First Surgeon General Report: Smoking and Health." Back then, tobacco zealots called for "reasonable" measures such as warning labels on cigarettes and restrictions on advertising. Emboldened by their success in getting these relatively benign measures, tobacco zealots moved on to seeking bans on smoking on airplanes and airports; suits against tobacco manufacturers; confiscatory taxes on cigarettes; denying child adoption to smokers; bans on smoking in bars, restaurants, and workplaces; even bans on outdoor smoking such as in stadiums, public beaches, and city streets. Had the tobacco zealots called for all of these measures, as a total package back in 1964, they would not have even gotten warning labels on cigarettes. That's the tyrant's strategy: Attacking people's rights to property and liberty on a piecemeal basis reduces resistance.

We Americans have given federal, state, and local governments the right to interfere with any aspect of our lives when it comes to issues of health. So should we be surprised when an emboldened Congress enacts Obamacare, even though most Americans were against it, that not only mandates that we purchase health insurance but will eventually control virtually every aspect of our health care? Should we be surprised when government tells us what food to give our children? Should we be surprised when government taxes soft drinks in the name of fighting obesity? Should we be surprised when governments order restaurants not to serve foie gras or cook with trans fats? If you think government has the right to look after our health, how far would you have it go? How about a congressional mandate for morning calisthenics, eight glasses of water a day, and eight hours of sleep each night?

A Killer Agency

February 9, 2011

Sam Kazman's "Drug Approvals and Deadly Delays" article in the *Journal of American Physicians and Surgeons* (Winter 2010) tells a story about how the US Food and Drug Administration's policies have led to the deaths of tens of thousands of Americans. Let's look at how it happens.

During the FDA's drug approval process, it confronts the possibility of two errors. If the FDA approves a drug that turns out to have unanticipated, dangerous side effects, people will suffer. Similarly, if the FDA denies or delays the marketing of a perfectly safe and beneficial drug, people will also suffer. Both errors cause medical harm.

Kazman argues that from a political point of view, there's a huge difference between the errors. People who are injured by incorrectly approved drugs will know that they are victims of FDA mistakes. Their suffering makes headlines. FDA officials face unfavorable publicity and perhaps congressional hearings.

It's an entirely different story for victims of incorrect FDA drug delays or denials. These victims are people who are prevented access to drugs that could have helped them. Their suffering or death is seen as reflecting the state of medicine rather than the status of an FDA drug application. Their doctor simply tells them there's nothing more that can be done to help them.

Beta-blockers reduce the risks of secondary heart attacks and were widely used in Europe during the mid-'70s. The FDA imposed a moratorium on beta-blocker approvals in the United States because of the drug's carcinogenicity in animals. Finally, in 1981, FDA approved the first such drug, boasting that it might save up to 17,000 lives per year. That meant as many as 100,000 people might have died from secondary heart attacks waiting for FDA approval.

In the early 1990s, it took the FDA more than three years to approve interleukin-2 as the first therapy for advanced kidney cancer.

By the time the FDA approved the drug, it was available in nine European countries. The FDA was worried about the drug's toxicity that resulted in the death of 5 percent of those who took it during testing trials. This concern obscures the fact that metastatic kidney cancer has the effect of killing 100 percent of its victims.

Kazman says that if we estimate that interleukin-2 would have helped 10 percent of those who would otherwise die of kidney cancer, then the FDA's delay might have contributed to the premature deaths of 3,000 people. Kazman asks whether we've seen any photos or news stories of the 3,000 victims of the FDA's interleukin-2 delay or the 100,000 victims of the FDA's beta-blocker delay.

These are the invisible victims of FDA policy. In the 1974 words of FDA commissioner Alexander M. Schmidt: "In all of FDA's history, I am unable to find a single instance where a congressional committee investigated the failure of FDA to approve a new drug. But, the times when hearings have been held to criticize our approval of new drugs have been so frequent that we aren't able to count them. . . . The message to FDA staff could not be clearer."

That message is to always err on the side of overcaution where FDA's victims are invisible and the agency is held blameless.

Kazman's day job is general counsel for the Washington, D.C.-based Competitive Enterprise Institute that's done surveys of physicians and their views of the FDA. On approval speed, 61 to 77 percent of physicians surveyed say the FDA approval process is too slow. Seventy-eight percent believe the FDA has hurt their ability to give patients the best care.

But so what? Physicians carry far less weight with the FDA than "public interest" advocates and politicians.

When the FDA announces its approval of a new drug or device, the question that needs to be asked is: If this drug will start saving lives tomorrow, how many people died yesterday waiting for the FDA to act?

Energy Manipulation

August 14, 2013

Why is it that natural gas sells in the United States for $3.94 per 1,000 cubic feet and in Europe and Japan for $11.60 and $17, respectively? Part of the answer is our huge supply. With high-tech methods of extraction and with discovery of vast gas-rich shale deposits, estimated reserves are about 2.4 quadrillion cubic feet. That translates into more than a 100-year supply of natural gas at current usage rates. What partially explains the high European and Japanese prices is the fact that global natural gas markets are not integrated. Washington has stringent export restrictions on natural gas.

Naturally, the next question is: Why are there natural gas export restrictions? Just follow the money. According to OpenSecrets.org, The Dow Chemical Co. "posted record lobbying expenditures last year, spending nearly $12 million, and is on pace to eclipse that number this year." The company has spent hundreds of thousands of dollars contributing to the political campaigns of congressmen who support export restrictions. Natural gas is a raw material for Dow. It benefits financially from cheap gas prices, which it fears would rise if Congress were to lift export restrictions. Dow argues, "Continuing optimism for US manufacturing is founded on the prospect of an adequate, reliable and reasonably priced supply of natural gas." Of course, Dow and other big users of natural gas get support from environmentalists, who are anti-drilling and anticipate that export restrictions will serve their ends.

Big natural gas users and environmentalists have foreign allies, suggested by the statement of Saudi Prince Alwaleed bin Talal, who told Saudi Arabia's oil minister, Ali al-Naimi, that rising American shale gas production is "an inevitable threat." Nigeria's oil minister, Diezani Alison-Madueke, agrees, saying that US shale oil is a "grave concern." In light of these foreign "concerns" about US energy production, one wonders whether foreign countries have given financial aid to US politicians, environmentalists, and other groups that are waging war against domestic oil and natural gas drilling. It would surely be in their interests to do everything in their power to keep the West dependent on OPEC nations for oil and gas.

Natural gas producers would like to export some of their product to Europe and Japan to take advantage of higher prices. One effect of those exports would be to raise natural gas prices in the United States and lower them in the recipient countries. Industrial giants such as Dow, Alcoa, Celanese, and Nucor are members of America's Energy Advantage, a lobby group that says it is unpatriotic to allow unlimited natural gas exports. It argues that export restrictions keep natural gas prices low and give US manufacturing companies a raw material advantage, which allows them to produce goods at lower prices.

I'd like to ask Dow, Alcoa, and other companies that lobby against natural gas exports whether their argument applies to them. After all, they ship a lot of their domestic product overseas. For example, Alcoa exports tons of aluminum. Export restrictions on aluminum would lower domestic aluminum prices, thereby benefiting the aircraft industry, as well as making other aluminum-using manufacturers more competitive. Unfortunately, I doubt whether Alcoa would see it that way. In general, it is poor economic policy to encourage domestic American industry through costly and inefficient methods such as export restrictions.

But there's another effect of the natural gas export restrictions. The huge supply and resulting low prices have begun to act as a deterrent to future energy exploration and production. According to a *Wall Street Journal* article by Dr. Thomas Tunstall, research director for the Institute for Economic Development at the University of Texas at San Antonio, titled "Exporting Natural Gas Will Stabilize US Prices" (May 29, 2013), natural gas production at three major shale oil fields in Texas has flattened out at 2012 output levels.

Tunstall concludes, "Over the long haul, market dynamics—which include the ability to export without undue uncertainty or restriction—will best manage global supply and demand curves for natural gas." I agree.

Our Fragile Planet
December 11, 2013

Let's examine a few statements reflecting a vision thought to be beyond question. "The world that we live in is beautiful but fragile." "The third rock from the sun is a fragile oasis." Here are a couple of Earth Day quotes: "Remember that Earth needs to be saved every single day." "Remember the importance of taking care of our planet. It's the only home we have!" Such statements, along with apocalyptic predictions, are stock in trade for environmental extremists and nonextremists alike. Worse yet is the fact that this fragile-Earth indoctrination is fed to our youth from kindergarten through college. Let's examine just how fragile the Earth is.

The 1883 eruption of the Krakatoa volcano, in present-day Indonesia, had the force of 200 megatons of TNT. That's the equivalent of 13,300 15-kiloton atomic bombs, the kind that destroyed Hiroshima in 1945. Preceding that eruption was the 1815 Tambora eruption, also in present-day Indonesia, which holds the record as the largest known volcanic eruption. It spewed so much debris into the atmosphere, blocking sunlight, that 1816 became known as the "Year Without a Summer" or "Summer That Never Was." It led to crop failures and livestock death in much of the Northern Hemisphere and caused the worst famine of the nineteenth century. The A.D. 535 Krakatoa eruption had such force that it blotted out much of the light and heat of the sun for eighteen months and is said to have led to the Dark Ages. Geophysicists estimate that just three volcanic eruptions, Indonesia (1883), Alaska (1912), and Iceland (1947), spewed more carbon dioxide and sulfur dioxide into the atmosphere than all of mankind's activities in our entire history.

How has our fragile Earth handled floods? China is probably the world capital of gigantic floods. The 1887 Yellow River flood cost between 900,000 and 2 million lives. China's 1931 flood was worse, yielding an estimated death toll between 1 million and 4 million. But

China doesn't have a monopoly on floods. Between 1219 and 1530, the Netherlands experienced floods costing about 250,000 lives.

What about the impact of earthquakes on our fragile Earth? There's Chile's 1960 Valdivia earthquake, coming in at 9.5 on the Richter scale, a force equivalent to 1,000 atomic bombs going off at the same time. The deadly 1556 earthquake in China's Shaanxi province devastated an area of 520 miles. There's the more recent December 2004 magnitude-9.1 earthquake in the Indian Ocean that caused the deadly Boxing Day tsunami, and a deadly March 2011 magnitude-9.0 earthquake struck eastern Japan.

Our fragile Earth faces outer space terror. Two billion years ago, an asteroid hit earth, creating the Vredefort crater in South Africa. It has a radius of 118 miles, making it the world's largest impact crater. In Ontario, there's the Sudbury Basin, resulting from a meteor strike 1.8 billion years ago, which has an 81-mile diameter, making it the second-largest impact structure on Earth. Virginia's Chesapeake Bay crater is a bit smaller, about 53 miles wide. Then there's the famous but puny Meteor Crater in Arizona, which is not even a mile wide.

I've pointed out only a tiny portion of the cataclysmic events that have struck the earth—ignoring whole categories, such as tornadoes, hurricanes, lightning strikes, fires, blizzards, landslides, and avalanches. Despite these cataclysmic events, the Earth survived. My question is: Which of these powers of nature can be matched by mankind? For example, can mankind duplicate the polluting effects of the 1815 Tambora volcanic eruption or the asteroid impact that wiped out dinosaurs? It is the height of arrogance to think that mankind can make significant parametric changes in the Earth or can match nature's destructive forces.

Occasionally, environmentalists spill the beans and reveal their true agenda. Barry Commoner said, "Capitalism is the Earth's number one enemy." Amherst College professor Leo Marx said, "On ecological grounds, the case for world government is beyond argument." With the decline of the USSR, communism has lost considerable respectability and is now repackaged as environmentalism and progressivism.

Who Owns You?

June 11, 2014

Darcy Olsen, president of the Arizona-based Goldwater Institute, and Richard Garr, president of Neuralstem, a biotech company, wrote "Right to Try Experimental Drugs" in *USA Today* (May 28, 2014). They pointed out that "this year, more than 5,000 Americans will lose their battle with ALS, commonly known as Lou Gehrig's disease." Up until recently, there was no medicine on the market that significantly improved the lives of ALS patients. But now there is one in clinical trials that holds considerable promise, but it has not been granted Food and Drug Administration approval. The average amount of time it takes to get a drug through the FDA approval process is ten years. That's time that terminal patients don't have.

Legislators in Colorado, Louisiana, and Missouri recently approved "Right to Try" legislation, and Arizona voters will vote on the measure this November. "Right to Try" is an initiative designed by the Goldwater Institute. It would give terminal patients access to investigational drugs that have completed basic safety testing. Under a doctor's supervision, people would be given the chance to try promising experimental drugs before they're given final FDA approval.

There's no denying that there's risk in taking a drug or medical procedure that hasn't completed clinical trials. The question is: Who has the right to decide how much risk a person will take—he or some faceless Washington bureaucrat? In my opinion, the answer depends upon the answer to the question: Who owns you? If one owns himself, then it is he who decides how much risk he takes. If government owns you, then you don't have the right to unilaterally decide how much risk you'll take.

The FDA's mission is to ensure the safety and effectiveness of pharmaceuticals. In doing so, FDA officials can make two types of errors. They can approve a drug that has unanticipated dangerous side effects, or they can disapprove or delay a drug that is both safe and effective.

FDA officials have unequal incentives to avoid these two types of errors. If the FDA official errs on the side of under-caution—approving a dangerous drug—the victims are visible, and he is held directly accountable. If he errs on the side of over-caution—holding up approval of a safe and effective drug—who's to know? The cost and the victims are invisible. Politicians and bureaucrats prefer invisible victims.

Here are a couple of notable examples. Clozapine was approved and used in 1972 in Europe. Clozapine's ability to treat schizophrenics who did not respond to other medicines became well-known by 1979. Yet the drug was not approved in the United States until 1989 because companies believed that the FDA would reject it on the grounds that 1 percent of patients who took the drug contracted a blood disease. As an article in *The New England Journal of Medicine* stated, "what is remarkable is that clozapine has a beneficial effect in a substantial proportion (30 to 50 percent) of patients who have an inadequate response to other . . . drugs." Nearly 250,000 people with schizophrenia suffered needlessly, when relief was at hand.

According to Robert M. Goldberg, writing for the journal *Regulation*, "Mevacor is a cholesterol-lowering drug that has been linked to reduction in death due to heart attacks. It was available in Europe in 1989 but did not become available in the United States until 1992. Studies confirm what doctors saw to be the case: taking the drug reduces death due to heart disease by about 55 percent. During that three-year period as many as a thousand people a year died from heart disease because of the FDA delay."

There is self-correction when a drug that has unanticipated dangerous side effects has been marketed. The drug is removed. But there's no self-correction when a safe, effective lifesaving drug is not approved or is delayed. Those 5,000 ALS patients who will die of their disease this year are invisible, and FDA officials are unaccountable. "Right to Try" legislation is a step in the right direction to remedy that.

PART VI

International

International trade makes for useful fodder for those who are against liberty in general. How often in our trade relationships do we hear the claim "I am for free, but fair, trade"? That is usually a claim made by an American producer who would like Congress to impose restrictions on foreign goods so that he can charge American consumers higher prices—of course, that is never his stated justification. Much of the mischief in thinking about international trade issues begins with the often-heard statement that the United States trades with other countries. That is nonsense but worse is that it leads to incorrect analysis and demagoguery. Why?

It is not the US Congress trading cars, televisions, and clothing with the Japanese Diet, the British Parliament, the German Bundestag, or the National People's Congress of the Republic of China. When I purchased my Mercedes-Benz, I did not do any business with the US Congress and Germany's Bundestag. I dealt exclusively with an intermediary for Mercedes-Benz, a multinational division of the German manufacturer Daimler AG. The only participation the Bundestag and the US Congress had to do with my purchase was to impede it through taxes and regulations.

The recognition that it is private persons in one country trading with private persons in another country raises at least one important moral question. If one person wishes to buy a product from another person, what gives a third party a right to interfere with that exchange? Put more explicitly, if I wish to purchase a suit from a Canadian manufacturer, what standard of personal liberty gives a third party the right to restrict that exchange?

Another issue in the international arena is Third World poverty. The typical response, in part motivated by Western guilt about colonialism, is to call for foreign aid programs. For over a half-century we have seen that foreign aid has not done much to help the common man. There's no complete explanation for why some countries are affluent while others are poor, but there are some clues. Rank countries according to whether they were closer to being free-market economies or whether they're closer to socialist or planned economies. Then rank countries by per-capita income. Doing so we will find a general, though not perfect, pattern whereby those having a larger measure of economic freedom also enjoy a higher standard of living. Also, if we ranked countries according to how Freedom House or International Amnesty rates their human rights protections, we will find that citizens of freer market economies enjoy a greater measure of human rights protections. You can bet the rent money that the correlation between free markets, wealth, and human rights protections are not coincidental. The best thing the West can do is to keep our money and instead encourage economic freedom in the world's poor nations.

Another topic in the international arena is the US political relationship with the rest of the world. The key factor in this arena is national defense. For the most part, our half-century Cold War is over. The USSR no longer exists. Despite that fact, we still face a number of international threats. Without question the United States is the most powerful military force in the world. It must adapt to the new threat that comes from Iran's design to acquire nuclear weapons. That threat is compounded by the fact that Iran is a state sponsor of terrorist activity. Right now Iran has cleared the biggest hurdle to creating a nuclear weapon. They have built facilities to separate the explosive uranium-235 isotope from uranium ore using gas centrifuges spinning at supersonic speeds.

The United States has both the intelligence and military capacity to eliminate Iran's capacity to enrich uranium. While we have the intelligence and capacity, we lack the will. In future years, if a terrorist is able to bring a nuclear weapon to destroy or make uninhabitable one of our cities, few people will attribute it to decisions that today's political leaders have made regarding Iran.

There are other international issues that have been the subject of my columns such as our forgetting that the horrors of World War II were a result of the failure of US, British, and French foreign policy toward the ambitions of Germany's tyrants. That failure led to the deaths of 60 million people during World War II.

The common theme throughout my vision of foreign policy is personal liberty. But sometimes, to protect personal liberty, military preemption is necessary.

Excused Horrors
November 18, 2009

Last Tuesday, I had the pleasurable task of being master of ceremonies for the Atlas Economic Research Foundation dinner in Washington, D.C., that celebrated the twentieth anniversary of the fall of the Berlin Wall. Founded in 1981, the Atlas Foundation assists the formation of free-market think tanks around the world to spread the ideas of personal liberty, private property rights, and limited government. So far, they have been successful in at least seventy countries. Attending the two-day celebration were think-tank representatives from many of these countries, including those from Croatia, Venezuela, Zimbabwe, Cote d'Ivoire, Kenya, Mozambique, South Korea, Russia, and Brazil.

Alan Kors, University of Pennsylvania history professor, gave the evening's keynote address. What he revealed about the dereliction and character weakness of academics, intellectuals, media elites, and politicians is by no means complimentary, but worse than that, dangerous. Professor Kors said that over the years, he has frequently asked students how many deaths were caused by Joseph Stalin and Mao Zedong and their successors. Routinely, they gave numbers in the thousands. Kors says that's equivalent to saying the Nazis are responsible for the deaths of just a few hundred Jews. But here's the record: Nazis were responsible for the deaths of 20 million of their own people and those in nations they conquered. Between 1917 and 1983, Stalin and his successors murdered, or were otherwise responsible for the deaths of, 62 million of their own people. Between 1949 and 1987, Mao Zedong and his successors were responsible for the deaths of 76 million Chinese.

Professor Kors asks why are the horrors of Nazism so well known and widely condemned, but not those of socialism and communism? For decades after World War II, people have hunted down and sought punishment for Nazi murderers. How much hunting down and seeking punishment for Stalinist and Maoist murderers? In Europe, especially Germany, hoisting the swastika-emblazoned Nazi flag is a crime.

It's acceptable to hoist and march under a flag emblazoned with the former USSR's hammer and sickle. Even in the United States, it's acceptable to praise mass murderers, as Anita Dunn, President Obama's communications director, did in a commencement address for St. Andrews Episcopal High School at Washington National Cathedral where she said Mao Zedong was one of her heroes. Whether it's the academic community, the media elite, or politicians, there is a great tolerance for the ideas of socialism—a system that has caused more deaths and human misery than all other systems combined.

Academics, media elites, and leftist politicians both in the United States and Europe protested the actions and military buildup of President Ronald Reagan and Prime Minister Margaret Thatcher that led to the fall of the Berlin Wall and ultimately the breakup of the Soviet Union. Recall the leftist hissy fit when Ronald Reagan called the Soviet Union the evil empire and predicted that communism would wind up on the trash heap of history.

Professor Alan Kors did not say this but the reason why the world's leftists give the world's most horrible murderers a pass is because they sympathize with their socioeconomic goals, which include government ownership and control over the means of production. In the United States, the call is for government control, through regulations, as opposed to ownership. Unfortunately, it matters little whether there is a Democratic- or Republican-controlled Congress and White House; the march toward greater government control continues. It just happens at a quicker pace with Democrats in charge.

You say, "Come on, Williams, there will never be the kind of socialist oppression seen elsewhere here!" You might be right because Americans have become very compliant with unconstitutional and immoral congressional edicts. But what do you think would happen if some Americans began to rise up and heed Thomas Jefferson's admonition "Whensoever the General Government assumes undelegated powers, its acts are unauthoritative, void, and of no force" and decided to disobey unconstitutional congressional edicts?

Untrue Beliefs

January 6, 2010

Here's a sample of last week's news reporting: "A new decade is about to start...," "What better way to start a new year and decade...," and "ABC 'World News' Decade Look-Back." One would think that the first decade of the third millennium came to an end midnight December 31 and the new decade began a minute after midnight. The truth of the matter is that we must wait another year before the new decade begins at 12:01 a.m. January 1, 2011. Just do the math: The end of 2001 was the first year of the decade; the end of 2002 completed the second year, and so forth. The end of 2009 completes the ninth year and the end of 2010 completes the tenth year and the end of the decade. One minute after midnight January 1, 2011, begins the second decade of the third millennium.

Many reporters and talking heads will read this column and will still refer to 2010 as the new decade. My question: What is the most suitable characterization we can give them? I think it's the same characterization we would make of a person who's shown that an object is white and he insists upon calling it black—stupid. Then there's the person who agrees that 2010 does not begin the next decade but prefers to say it's the next decade anyway. For that person, reality is optional. Then there's the person who steadfastly holds that 2010 begins the next decade because that's what most people believe. He might be a politician.

Politicians, businessmen, and labor union spokesmen have whined about the decline in US manufacturing. Before looking into what they say is the sad decline in US manufacturing, let's examine what has happened in agriculture. In 1790, farmers were 90 percent of the US labor force. By 1900, only about 41 percent of our labor force was employed in agriculture. By 2008, less than 3 percent of Americans are employed in agriculture. What would you have Congress do in the face of this precipitous loss of agricultural jobs? One thing Congress could do is outlaw all of the technological advances and machinery that have made our farmers the world's most productive. Our farmers are so productive that if needed, they could feed the entire world.

Let's look at manufacturing. According to Dr. Mark Perry's Department of Labor employment data, in his article "Manufacturing's Death Greatly Exaggerated" (http://blog.american.com/?p=8593), US manufacturing employment peaked at 19.5 million jobs in 1979. Since 1979, the manufacturing workforce has shrunk by 40 percent and there's every indication that manufacturing employment will continue to shrink. Before you buy into the call for Congress to do something about manufacturing job loss, there are some other facts to be considered.

According to the Federal Reserve, the dollar value of US manufacturing output in November was $2.72 trillion (in 2000 dollars). Today's manufacturing worker is so productive that the value of his average output is $234,220. Output per worker is three times as high as it was in 1980 and twice as high as it was in 1990. For the year 2008, the Federal Reserve estimates that the value of US manufacturing output was about $3.7 trillion (in 2008 dollars). If the US manufacturing sector were a separate economy, with its own GDP, it would be tied with Germany as the world's fourth-richest economy. The GDPs are: United States ($14.2 trillion), Japan ($4.9 trillion), China ($4.3 trillion), US manufacturing ($3.7 trillion), Germany ($3.7 trillion), France ($2.9 trillion), and the United Kingdom ($2.7 trillion).

These facts put a lie to claims we hear about how we are a country that "doesn't produce anything anymore," and how we have "outsourced our production to China," and there's been a "demise of US manufacturing." US manufacturing has gone through the same kind of labor-saving technological innovation as agriculture. Should we discard that innovation in the name of saving jobs?

Haiti's Avoidable Death Toll
January 20, 2010

Some expect Haiti's 7.0 earthquake death toll to reach over 200,000 lives. Why the high death toll? Northern California's 1989 Loma Prieta earthquake was more violent, measuring 7.1 on the Richter scale, resulting in 63 deaths and 3,757 injuries. The 1906 San Francisco earthquake measured 7.8 on the Richter scale, about eight times more violent than Haiti's, and cost 3,000 lives.

As tragic as the Haitian calamity is, it is merely symptomatic of a far deeper tragedy that's completely ignored, namely self-inflicted poverty. The reason why natural disasters take fewer lives in our country is because we have greater wealth. It's our wealth that permits us to build stronger homes and office buildings. When a natural disaster hits us, our wealth provides the emergency personnel, heavy machinery, and medical services to reduce the death toll and suffering. Haitians cannot afford the life-saving tools that we Americans take for granted. President Barack Obama called the quake "especially cruel and incomprehensible." He would be closer to the truth if he had said that the Haitian political and economic climate that make Haitians helpless in the face of natural disasters are "especially cruel and incomprehensible."

The biggest reason for Haiti being one of the world's poorest countries is its restrictions on economic liberty. Let's look at some of it. According to the 2009 Index of Economic Freedom, authorization is required for some foreign investments, such as in electricity, water, public health, and telecommunications. Authorization requires bribing public officials and, as a result, Haiti's monopolistic telephone services can at best be labeled primitive. That might explain the difficulty Haitian-Americans have in finding out about their loved ones.

Corruption is rampant. Haiti ranks 177th out of 179 countries in the 2007 Transparency International's Corruption Perceptions Index.

Its reputation as one of the world's most corrupt countries is a major impediment to doing business. Customs officers often demand bribes to clear shipments. The Heritage Foundation's Index of Economic Freedom says that because of burdensome regulations and bribery, starting a business in Haiti takes an average of 195 days, compared with the world average of 38 days. Getting a business license takes about five times longer than the world average of 234 days—that's over three years.

Crime and lawlessness are rampant in Haiti. The US Department of State website (travel.state.gov), long before the earthquake, warned, "There are no 'safe' areas in Haiti. . . . Kidnapping, death threats, murders, drug-related shootouts, armed robberies, home break-ins and car-jacking are common in Haiti." The Australian Department of Foreign Affairs and Trade warns its citizens that, "The level of crime in Haiti is very high and the police have little ability to enforce laws. Local authorities often have limited or no capacity to provide assistance, even if you are a victim of a serious crime." Crime anywhere is a prohibitive tax on economic development and the poorest people are its primary victims.

Private property rights are vital to economic growth. The Index of Economic Freedom reports that "Haitian protection of investors and property is severely compromised by weak enforcement, a paucity of updated laws to handle modern commercial practices, and a dysfunctional and resource-poor legal system." That means commercial disputes are settled out of court often through the bribery of public officials; settlements are purchased.

The way out of Haiti's grinding poverty is not rocket science. Ranking countries according to: (1) whether they are more or less free market, (2) per-capita income, and (3) ranking in Amnesty International's human rights protection index, we would find that those nations with a larger free market sector tend also to be those with the higher income and greater human rights protections. Haitian President Rene Preval is not enthusiastic about free markets; his heroes are none other than the hemisphere's two brutal communist tyrants: Venezuela's Hugo Chavez and Cuba's Fidel Castro.

Haiti's disaster demands immediate Western assistance but it's only the Haitian people who can relieve themselves of the deeper tragedy of self-inflicted poverty.

Immigration and Liberty
May 19, 2010

My sentiments on immigration are expressed by the welcoming words of poet Emma Lazarus' that grace the base of our Statue of Liberty: "Give me your tired, your poor, your huddled masses yearning to breathe free." Those sentiments are probably shared by most Americans and for sure by my libertarian fellow travelers, but their vision of immigration has some blind spots. This has become painfully obvious in the wake Arizona's law that cracks down on illegal immigration. Let's look at the immigration issue step by step.

There are close to 7 billion people on our planet. I'd like to know how the libertarians answer this question: Does each individual on the planet have a natural or God-given right to live in the United States? Unless one wishes to obfuscate, I believe that a yes or no can be given to that question just as a yes or no answer can be given to the question whether Williams has a right to live in the United States.

I believe most people, even my open-borders libertarian friends, would not say that everyone on the planet had a right to live in the United States. That being the case suggests there will be conditions that a person must meet to live in the United States. Then the question emerges: Who gets to set those conditions? Should it be the United Nations, the European Union, the Japanese Diet, or the Moscow City Duma? I can't be absolutely sure, but I believe that most Americans would recoil at the suggestion that somebody other than Americans should be allowed to set the conditions for people to live in the United States.

What those conditions should be is one thing and whether a person has a right to ignore them is another. People become illegal immigrants in one of three ways: entering without authorization or inspection, staying beyond the authorized period after legal entry, or violating the terms of legal entry. Most of those who risk prosecution under Arizona's new law fit the first category—entering without authorization or inspection.

Probably, the overwhelming majority of Mexican illegal immigrants are hardworking, honest, and otherwise law-abiding members of the communities in which they reside. It would surely be a heartwrenching scenario for such a person to be stopped for a driving infraction, have his illegal immigrant status discovered, and face deportation proceedings. Regardless of the hardship suffered, being in the United States without authorization is a crime.

When crimes are committed, what should be done? Some people recommend amnesia, which turns out to be the root word for amnesty. But surely they don't propose it as a general response to crime where criminals confess their crime, pay some fine, and apply to have their crimes overlooked. Amnesty supporters probably wish amnesty to apply to only illegal immigrants. That being the case, one wonders whether they wish it to apply to illegals past, present, and future, regardless of race, ethnicity, or country of origin.

Various estimates put the illegal immigrant population in the United States between 10 and 20 million. One argument says we can't round up and deport all those people. That argument differs little from one that says since we can't catch every burglar, we should grant burglars amnesty. Catching and imprisoning some burglars sends a message to would-be burglars that there might be a price to pay. Similarly, imprisoning some illegal immigrants and then deporting them after their sentences were served would send a signal to others who are here illegally or who are contemplating illegal entry that there's a price to pay.

Here's Williams's suggestion in a nutshell. Start strict enforcement of immigration law, as Arizona has begun. Strictly enforce border security. Most importantly, modernize and streamline our cumbersome immigration laws so that people can more easily migrate to our country.

Invisible Victims

October 16, 2010

The National Transportation Safety Board has again recommended that airlines require a separate seat for all children, regardless of age, eliminating the current practice of permitting children under the age of two to fly for free on the lap of a parent. Will mandating child restraint systems make air travel safer? The answer is probably yes but that's the visible.

Having to purchase an extra airplane ticket, some families will opt to drive to their destination instead. Thus, mandated CRS will force some families to switch to a less safe method of travel and some highway fatalities will represent the invisible victims of NTSB policy. By the way, if parents wanted a greater measure of safety for their infant, it's available to them right now. They can purchase a seat and seat restraint for their infant.

The US Food and Drug Administration is charged with ensuring that drugs are safe and effective. Drugs must meet FDA approval before they can be marketed. FDA officials can make two kinds of errors. They can approve a drug that has unanticipated, dangerous side effects that might cause illness and death. Or, they can err by either not approving or causing huge delays in the marketing of a safe and effective drug. Statistically, these are known as the Type I and Type II errors.

FDA officials have a bias toward erring on the side of over-caution. If FDA officials err on the side of under-caution, approving an unsafe drug, they are attacked by the media, patient groups, and investigated by Congress. Their victims, sick and dead people, are highly visible. If FDA officials err on the side of over-caution, keeping a safe and effective drug off the market, who's to know? The victims are invisible.

If you conclude that FDA officials have a bias toward errors that create invisible victims, who don't know whom to blame for their illness or death, step to the head of the class. Particularly egregious examples are: The FDA's ten-year delay in approving alprenolol, a beta-blocker, sold for three years in Europe, cost more than 10,000 lives per year. The three-year delay in the approval of misoprostol, a drug for the treatment of gastric bleeding that cost between 8,000 and 15,000 lives per year. The lag in the approval of streptokinase for the treatment of occluded coronary arteries cost more than 10,000 lives per year.

FDA erring on the side of over-caution makes the average cost of bringing a drug to the market close to $1 billion. When an FDA official proudly announces the approval of a major new drug, someone should ask him: If this drug is going to start saving lives tomorrow, how many people died yesterday, last week, last month, or last year waiting for the drug to be approved? A drug company CEO could give you the answer if he weren't fearful of FDA retaliation.

Corporate Average Fuel Economy (CAFE) represents Congress's way to force manufacturers to produce more fuel-efficient cars. Manufacturers meet CAFE standards by producing lighter weight and hence less crash-worthy cars. According to a Brookings Institution study, a 500-pound weight reduction of the average car increased annual highway fatalities by 2,200–3,900 and serious injuries by 11,000 and 19,500 per year. A National Highway Transportation and Safety Administration study demonstrated that reducing a vehicle's weight by only 100 pounds increased the fatality rate by as much as 5.63 percent for light cars, 4.70 percent for heavier cars, and 3.06 percent for light trucks. These rates translated into additional traffic fatalities of 13,608 for light cars, 10,884 for heavier cars, and 14,705 for light trucks between 1996 and 1999.

Congressmen have full knowledge of these life and death statistics but doing the bidding of environmentalists and other interest groups is more important than American lives. There ought to be a way to make the invisible victims of Congress visible.

Free or Fair?

December 29, 2010

At first blush, the mercantilists' call for "free trade but fair trade" sounds reasonable. After all, who can be against fairness? Giving the idea just a bit of thought suggests that fairness as a guide for public policy lays the groundwork for tyranny. You say, "Williams, I've never heard anything so farfetched! Explain yourself."

Think about the First Amendment to our Constitution that reads: Congress shall make no law respecting an establishment of religion, or prohibiting the free exercise thereof; or abridging the freedom of speech, or of the press; or the right of the people peaceably to assemble, and to petition the Government for a redress of grievances."

How many of us would prefer that the founders had written the First Amendment so as to focus on fairness rather than freedom and instead wrote: "Congress shall make no unfair laws respecting an establishment of religion, or prohibiting the fair exercise thereof; or abridging the fairness of speech, or of the press; or the right of the people to peaceably assemble in a fair fashion, and to fairly petition the Government for a redress of grievances"?

How supportive would you be to a person who argued that he was for free religion but fair religion, or he was for free speech but fair speech? Would you be supportive of government efforts to limit unfair religion and unfair speech? How might life look under a regime of fairness of religion, speech and the press?

Suppose a newspaper published a statement like "President Obama might easily end his term alongside Jimmy Carter as one of America's worst presidents." Some people might consider that fair speech while other people denounce it as unfair speech. What to do? A tribunal would have to be formed to decide on the fairness or unfairness of the statement. It goes without saying that the political makeup of the tribunal would be a matter of controversy. Once such a tribunal was set up, how much generalized agreement would there be on what it decreed? And, if deemed unfair speech, what should the penalties be?

The bottom line is that what's fair or unfair is an elusive concept and the same applies to trade. Last summer, I purchased a 2010 LS 460 Lexus, through a US intermediary, from a Japanese producer for $70,000. Here's my question to you: Was that a fair or unfair trade? I was free to keep my $70,000 or purchase the car. The Japanese producer was free to keep his Lexus or sell me the car. As it turned out, I gave up my $70,000 and took possession of the car, and the Japanese producer gave up possession of the car and took possession of my money. The exchange occurred because I saw myself as being better off and so did the Japanese producer. I think it was both free and fair trade, and I'd like an American mercantilist to explain to me how it wasn't.

Mercantilists have absolutely no argument when we recognize that trade is mostly between individuals. Mercantilists pretend that trade occurs between nations such as US trading with England or Japan to appeal to our jingoism. First, does the US trade with Japan and England? In other words, is it members of the US Congress trading with their counterparts in the Japanese Diet or the English Parliament? That's nonsense. Trade occurs between individuals in one country, through intermediaries, with individuals in another country.

Who might protest that my trade with the Lexus manufacturer was unfair? If you said an American car manufacturer and their union workers, go to the head of the class. They would like Congress to restrict foreign trade so that they can sell their cars at a pleasing price and their workers earn a pleasing wage. As a matter of fact, it's never American consumers who complain about cheaper prices. It's always American producers and their unions who do the complaining. That ought to tell us something.

True or False

January 5, 2011

So many statements we accept as true, plausible, or beyond question; but are they? Let's look at a couple of important ones: global warming and US manufacturing decline.

In 2000, Dr. David Viner of University of East Anglia's disgraced Climatic Research Unit advised, "Within a few years winter snowfall will become a very rare and exciting event." "Children just aren't going to know what snow is." Britain's Meteorological Office said this December was "almost certain" to become the coldest since records began in 1910. Paul Michaelwaite, forecaster for NetWeather.tv, said, "It is looking like this winter could be in the top twenty cold winters in the last hundred years."

In reference to the last decade of the Earth's cooling, geologist Dr. Don J. Easterbrook, emeritus professor at Western Washington University, says, "Recent solar changes suggest that it could be fairly severe, perhaps more like the 1880 to 1915 cool cycle than the more moderate 1945–1977 cool cycle. A more drastic cooling, similar to that during the Dalton and Maunder minimums, could plunge the Earth into another Little Ice Age, but only time will tell if that is likely." Global warming hype is nothing less than a gambit for more government control over our lives.

How about statements like these: "The United States got to where it is today by making things." "There's nothing made here anymore." "One-third of the nation's manufacturing jobs have vanished in the past decade." These statements suggest that we are no longer the world's top manufacturer; we have all but turned into a nation of "hamburger flippers."

According to data assembled by Dr. Mark Perry, in his article in *The American* (December 23, 2009) titled "Manufacturing's Death Greatly Exaggerated," "For the year 2008, the Federal Reserve estimates that the value of US manufacturing output was about $3.7 trillion." If the US manufacturing sector were a separate economy, with its own GDP, it would be tied with Germany as the world's fourth-richest economy. The 2008 GDPs were: United States ($14.2 trillion), Japan ($4.9 trillion), China ($4.3 trillion), US manufacturing ($3.7 trillion), Germany ($3.7 trillion), France ($2.9 trillion), and the United Kingdom ($2.7 trillion).

US manufacturing employment peaked at 19.5 million jobs in 1979. Since 1979, the manufacturing workforce has shrunk by 40 percent, and there's every indication that manufacturing employment will continue to shrink. Because of automation, the US worker is now three times as productive as in 1980 and twice as productive as in 2000. It's productivity gains, rather than outsourcing and imports, that explains most of our manufacturing job loss.

US manufacturing is going through the same kind of labor-saving technological innovation as agriculture. In 1790, farmers were 90 percent of the US labor force. By 1900, only about 41 percent of our labor force was employed in agriculture. By 2008, less than 3 percent of Americans were employed in agriculture. What would you have had Congress do in the face of this precipitous loss of agricultural jobs? Should Congress have outlawed all of the technological advances and machinery that cost millions of agricultural jobs and made our farmers the world's most productive? Also, had Congress done something to save those agricultural jobs, where would we have gotten the workers to produce the millions of things we enjoy that weren't even around in 1790? We would have been poorer.

Let's not stop with agriculture. In 1970, the telecommunications industry employed 421,000 workers, in good-paying jobs as switchboard operators, handling 9.8 billion long-distance calls yearly. Today, the telecommunications industry employs fewer than 60,000 operators, and they handle more than 100 billion long-distance calls yearly. That's an 85 percent job loss. The spectacular advances in telecommunications, which raised productivity, made the cost of long-distance calls a tiny fraction of what they were.

What we're witnessing in many of our industries is what economic historian Joseph Schumpeter called "creative destruction." The adjustment to it can be painful, but to stand in its way will make us a poorer nation.

Smugglers as Heroes
April 27, 2011

Smugglers are heroes of sorts. The essence of what a smuggler offers is: "Government tyrants want to either prevent or interfere with peaceable voluntary exchange among individuals. I can reduce the impact of that interference." Let's look at smuggling, keeping in mind that not everything illegal is immoral and not everything legal is moral.

Leading up to our War of Independence, the British, under the Navigation Acts, had levied taxes on a wide range of imports. One of those taxes was on molasses imported from non-British islands. John Hancock, whose flamboyant signature graces our Declaration of Independence, had a thriving business smuggling an estimated 1.5 million gallons of molasses a year. His smuggling practices financed much of the resistance to British authority. In fact, a joke of the time was "Sam Adams writes the letters [to newspapers] and John Hancock pays the postage."

Hancock's smuggling, as well as that of many others, made the people of our nation better off by providing cheaper prices for molasses used for making rum. British oppressors were worse off by having lower tax revenues.

In 1920, the Eighteenth Amendment, prohibiting the production, distribution, and sale of alcoholic beverages in the United States, went into effect. It had wide public support. In my opinion, no case can be made for stopping another person from enjoying beer, wine, and whiskey. That's oppression, but along came heroes to the rescue. The ink hadn't dried on the Eighteenth Amendment before smugglers started smuggling beer and whiskey from Canada and Mexico. Ships lined up along our shores, just beyond the three-mile limit, to off-load whiskey onto speedboats. Smugglers and bootleggers spared millions of Americans from do-gooder oppression.

While the smuggler qua smuggler is my hero, several important negative effects surround his activity. Smuggling is illegal. It becomes a sometimes-nasty criminal enterprise because those who engage in it tend to be people with an overall lower regard for the law. Since smuggling is illegal, disputes must be settled with guns and violence instead of courts. Plus, police and other public officials are corrupted. Worse of all is the reduced respect for laws by the public at large. After the Eighteenth Amendment's repeal, virtually all of the crime and corruption associated with Prohibition disappeared.

Not many Americans are aware of today's big smuggling activity—cigarette smuggling. Confiscatory taxes that are as high as $7 a pack, in New York City, making one pack of cigarettes sell for $13, have encouraged a thriving smuggling business across our country. Like Prohibition, confiscatory tobacco taxes are popular with Americans.

A recent study by Michael LaFaive and Todd Nesbit of the Midland, Michigan-based Mackinac Center for Public Policy titled "Cigarette Taxes and Smuggling" shows that states with the highest cigarette-smuggling rates are those with the highest tobacco taxes such as Arizona (51.8 percent of the state's total consumption are smuggled), New York (47.5 percent), Rhode Island (40.5 percent), New Mexico (37.2 percent), and California (36.3 percent).

Cigarette smuggling, like yesteryear's whiskey smuggling, has become a livelihood for criminals. The Bureau of Alcohol, Tobacco, Firearms and Explosives has found that Russian, Armenian, Ukrainian, Chinese, Taiwanese, and Middle Eastern (mainly Pakistani, Lebanese, and Syrian) organized crime groups are highly involved in the trafficking of contraband and counterfeit cigarettes. What's worse is that some of these groups use their earnings to provide financial assistance to terrorist organizations such as Hezbollah and Hamas. That means tax-hungry politicians and anti-tobacco zealots are providing the means for aid to America's enemies.

The solution to cigarette smuggling, and the criminal activities associated with it, is to eliminate the confiscatory taxes. Unfortunately for tax-hungry politicians and anti-tobacco zealots, who see confiscatory taxes as a tool in their moral crusade against tobacco, only benefits count. For them, the costs of their agenda are irrelevant or secondary at best. And, as novelist C. S. Lewis put it, "Of all tyrannies a tyranny sincerely exercised for the good of its victims may be the most oppressive."

Ominous Parallels

August 17, 2011

People are beginning to compare Barack Obama's administration to the failed administration of Jimmy Carter, but a better comparison is to the Roosevelt administration of the 1930s and '40s. Let's look at it with the help of a publication from the Mackinac Center for Public Policy and the Foundation for Economic Education titled "Great Myths of the Great Depression," by Dr. Lawrence Reed.

During the first year of President Franklin D. Roosevelt's New Deal, he called for increasing federal spending to $10 billion while revenues were only $3 billion. Between 1933 and 1936, government expenditures rose by more than 83 percent. Federal debt skyrocketed by 73 percent. Roosevelt signed off on legislation that raised the top income tax rate to 79 percent and then later to 90 percent. Hillsdale College economics historian and professor Burt Folsom, author of *New Deal or Raw Deal?*, notes that in 1941, Roosevelt even proposed a 99.5 percent marginal tax rate on all incomes more than $100,000. When a top adviser questioned the idea, Roosevelt replied, "Why not?"

Roosevelt had other ideas for the economy, including the National Recovery Act. Dr. Reed says: "The economic impact of the NRA was immediate and powerful. In the five months leading up to the act's passage, signs of recovery were evident: factory employment and payrolls had increased by 23 and 35 percent, respectively. Then came the NRA, shortening hours of work, raising wages arbitrarily, and imposing other new costs on enterprise. In the six months after the law took effect, industrial production dropped 25 percent."

Blacks were especially hard hit by the NRA. Black spokesmen and the black press often referred to the NRA as the "Negro Run Around," "Negroes Rarely Allowed," "Negroes Ruined Again," "Negroes Robbed Again," "No Roosevelt Again," and the "Negro Removal Act." Fortunately, the courts ruled the NRA unconstitutional. As a result, unemployment fell to 14 percent in 1936 and lower by 1937.

Roosevelt had more plans for the economy, namely the National Labor Relations Act, better known as the "Wagner Act." This was a payoff to labor unions, and with these new powers, labor unions went on a militant organizing frenzy that included threats, boycotts, strikes, seizures of plants, widespread violence, and other acts that pushed productivity down sharply and unemployment up dramatically. In 1938, Roosevelt's New Deal produced the nation's first depression within a depression. The stock market crashed again, losing nearly 50 percent of its value between August 1937 and March 1938, and unemployment climbed back to 20 percent. Columnist Walter Lippmann wrote in March 1938 that "with almost no important exception every measure [Roosevelt] has been interested in for the past five months has been to reduce or discourage the production of wealth."

Roosevelt's agenda was not without its international admirers. The chief Nazi newspaper, *Volkischer Beobachter*, repeatedly praised "Roosevelt's adoption of National Socialist strains of thought in his economic and social policies" and "the development toward an authoritarian state" based on the "demand that collective good be put before individual self-interest." Roosevelt himself called Benito Mussolini "admirable" and professed that he was "deeply impressed by what he [had] accomplished."

FDR's very own treasury secretary, Henry Morgenthau, saw the folly of the New Deal, writing: "We have tried spending money. We are spending more than we have ever spent before and it does not work. . . . We have never made good on our promises. . . . I say after eight years of this Administration we have just as much unemployment as when we started . . . and an enormous debt to boot!" The bottom line is that Roosevelt's New Deal policies turned what would have been a three- or four-year sharp downturn into a sixteen-year affair.

The 1930s depression was caused by and aggravated by acts of government, and so was the current financial mess that we're in. Do we want to repeat history by listening to those who created the calamity? That's like calling on an arsonist to help put out a fire.

The Financial Mess in the United States and Europe

September 28, 2011

What's the common thread between Europe's financial mess, particularly among the PIIGS (Portugal, Ireland, Italy, Greece, and Spain), and the financial mess in the United States? That question could be more easily answered if we asked instead: What's necessary to cure the financial mess in Europe and the United States? If European governments and the US Congress ceased the practice of giving people what they have not earned, budgets would be more than balanced. For government to guarantee a person a right to goods and services he has not earned, it must diminish someone else's right to what he has earned, simply because governments have no resources of their very own.

The first order of business in reaching a solution to the financial mess in Europe and the United States must be the recognition that governments have been doing a class of unsustainable things, mostly giving people special privileges and things that they have not earned. It's a matter of not simply what's good or bad for the beneficiaries but what its effect is on society at large and the welfare of a nation.

Take the understandably humane motivation to provide health care services for the medically indigent. If one is concerned about the health needs of a person, why shouldn't the government also provide him with resources for nutrition? Good health is not just medical services and food but a decent place to live. Furthermore, good health is a matter of not just physical well-being but mental well-being as well, so why not have government-sponsored vacations? That's not such a far-fetched idea as one might imagine. Antonio Tajani, the European commissioner for industry and entrepreneurship, has declared vacationing to be a "human right."

Growing social spending in the name of health is just one example of a much larger process affecting the whole of our societies. There's a process that we might call contagion, in which spending automatically and unavoidably breeds more spending. For example, if government provides subsidies for wheat farmers, corn farmers will organize and protest that it's unfair not to grant them subsidies. What case can be made for government's not granting subsidies to all farmers? Then there's contagion across borders. If European farmers get subsidies, American farmers are going to demand subsidies to "even the playing field." How about government bailouts? There's contagion there as well. If Congress bails out General Motors, what's the justification for not also bailing out Chrysler and JPMorgan Chase, Bank of America, Fannie Mae, AIG, Citigroup, and other failed enterprises? Bailouts are contagious both in the short and the long run. Bailouts create what's known as a moral hazard, in which people have reduced incentive to mend their ways.

The bottom line is that the sole tendency of the welfare state is for it to grow and consume more and more of a nation's income. According to "Measuring the Unfunded Obligations of European Countries" (January 2009), by the Dallas-based National Center for Policy Analysis, by 2050, the average EU country will need more than 60 percent of its gross domestic product to fulfill its obligations. According to the 2008 Social Security and Medicare trustees reports, the combined unfunded liability of just these two government programs has reached $101.7 trillion in today's dollars.

It turns out that if Congress taxed away our entire $14 trillion 2011 GDP and put it in the bank, it would just barely cover Social Security and Medicare liabilities. That observation suggests that we can't tax our way out of our fiscal mess. In order to avoid permanent stagnation or total economic collapse, governments must start the process of reducing welfare spending. I wouldn't recommend cold turkey for a heroin addict, neither would I recommend cold turkey for all those people who have been addicted and made dependent upon government handouts. We must find a compassionate way to wean people off government.

Hating America

May 15, 2013

Brothers Tamerlan and Dzhokhar Tsarnaev, who are accused of setting the bombs that exploded at the Boston Marathon, attended the University of Massachusetts. Maybe they hated our nation before college, but if you want lessons on hating America, college attendance might be a good start. Let's look at it.

"We need to think very, very clearly about who the enemy is. The enemy is the United States of America and everyone who supports it." That's taught to University of Hawaii students by Professor Haunani-Kay Trask. Richard Falk, professor emeritus at Princeton University and the U.N. Human Rights Council's Palestine monitor, explained the Boston bombings by saying, "The American global domination project is bound to generate all kinds of resistance in the post-colonial world." Professor Falk has also stated that President George W. Bush ordered the destruction of the twin towers.

University of Southern California professor Darry Sragow preaches hate to his students in his regulation of elections and political finance class, recently telling them that Republicans are stupid, racist losers and that they are angry old white people. A few years ago, Rod Swanson, a UCLA economics professor, told his class, "The United States of America, backed by facts, is the greediest and most selfish country in the world." Penn State University professor Matt Jordan compared supporters of the voter ID laws to the Ku Klux Klan. Professor Sharon Sweet, an algebra teacher at Brevard Community College, told her students to sign a pledge that read, "I pledge to vote for President Obama and Democrats up and down the ticket." Fortunately, the college's trustees fired her.

University of Rhode Island history professor Erik Loomis tweeted, "I want [National Rifle Association executive vice president] Wayne LaPierre's head on a stick." He asked, "Can [we] define NRA membership as dues contributing to a terrorist organization?" Here's a sample of how Professor Loomis frequently expresses himself: "Mother-f———ing f———heads f———ing f———." Then there's Georgetown law professor Louis Michael Seidman, who explained our national problems by saying, "But almost no one blames the culprit: our insistence on obedience to the Constitution, with all its archaic, idiosyncratic and downright evil provisions." Professor Seidman worked for The Public Defender Service for the District of Columbia. When he was sworn in as an officer of the court, I wonder what constitution he swore to uphold and defend.

Parents don't have to wait for college admission for their youngsters to receive America-hating lessons. Scott Compton, an English teacher at Chapin High School in Chapin, S.C., was put on administrative leave after he allegedly threw an American flag on the floor and stomped on it in front of his students. He has chosen to resign.

An Advanced Placement world geography teacher at Lumberton High School in Texas encouraged students to dress in Islamic clothing and instructed them to refer to the 9/11 hijackers not as terrorists but as "freedom fighters." They were also told to stop referring to the Holocaust as genocide. John Valastro, the superintendent of the Lumberton Independent School District, told Fox News that the teacher did absolutely nothing wrong.

In McAllen, Texas, teachers tried to force a teenager to sing the Mexican national anthem and recite Mexico's pledge of allegiance. The teen refused, saying it was against her beliefs as an American. She was thrown out of the class and given a failing grade for that day's assignment. Her father has filed a lawsuit on behalf of his daughter against the McAllen Independent School District.

Investor's Business Daily ran a story that shows student indoctrination is official union policy: "A New Low from the California Federation of Teachers: Urine Indoctrination" (December 5, 2012). The union's website has a cartoon narrated by leftist Hollywood actor Ed Asner. In tones used when reading to children, Asner says: "[Rich people] love their money more than anything in the whole world. . . .

Over time, rich people decided they weren't rich enough, so they came up with ways to get richer." The cartoon finishes its class warfare message by graphically depicting "the rich" urinating on the poor.

These people running our education system are destroying the minds and values of our young people, and we allow them to do it.

What Egyptians Need

July 17, 2013

What Egyptian citizens must recognize is that political liberty thrives best where there's a large measure of economic liberty. The Egyptian people are not the problem; it's the environment they're forced to live in. Why is it that Egyptians do well in the United States but not Egypt? We could make the same observation about Nigerians, Cambodians, Jamaicans, and many other people who leave their homeland and immigrate to the United States. For example, Indians in India suffer great poverty. But that's not true of Indians who immigrate to the United States. They manage to start more Silicon Valley companies than any other immigrant group, and they do the same in Massachusetts, Texas, Florida, New York, and New Jersey.

According to various reports, about 50 percent of Egypt's 83 million people live on or below the $2-per-day poverty line set by the World Bank. Overall, unemployment is 13 percent, and among youths, it's 25 percent. Those are the official numbers. The true rates are estimated to be twice as high.

Much of Egypt's economic problems are directly related to government intervention and control, which have resulted in weak institutions so vital for prosperity. As Hernando de Soto, president of Peru's Institute for Liberty and Democracy, wrote in his *Wall Street Journal* article titled "Egypt's Economic Apartheid" (February 3, 2011), more than 90 percent of Egyptians hold their property without legal title. De Soto said: "Without clear legal title to their assets and real estate, in short, these entrepreneurs own what I have called 'dead capital'—property that cannot be leveraged as collateral for loans, to obtain investment capital, or as security for long-term contractual deals. And so the majority of these Egyptian enterprises remain small and relatively poor."

Egypt's legal private sector employs 6.8 million people, and the public sector has 5.9 million. More than 9 million people work in the extra-legal sector, making Egypt's underground economy the nation's biggest employer. Why are so many Egyptians in the underground economy? De Soto answered by giving a typical example: "To open a small bakery, our investigators found, would take more than 500 days. To get legal title to a vacant piece of land would take more than 10 years of dealing with red tape. To do business in Egypt, an aspiring poor entrepreneur would have to deal with 56 government agencies and repetitive government inspections." According to the World Bank, in terms of the difficulty of doing business, Egypt ranks 109th out of 185 countries.

What needs to be done? Although it shouldn't be seen as a general strategy, there is at least one notable case in which a military coup and subsequent rule worked to the great benefit of a nation. A July 5 *Investor's Business Daily* editorial (http://tinyurl.com/klkjrmf) was about Chile's 1973 coup, which toppled the democratically elected Salvador Allende government and put Chilean military commander Augusto Pinochet in charge. Pinochet used his military dictatorship to create free-market reforms by eliminating thousands of restrictive laws governing labor, mining, fishing, vineyards, startups, and banking that were choking Chile's economy. As a result, Chile became Latin America's best economy and today has Latin America's most durable democracy. That's the upside to Pinochet's rule. The downside was the regime's corruption and atrocities.

Western intellectuals, pundits, and politicians are mistakenly calling for democracy in Egypt. But there's a problem. In most countries in the Arab world, what we know as personal liberty is virtually nonexistent. Freedom House's 2011 "Freedom in the World" survey and Amnesty International's annual report for 2011 labeled most North African and Middle Eastern countries as either "repressive" or "not free." These nations do not share the philosophical foundations that delivered the West from its history of barbarism, such as the Magna Carta (1215) and later the teachings of such philosophers as Francis Bacon, John Locke, Thomas Hobbes, David Hume, Montesquieu, and Voltaire.

Personal liberty is important, but the best route to that goal is what Egypt needs most—reforms that create economic liberty.

How to Assist Evil

April 9, 2014

"Engineering Evil" is a documentary recently shown on the Military History channel. It's a story of Nazi Germany's murder campaign before and during World War II. According to some estimates, 16 million Jews and other people died at the hands of Nazis (http://tinyurl .com/6duny9).

Though the Holocaust ranks high among the great human tragedies, most people never consider the most important question: How did Adolf Hitler and the Nazis gain the power that they needed to commit such horror? Focusing solely on the evil of the Holocaust won't get us very far toward the goal of the Jewish slogan "Never Again."

When Hitler came to power, he inherited decades of political consolidation by Otto von Bismarck and later the Weimar Republic that had weakened the political power of local jurisdictions. Through the Enabling Act (1933), whose formal name was "A Law to Remedy the Distress of People and Reich," Hitler gained the power to enact laws with neither the involvement nor the approval of the Reichstag, Germany's parliament. The Enabling Act destroyed any remaining local autonomy. The bottom line is that it was decent Germans who made Hitler's terror possible—Germans who would have never supported his territorial designs and atrocities.

The twentieth century turned out to be mankind's most barbaric. Roughly 50 million to 60 million people died in international and civil wars. As tragic as that number is, it pales in comparison with the number of people who were killed at the hands of their own government. Recently deceased Rudolph J. Rummel, professor of political science at the University of Hawaii and author of *Death by Government*, estimated that since the beginning of the twentieth century, governments have killed 170 million of their own citizens. Top government killers were the Soviet Union, which, between 1917 and 1987, killed 62 million of its own citizens, and the People's Republic of China, which, between 1949 and 1987, was responsible for the deaths of 35 million to 40 million of its citizens. In a distant third place were the Nazis, who murdered about 16 million Jews, Slavs, Serbs, Czechs, Poles, Ukrainians, and others deemed misfits, such as homosexuals and the mentally ill.

We might ask why the twentieth century was so barbaric. Surely, there were barbarians during earlier ages. Part of the answer is that during earlier times, there wasn't the kind of concentration of power that emerged during the twentieth century. Had Josef Stalin, Mao Zedong, and Hitler been around in earlier times, they could not have engineered the slaughter of tens of millions of people. They wouldn't have had the authority. There was considerable dispersion of jealously guarded political power in the forms of heads of provincial governments and principalities and nobility and church leaders whose political power within their spheres was often just as strong as the monarch's.

Professor Rummel explained in the very first sentence of *Death by Government* that "Power kills; absolute Power kills absolutely. . . . The more power a government has, the more it can act arbitrarily according to the whims and desires of the elite, and the more it will make war on others and murder its foreign and domestic subjects." That's the long, tragic, ugly story of government: the elite's use of government to dupe and forcibly impose its will on the masses. The masses are always duped by well-intentioned phrases. After all, what German could have been against "A Law to Remedy the Distress of People and Reich"? It's not just Germans who have fallen prey to well-intentioned phrases. After all, who can be against the "Patient Protection and Affordable Care Act"?

We Americans ought to keep the fact in mind that Hitler, Stalin, and Mao would have had more success in their reign of terror if they had the kind of control and information about their citizens that agencies such as the National Security Agency, the Internal Revenue Service, and the Alcohol, Tobacco, and Firearms (ATF) have about us. You might ask, "What are you saying, Williams?" Just put it this way: No German who died before 1930 would have believed the Holocaust possible.

Our Unwillingness to Defend Ourselves
July 16, 2014

The US Justice Department's Bureau of Justice Statistics (BJS) reports that 2012 losses because of personal identity theft totaled $24.7 billion (http://tinyurl.com/mdncmmw). The money losses from identity theft pale in comparison with the costs of paperwork, time, and inconvenience imposed on the larger society in an effort to protect ourselves. According to LifeLock, while the laws against identity theft have gotten tougher, identity theft criminal prosecution is relatively rare. Unless we develop a low tolerance and a willingness to impose harsh sentences, identity thieves will continue to impose billions of dollars of costs on society.

Today's Americans tolerate what would have been unthinkable years ago. According to the National Center for Education Statistics and the BJS, 209,800 primary- and secondary-school teachers reported being physically attacked by a student during the 2011–12 academic year (http://tinyurl.com/nltrzaz). Hundreds of thousands more are threatened with injury. On average, 1,175 teachers are physically attacked each day of the school year. These facts demonstrate an unwillingness to defend ourselves against these young barbarians, who often will grow into big barbarians.

During the 1940s and early '50s, when I was in school, assaulting or threatening teachers was unthinkable. Corporal punishment in school or at home would have been the result of an assault or threat against a teacher. Starting in the '50s, following Dr. Benjamin Spock's advice, what worked for centuries was exchanged with what sounded good. In 1970, Thomas Gordon, best-selling author of *Parent Effectiveness Training*, told parents to stop punishing their children and to start treating them "much as we treat friends or a spouse." Corporal punishment has been criminalized. Other forms of punishment have been replaced with "timeout" and other such nonsense.

When young barbarians grow up to become big barbarians, often there's still an unwillingness to defend ourselves. In many poor neighborhoods, the police know who the criminals are, but their hands are tied by the courts. These criminals are permitted to prey on the overwhelmingly law-abiding members of the community, who, because of ineffective police protection, are huddled behind bars in their homes. Sometimes these criminals go downtown to single out white people, whom they sometimes refer to as "polar bears," to play the "knockout" game. What's worse is that sometimes, as in the case of Rochester, New York, the police characterize these brazen attacks as harassment rather than assaults. Though most of these attacks are against white people, the news media and police are reluctant to call them racist hate crimes.

It's in the international arena where we face the greatest threat from our unwillingness to protect ourselves. Most of the international community sees Iran as a sponsor and exporter of terrorism. There's no question that if Iran develops nuclear weapons, it doesn't bode well for the world. But what does the world do, led by the United States? It allows Iran to go full speed ahead in the name of what the Iranian press calls "the Iranian nation's nuclear rights." The United States alone has the power to tell Iran to permit unimpeded inspection of the country's nuclear facilities, with the threat of bombing if it doesn't comply.

The West, led by our country, is doing exactly what it did in the run-up to World War II. It knowingly allowed Adolf Hitler to rearm—in violation of treaties—which led to a war that cost 60 million lives. In 1936, France alone could have stopped Hitler.

We have a similar lack of willingness to effectively deal with terrorists. Our intelligence community knows the national origin of those who attack Americans. At least one part of our strategy should be to inform nations that we will exact a heavy price from them if they become a staging ground for terrorists.

Unfortunately, for the future of our nation and the world, we are too focused on government handouts rather than the most basic function of government: defending us from barbarians.

Western Anti-Semitism

August 6, 2014

Navi Pillay, U.N. high commissioner for human rights, has accused both Israel and Hamas militants of committing war crimes in the Gaza conflict. Her harshest criticism, as well as that of most nations, has been reserved for the Israeli government, charging that it has committed war crimes in direct violation of the Geneva Conventions. In the wake of the huge difference in casualties and property destruction, many in the West have accused the Israeli government of making a grossly disproportionate response to terrorist rocket attacks. A *New York Times* (July 23, 2014) article titled "As Much of the World Frowns on Israel, Americans Hold Out Support" says that a number of "world leaders and demonstrators pointed to the lopsided number of Palestinian casualties—more than 650, most of them civilians—versus 35 on the Israeli side, 32 of them soldiers." By now, those numbers have tripled, but let's think about some of the arguments being made.

First, let's take a historical look at proportionality in response to an attack. In February 1945, in Dresden, Germany, 25,000 lives were lost in one night and the city was reduced to rubble as a result of British and US bombers firebombing. In March 1945, 300 US B-29 planes dropped incendiary bombs on Tokyo, killing more than 100,000 people, with millions injured and made homeless. Later, atomic bombs were dropped on Hiroshima and Nagasaki, leading to even greater loss of life and property destruction. Who's willing to criticize the Allies for lack of proportionality in response to Germany's and Japan's attacks? Though the Allies brought about a horrible loss of life and massive destruction, one thing is very clear and indisputable: Neither country has attacked ever since.

Anti-Semitic attacks have skyrocketed in Europe in the wake of the Israeli-Palestinian conflict. It's not just a criticism of Israel's foreign policy; it's an attack on Jews. Synagogues have faced Molotov cocktails, bomb threats, and vandalism. Several European cities have seen slogans such as "Dirty Jews," "Jews your end is near," "Out with Zionists," "Israel executioner," and "Save Gaza! Hitler, you were right!" According to RT News, over the past month there has been a 50 percent increase in hate crimes against Jews in Britain.

The Western anti-Semitic and anti-Israel response is amazing and somewhat disconcerting. Israel is the only democratic nation in the Middle East. It has respect for relatively free markets, personal liberty, and private property rights. Many Westerners give their moral support to Muslims who, as a matter of religion, practice brutal control of women that includes honor killings. Many Muslims consider homosexuality to be not only a sin but a crime under Islamic law punishable by death. What Westerners consider basic human rights are often outlawed in Islamic nations. The Quran is the religious guide of Islam, and Muslims believe it to be a revelation from God. It contains more than a hundred verses that call Muslims to war with nonbelievers for the sake of Islamic rule. Westerners who condemn Israel and support the recent anti-Semitic attacks—or remain silent in the face of them—are by no means spared from Islamic condemnation as infidels.

It has to be heart-rending to any decent person to witness the suffering of the Palestinians, who're experiencing a major tragedy both in casualties and in property destruction. Though it is Hamas firing rockets into Israel, the ordinary Palestinian is not to be held blameless. Palestinians know that Hamas is storing rockets and building tunnels in civilian areas and that if Israel tries to take out these rockets and tunnels, civilian casualties will be part of the collateral damage. Their silence and acceptance implies support for the tactics of Hamas.

Gen. William T. Sherman told the 1879 graduating class of the Michigan Military Academy, "War is hell." There's no nice war, and that's why war should be a last alternative. Those Westerners who criticize Israel's response to close to 3,000 rocket attacks might tell us what Israel should do in response—just take the rockets, surrender or leave the Middle East?

Multiculturalism Is a Failure

September 17, 2014

German Chancellor Angela Merkel declared that in Germany, multiculturalism has "utterly failed." Both Australia's ex-prime minister John Howard and Spain's ex-prime minister Jose Maria Aznar reached the same conclusion about multiculturalism in their countries. British Prime Minister David Cameron has warned that multiculturalism is fostering extremist ideology and directly contributing to homegrown Islamic terrorism. UK Independence Party leader Nigel Farage said the United Kingdom's push for multiculturalism has not united Britons but pushed them apart. It has allowed for Islam to emerge despite Britain's Judeo-Christian culture. Former British Prime Minister Tony Blair said the roots of violent Islamism are not "superficial but deep" and can be found "in the extremist minority that now, in every European city, preach hatred of the West and our way of life."

The bottom line is that much of the Muslim world is at war with Western civilization. There's no question that the West has the military might to thwart radical Islam's agenda. The question up for grabs is whether we have the intelligence to recognize the attack and the will to defend ourselves from annihilation.

Multiculturalism is Islamists' foot in the door. At the heart of multiculturalism is an attack on Western and Christian values. Much of that attack has its roots on college campuses among the intellectual elite who see their mission as indoctrinating our youth. In past columns, I've documented professorial hate-America teaching, such as a UCLA economics professor's telling his class, "The United States of America, backed by facts, is the greediest and most selfish country in the world." A history professor told her class: "Capitalism isn't a lie on purpose. It's just a lie." She also said: "[Capitalists] are swine. . . . They're bastard people." Students sit through lectures listening to professorial rants about topics such as globalism and Western exploitation of the Middle East and Third World peoples.

Some public school boards have banned songs and music containing references to Santa Claus, Jesus, or other religious Christmas symbols. The New York City school system permits displays of Jewish menorahs and the Muslim star and crescent, but not the Christian Nativity scene. One school district banned a teacher from using excerpts from historical documents in his classroom because they contained references to God and Christianity. The historical documents in question were the Declaration of Independence and "The Rights of the Colonists," by Samuel Adams.

The United States is a nation of many races, ethnicities, religions, and cultures. Since our inception, people from all over the world have immigrated here to become Americans. They have learned English and American history and celebrated American traditions and values. They have become Americans while also respecting and adapting some of the traditions of the countries they left behind. By contrast, many of today's immigrants demand that classes be taught—and official documents be printed—in their native language. Other immigrants demand the use of Shariah, practices that permit honor killing and female genital mutilation.

Multiculturalists argue that different cultural values are morally equivalent. That's nonsense. Western culture and values are superior. For those who'd accuse me of Eurocentrism, I'd ask: Is forcible female genital mutilation, as practiced in nearly thirty sub-Saharan African and Middle Eastern countries, a morally equivalent cultural value? Slavery is practiced in Mauritania, Mali, Niger, Chad, and Sudan; is it morally equivalent? In most of the Middle East, there are numerous limits placed on women, such as prohibitions on driving, employment, and education. Under Islamic law, in some countries, female adulterers face death by stoning, and thieves face the punishment of having their hand severed. In some countries, homosexuality is a crime punishable by death. Are these cultural values morally equivalent, superior, or inferior to Western values?

Multiculturalism has not yet done the damage in the United States that it has in western European countries—such as England, France, and Germany—but it's on its way. By the way, one need not be a Westerner to hold Western values. Mainly, you just have to accept the supremacy of the individual above all else.

PART VII

Potpourri

This section consists of columns that do not quite fit the previous topics. Some readers might consider them bizarre, such as why I love greed, why the right to discriminate is a part of personal liberty, and my petty annoyances. Also, in this section is a lecture delivered to the Foundation for Economic Education on July 14, 2014, to commemorate the closing of its historic home in Irvington, New York, titled "Markets, Governments, and the Common Good."

Rich People versus Politicians

January 7, 2009

Sometimes I wish there were a humane way to get rid of the rich. Without the rich for whipping boys, we might be able to concentrate on what's best for the 99.5 percent of the rest of us.

Warren Buffett and Bill Gates, with about $60 billion in assets each, are America's richest men. With all that money, what can they force us to do? Can they take our house to make room so that another person can build an auto dealership or a casino parking lot? Can they force us to pay money into the government-run retirement Ponzi scheme called Social Security? Can Buffett and Gates force us to bus our children to schools out of our neighborhood in the name of diversity? Unless they are granted power by politicians, rich people have little power to force us to do anything.

A GS-9, or a lowly municipal clerk, has far more life-and-death power over us. It's they to whom we must turn to for permission to build a house, ply a trade, open a restaurant, and myriad other activities. It's government people, not rich people, who have the power to coerce and make our lives miserable. Coercive power goes a long way toward explaining political corruption.

Gov. Rod Blagojevich's hawking of Barack Obama's vacated US Senate seat; Ways and Means Committee Chairman Charlie Rangel's alleged tax-writing favors; former Rep. William Jefferson's business bribes; and the Jack Abramoff scandal are mere pimples on the government corruption landscape. We can think of these and similar acts as jailable illegal corruption. They pale in comparison to what's for all practical purposes the same thing, but simply legal corruption.

For example, according to the *Miami Herald*, by March 2008, the powerful Florida Fanjul sugar family had given over $300,000 to politicians and political committees. They didn't fork over all that money to help politicians to uphold and defend the US Constitution. Like businessmen who approach Charlie Rangel, Rod Blagojevich, and William Jefferson, they give politicians money because they want a favor in return—namely import restrictions on sugar so they can charge Americans higher prices. In the case of the Fanjuls, and thousands of others buying favors, they are engaged in legal corruption.

Legalized corruption is widespread and that's the job of 35,000 Washington, D.C. lobbyists earning millions upon millions of dollars. They represent America's big and small corporations, big and small labor unions, and even foreign corporations and unions. They are not spending billions of dollars in political contributions to encourage and assist the White House and Congress to uphold and defend the US Constitution. They are spending that money in the expectations of favors that will be bestowed upon them at the expense of some other American or group of Americans.

This power helps explain, for example, why a seat on the House Ways and Means Committee, not to mention its chairmanship, is so highly coveted. For the right price, a tax loophole, saving a company tens of millions of dollars, can be inserted into tax law, a la the Charlie Rangel scandal. At state levels, governors can award public works contracts to a generous constituent. At the local levels mayors can confer favors such as providing subsidies for sports stadiums and convention centers. When politicians can give favors, they will find buyers.

The McCain-Feingold law was to get "money out of politics" but more money was spent in the 2008 election cycle than ever. The only way to reduce corruption and money in Washington is to reduce the power politicians have over our lives. James Madison was right when he suggested, "All men having power ought to be distrusted to a certain degree." Thomas Jefferson warned, "The greatest calamity which could befall us would be submission to a government of unlimited powers." That's what today's Americans have given Washington— unlimited powers.

Empathy versus Law

May 20, 2009

President Obama's articulated criteria for his nominee to the US Supreme Court is: "We need somebody who's got the heart to recognize—the empathy to recognize what it's like to be a young teenage mom, the empathy to understand what it's like to be poor or African-American or gay or disabled or old. And that's the criteria by which I'm going to be selecting my judges."

What is the role of a US Supreme Court justice? A reasonable start for an answer is the recognition that our Constitution represents the rules of the game. A Supreme Court justice has one job and one job only, namely, he is a referee. There is nothing complicated about this. A referee's job, whether he is a football referee or a Supreme Court justice, is to know the rules of the game and make sure that they are evenly applied without bias. Do we want referees to allow empathy to influence their decisions? Let's look at it using this year's Super Bowl as an example.

The Pittsburgh Steelers have won six Super Bowl titles, seven AFC championships, and hosted ten conference games. No other AFC or NFC team can match this record. By contrast, the Arizona Cardinals' last championship victory was in 1947 when they were based in Chicago. In anyone's book, this is a gross disparity. Should the referees have the empathy to understand what it's like to be a perennial loser and what would you think of a referee whose decisions were guided by his empathy? Suppose a referee, in the name of compensatory justice, stringently applied pass interference or roughing the passer violations against the Steelers and less stringently against the Cardinals. Or, would you support a referee who refused to make offensive pass interference calls because he thought it was a silly rule? You'd probably remind him that the league makes the rules, not referees.

I'm betting that most people would agree that football justice requires that referees apply the rules blindly and independent of the records or any other characteristic of the two teams. Moreover, I believe that most people would agree that referees should evenly apply the rules of the games even if they personally disagreed with some of the rules.

The relationship between Supreme Court justices and the US Constitution should be identical to that of referees and football rules. The status of a person appearing before the court should have absolutely nothing to do with the rendering of decisions. That's why Lady Justice, often appearing on court buildings, is shown wearing a blindfold. It is to indicate that justice should be meted out impartially, regardless of identity, power, or weakness. Also, as Justice Oliver Wendell Holmes said, "Men should know the rules by which the game is played. Doubt as to the value of some of those rules is no sufficient reason why they should not be followed by the courts." The legislative branch makes the rules, not judges.

Interventionists often make their case for bending the rules based on the unfairness of outcomes such as differences in income, education, and wealth. After all, how can the game of life possibly be fair when some people's yearly income totals in the hundreds of thousands, even millions of dollars, while many others scarcely earn twenty or thirty thousand dollars? Some people find that argument persuasive but it's nonsense. Income distribution is an outcome and fairness cannot be determined by outcomes. It's the same with football. The Steelers winning six Super Bowl titles and Arizona winning none is an outcome and cannot be used to determine football fairness. Fairness in either case must be settled by process questions such as: Were the rules unbiased and evenly applied? If so, any outcome is just and actions based on empathy would make it unjust.

Markets: Pro-Rich or Pro-Poor
May 12, 2010

Listening to America's liberals, who now prefer to call themselves progressives, one would think that free markets benefit the rich and harm the poor, but little can be further from the truth. First, let's say what free markets are. Free markets, or laissez-faire capitalism, refer to an economic system where there is no government interference except to outlaw and prosecute fraud and coercion. It ought to be apparent that our economy cannot be described as free market because there is extensive government interference. We have what might be called a mixed economy, one with both free-market and socialistic attributes. If one is poor or of modest means, where does he fare better: in the freer and more open sector of our economy or in the controlled and highly regulated sector? Let's look at it.

Did Carnegie, Mellon, Rockefeller, and Guggenheim start out rich? Andrew Carnegie worked as a bobbin boy, changing spools of thread in a cotton mill twelve hours a day, six days a week, earning $1.20 a week. A young John D. Rockefeller worked as a clerk. Meyer Guggenheim started out as a peddler. Andrew Mellon did have a leg up; his father was a lawyer and banker. Sam Walton milked the family's cows, bottled the milk, and delivered it and newspapers to customers. Richard Sears was a railroad station agent. Alvah Roebuck began work as a watchmaker. Together, they founded Sears, Roebuck and Company in 1893. John Cash Penney (founder of JCPenny department stores) worked for a local dry-goods merchant.

It wasn't just whites who went from rags to riches through open markets; there were a few blacks. Madam C. J. Walker, born Sarah Breedlove, just two years after the end of slavery, managed to build an empire from developing and selling hair products. John H. Johnson founded Johnson Publishing Company, which became an international media and cosmetics empire. There are many modern-day black millionaires who, like other millionaires, black and white, found the route to their fortunes mostly through the open, highly competitive, and more free market end of our economy.

Restricted, regulated, and monopolized markets are especially handicapping to people who are seen as less preferred, latecomers, and people with little political clout. For example, owning and operating a taxi is one way out of poverty. It takes little skills and capital. But in most cities, one has to purchase a license costing tens of thousands of dollars. New York City's taxicab licensing law is particularly egregious, requiring a person, as of May 2007, to pay $600,000 for a license to own and operate one taxicab. Business licensing laws are not racially discriminatory as such, but they have a racially discriminatory effect.

The Davis-Bacon Act of 1931, still on the books today, had a racially discriminatory intent and has a racially discriminatory effect. The Davis-Bacon Act is a federal law that mandates "prevailing wages" be paid on all federally financed or assisted construction projects and as such discriminates against nonunionized black construction contractors and black workers. During the 1931 legislative debate, quite a few congressmen expressed racist motives in their testimony in support of the law, such as Rep. Clayton Allgood, D-Ala., who said, "Reference has been made to a contractor from Alabama who went to New York with bootleg labor. This is a fact. That contractor has cheap colored labor that he transports, and he puts them in cabins, and it is labor of that sort that is in competition with white labor throughout the country." Today's supporters of the Davis-Bacon Act use different rhetoric, but its racially discriminatory effects are the same.

The market is a friend in another unappreciated way. In poor black neighborhoods, one might see some nice clothing, some nice food, some nice cars, but no nice schools. Why not at least some nice schools? Clothing, food and cars are distributed by the market mechanism while schools are distributed by the political mechanism.

Liberal Crackup

September 15, 2010

Charles Krauthammer, in his *Washington Post* column (August 27, 2010), said, "Liberalism under siege is an ugly sight indeed," pointing out that overwhelming majorities of Americans have repudiated liberal agenda items such as: Obamacare, Obama's stimulus, building an Islamic center and mosque near Ground Zero, redefinition of marriage to include same-sex marriage, lax immigration law enforcement, and vast expansion of federal power that includes unprecedented debt and deficits.

The nation's elite and the news media see being against the Obama-led agenda as being racist, homophobic, xenophobic, Islamaphobic, mean-spirited, and insensitive. Paul Krugman, columnist for *The New York Times*, has a different twist expressed in "It's Witch-Hunt Season" (August 29, 2010). Krugman says that the last time a Democrat sat in the White House, Bill Clinton, he faced a witch-hunt by his political opponents. "Now," Krugman says, "it's happening again— except that this time it's even worse," asking, "So where is this rage coming from? Why is it flourishing? What will it do to America?"

Professor Krugman and others among America's elite blame some of the rage on talk-show hosts such as Rush Limbaugh, Glenn Beck, and Sean Hannity. They are only partially correct. What talk shows have accomplished is they've ended the isolation of many ordinary Americans. When the liberal mainstream media dominated the airwaves, Americans who were against race and sex quotas were made to feel as though they were racists and sexists. Americans who were against big government were portrayed as mean-spirited and uncaring. What talk radio and the massive expansion in nontraditional media have done is not only end the isolation, but more important, the silence amongst ordinary Americans.

Krugman says that what we're witnessing is "political craziness." Therefore, the overwhelming majority of Americans who think our borders ought to be secure and think we should have the right to determine who enters our country are politically crazy. Americans who can find nothing in the US Constitution granting Congress the power to take over our health care system are politically crazy. Americans who think a mosque should not be built in the shadows of the Muslim-destroyed World Trade Center are simply religious bigots. By the way, those who oppose the building are not saying there's no legal or constitutional right to do so any more than they would say a person has no legal or constitutional right to curse his parents, but neither is a good idea. In Thomas Sowell's column on the topic (August 31, 2010), he reminds us that "If we all did everything that we have a legal right to do, we could not even survive as individuals, much less as a society."

Krugman predicts that political craziness, and by inference crazy Americans, will result in a Republican takeover of the House of Representatives and play chicken with the federal budget. Chicken with the budget is precisely what Defundit.org has called for. Already they've obtained the pledges of 165 congressional candidates not to fund any part of Obamacare.

While America's liberal elite have not reached the depths of tyrants such as Lenin, Stalin, Mao, and Hitler, they share a common vision and, as such, differ only in degree but not kind. Both denounce free markets and voluntary exchange. They are for control and coercion by the state. They believe they have superior wisdom to the masses and they have been ordained to forcibly impose that wisdom on the rest of us. They, like any other tyrant, have what they see as good reasons for restricting the freedom of others.

Their agenda calls for the elimination or attenuation of the market. Why? Free markets imply voluntary exchange. Tyrants do not trust that people behaving voluntarily will do what the tyrants think they should do. Therefore, they seek to replace the market with economic planning control and regulation.

Why liberalism has become an ugly sight, as Krauthammer claims, is because more and more Americans have wised up to their agenda.

Profit versus Nonprofit

September 22, 2010

"Philadelphia Scandal Underscores Pitiful State of Public Housing Oversight," read Jonathan Berr's August 28 report in the *Daily Finance*. It was a story about Carl Greene, the embattled director of the Philadelphia Housing Authority (PHA). He was put on paid leave while the board investigates charges that he settled four sexual harassment claims against him without notifying the PHA, doled out work to politically connected law firms and pressured employees to donate to his favorite nonprofit. Greene is also being investigated by the US Attorney General's Office for the Eastern District of Pennsylvania and Housing and Urban Development's Office of Inspector General. They have yet to bring criminal charges against him.

People always act surprised by revelations of political corruption but the Philadelphia Housing Authority corruption is highly probable in nonprofit entities such as government. Because of ignorance and demagoguery, being profit-motivated has become suspicious and possibly a dirty word. Nonprofit is seen as more righteous. Very often, people pompously stand before us and declare, "We're a non-profit organization." They expect for us to believe that since they're not in it for money, they are somehow above self-interest and have the public interest as their motivation. There's little much further from the truth.

People are always self-interested. It's just when they manage a nonprofit organization such as the Philadelphia Housing Authority, government entities in general, universities, and charitable organizations, they face a different set of constraints on their behavior. The fundamental difference between nonprofit organizations and their profit-making counterparts is that nonprofits tend to take a greater portion of their compensation from easier working conditions, more time off, favors, and under-the-table payments. Profit-making organizations take a greater portion of their compensation in cash, except those that are highly regulated.

In the profit-making world, there is much greater monitoring of the behavior of people who act for the organization. Profit-making organizations have a financial bottom line they must meet, or sooner or later, heads will roll. Not so with nonprofits, who have no bottom line to meet. On top of that, incompetence for nonprofits means bigger budgets, higher pay and less oversight. That description aptly fits one of the nation's largest nonprofit organizations—the public education establishment.

Profit is vital to human well-being. Profit is the payment to entrepreneurs just as wages are payments to labor, interest to capital, and rent to land. In order to earn profits in free markets, entrepreneurs must identify and satisfy human wants and do so in a way that economizes on society's scarce resources.

Here's a little test. Which entities produce greater customer satisfaction: for-profit enterprises such as supermarkets, computer makers, and clothing stores, or nonprofit entities such as public schools, post offices, and motor vehicle departments? I'm guessing you'll answer the former. Their survival depends on pleasing customers. Nonprofits, such as public schools, post offices, and motor vehicle departments, survival depends mostly on pleasing politicians.

When a firm fails to please its customers and thereby fails to earn a profit, it goes bankrupt, making those resources available to another who might do better. That's unless government steps in to bail it out. Bailouts permit a business to continue doing a poor job of pleasing customers and husbanding resources. Government-owned nonprofit entities are immune to the ruthless market discipline of being forced to please customers. The same can be said of businesses that receive government handouts.

It's this ruthlessness of market discipline that forces firms to please customers, economize on resources, and thereby earn profits or go out of business and goes a long way toward explaining hostility toward free market capitalism. And much of the hostility toward free-market capitalism is held by businessmen. Adam Smith recognized this in his *Wealth of Nations* when he said, "People of the same trade seldom meet together, even for merriment and diversion, but the conversation ends in a conspiracy against the public, or in some contrivance to raise prices." Their co-conspirator is always government.

Job Destruction Makes Us Richer

July 27, 2011

Here's what President Barack Obama said about our high rate of unemployment in an interview with NBC's Ann Curry: "The other thing that happened, though—and this goes to the point you were just making—is there are some structural issues with our economy, where a lot of businesses have learned to become much more efficient with a lot fewer workers," adding that "you see it when you go to a bank and you use an ATM; you don't go to a bank teller. Or you go to the airport and you're using a kiosk instead of checking in at the gate." The president's statements suggest that he sees labor-saving technological innovation as a contributor to today's high rate of unemployment. That's unmitigated nonsense. Let's see whether technological innovation causes unemployment.

In 1790, farmers were 90 percent, out of a population of nearly 3 million, of the US labor force. By 1900, only about 41 percent of our labor force was employed in agriculture. By 2008, fewer than 3 percent of Americans were employed in agriculture. Through labor-saving technological advances and machinery, our farmers are the world's most productive. As a result, Americans are better off.

In 1970, the telecommunications industry employed 421,000 workers as switchboard operators, annually handling 9.8 billion long-distance calls. Today the telecommunications industry employs only 78,000 operators. That's a tremendous 80 percent job loss. What happened? The answer: There have been spectacular labor-saving advances in telecommunications. Today more than 100 billion long-distance calls a year require only 78,000 switchboard operators. What's more is the cost of making a long-distance call is a tiny fraction of what it was in 1970. Can we say these technological innovations made the nation worse off?

Professor Russell Roberts, my George Mason University colleague, gives other examples in his *Wall Street Journal* article (June 22, 2011)

"Obama vs. ATM's: Why Technology Doesn't Destroy Jobs." He says that today just a couple of workers can manage the egg-laying operation of nearly a million chickens laying 240 million eggs a year, through a highly mechanized and computerized process. Thousands of toll collectors are replaced by E-ZPass machines. Autoworkers are replaced by robots. Fifty years ago, a typical textile worker operated five machines capable of running thread through a loom a hundred times a minute. Today machines run six times as fast, and one worker can oversee a hundred of them.

You say, "Williams, certain jobs are destroyed by technology." You're right, but many more are created. Think about it. If 90 percent of Americans still had been farmers in 1900, where in the world would we have gotten workers to produce all those goods that were not even heard of in 1790, such as telephones, steamships, and oil wells? We need not go back that far. If there hadn't been the kind of labor-saving technical innovation we've had since the 1950s—in the auto, construction, telephone industries, and many others—where in the world would we have gotten workers to produce things that weren't heard of in the '50s, such as desktop computers, cellphones, HDTVs, digital cameras, MRI machines, pharmaceuticals, and myriad other goods and services?

What technological innovation does is reduce the value of some jobs, raise the value of others, and create many more jobs. Some workers are made better off through greater employment opportunities. Others are made worse off by having to accept less attractive employment opportunities, an adjustment process that can be painful. Since technological progress makes goods and services cheaper, and of higher quality, to stand in its way, in the name of saving jobs, will make us a poorer nation. What we're witnessing in our economy is what economic historian Joseph Schumpeter termed "creative destruction," the process in which something new replaces something older.

By the way, we can always count upon an infinite number of potential jobs. The reason is that human wants are insatiable. People always want more of something. That want will create jobs for someone else.

Profits Are for People

October 26, 2011

The Occupy Wall Street demonstrators are demanding "people before profits"—as if profit motivation were the source of mankind's troubles—when it's often the absence of profit motivation that's the true villain.

First, let's get both the definition and magnitude of profits out of the way. Profits represent the residual claim earned by entrepreneurs. They're what are left after other production costs—such as wages, rent, and interest—have been paid. Profits are the payment for risk taking, innovation, and decision-making. As such, they are a cost of business just as are wages, rent, and interest. If those payments are not made, labor, land and capital will not offer their services. Similarly, if profit is not paid, entrepreneurs won't offer theirs. Historically, corporate profits range between 5 and 8 cents of each dollar, and wages range between 50 and 60 cents of each dollar.

Far more important than simple statistics about the magnitude of profits is the role played by profits, namely that of forcing producers to cater to the wants and desires of the common man. When's the last time we've heard widespread complaints about our clothing stores, supermarkets, computer stores, or appliance stores? We are far likelier to hear people complaining about services they receive from the post office, motor vehicle and police departments, boards of education, and other government agencies. The fundamental difference between the areas of general satisfaction and dissatisfaction is the pursuit of profits is present in one and not the other.

The pursuit of profits forces producers to be attentive to the will of their customers, simply because the customer of, say, a supermarket can fire it on the spot by taking his business elsewhere. If a state motor vehicle department or post office provides unsatisfactory services, it's not so easy for dissatisfied customers to take action against it. If a private business had as many dissatisfied customers as our government schools have, it would have long ago been out of business.

Free-market capitalism is unforgiving. Producers please customers, in a cost-minimizing fashion, and make a profit, or they face losses or go bankrupt. It's this market discipline that some businesses seek to avoid. That's why they descend upon Washington calling for crony capitalism—government bailouts, subsidies, and special privileges. They wish to reduce the power of consumers and stockholders, who hold little sympathy for blunders and will give them the ax on a moment's notice.

Having Congress on their side means business can be less attentive to the will of consumers. Congress can keep them afloat with bailouts, as it did in the cases of General Motors and Chrysler, with the justification that such companies are "too big to fail." Nonsense! If General Motors and Chrysler had been allowed to go bankrupt, it wouldn't have meant that their productive assets, such as assembly lines and tools, would have gone poof and disappeared into thin air. Bankruptcy would have led to a change in ownership of those assets by someone who might have managed them better. The bailout enabled them to avoid the full consequences of their blunders.

By the way, we often hear people say, with a tone of saintliness, "We're a nonprofit organization," as if that alone translates into decency, objectivity, and selflessness. They want us to think they're in it for the good of society and not for those "evil" profits. If we gave it just a little thought and asked what kind of organization throughout mankind's history has accounted for his greatest grief, the answer wouldn't be a free-market, private, profit-making enterprise; it would be government, the largest nonprofit organization.

The Occupy Wall Street protesters are following the path predicted by the great philosopher-economist Frederic Bastiat, who said in *The Law* that "instead of rooting out the injustices found in society, they make these injustices general." In other words, the protesters don't want to end crony capitalism, with its handouts and government favoritism; they want to participate in it.

Should the Rich Be Condemned?

November 23, 2011

Thomas Edison invented the incandescent bulb, the phonograph, the DC motor, and other items in everyday use and became wealthy by doing so. Thomas Watson founded IBM and became rich through his company's contribution to the computation revolution. Lloyd Conover, while in the employ of Pfizer, created the antibiotic tetracycline. Though Edison, Watson, Conover, and Pfizer became wealthy, whatever wealth they received pales in comparison with the extraordinary benefits received by ordinary people. Billions of people benefited from safe and efficient lighting. Billions more were the ultimate beneficiaries of the computer, and untold billions benefited from healthier lives gained from access to tetracycline.

President Barack Obama, in stoking up class warfare, said, "I do think at a certain point you've made enough money." This is lunacy. Andrew Carnegie's steel empire produced the raw materials that built the physical infrastructure of the United States. Bill Gates cofounded Microsoft and produced software products that aided the computer revolution. But Carnegie had amassed quite a fortune long before he built Carnegie Steel Co., and Gates had quite a fortune by 1990. Had they the mind of our president, we would have lost much of their contributions, because they had already "made enough money."

Class warfare thrives on ignorance about the sources of income. Listening to some of the talk about income differences, one would think that there's a pile of money meant to be shared equally among Americans. Rich people got to the pile first and greedily took an unfair share. Justice requires that they "give back." Or, some people talk about unequal income distribution as if there were a dealer of dollars. The reason some people have millions or billions of dollars while others have very few is the dollar dealer is a racist, sexist, a multinationalist, or just plain mean. Economic justice requires a redealing of the dollars, income redistribution, or spreading the wealth, where the ill-gotten gains of the few are returned to their rightful owners.

In a free society, for the most part, people with high incomes have demonstrated extraordinary ability to produce valuable services for—and therefore please—their fellow man. People voluntarily took money out of their pockets to purchase the products of Gates, Pfizer, or IBM. High incomes reflect the democracy of the marketplace. The reason Gates is very wealthy is millions upon millions of people voluntarily reached into their pockets and handed over $300 or $400 for a Microsoft product. Those who think he has too much money are really registering disagreement with decisions made by millions of their fellow men.

In a free society, in a significant way income inequality reflects differences in productive capacity, namely one's ability to please his fellow man. For example, I can play basketball and so can LeBron James, but would the Miami Heat pay me anything close to the $43 million they pay him? If not, why not? I think it has to do with the discriminating tastes of basketball fans who pay $100 or more to watch the game. If the Miami Heat hired me, they would have to pay fans to watch.

Stubborn ignorance sees capitalism as benefiting only the rich, but the evidence refutes that. The rich have always been able to afford entertainment; it was the development and marketing of radio and television that made entertainment accessible to the common man. The rich have never had the drudgery of washing and ironing clothing, beating out carpets, or waxing floors. The mass production of washing machines, wash-and-wear clothing, vacuum cleaners, and no-wax floors spared the common man this drudgery. At one time, only the rich could afford automobiles, telephones, and computers. Now all but a small percentage of Americans enjoy these goods.

The prospects are dim for a society that makes mascots out of the unproductive and condemns the productive.

I Love Greed

January 4, 2012

What human motivation gets the most wonderful things done? It's really a silly question, because the answer is so simple. It turns out that it's human greed that gets the most wonderful things done. When I say greed, I am not talking about fraud, theft, dishonesty, lobbying for special privileges from government, or other forms of despicable behavior. I'm talking about people trying to get as much as they can for themselves. Let's look at it.

This winter, Texas ranchers may have to fight the cold of night, perhaps blizzards, to run down, feed, and care for stray cattle. They make the personal sacrifice of caring for their animals to ensure that New Yorkers can enjoy beef. Last summer, Idaho potato farmers toiled in blazing sun, in dust and dirt, and maybe being bitten by insects to ensure that New Yorkers had potatoes to go with their beef.

Here's my question: Do you think that Texas ranchers and Idaho potato farmers make these personal sacrifices because they love or care about the well-being of New Yorkers? The fact is whether they like New Yorkers or not, they make sure that New Yorkers are supplied with beef and potatoes every day of the week. Why? It's because ranchers and farmers want more for themselves. In a free-market system, in order for one to get more for himself, he must serve his fellow man. This is precisely what Adam Smith, the father of economics, meant when he said in his classic *An Inquiry into the Nature and Causes of the Wealth of Nations* (1776), "It is not from the benevolence of the butcher, the brewer, or the baker, that we expect our dinner, but from their regard to their own interest." By the way, how much beef and potatoes do you think New Yorkers would enjoy if it all depended upon the politically correct notions of human love and kindness? Personally, I'd grieve for New Yorkers. Some have suggested that instead of greed, I use "enlightened self-interest." That's OK, but I prefer greed.

Free-market capitalism is relatively new in human history. Prior to the rise of capitalism, the way people amassed great wealth was by looting, plundering, and enslaving their fellow man. Capitalism made it possible to become wealthy by serving one's fellow man. Capitalists seek to discover what people want and then produce it as efficiently as possible. Free-market capitalism is ruthless in its profit and loss discipline. This explains much of the hostility toward free-market capitalism; some of it is held by businessmen. Smith recognized this hostility when he said, "People of the same trade seldom meet together, even for merriment and diversion, but the conversation ends in a conspiracy against the public, or in some contrivance to raise prices." He was hinting at government-backed crony capitalism, which has come to characterize much of today's businesses.

Free-market capitalism has other enemies—mostly among the intellectual elite and political tyrants. These are people who believe that they have superior wisdom to the masses and that God has ordained them to forcibly impose that wisdom on the rest of us. Of course, they have what they consider to be good reasons for restricting liberty, but every tyrant who has ever lived has had what he considered good reason for restricting liberty. A tyrant's agenda calls for the attenuation or the elimination of the market and what is implied by it—voluntary exchange. Tyrants do not trust that people acting voluntarily will do what the tyrant thinks they should do. They want to replace the market with economic planning and regulation.

The Wall Street occupiers and their media and political allies are not against the principle of crony capitalism, bailouts, and government special privileges and intervention. They share the same hostility to free market capitalism and peaceable voluntary exchange as tyrants. What they really want is congressional permission to share in the booty from looting their fellow man.

In Greed I Trust

January 11, 2012

Last week's column started off asking: "What human motivation gets the most wonderful things done?" The answer is that human greed is what gets wonderful things done. I wasn't talking about fraud, theft, dishonesty, special privileges from government, or other forms of despicable behavior. I was talking about people trying to get as much as they can for themselves.

Think about greed and racial discrimination. In 1947, when the Brooklyn Dodgers hired Jackie Robinson, why did racial discrimination by major league teams begin to drop like a hot potato? It wasn't feelings of guilt by white owners, affirmative action, or antidiscrimination laws. It turned out that there was a huge pool of black baseball talent in the Negro leagues. It became too costly for teams to allow the Dodgers to gain a monopoly on this talent. Black players won the National League's Most Valuable Player award for seven consecutive seasons. Had other teams not stepped in to hire black players, allowing the Dodgers to hire them, it might have given the Dodgers a virtual monopoly on world championships.

During South Africa's apartheid era, whites were in control, both economically and politically, and enacted some of the harshest racially discriminatory employment laws. There were job reservation laws that reserved certain jobs for whites only. Many white employers went to considerable lengths to contravene and violate those laws. White building trade unions complained to the South African government that laws reserving skilled jobs for whites had broken down.

What was happening? White contractors found out that often they could earn greater profits by hiring a black worker to do the job of a white worker for only a fraction of the wage. That raised the cost of discriminating against black workers. Racist white workers did what any good liberal or labor union supporter would do; they got behind support for minimum wage laws and what produces the same effect, equal-pay-for-equal-work laws. South Africa's Wage Board said, "The method would be to fix a minimum rate for an occupation or craft so high that no Native would likely be employed." "Equal pay for equal work" became the rallying slogan of the South African white labor movement. They knew that if employers were forced to pay black workers the same wages as white workers, there'd be reduced incentive to hire blacks.

Unionists in the United States also wanted to suppress employer quests for greater profits. After a bitter 1909 strike by the Brotherhood of Locomotive Firemen, an arbitration board decreed that blacks and whites were to be paid equal wages. Union members expressed their delight, saying, "If this course of action is followed by the company and the incentive for employing the Negro thus removed, the strike will not have been in vain."

The Davis-Bacon Act sets minimum wages on federally financed or assisted construction projects. It was racially motivated in 1931, and it's still on the books. During congressional debate leading to its passage, Rep. John Cochran of Missouri said he had "received numerous complaints in recent months about Southern contractors employing low-paid colored mechanics getting work and bringing the employees from the South." Rep. Miles Allgood of Alabama complained: "Reference has been made to a contractor from Alabama who went to New York with bootleg labor. This is a fact. That contractor has cheap colored labor that he transports, and he puts them in cabins, and it is labor of that sort that is in competition with white labor throughout the country." Rep. William Upshaw of Georgia complained of the "superabundance or large aggregation of Negro labor," which, to him, was a real problem. American Federation of Labor President William Green made clear his union's interests, saying, "Colored labor is being sought to demoralize wage rates."

There are many examples from around the world of how people have used legal and extralegal means to thwart people trying to get more for themselves, or what I like to call greed. The suppression of these motives has always worked against the best interest of discriminated-against people.

Good Economists

April 18, 2012

It's difficult to be a good economist and simultaneously be perceived as compassionate. To be a good economist, one has to deal with reality. To appeal compassionate, often one has to avoid unpleasant questions, use "caring" terminology and view reality as optional.

Affordable housing and health care costs are terms with considerable emotional appeal that politicians exploit but have absolutely no useful meaning or analytical worth. For example, can anyone tell me in actual dollars and cents the price of an affordable car, house, or myomectomy? It's probably more pleasant to pretend that there is universal agreement about what is or is not affordable.

If you think my criticism of affordability is unpleasant, you'll hate my vision of harm. A good economist recognizes that harm is not a one-way street; it's reciprocal. For example, if I own a lot and erect a house in front of your house and block your view of a beautiful scene, I've harmed you; however, if I am prevented from building my house in front of yours, I'm harmed. Whose harm is more important? You say, "Williams, you can't tell." You can stop me from harming you by persuading some government thugs to stop me from building. It's the same thing with smoking. If I smoke a cigarette, you're harmed—or at least bothered. If I'm prevented from smoking a cigarette, I'm harmed by reduced pleasure. Whose harm is more important? Again, you can't tell. But as in the building example, the person who is harmed can use government thugs to have things his way.

How many times have we heard that "if it will save just one human life, it's worth it" or that "human life is priceless"? Both are nonsense statements. If either statement were true, we'd see lower speed limits, bans on auto racing, and fewer airplanes in the sky. We can always be safer than we are. For example, cars could be produced such that occupants could survive unscathed in a 50-mph head-on collision, but how many of us could buy such a car? Don't get me wrong; I might think my life is priceless, but I don't view yours in the same light. I admire Greta Garbo's objectivity about her life. She said, "I'm a completely worthless woman, and no man should risk his life for me."

Speaking of worthlessness, I'd be worthless as an adviser to either the White House or Congress because if they asked me what they should do to get the economy going, I'd answer, "Do nothing!" Let's look at it. Between 1787 and 1930, our nation suffered both mild and severe economic downturns. There was no intervention to stimulate the economy, but the economy always recovered.

During the 1930s, there were massive interventions, starting with President Herbert Hoover and later with President Franklin D. Roosevelt. Their actions turned what would have been a sharp three- or four-year economic downturn into a ten-year affair. In 1930, when Hoover began to "fix" the economy, unemployment was 6 percent. FDR did even more to "fix" the economy. As a result, unemployment remained in double digits throughout the decade and reached 20 percent in 1939. President Roosevelt blamed the high unemployment on his predecessor. Presidential blaming of predecessors is a practice that continues to this day.

You say, "Williams, the White House and Congress should do something." The track record of doing nothing is pretty good compared with doing something. None of our economic downturns in the century and a half prior to 1930 lasted as long as the Great Depression.

It would be political suicide for a politician to follow my counsel— and for good reason. Americans have been miseducated into thinking that Roosevelt's New Deal saved our economy. That miseducation extends to most academics, including economists, at our universities, who are arrogant enough to believe that it's possible for a few people in Washington to have the information and knowledge necessary to manage the economic lives of 313 million people. Good economists recognize our limitations, making us not nice people to be around.

The Rich Don't Pay Enough?

August 29, 2012

If you listen to America's political hacks, mainstream media talking heads, and their socialist allies, you can't help but reach the conclusion that the nation's tax burden is borne by the poor and middle class while the rich get off scot-free.

Stephen Moore, senior economics writer for the *Wall Street Journal*, and I'm proud to say former GMU economics student, wrote "The US Tax System: Who Really Pays?" in the Manhattan Institute's Issue 2012 (August 2012). Let's see whether the rich are paying their "fair" share.

According to IRS 2007 data, the richest 1 percent of Americans earned 22 percent of national personal income but paid 40 percent of all personal income taxes. The top 5 percent earned 37 percent and paid 61 percent of personal income tax. The top 10 percent earned 48 percent and paid 71 percent of all personal income taxes. The bottom 50 percent earned 12 percent of personal income but paid just 3 percent of income tax revenues.

Some argue that these observations are misleading because there are other federal taxes the bottom 50 percenters pay such as Social Security and excise taxes. Moore presents data from the Tax Policy Center, run by the liberal Urban Institute and the Brookings Institution, that takes into account payroll and income taxes paid by different income groups. Because of the earned income tax credit, most of America's poor pay little or nothing. What the Tax Policy Center calls working class pay 3 percent of all federal taxes, middle class 11 percent, upper middle class 19 percent, and wealthy 67 percent.

President Obama and the Democratic Party harp about tax fairness. Here's my fairness question to you: What standard of fairness dictates that the top 10 percent of income earners pay 71 percent of the federal income tax burden while 47 percent of Americans pay absolutely nothing?

President Obama and his political allies are fully aware of IRS data that shows who pays what. Their tax demagoguery knowingly exploits American ignorance about taxes. A complicit news media is only happy to assist. We might ask ourselves what's to be said about the decency of people who knowingly mislead the public about taxes. Of course, I might be all wrong, and true tax fairness dictates that the top 10 percent pay all federal income taxes.

Aside from the fairness issue, 47 percent of taxpayers having no federal income tax liability is dangerous for our nation. These people become natural constituents for big-spending, budget-wrecking, debt-creating politicians. After all, if you have no income tax liability, what do you care about either raising or lowering taxes? That might explain why the so-called Bush tax cuts were not more popular. If you're not paying income taxes, why should you be happy about an income tax cut? Instead, you might view tax cuts as a threat to various handout programs that nearly 50 percent of Americans enjoy.

Tax demagoguery is useful for politicians who prey on the politics of envy to get reelected, but is it good for Americans? We're witnessing the disastrous effects of massive spending in Greece, Italy, Ireland, Portugal, and other European countries where a greater number of people live off of government welfare programs than pay taxes. Government debt in Greece is 160 percent of gross domestic product, 120 percent in Italy, 104 in Ireland, and 106 in Portugal.

Here's the question for us: Is the United States moving toward or away from the troubled EU nations? It turns out that our national debt to GDP ratio in the 1970s was 35 percent; now it's 106 percent of GDP. If you think we're immune from the economic chaos in some of the EU countries, you're whistling "Dixie." And when economic chaos comes, whom do you think will be more affected by it: rich people or poor people?

A Modest Proposal
October 10, 2012

California was once the land of opportunity, but it is going down the tubes. Several of California's prominent cities have declared bankruptcy, such as Vallejo, Stockton, Mammoth Lakes, and San Bernardino. Others are on the precipice, and that includes Los Angeles, California's largest city. California's 2012 budget deficit is expected to top $28 billion, and its state debt is $618 billion. That's more than twice the size of New York's state debt, which itself is the second highest in the nation.

Democrats control California's legislature, and its governor, Jerry Brown, is a Democrat. California is home to some of America's richest people and companies. It would then appear that the liberals' solution to deficit and debt would be easy. They need only to raise taxes on California's rich to balance the budget and pay down the debt—or, as President Barack Obama would say, make the rich pay their fair share.

The downside to such a tax strategy is the fact that people are already leaving California in great numbers. According to a Manhattan Institute study, "The Great California Exodus: A Closer Look," by Thomas Gray and Robert Scardamalia (October 2012), roughly 225,000 residents leave California each year—and have done so for the past ten years. They take their money with them. Using census and Internal Revenue Service data, Gray and Scardamalia estimate that California's outmigration results in large shares of income going to other states, mostly to Nevada ($5.67 billion), Arizona ($4.96 billion), Texas ($4.07 billion), and Oregon ($3.85 billion). That's the problem. California politicians can fleece people in 2012, but there's no guarantee that they can do the same in 2013 and later years; people can leave. Also, keep in mind that rich people didn't become rich by being stupid. They have ingenious ways to hide their money.

California has one-eighth of the nation's population but one-third of its welfare recipients. According to *Businessweek*, "it is one of the few states that continue to provide welfare checks for children once their parents are no longer eligible." There's nothing new about the handout strategy. As far back as 140 B.C., Roman politicians found that the way to win votes is to give out cheap food and entertainment, what came to be known as "bread and circuses."

Given the widespread contempt for personal liberty and constitutional values, there might be a way for California politicians to solve their fiscal mess. They can simply stop wealthy people from leaving the state or, alternatively, like some Third World nations, set limits on the amount of assets a resident can take out of the state. This would surely be within their jurisdiction and would not raise any constitutional issues, because it would serve a compelling state purpose. In other words, if California were to set up border controls to stop people, as East Germans did at Checkpoint Charlie, before they cross the state line, such action would be protected by the Tenth Amendment.

The fact that many Californians have managed to get their assets out of the state complicates the issue. Article 1, Section 8, of the US Constitution authorizes Congress "To regulate Commerce with foreign Nations, and among the several States, and with the Indian Tribes." This is known as the commerce clause. There's no question that people who pull up stakes and leave California affect interstate commerce; California has less tax revenue, and recipient states have more. What California Attorney General Kamala D. Harris might do is sue Nevada, Arizona, Texas, and Oregon in the federal courts for enticing, through lower taxes and less onerous regulations, wealthy California taxpayers.

Were California to take such measures and have a modicum of success, one wonders how many Americans would be offended by such an encroachment on personal liberty. After all, how would forcing an American to remain in a state differ in principle from forcing him to purchase health insurance?

What You Can't Say

October 24, 2012

Jon Hubbard, a Republican member of the Arkansas House of Representatives, has a book, titled *Letters to the Editor: Confessions of a Frustrated Conservative*. Among its statements for which Hubbard has been criticized and disavowed by the Republican Party is, "The institution of slavery that the black race has long believed to be an abomination upon its people may actually have been a blessing in disguise. The blacks who could endure those conditions and circumstances would someday be rewarded with citizenship in the greatest nation ever established upon the face of the Earth."

Hubbard's observation reminded me of my 1972 job interview at the University of Massachusetts. During a reception, one of the Marxist professors asked me what I thought about the relationship between capitalism and slavery. My response was that slavery has existed everywhere in the world, under every political and economic system, and was by no means unique to capitalism or the United States. Perturbed by my response, he asked me what my feelings were about the enslavement of my ancestors. I answered that slavery is a despicable violation of human rights but that the enslavement of my ancestors is history, and one of the immutable facts of history is that nothing can be done to change it.

The matter could have been left there, but I volunteered that today's American blacks have benefited enormously from the horrible suffering of our ancestors. Why? I said the standard of living and personal liberty of black Americans are better than what blacks living anywhere in Africa have. I then asked the professor what it was that explained how tens of millions of blacks came to be born in the United States instead of Africa. He wouldn't answer, but an answer other than slavery would have been sheer idiocy. I attempted to assuage the professor's and his colleagues' shock by explaining to them that to morally condemn a practice such as slavery does not require one to also deny its effects.

My yet-to-be-learned lesson—and perhaps that of Rep. Hubbard—is that there are certain topics or arguments that one should not bring up in the presence of children or those with little understanding. Both might see that explaining a phenomenon is the same as giving it moral sanction or justification. It's as if one's explanation that the independent influence of gravity on a falling object is to cause it to accelerate at 32 feet per second per second could be interpreted as giving moral sanction and justification to gravity.

Slavery is widely misunderstood, and as such has been a tool for hustlers and demagogues. Slavery has been part of the human condition throughout recorded history and everywhere on the globe. Romans enslaved other Europeans; Greeks enslaved other Greeks; Asians enslaved Asians; Africans enslaved Africans; and in the New World, Aztecs enslaved Aztecs and other native groups. Even the word slave is derived from the fact that Slavic people were among the early European slaves.

Though racism has been used to justify slavery, the origins of slavery had little to do with racism. In recent history, the major slave traders and slave owners have been Arabs, who enslaved Europeans, black Africans, and Asians. A unique aspect of slavery in the Western world was the moral outrage against it, which began to emerge in the eighteenth century and led to massive efforts to eliminate it. It was Britain's military might and the sight of the Union Jack on the high seas that ultimately put an end to the slave trade.

Unfortunately, the facts about slavery are not the lessons taught in our schools and colleges. The gross misrepresentation and suggestion in textbooks and lectures is that slavery was a uniquely American practice done by racist white people to black people. Despite abundant historical evidence, youngsters are taught nothing about how the Founding Fathers quarreled, debated, and agonized over the slave issue.

Women in Combat

February 6, 2013

A senior Defense Department official said the ban on women in combat should be lifted because the military's goal is "to provide a level, gender-neutral playing field." I'd like to think the goal of the military should be to have the toughest, meanest fighting force possible. But let's look at "gender-neutral playing field."

The Army's physical fitness test in basic training is a three-event physical performance test used to assess endurance. The minimum requirement for seventeen- to twenty-one-year-old males is thirty-five pushups, forty-seven situps, and a two-mile run in sixteen minutes, thirty-six seconds or less. For females of the same age, the minimum requirement is thirteen pushups, forty-seven situps, and a 19:42 two-mile run. Why the difference in fitness requirements? "USMC Women in the Service Restrictions Review" found that women, on average, have 20 percent lower aerobic power, 40 percent lower muscle strength, 47 percent less lifting strength, and 26 percent slower marching speed than men.

William Gregor, professor of social sciences at the Army's Command and General Staff College, reports that in tests of aerobic capacity, the records show that only 74 of 8,385 Reserve Officers' Training Corps women attained the level of the lowest 16 percent of men. The "fight load"—the gear an infantryman carries on patrol—is 35 percent of the average man's body weight but 50 percent of the average Army woman's weight. In his examination of physical fitness test results from the ROTC, dating back to 1992, and 74,000 records of male and female commissioned officers, only 2.9 percent of women were able to attain the men's average pushup ability and time in the two-mile run.

In a January report titled "Defense Department 'Diversity' Push for Women in Land Combat" (http://tinyurl.com/axn9l93) Elaine Donnelly, director of the Center for Military Readiness, points to US Army studies showing that women are twice as likely to suffer injuries and are three times more undeployable than men. Women are less likely to be able to march under load—12.4 miles in five hours with an 83-pound assault load—and to be able to crawl, sprint, negotiate obstacles with that load or move a casualty weighing 165 pounds or more while carrying that load. Plus, there are muscle-challenging feats, even for men, such as field repairs on an M1A1 Abrams tank.

Then there's the pregnancy issue, which makes women three to four times as likely as men to be undeployable. And once deployed, they often have to be medically evacuated, leaving units understrength. Finally, there's another difference between men and women rarely considered in deliberation about whether women should be in combat. All measures of physical aggressiveness show that men, maybe because of testosterone levels ten times higher, are more aggressive, competitive, and hostile than women. Those attributes are desirable for combat.

Here are a couple of what-if questions. Suppose a combat unit is retreating in mountainous terrain in Afghanistan, where a person's aerobic capacity really makes a difference, and the women in the unit can't keep up with the men. What would you propose, leaving the women behind to possibly be captured by the Taliban or having the unit slow down so the women can keep up, thereby risking causalities or capture? What if a male soldier is washed out of the Army's Advanced Infantry Training program because he cannot pass its physical fitness test whereas a female soldier who can't perform at his level is retained? Should male soldiers be able to bring suit and be awarded damages for sex discrimination? How much respect can a male soldier have for his female counterpart, who is held to lower performance standards?

There's another issue. The Selective Service System's website has the following message about draft registration: "Even though the Secretary of Defense has decided to allow women in combat jobs, the law has not been changed to include this. Consequently, only men are currently required to register by law with Selective Service during ages 18 thru 25. Women still do not register." How can that, coupled with differences in performance standards, possibly be consistent with the Defense Department's stated agenda "to provide a level, gender-neutral playing field"?

Understanding Liberals and Progressives
June 5, 2013

In order to understand the liberal and progressive agenda, one must know something about their world vision and values. Let's examine some of the evidence.

Why the 1970s struggle to ban DDT? Alexander King, founder of the Malthusian Club of Rome, wrote in a 1990 biographical essay: "My own doubts came when DDT was introduced for civilian use. In Guyana, within two years, it had almost eliminated malaria, but at the same time the birth rate had doubled. So my chief quarrel with DDT, in hindsight, is that it has greatly added to the population problem."

Dr. Charles Wurster, former chief scientist for the Environmental Defense Fund, was once asked whether he thought a ban on DDT would result in the use of more dangerous chemicals and more malaria cases in Sri Lanka. He replied: "Probably. So what? People are the cause of all the problems. We have too many of them. We need to get rid of some of them, and [malaria] is as good a way as any."

According to *Earthbound*, a collection of essays on environmental ethics, William Aiken said: "Massive human diebacks would be good. It is our duty to cause them. It is our species' duty, relative to the whole, to eliminate 90 percent of our numbers."

Former National Park Service research biologist David Graber opined, "Human happiness, and certainly human fecundity, are not as important as a wild and healthy planet. . . . We have become a plague upon ourselves and upon the Earth . . . . Until such time as Homo sapiens should decide to rejoin nature, some of us can only hope for the right virus to come along."

Speaking of viruses, Prince Philip—Duke of Edinburgh and patron of the World Wildlife Fund—said, "If I were reincarnated, I would wish to be returned to Earth as a killer virus to lower human population levels." The late Jacques Cousteau told *The UNESCO Courier*: "One America burdens the earth much more than twenty

Bangladeshes. This is a terrible thing to say. In order to stabilize world population, we must eliminate 350,000 people per day. It is a horrible thing to say, but it's just as bad not to say it."

That represents the values of some progressives, but what about their predictions? In 1972, a report was written for the Club of Rome to warn that the world would run out of gold by 1981, mercury and silver by 1985, tin by 1987, and petroleum, copper, lead, and natural gas by 1992. It turns out that each of these resources is more plentiful today. Gordon Taylor, in his 1970 book, *The Doomsday Book*, said that Americans were using 50 percent of the world's resources and that "by 2000 [Americans] will, if permitted, be using all of them." In 1975, the Environment Fund took out full-page ads warning, "The World as we know it will likely be ruined by the year 2000." Harvard University Nobel laureate biologist George Wald in 1970 warned, "Civilization will end within 15 or 30 years unless immediate action is taken against problems facing mankind." Former Sen. Gaylord Nelson, quoting Dr. S. Dillon Ripley, warned, in *Look* magazine (1970), that by 1995, "somewhere between 75 and 85 percent of all the species of living animals will be extinct." In 1974, the US Geological Survey said the United States had only a ten-year supply of natural gas. The fact of the matter, according to the American Gas Association, is that there's more than a 110-year supply.

In 1986, Lester Brown, who had been predicting global starvation for forty years, received a MacArthur Foundation "genius" award, along with a stipend. The foundation also gave Dr. Paul Ehrlich, who predicted millions of Americans would die of starvation, the "genius" award in 1990. Note that these $300,000 to $400,000 awards were granted well after enough time had passed to demonstrate that Brown and Ehrlich were insanely wrong.

Just think: Congress listens to people like these and formulates public policy on their dire predictions that we're running out of something.

Touchy Topics
September 4, 2013

Here's a question: What is the true test of one's commitment to freedom of expression? Is it when one permits others to express ideas with which he agrees? Or is it when he permits others to express ideas he finds deeply offensive? I'm betting that most people would wisely answer that it's the latter, and I'd agree. How about this question: What is the true test of one's commitment to freedom of association? Is it when people permit others to freely associate in ways of which they approve? Or is it when they permit others to freely associate in ways they deem despicable? I'm sure that might be a considerable dispute about freedom of association compared with the one over freedom of expression. To be for freedom in either case requires that one be brave enough to accept the fact that some people will make offensive expressions and associate in offensive ways. Let's explore this with an example from the past.

In 1958, Richard Loving, a white man, and Mildred Jeter, a black woman, two Virginia residents, traveled to Washington, D.C., to marry. Upon their return to Virginia, they were charged with and found guilty of violation of Virginia's anti-miscegenation laws. In 1967, the US Supreme Court, in Loving v. Virginia, held that laws banning interracial marriages violated the equal protection and due process clauses of the Fourteenth Amendment. The couple's conviction was reversed. Thus, Virginia's anti-miscegenation laws not only violated the US Constitution but also violated the basic human right of freedom of association.

Now let's ask ourselves: Would Virginia's laws have been more acceptable if, instead of banning interracial marriages, they had mandated interracial marriages? Any decent person would find such a law just as offensive—and for the same reason: It would violate freedom of association. Forced association is not freedom of association.

Before you say, "Williams, where you're going with this discussion isn't very good," there's another case from our past. Henry Louis Mencken, writing in *The Baltimore Evening Sun* (November 9, 1948), brought to light that the city's parks board had a regulation forbidding white and black citizens from playing tennis with each other in public parks. Today most Americans would find such a regulation an offensive attack on freedom of association. I imagine that most would find it just as offensive if the regulation had required blacks and whites to play tennis with each other. Both would violate freedom of association.

Most Americans probably agree there should be freedom of association in the cases of marriage and tennis, but what about freedom of association as a general principle? Suppose white men formed a club, a professional association, or any other private association and blacks and women wanted to be members. Is there any case for forcing them to admit blacks and women? What if it were women or blacks who formed an association? Should they be forced to admit men or whites? Wouldn't forced membership in either case violate freedom of association?

What if you wanted to deal with me but I didn't want to deal with you? To be more concrete, suppose I own a private company and I'm looking to hire an employee. You want to deal with me, but I don't want to deal with you. My reasons might be that you're white or a Catholic or ugly or a woman or anything else that I find objectionable. Should I be forced to hire you? You say, "Williams, that's illegal employment discrimination." You're absolutely right, but it still violates peaceable freedom of association.

Much of the racial discrimination in our history was a result of legal or extralegal measures to prevent freedom of association. That was the essence of Jim Crow laws, which often prevented blacks from being served in restaurants, admitted into theaters, allowed on public conveyances, and given certain employment. Whenever one sees laws or other measures taken to prevent economic transactions, you have to guess that the reason there's a law is that if there were no law, not everyone would behave according to the specifications of the law.

Honesty and Trust

September 25, 2013

Dishonesty, lying, and cheating are not treated with the right amount of opprobrium in today's society. To gain an appreciation for the significance of honesty and trust, consider what our day-to-day lives would be like if we couldn't trust anyone. When we purchase a bottle of a hundred pills from our pharmacist, how many of us bother to count the pills? We pull in to a gasoline station and pay $35 for 10 gallons of gasoline. How do we know for sure whether we in fact received 10 gallons instead of 9–3/4? You pay $7 for a 1-pound package of filet mignon. Do you ever independently verify that you in fact received 1 pound? In each of those cases, and thousands more, we simply trust the seller.

There are thousands of cases in which the seller trusts the buyer. Having worked forty hours, I trust that George Mason University, my employer, will pay me. People place an order with their stockbroker to purchase a hundred shares of AT&T stock, and the stockbroker trusts that he'll be paid. Companies purchase 5 tons of aluminum with payment due thirty days later.

Examples of honesty and trust abound, but imagine the cost and inconvenience if we couldn't trust anyone. We would have to lug around measuring instruments to make sure that it was in fact 10 gallons of gas and 1 pound of steak that we purchased. Imagine the hassle of having to count out the number of pills in a bottle. If we couldn't trust, we'd have to bear the costly burden of writing contracts instead of relying on a buyer's or a seller's word. We'd have to bear the monitoring costs to ensure compliance in the simplest of transactions. It's safe to say that whatever undermines honesty and trust raises the costs of transactions, reduces the value of exchange and makes us poorer.

Honesty and trust come into play in ways that few of us even contemplate. In my neighborhood, workers for FedEx, UPS, and other delivery companies routinely leave packages that contain valuable merchandise on the doorstep if no one answers the door. The local supermarket leaves plants, fertilizer, and other home and garden items outdoors overnight unattended. What's more, the supermarket displays loads of merchandise at entryways and exits. In neighborhoods where there's less honesty, deliverymen's leaving merchandise on doorsteps and stores leaving merchandise outdoors unattended or at entryways and exits would be equivalent to economic suicide.

Dishonesty is costly. Delivery companies cannot leave packages when the customer is not home. The company must bear the costs of making return trips, or the customer has to bear the costs of going to pick up the package. If a supermarket places merchandise outside, it must bear the costs of hiring an attendant—plus retrieve the merchandise at the close of business; that's if it can risk having merchandise outdoors in the first place.

Honesty affects stores such as supermarkets in another way. A supermarket manager's goal is to maximize the rate of merchandise turnover per square foot of leased space. When theft is relatively low, the manager can use all of the space he leases, including outdoor and entryway space, thereby raising his profit potential. That opportunity is denied to supermarkets in localities where there's less honesty. That in turn means a higher cost of doing business, which translates into higher prices, less profit and fewer customer amenities.

Crime, distrust, and dishonesty impose huge losses that go beyond those suffered directly. Much of the cost of crime and dishonesty is borne by people who can least afford it—poor people. It's poor people who have fewer choices and pay higher prices or must bear the transportation costs of going to suburban malls to shop. It's poor people in high-crime neighborhoods who are refused pizza delivery and taxi pickups. The fact that honesty and trust are so vital should make us rethink just how much tolerance we should have for criminals and dishonest people.

Are Guns the Problem?

October 2, 2013

Every time there's a shooting tragedy, there are more calls for gun control. Let's examine a few historical facts. By 1910, the National Rifle Association had succeeded in establishing seventy-three NRA-affiliated high-school rifle clubs. The 1911 second edition of the *Boy Scout Handbook* made qualification in NRA's junior marksmanship program a prerequisite for obtaining a Boy Scout of America merit badge in marksmanship. In 1918, the Winchester Repeating Arms Co. established its own Winchester Junior Rifle Corps. The program grew to 135,000 members by 1925. In New York City, gun clubs were started at Boys, Curtis, Commercial, Manual Training and Stuyvesant high schools. With so many guns in the hands of youngsters, did we see today's level of youth violence?

What about gun availability? Catalogs and magazines from the 1940s, '50s, and '60s were full of gun advertisements directed to children and parents. For example, "What Every Parent Should Know When a Boy or Girl Wants a Gun" was published by the National Shooting Sports Foundation. The 1902 Sears mail-order catalog had thirty-five pages of firearm advertisements. People just sent in their money, and a firearm was shipped. For most of our history, a person could simply walk into a hardware store, virtually anywhere in our country, and buy a gun. Few states bothered to have even age restrictions on buying guns.

Those and other historical facts should force us to ask ourselves: Why—at a time in our history when guns were readily available, when a person could just walk into a store or order a gun through the mail, when there were no FBI background checks, no waiting periods, no licensing requirements—was there not the frequency and kind of gun violence that we sometimes see today, when access to guns is more restricted? Guns are guns. If they were capable of behavior, as some people seem to suggest, they should have been doing then what they're doing now.

Customs, traditions, moral values, and rules of etiquette, not just laws and government regulations, are what make for a civilized society, not restraints on inanimate objects. These behavioral norms—transmitted by example, word of mouth, and religious teachings—represent a body of wisdom distilled through ages of experience, trial and error, and looking at what works. The benefit of having customs, traditions, and moral values as a means of regulating behavior is that people behave themselves even if nobody's watching. In other words, it's morality that is society's first line of defense against uncivilized behavior.

Moral standards of conduct, as well as strict and swift punishment for criminal behaviors, have been under siege in our country for more than a half-century. Moral absolutes have been abandoned as a guiding principle. We've been taught not to be judgmental, that one lifestyle or value is just as good as another. More often than not, the attack on moral standards has been orchestrated by the education establishment and progressives. Police and laws can never replace these restraints on personal conduct so as to produce a civilized society. At best, the police and criminal justice system are the last desperate line of defense for a civilized society. The more uncivilized we become the more laws are needed to regulate behavior.

What's worse is that instead of trying to return to what worked, progressives want to replace what worked with what sounds good or what seems plausible, such as more gun locks, longer waiting periods, and stricter gun possession laws. Then there's progressive mindlessness "cures," such as "zero tolerance" for schoolyard recess games such as cops and robbers and cowboys and Indians, shouting "bang bang," drawing a picture of a pistol, making a gun out of Lego pieces, and biting the shape of a gun out of a Pop-Tart. This kind of unadulterated lunacy—which focuses on an inanimate object such as a gun instead of on morality, self-discipline, and character—will continue to produce disappointing results.

Equality in Discipline
April 16, 2014

George Leef, director of research for the North Carolina-based John William Pope Center for Higher Education Policy, authored a *Forbes* op-ed article titled "Obama Administration Takes Groupthink to Absurd Lengths." The subtitle is "School Discipline Rates Must Be 'Proportionate'" (http://tinyurl.com/mxnlg9h). Let's examine some of the absurdity of the Obama administration's take on student discipline.

Last January, the departments of Justice and Education published a "guidance" letter describing how schools can meet their obligations under federal law to administer student discipline without discriminating on the basis of race, color, or national origin. Its underlying threat is that if federal bureaucrats learn of racial disproportionality in the punishments meted out for misbehavior, they will descend upon a school's administrators. If schools cannot justify differentials in rates of punishment by race or ethnic group, they will face the loss of federal funds and be forced to undertake costly diversity training.

The nation's educators can avoid sanctions by adopting a racial quota system for student discipline. So as Roger Clegg, president and general counsel of the Center for Equal Opportunity, predicts, "school officials will either start disciplining students who shouldn't be, or, more likely, will not discipline some students who ought to be." I can imagine school administrators reasoning this way: "Blacks are 20 percent of our student body, and 20 percent of suspensions this year have been of black students. In order to discipline another black student while maintaining our suspension quota, we will have to suspend some white students, whether they're guilty or not." Some administrators might see some injustice in that approach and simply ignore the misbehavior of black students.

Leef cites Manhattan Institute's Heather Mac Donald, who wrote in *City Journal* (http://tinyurl.com/9k648fj) that "the Departments of Education and Justice have launched a campaign against disproportionate minority discipline rates, which show up in virtually every school district with significant numbers of black and Hispanic students. The possibility that students' behavior, not educators' racism, drives those rates lies outside the Obama administration's conceptual universe." She quoted Aaron Benner, a black teacher in a St. Paul, Minn., school who abhors the idea that school officials should go easy on black students who act up because (as a "facilitator" said) that's what black culture is. "They're trying to pull one over on us. Black folks are drinking the Kool-Aid; this 'let-them-clown' philosophy could have been devised by the KKK." Benner is right. I can't think of a more racist argument than one that holds that disruptive, rude behavior and foul language are a part of black culture.

If Barack Obama's Department of Justice thinks that disproportionality in school punishments is probative of racial discrimination, what about our criminal justice system, in which a disproportionate number of blacks are imprisoned, on parole or probation, and executed? According to the NAACP's criminal justice fact sheet, blacks now constitute nearly 1 million of the total 2.3 million people who are incarcerated. Blacks are incarcerated at nearly six times the rate of whites. The NAACP goes on to report that if blacks and Hispanics were incarcerated at the same rate as whites, today's prison and jail populations would decline by approximately 50 percent (http://tinyurl.com/7g2b32h).

So what to do? For example, blacks are 13 percent of the population but over 50 percent of homicide victims and about 46 percent of convicted murderers. Seeing as the Obama administration is concerned about punishment disproportionality, should black convicts be released so that only 13 percent of incarcerated murderers are black? Or should the Department of Justice order the conviction of whites, whether they're guilty or not, so that the number of people convicted of murder by race is equal to their number in the general population? You say, "Williams, that not only is a stupid suggestion but violates all concepts of justice!" You're absolutely right, but isn't it just as stupid and unjust for the Obama administration to seek punishment equality in schools?

Petty Annoyances
June 4, 2014

Most who read my columns think that I'm only annoyed by politicians, growing government, and Americans who have little respect or love for liberty and our Constitution. There are other things that annoy me.

One annoyance is people's seeming inability or unwillingness to differentiate between the number zero and the letter "o." I've had conversations with telephone operators who have told me that I can reach my party by dialing, for example, 31o-3o55. Sometimes I've asked, "If I follow your instructions, by dialing the letter 'o' instead of the number zero, will I reach my party?" They always answer no and that I must dial the zero. Then I ask, "Why did you tell me 'o' when you meant zero?" Our chitchat usually degrades after that. It's not only telephone operators. How many times have you heard a student or teacher say, "He has a 4 point o GPA"?

I wonder whether the confusion stems from the fact that both o's and zeroes are round. Here's a definition that distinguishes them: "O" is a vowel and the fifteenth letter of the alphabet. Zero is defined as any number that when added to or subtracted from another number does not change the value of that number.

I recently made Microsoft Outlook my default email client, but I'm having a bit of a problem with it. When it's initially turned on, there's a message that reads, "Trying to connect." Similarly, on a cloudy morning, I hear weathermen say that the sun will try to come out later. So if Microsoft Outlook didn't connect or the afternoon didn't turn out to be sunny, could we say it was because Microsoft Outlook or the sun didn't try hard enough? But it's not just computer software technicians and weathermen who use teleological explanations that ascribe purposeful behavior to inanimate objects. Recently, I listened to brilliant lectures on particle physics by a distinguished physics professor, who said that strange quarks want to decay. In a cellular respiration lecture, another professor said that one mole of glucose wants to become thirty-eight units of adenosine triphosphate. I'm wondering how these professors know what strange quarks and glucose moles want to do; have they spoken to them?

You say, "Williams, you're being too picky! What's the harm?" There's a great potential for harm when people come to believe that inanimate objects are capable of purposeful behavior. That's the implied thinking behind the pressure for gun control. People behave as if a gun could engage in purposeful behavior such as committing crime; thereby, our focus is directed more toward controlling inanimate objects than it is toward controlling evil people.

How many times have you heard a statement such as "Harold and myself were studying"? When one of my students makes such a statement, I sometimes ask, "What if Harold were not studying with you? Would you say, 'Myself was studying'?" That'd be silly. Words such as "myself" and "himself" are reflexive pronouns. Their proper use requires reference to the subject of the sentence. For example, "Harold injured himself." A reflexive pronoun can also be used intensively for emphasis, for example, "Harold himself was injured."

I have another grammar annoyance. How about when people make a statement such as "He is taller than me"? Whenever I hear such an error, I visualize Dr. Martin Rosenberg, my high school English teacher during the early '50s, putting both hands on his waist and sarcastically asking the student, "Do you mean 'He is taller than me am'?" "Am" is the elliptical, or understood or left-out, verb at the end of the sentence. The subject of a verb must be in the nominative case. To be grammatically correct, the sentence should be, "He is taller than I."

Considerable evidence demonstrates that most people are not bothered by my petty annoyances. I'm willing to give them the benefit of the doubt. It may be that it's I who is getting old and out of touch, having been educated during ancient times when nonsense was less acceptable.

Things I Don't Understand
September 3, 2014

There are things that really puzzle me. Some life insurance companies charge lower premiums if you haven't made a life-shortening lifestyle choice. Being a nonsmoker is one of them. Actuarially, that makes sense because the life expectancy for smokers is at least ten years shorter than for nonsmokers.

Insurance company policies charge higher premiums to those who are obese. The National Institutes of Health reports that those with a body mass index greater than 40 have a six- to fourteen-year lower life expectancy. Again, actuarially, that makes sense. Indeed, there's a strong advocacy for higher life insurance, as well as health insurance, premiums for those whose lifestyle choices impose a greater financial burden on society, which obesity does. But there's one important exception.

According to the *International Journal of Epidemiology*, life expectancy at age twenty for homosexual and bisexual men is eight to twenty years less than for all men. That's a lifestyle shortening of life expectancy greater than obesity and tobacco use. Yet one never hears of insurance companies advertising lower premiums for heterosexual men. You say, "That would be discrimination." You're right, but why is it acceptable for insurance companies to discriminate against smokers and the obese but not homosexuals? After all, they are all Americans and protected by the Constitution. It's really a matter of politics, as seen by the journal's publication of an article titled "Gay life expectancy revisited" (http://tinyurl.com/25ejq2d). The publication had to soft-pedal its study results because of complaints that pointing out life expectancy differences between heterosexuals and homosexuals had become fuel for homophobia. The bottom line is that homosexuals have far greater political power and sympathy than smokers and the obese.

Sticking with medical issues, Dr. Tom Frieden, head of the Centers for Disease Control and Prevention, said, "Ebola poses little risk to the US general population." If one cannot contract Ebola, as the CDC claims, except through the exchange of bodily fluids, then why were millions of dollars spent transporting Ebola patients Dr. Kent Brantly and Nancy Writebol from Liberia to a US hospital under extreme isolation procedures? The CDC's Ebola claim strikes me as fishy. To use a line spoken by Marcellus in William Shakespeare's "Hamlet," "something is rotten in the state of Denmark."

There are warning labels that puzzle me, engendering considerable disrespect for my fellow Americans' intellect. How about the warning, "Do not hold the wrong end of a chain saw." On packaging for a clothes iron is the warning, "Do not iron clothes on body." A Superman costume contained the warning, "Wearing of this garment does not enable you to fly."

Then there are the "do not take internally" warnings. Most often, the product containing this warning isn't something one reasonably takes internally, such as butter, soda, or cough syrup. The warnings are on products such as paint, bleach, and other cleaning fluids. I'm wondering how many grown Americans actually took a swig of something like Minwax, bleach, or paint thinner. Then there's a warning label that appears on some automobile windshield sun screens, which people purchase to keep their cars cool: "Do Not Drive with Screen in Place."

Here's my take. The warning labels are all a waste. A person dumb enough to drink Minwax, bleach, or paint thinner or drive with a sun screen in place is probably also too dumb to read. Speaking of warning labels, there's a debate about whether mother's milk is good or bad for infants—a preposterous debate, considering the historical success of nursing manifested by a world population of 7 billion. If government authorities, such as the Food and Drug Administration, conclude that mother's milk is hazardous, I'm wondering where they're going to put the warning label.

Do Statistical Disparities Mean Injustice?
September 24, 2014

How many times have we heard laments such as "women are 50 percent of the population but only 5 percent of Fortune 500 CEOs" and, as the Justice Department recently found, "blacks are 54 percent of the population in Newark, New Jersey, but 85 percent of pedestrian stops and 79 percent of arrests"? If one believes that people should be represented socioeconomically according to their numbers in the population, then statistical disparities represent injustices that demand government remedies. Before we jump to conclusions about what disparities mean and whether they are indicators of injustice, we might examine some other disparities to see what we can make of them.

According to a recent study conducted by Bond University in Australia, sharks are nine times as likely to attack and kill men than they are women. If sinister motivation is attributed for this disparity, as is done in the cases of sex and racial disparities, we can only conclude that sharks are sexist. Another sex disparity is despite the fact that men are 50 percent of the population and so are women, men are struck by lightning six times as often as women. I wonder what whoever is in charge of lightning has against men.

Another gross statistical disparity is despite the fact that Jews are less than 3 percent of the US population and a mere 0.2 percent of the world's population, between 1901 and 2010, Jews were 35 percent of American and 22 percent of the world's Nobel Prize winners.

There are other disparities that we might acknowledge with an eye to corrective public policy. Asian-Americans routinely score the highest on the math portion of the SAT, whereas blacks score the lowest. The population statistics for South Dakota, Iowa, Maine, Montana, and Vermont show that not even 1 percent of their populations is black. In states such as Georgia, Alabama, and Mississippi, blacks are overrepresented in terms of their percentages in the general population. When this kind of "segregation" is found in schooling, the remedy is busing.

There are loads of international examples of ethnic disparities. During the 1960s, the Chinese minority in Malaysia, where Malays politically dominate, received more university degrees than the Malay majority—including four hundred engineering degrees, compared with just four for the Malays. In Brazil's state of Sao Paulo, more than two-thirds of the potatoes and 90 percent of the tomatoes produced have been produced by people of Japanese ancestry.

Blacks are 13 percent of our population but 80 percent of professional basketball players and 65 percent of professional football players and among the highest-paid players in both sports. By stark contrast, blacks are only 2 percent of the NHL's professional ice hockey players. Basketball, football, and ice hockey represent gross racial disparities and come nowhere close to "looking like America."

Even in terms of sports achievement, racial diversity is absent. In Major League Baseball, three out of the four hitters with the most career home runs are black. Since blacks entered the major leagues, of the eight times more than hundred bases have been stolen in a season, all were by blacks. In basketball, fifty of the fifty-nine MVP awards have been won by black players.

If America's diversity worshippers see underrepresentation as "probative" of racial discrimination, what do they propose be done about overrepresentation? After all, overrepresentation and underrepresentation are simply different sides of injustice. If those in one race are over-represented, it might mean they're taking away what rightfully belongs to another race. For example, is it possible that Jews are doing things that sabotage the chances of a potential Indian, Alaska Native, or Mexican Nobel Prize winner? What about the disgraceful lack of diversity in professional basketball and ice hockey? There's not even geographical diversity in professional ice hockey; not a single player can boast of having been born and raised in Hawaii, Louisiana, or Mississippi.

Courts, bureaucrats, and the intellectual elite have consistently concluded that "gross" disparities are probative of a pattern and practice of discrimination. Given all of the differences among people, such a position is pure nonsense.

Walter Williams at Foundation for Economic Education

Professor Williams delivered the following to an audience in Irvington, New York, on June 28, 2014. Williams's lecture is one in a series designed to share ideas, honor FEE's rich tradition, and say goodbye to the Irvington property.

Markets, Governments, and the Common Good

Let us begin with a discussion of a working definition of markets. Markets are simply millions upon millions, and internationally billions upon billions, of individual decision-makers, engaged in the pursuit of what they determine to be their best interests. We say that the market is free if it is characterized by peaceable, voluntary exchange, private property rights, rule of law, and limited government intervention and control. While some people denounce free markets as immoral, the reality is exactly the opposite. Free markets are more moral than any other system of resource allocation. Let's talk about the moral superiority of free markets.

Suppose you hire me to mow your lawn and afterwards you pay me $30. The money you pay me might be thought of as a certificate of performance—proof that I served you. With these certificates of performance (money) in hand, I go to my grocer and demand 3 pounds of steak and a six-pack of beer that my fellow man produced. In effect, the grocer says, "Williams, you're asking that your fellow man, as ranchers and brewers, serve you. What did you do in turn to serve your fellow man?" I say, "I mowed my fellow man's lawn." The grocer says, "Prove it!" That's when I hand over my certificates of performance—the $30.

A system that requires that I serve my fellow man in order to have a claim on what he produces is far more moral than government resource allocation. The government can, in effect say, justifying it with one reason or another, "Williams, you don't have to serve your fellow man in order to have a claim on what he produces. Through the tax code, we'll take what he produces and give it to you." Of course, if I were to privately take what my fellow man produced, we'd call it theft. The only difference is when the government does it, that theft is legal but nonetheless theft—which is defined as taking of one person's rightful property to give to another.

The essence of free markets is good-good exchanges, or what I like to think of as seduction. Exchanges of this sort are featured by the proposition: "I'll do something good for you if you do something good for me." Game theorists recognize this as a positive-sum game—a transaction where both parties, in their own estimation, are better off as a result. When I go to my grocer and offer him the following proposition: If you do something good for me—give me that gallon of milk—I'll do something good for you—give you three dollars. As a result, I am better off because I valued the milk more than I valued the three dollars and he is better off because he valued the three dollars more than he valued the gallon of milk.

Of course there's another type of exchange not typically, voluntarily entered into, namely good-bad exchanges, or what we might call rape. An example of that kind of exchange would be where I approached my grocer with a pistol, telling him that if he didn't do something good for me (give me that gallon of milk) I'd do something bad to him: blow his brains out. Clearly, I would be better off, but he would be worse off. Game theorists call that a zero-sum game. That's the case where in order for one person to be better off, of necessity the other must be worse off. Zero-sum games are transactions mostly initiated by thieves and governments, both are involved in what is euphemistically called income redistribution. The only difference is one does it under the color of the law and the other doesn't.

The Wonders of Greed

What human motivation is responsible for getting the most wonderful things done? I would say greed. When I use the term greed, I do not mean cheating, stealing, fraud, and other acts of dishonesty, I mean people seeking to get the most for themselves. Unfortunately, many people are naive enough to believe that compassion, concern, and "feeling another's pain" are the superior human motivations. As such we fall easy prey to charlatans, quacks, and hustlers. Since it's not considered polite, and surely not politically correct to come out and actually say that greed gets wonderful things done, let me go through a few of the millions of examples of the wonders of greed. It's a wonderful thing that most of us own cars. Is there anyone who believes that the reason we have cars is because Detroit assembly line workers care about us? It's also wonderful that Texas cattle ranchers make the sacrifices of time and effort caring for steer so that New Yorkers can have beef on their supermarket shelves. It is also wonderful that Idaho potato growers arise early to do back-breaking work in the hot sun to ensure that New Yorkers also have potatoes on their supermarket shelves. Again, is there anyone who believes that ranchers and potato growers, who make these sacrifices, do so because they care about New Yorkers? They might hate New Yorkers. New Yorkers have beef and potatoes because Texas cattle ranchers and Idaho potato growers care about themselves and they want more for themselves. How much steak and potatoes would New Yorkers have if it all depended on human love and kindness? I would feel sorry for New Yorkers. Reasoning this way bothers some people because they are more concerned with the motives behind a set of actions rather than the results.

This is what Adam Smith, the father of economics, meant in *The Wealth of Nations* when he said, "It is not from the benevolence of the butcher, the brewer, or the baker, that we expect our dinner, but from their regard to their own interests." In other words, the public good is promoted best by people pursuing their own private interests.

Parity of the Market

There is another feature of the free market that often goes unappreciated. That is a sort of parity of the marketplace. The market is an extreme form of democracy: one man, one vote. While the rich have many more dollars than I have, my one dollar is just as valuable as a rich man's one dollar. One might assert that common people do not have access to Rolls Royces and yachts. You would be wrong. Microsoft's Bill Gates is super-rich and can afford to ride in a Rolls Royce and go yachting; but so can the common man—just not for as long. He can rent a Rolls or a yacht for a day, half-day, or an hour. This is something often forgotten: People can bid on quantity as well as price.

The fruits of the free market are the best thing that ever happened to the common man. The rich have always had access to entertainment, often in the comfort of their palaces and mansions. The rich have never had to experience the drudgery of having to beat out carpets, iron their clothing, or slave over a hot stove all day in order to have a decent dinner. They could afford to hire people. Mass production and marketing have made radios and televisions, vacuum cleaners, wash-and-wear clothing, and microwave ovens available and well within the means of the common man; thus sparing him of the boredom and drudgery of the past. Today, the common man has the power to enjoy much (and more) of what only the rich could afford yesteryear.

What about those who became wealthy producing these comforts available to the common man? Henry Ford benefited immensely from mass-producing automobiles but the benefits received by the common man, from being able to buy a car, dwarfs anything Ford received. Individuals who founded companies that produced penicillin, polio, and typhoid vaccines may have become very wealthy—but again, it was the common man who was the major beneficiary. In more recent times, computers and software products have benefited our health, safety, and quality of life in ways that dwarf whatever wealth received by their creators.

Capitalism is relatively new in human history. Prior to the rise of capitalism, the way people amassed great wealth was by looting, plundering, and enslaving their fellow man. Capitalism made it possible to become wealthy by serving one's fellow man. Capitalists seek to discover what people want and then produce and market it as efficiently as possible. Here's a question that we should ponder in light of anti-market demagoguery: Are people who by their actions created unprecedented convenience, longer life expectancy, and made more fun available for the ordinary person—and became wealthy in the process—deserving of all the scorn and ridicule heaped upon them by intellectuals and politicians? Are the wealthy really obliged to "give something back"? After all, for example, what more do the wealthy discoverers and producers of, say, life-saving antibiotics owe us? They've already saved lives and made us healthier.

Despite the miracles of capitalism, it doesn't do well in popularity polls. One of the reasons is that capitalism is always evaluated against the nonexistent, unrealizable utopias of socialism or communism. Any earthly system, when compared to a Utopia, will pale in comparison. But for the ordinary person, capitalism, with all of its warts, is superior to any system yet devised to deal with our everyday needs and desires.

Rights versus Wishes

Often people speak of rights to housing, medical care, food, and other goods and services deemed necessary for the sustenance of life. That vision leads to gross violations of most standards of morality. In standard usage of the term, a right, sometimes called negative rights, is something that exists simultaneously among people. A right confers no obligation on another. For example, the right to free speech is something we all possess simultaneously. My right to free speech imposes no obligation upon another except that of noninterference. Similarly, I have a right to travel freely. That right imposes no obligation upon another except that of noninterference.

Contrast those rights to the supposed right to medical care or decent housing whether one can afford them or not. Through government actions, those supposed rights do impose obligations upon others. Government has no resources of its very own. The money coming from federal, state, and local governments to pay for those "rights" does not come from politicians reaching into their own pockets. Moreover, there is no Santa Claus or Tooth Fairy who provides the money.

The recognition that government has no resources of its very own forces one to recognize that the only way government can give one person a dollar is to first take it from someone else. A government-granted right to medical care, housing, or anything else imposes an obligation on another, namely one American have less of something else—diminished rights to his earnings. That is, if one person has a right to something he did not earn, it requires another to not have a right to something he did earn. Let's apply this bogus concept of rights—some might call it positive rights—to free speech and the right to travel freely. In that case, my free speech rights would require others to supply me with an auditorium, microphone, and audience. My right to travel would require that others provide me with airplane tickets and hotel accommodations. Most Americans, I would imagine, would tell me, "Williams, yes, you have rights to free speech and travel rights, but I'm not obligated to pay for them!"

As human beings we all have certain unalienable rights, as so eloquently stated in our Declaration of Independence. Of the rights we possess, we have a right to delegate to government. For example, we all have a right to defend ourselves against predators. Since we possess that right, we can delegate it to government. In other words, we can say to government, "We have the right to defend ourselves but for a more orderly society, we delegate to you the authority to defend us." By contrast, I do not possess the right to take the property of one person to give to another. Since I do not possess such a right, I cannot delegate it to government. If you're a Christian or simply a moral human being, you should be against these so-called rights. After all, when God gave Moses the Seventh Commandment—"Thou shalt not steal"—I'm sure that he didn't mean thou shalt not steal unless there was a majority vote in Congress. Moreover, I'm sure that if you were to have a heart-to-heart talk with God and ask him, "God, is it okay to be a recipient of stolen property?" I'm guessing He would say that being a recipient of stolen property is a sin as well. I strongly believe in helping our fellow man in need. Doing so by reaching into one's own pockets to help him is praiseworthy and laudable. Reaching into someone else's pockets to do so is despicable and worthy of condemnation.

The Common Good

If the common good or social justice has any operational meaning at all, it means that there is a system of governance where the purpose of laws is to prevent one person from violating another person's right to acquire, keep, and dispose of property in any manner so long as he does not violate another's similarly held rights. In other words, laws should be written to prevent force and fraud. Laws that force one person to serve the purposes of another are immoral.

Today, our government has become increasingly destructive of the ends it was created to serve. Americans have become increasingly hostile and alien to the liberties envisioned by the framers. We have disregarded the inscription that graces the wall at the US Department of Justice warning, "Where the law ends tyranny begins." Benjamin Franklin said, "A frequent reference to the fundamental principles is absolutely necessary to preserve the blessings of liberty, and keep a free government." That's the job that the Foundation for Economic Education has done so well over the decades.

About the Author

Born in Philadelphia, Pennsylvania, **Dr. Walter E. Williams** holds a BA in economics from California State University, Los Angeles, and MA and PhD degrees in economics from UCLA. He also holds a Doctor of Humane Letters from Virginia Union University and Grove City College, Doctor of Laws from Washington and Jefferson College and Doctor Honoris Causa en Ciencias Sociales from Universidad Francisco Marroquin, in Guatemala, where he is also Professor Honorario.

Dr. Williams has served on the faculty of George Mason University in Fairfax, Virginia, as John M. Olin Distinguished Professor of Economics, since 1980; from 1995 to 2001, he served as department chairman. He has also served on the faculties of Los Angeles City College, California State University Los Angeles, Temple University in Philadelphia, and Grove City College, Grove City, Pennsylvania

Dr. Williams is the author of over 150 publications which have appeared in scholarly journals such as *Economic Inquiry, American Economic Review, Georgia Law Review, Journal of Labor Economics, Social Science Quarterly,* and *Cornell Journal of Law and Public Policy* and popular publications such as *Newsweek, Ideas on Liberty, National Review, Reader's Digest, Cato Journal,* and *Policy Review.* He has authored ten books: *America: A Minority Viewpoint, The State Against Blacks* (which was later made into the PBS documentary *Good Intentions*), *All It Takes Is Guts, South Africa's War Against Capitalism* (which was later revised for South African publication), *Do the Right Thing: The People's Economist Speaks, More Liberty Means Less Government, Liberty vs. the Tyranny of Socialism, Up From The Projects: An Autobiography,* and *Race and Economics: How Much Can Be Blamed On Discrimination?*

He has made scores of radio and television appearances which include *Nightline, Firing Line, Face the Nation,* Milton Friedman's *Free To Choose, Crossfire, MacNeil/Lehrer, Wall Street Week,* and was a regular commentator for *Nightly Business Report.* He is also occasional substitute host for the *Rush Limbaugh* show. In addition Dr. Williams writes a nationally syndicated weekly column that is carried by approximately 140 newspapers and several web sites.

Dr. Williams serves on several boards of trustees/directors: Grove City College, Reason Foundation, and Chase Foundation. He also serves on numerous advisory boards including: Cato Institute, Landmark Legal Foundation, Institute of Economic Affairs, and Heritage Foundation.

Dr. Williams has received numerous fellowships and awards including: the Fund for American Studies David Jones Lifetime Achievement Award, Foundation for Economic Education Adam Smith Award, Hoover Institution National Fellow, Ford Foundation Fellow, Valley Forge Freedoms Foundation George Washington Medal of Honor, Veterans of Foreign Wars U.S. News Media Award, Adam Smith Award, California State University Distinguished Alumnus Award, George Mason University Faculty Member of the Year, and Alpha Kappa Psi Award.

Dr. Williams has participated in numerous debates, conferences and lectures in the United States and abroad. He has frequently given expert testimony before Congressional committees on public policy issues ranging from labor policy to taxation and spending. He is a member of the Mont Pelerin Society, and the American Economic Association.

Index